I KISS YOUR HANDS MANY TIMES

I KISS YOUR HANDS
MANY TIMES

Hearts, Souls, and Wars in Hungary

MARIANNE
SZEGEDY-MASZÁK

SPIEGEL & GRAU

NEW YORK

Published in the United States by Spiegel & Grau,
an imprint of The Random House Publishing Group,
a division of Random House, Inc., New York.

SPIEGEL & GRAU and the HOUSE colophon are
registered trademarks of Random House, Inc.

LIBRARY OF CONGRESS CATALOGING-IN-PUBLICATION DATA
Szegedy-Maszák, Marianne.
I kiss your hands many times : hearts, souls, and wars in Hungary /
Marianne Szegedy-Maszák.
pages cm
Includes bibliographical references.
ISBN 978-0-385-52485-8
eBook ISBN 978-0-679-64522-1
1. Szegedy-Maszák, Marianne.   2. Hungarians—United States—Biography.
3. World War, 1939–1945—Hungary.   4. Holocaust, Jewish (1939–1945)—Hungary.
5. Jews—Hungary—Biography.   6. Hungary—Biography.   I. Title.
E184.H95S85 2013
940.53'18092—dc23 [B]   2012043179

Printed in the United States of America on acid-free paper

www.spiegelandgrau.com

2 4 6 8 9 7 5 3 1

FIRST EDITION

Book design by Barbara M. Bachman

To Hanna and Aladár,

my mother and father

"For the significance of a noble family lies entirely in its traditions, that is in its vital memories: and he was the last to have any unusual memories, anything different from those of other families."

—GIUSEPPE DI LAMPEDUSA, *The Leopard*

CONTENTS

THE
WEISS FAMILY

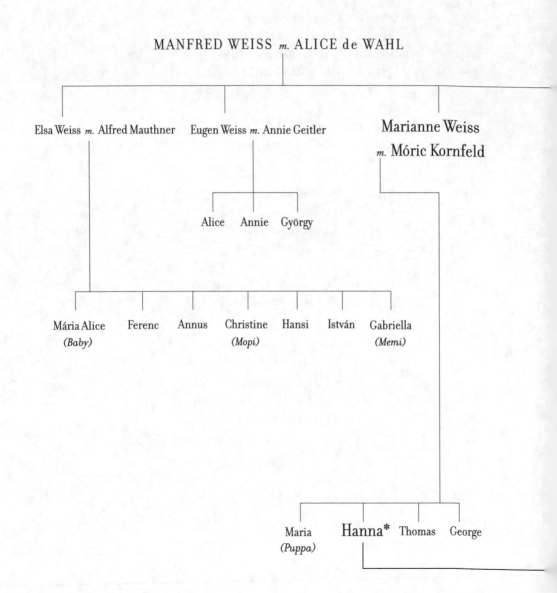

MANFRED WEISS *m.* ALICE de WAHL

Elsa Weiss *m.* Alfred Mauthner   Eugen Weiss *m.* Annie Geitler   Marianne Weiss
m. Móric Kornfeld

Alice   Annie   György

Mária Alice   Ferenc   Annus   Christine   Hansi   István   Gabriella
(Baby)   *(Mopi)*   *(Memi)*

Maria   Hanna*   Thomas   George
(Puppa)

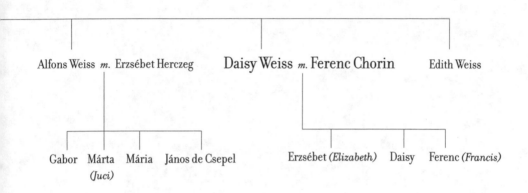

Alfons Weiss *m.* Erzsébet Herczeg   Daisy Weiss *m.* Ferenc Chorin   Edith Weiss

Gabor   Márta   Mária   János de Csepel   Erzsébet *(Elizabeth)*   Daisy   Ferenc *(Francis)*
        (Juci)

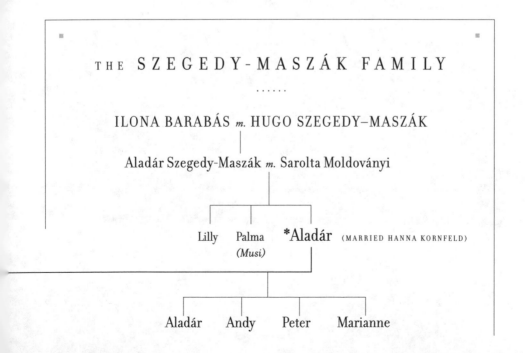

■   ■

THE S Z E G E D Y - M A S Z Á K F A M I L Y

......

ILONA BARABÁS *m.* HUGO SZEGEDY–MASZÁK

Aladár Szegedy-Maszák *m.* Sarolta Moldoványi

Lilly   Palma   *Aladár   (MARRIED HANNA KORNFELD)
        (Musi)

Aladár   Andy   Peter   Marianne

Prologue

I was brought to our house on Patterson Street, in Washington, D.C., four days after I was born in the spring of 1955, and I grew up to the sound of languages I couldn't understand. My father was fifty-one when I was born, my mother thirty-nine, and my brothers, Peter and Andrew, were much older than I, five and seven years respectively. My mother's parents and older sister lived with us, so I spent much of my childhood observing the complex interplay of the many adults in my life, longing to be included in the combative exclusive society of older boys, and sitting silent, daydreaming, picking up the gist of topics, as conversations in the many secret languages in which they were all fluent—Hungarian, French, German, to a lesser extent Portuguese—swirled around me.

My older brother Andy spoke German and Hungarian but at age five had concluded that these were far less useful than English, which was what was spoken in kindergarten. Following the tradition of immigrant children everywhere, he refused to speak German and Hungarian when at home, thereby persuading all the elders that in America children needed to assimilate, and assimilation meant speaking only English.

By the time I appeared, smack dab in the middle of the Eisenhower era, Hungarian belonged exclusively to the adults, its alchemy of pervasiveness and inaccessibility creating in me a potent and powerful and frustrated longing for linguistic versatility that has lasted a lifetime. Like someone who lacks one of the five senses, I learned how to compensate and became fluent in understanding gestures, facial expressions, and emotions that were unexpressed, at least verbally.

The speed with which my father rubbed his index finger over his thumbnail could signal his level of parental anxiety. The intensity of my mother's focus on something—a conversation, a crossword puzzle, a person, a telephone call—was demonstrated when she bent her left arm, her hand playing with her pearls, while her right hand held the elbow. If my grandmother tilted her head to the right, an echo of girlish flirtation, I knew that she liked the person with whom she was speaking, but the vertical position was simple politeness. My grandfather's hands folded a few inches away from his face, elbows propped on the armrests, indicated that what he was about to say would be profound. My aunt's cigarette prop—the long inhale, say, or the longer untapped ash—was so articulate, she could have spoken only Chinese, and I would have known how she felt about a subject.

The house on Patterson Street was big and red brick and the largest on the block. Set back from the street, shrouded by a tangle of boxwood, holly trees, and azaleas, it so overshadowed our lives that when we referred to it, we simply said Patterson Street, as if it were the only house there. And for us, it was. My grandmother had shopped for the house with my mother in 1954. She bought furniture at an auction, managed to salvage some family art stored in France, and aside from a few changes of carpet, lightbulbs, and paint, for over fifty years the furniture remained just where she put it, and the pictures hung just where she hammered the nails.

It wasn't a shrine, though. In fact it was an active, jolly place with lots of coming and going, many guests and parties, a fortress against the impositions of the outside world. An enclave of civility and good conversation and utter predictability, it was more Budapest in 1935 than Washington in the latter half of the twentieth century. Each season came accompanied by a particular smell immediately noticeable when you walked into the front hall: my favorite was summer, a perfume of cigarettes, flowers, sherry, and warm dust.

We were not a conventional nuclear family but a sprawling, diffuse, middle-European, three-generation household dominated by the Kornfelds, my mother's people, converted aristocratic Jews. The dinner table was a diorama of the power structure in the household, with my baroness grandmother, Marianne, presiding. Once a noted beauty in Budapest, she possessed a kind of regal quality even as an old woman—her nails always painted a dusky pink, her white hair in a bun held by tortoiseshell pins, and large, heavy-lidded blue eyes that contained, if not sadness, then resignation.

On her right sat my grandfather, Baron Maurice de Kornfeld. He was always dapper in a three-piece suit and spats—a sartorial requirement that became increasingly difficult to satisfy in the United States—despite the fact that he rarely left the house and spent his days reading, writing, and playing solitaire in his little office. Even in his eighties he was never stooped, though he also never seemed to go very many places. As a child, I would visit him in his study as he played solitaire, and together we would arrange the cards. Bald, with a tidy mustache and a wise and gentle face, he exerted the compelling poetic force of a patient and deep intellectual; there was not a book not worth reading for him, whether philosophy or agrarian tracts or anything historical or merely entertaining like Wodehouse or Maigret.

My mother's unmarried, older, and dazzling sister, Mária, had been as beautiful as a porcelain doll as a child, and in the family craze for diminutives, she became Puppa. She had dark hair that she permitted to gray and then whiten, and her mother's heavy-lidded eyes, though in a soft brown. She always wore glasses and, astonishing to me, had so much trouble with her teeth, she actually decided to have them all pulled and wore unobtrusive dentures. (I had always assumed that adults would not have their own teeth, but this seemed a bit radical.)

A beloved prodigal, now an even more beloved working woman, she sat next to her father, exerting a quiet unspoken force that shaped all our lives but I think mine particularly. While she was only a modest laboratory technician, first at Suburban Hospital and then for a private group of physicians, she had lived a romantic and defiant life until she was thirty-six, when she gave herself over to work, service to the family, and learning as much as she could about religion and history and ancient times. What lab technician was reading Maimonides or was immersed in African archeology?

Like some superhero, she spent her days masquerading as a servile drone, while her real identity, or the identity that I bestowed on her, was the feminist (though she loathed feminists) intellectual. She spoke disparagingly of marriage—at least for herself—but was candid about her two great love affairs. One had been in Budapest, with her mother's first cousin's husband (how Hungarian) who was over twenty years older than she and was the Great Love of Her Life. The other was in Portugal, with a Catalan painter who also adored her but was jealous of her autonomous nature. She left Portugal in 1950, telling Luis she was going for only a brief visit with her family in America. She never returned.

To the left of my grandmother sat my father, Aladár, who kept his handsome-movie-star looks well into his sixties. Pictures from his youth suggest a young James Mason, with a broad smile and a pointed widow's peak. Hanna, my mother, sat next to him, as lean as her sister was voluptuous. She had a long Modigliani face with a prominent nose that was apparently a singular sorrow for my grandmother. My grandmother's tendency to compare the two sisters, and to judge my mother unfavorably, was contagious. Even as a child, I somehow knew that my mother had a more difficult life because of the obvious perfection of her older sister. And as an adolescent in the late 1960s and early 1970s, the role model who had the more compelling feminine mystique was obvious. Yet my mother was the one who had been chosen by the most eligible bachelor in Budapest, the one everyone considered a rising political star.

For me, as I grew older, she was embarrassing. She was much too present in my daily life, with her accent and her stockings and her refusal to listen to anything but classical music in the car. Of course, with three children, she was the only member of the household who was truly engaged in the new world, and she was fierce about her engagement, organizing carpools, becoming a lunch mother, and—heaven help me— having a brief stint as a Girl Scout leader. Though she never voluntarily wore pants, she bought a pair of tailored gray-flannel trousers when we went away camping, and she dutifully did all that was required of her with the other leaders, until lights out, when she drove all the way home to sleep in her own bed and use her own bathroom, returning before dawn for uncooked pancakes and cocoa.

Down the table, below the silver saltcellars, appended to the dominant structure, were the three of us, my older brothers and me. The room was formal, with heavy drapes, silk curtains that set it apart from the hall, oil paintings, and silver service on the credenza. A Filippino Lippi painting of Saint John the Baptist as a rather formidable child—it had once been part of a triptych, we were told—looked down on us from the wall. Today the notion that adults in a household could outnumber three children is bizarre; for us it was a fact of life.

But a far more significant fact of life—the polar opposite of both the American dream and the immigrant experience—was the fundamental awareness, so fundamental that even now I hardly question it, that the lives of the younger generation were destined to be less interesting, less accomplished, less erudite, and less meaningful than those of the adults.

Even though the civilized and soft-spoken members of the older generation who dominated the household had settled into a life of reflection
instead of action, it didn't matter. What mattered was what preceded us.
The life *before* America. The life *before* the war. Yes, even life *during* the
war. The daily grind in America paled in comparison to the eradicated
Hungarian world; the past trumped the present.

Evidence abounded. The oil portraits in the living room were painted
by one of Hungary's most famous artists, Miklós Barabás, my father's
grandfather. Watercolor scenes from the country estate of my mother's
family, of workers collecting hay, a peasant mother holding a baby, the
inside of a country church that had the family crest on one of its walls
were painted by my grandmother's cousin, a brilliant Viennese artist who
died in Auschwitz. Fragments of this lost life covered the walls, filled the
bookcases, and decorated tabletops. Or came to dinner. Or arrived in the
mail.

Thirty-seven yellowed photographs hung on the walls of my grandparents' bedroom. I had ample time to become acquainted with the images since their room was adjacent to mine and as a child I could wander
there freely. In their sunbathed room, I would look at sepia-toned prints
of my mother and aunt in riding breeches, at my uncle Tom peeping
around the huge curved staircase of their country home in Ireg, at my
uncle George, a stunningly beautiful boy with lush blond hair and my
grandmother's melting blue eyes. There were photographs of weddings
in the countryside, manors in the city, and the porches of spectacular
country houses. One was an aerial view of an enormous dining room
table, replanted in a garden, beautifully set with Herend porcelain for
fifty.

Hanging over my grandparents' beds was a photograph of my grandmother, her five brothers and sisters, and her mother and father, sitting
behind a large table in their Budapest house. It must have been in 1899
because my great-aunt Edith was just a baby. My great-grandfather
Manfred Weiss, the owner of Csepel, the largest iron- and steel-
manufacturing factory in Hungary that at one time employed forty thousand people, stands behind his brood. My great-aunt Elsa, the oldest girl,
defiantly glares at the camera. Their mother—who would be dead of
pernicious anemia only four years later, but here still young and
beautiful—looks down at her youngest daughter, Edith, the baby swad-
dled in streams of lace. Lace hung everywhere, really—on the bibs of my

two great-uncles' shirts, on the cuffs and bodice of my grandmother and her sisters Elsa and Daisy. The children look so solemn, as if their powerful father has sternly advised them to behave.

I don't know what was so touching about that picture: the looming death of their mother, perhaps, or the innocent perfection of that frozen moment. Or the fact that once the moment passed, once the shutter had opened and shut for the last time, they were all one millimeter closer to the utter obliteration of all that was contained so simply and serenely in that frame.

Once they were great and important people. Once being barons and baronesses entailed true noblesse oblige. They really did help others— orphan girls, factory workers, artists and poets, and some of the most prominent writers in interwar Hungary. Once they owned and organized publications, newspapers, and journals like the *Hungarian Quarterly* and *La Nouvelle Revue d'Hongrie*. Once nearly everyone in Budapest knew their names, ate their jams, sewed with their needles, and rode their bicycles. Some even drove their cars and flew airplanes with their engines.

Once they lived lives of splendor and privilege, but the people I knew lived in a large but not imposing house in Washington, entertained other émigrés, sent money to many who were left behind, and accepted their reduced circumstances with grace. Our dining room table seemed like an inverted evolutionary model, descending from the creatures at the pinnacle of civilization to the barely couth children of middle-class America. The elders were not arrogant about it—indeed, they were all deeply grateful to have made a home in the United States. But their quiet self-confidence and forebearance only emphasized the gap between one end of the table and the other.

I never questioned the position of my parents in the hierarchy, though in retrospect I see that their deference to my mother's family was exquisitely tragic. My parents, especially my father, assumed the position of marginal figures. While my energetic mother did the motherly things expected of her, my father seemed as much a foreigner in his immediate family as he was in America.

It's not that he was so remote I didn't know him. I was, after all, thirty-three years old when he died in 1988, and for most of those thirty-three years I had a loving, respectful, albeit slightly formal relationship with him. I loved him. Of course I loved him. But in the universal algorithm of misunderstanding that is built into the experience of children and their parents, I loved only a *version* of him: the depressed, defeated, disengaged, elderly Hungarian émigré version, protected from either criticism or great expectations because of his illustrious, indeed his heroic, past.

My parents arrived in the United States in January 1946, my father as the Hungarian ambassador, actually the Hungarian minister, during the brief coalition government, and my mother as his brand-new bride. He had received the prize appointment after his opposition to the Nazis, when he was head of the political division of the Hungarian Foreign Ministry, landed him in Dachau. In June 1947 my father refused to recognize the new Communist government and resigned and remained in America.

It was obvious that my father was sad, even to a child. He was a pessimist, he said emphatically and often. None of us realized that what this really meant was that he was clinically depressed. If you admired a particular suit he wore during an evening dinner party, for example, he would reply, "Thank you. It is the suit I will be buried in."

My father was fifty-one when I was born, and had resigned himself to a much-diminished life. His favorite sister was still imprisoned in Hungary for his defection. His elderly parents not only lost their pension but had been deported to a house in the countryside, a shack really, and they were forced to share it with a family of strangers. His father died in those circumstances. A cousin had been murdered by the notorious secret police.

My father faded into his parallel universe of books, his garden, and his responsibilities as the editor of the Hungarian department of the Voice of America. He worked Tuesday through Saturday, so our exposure to him was largely limited to mass on Sunday and the noonday dinner that followed it. After that he would work in his garden or tend the seedlings under the grow lights in his basement office. He would retreat into the Sunday papers and his books. One of my cousins actually thought he was the gardener, so disconnected was he from the warp and woof of our lives. On some level I assumed that my parents had both loved others but married each other as a kind of accommodation. Only as I grew older did I begin to see that his thwarted ambition, his lost country, and his experience in the concentration camp trailed behind him like the ghost of a dead twin.

The mosaic of all these lives became more richly detailed as I grew older. And the story, no longer restricted to the house on Patterson Street, became the stuff of history. Who could not find compelling the powerful paradox of my mother's family, who had survived the massive extermination of Hungarian Jewry by having made a deal with Heinrich Himmler, in which they received passage to Portugal in exchange for their factories and much of their wealth. Miraculously, Himmler kept his side of the bargain. And then there was the paradox of my father the Gentile who had sat in Dachau. The broader historical significance of it all, the importance of this family in shaping the political, industrial, and cultural landscape of Hungary during the interwar years, haunted me yet remained just out of reach.

Much later I found a small cache of letters in my mother's bedside table. She died on a mild January day in 2002 from pancreatic cancer. She succumbed, exactly as she had dreaded, in a hospital, with tubes in too many places. My aunt stood with us and said goodbye to her younger sister. Together they had buried their parents and my father. Together they had traveled to Europe and California and New Mexico and New York; together they had hosted dinner parties and celebrated every holiday and birthday and watched *Jeopardy!* and the opera on public television. With the exception of five years—from 1945 until 1950—they had never lived apart, for the rest of my mother's eighty-five years.

Two years after the funeral we finally sold Patterson Street, and it was time to finally clean out all the drawers, the papers, the closets, the detritus of the eight lives that had called the place home for over fifty years. In my mother's nightstand, I found four yellowed envelopes marked in her handwriting, in pencil, 1940, 1941, 1942, and 1943. They contained letters from my father as my mother summered at her family's country estate. I had grown accustomed to a kind of exhausted passivity when faced with pages of handwritten Hungarian, similar to the old feelings at the dinner table surrounded by all those languages. I put them in a box and emptied the box into family files. It took a year before I hired a translator.

Two mornings a week for a month, Judy Katona would appear, sit in my office, and translate the letters as I typed the words. Sentence by sentence the ghost of the dead twin came to life. I became acquainted with the father I had never known but had always hoped was there—luminous, ambitious, wise, even funny.

He was thirty-six when the letters began on July 4, 1940. He had met my mother several months before at a dinner party and had already been befriended by my grandfather, who was always on the lookout for brilliant young men with whom he could talk and sometimes help. My father began this letter by discussing burning political questions and said he hoped "that world politics will not make the realization of my twenty-year plan impossible." Gradually, he ventured into slightly more personal questions: if her summer was pleasant, if her mother was worried about her brothers, if she could garden.

The details of their courtship and of his life slowly emerged, like a film soaking in developing solution. He would write every week, often more frequently. He wrote about politics, about his work, about dinner parties and visiting delegations, about his parents and sister, about the books he was reading and the trips he was planning. He collected poems he thought "worthwhile to read . . . because I am curious what you think about them." He wished her "sunshine, few frustrations and the knowledge that I kiss your hands many times."

My mother's letters to him are lost. My father probably burned them along with many of his incriminating papers on March 19, 1944, when the Nazis invaded Hungary. Nonetheless glimmers of her responses emerge in his letters. She is his fortune teller, and he assures her that "I think I am going to turn to you for any prediction." Gently he tells her that she doesn't need to write a first draft of her letters to him—that he will be happy with her thoughts "just as they come off of your pen."

I can see my mother, her intellectual inferiority complex in full flower, worried about impressing this dazzling intellectual, the first-prize winner at École Libre des Sciences Politiques and a diplomat who had distinguished himself in Berlin and now in Budapest. I can also see her being flirtatious, teasing him, being hilariously funny and brilliant in her insights about people. I imagine her charming him with her youth—this all began when she was twenty-four—and with her enormous capacity for love and friendship. And she must have blossomed after having been chosen by him: for the first time in her life, she excelled at something other than sports.

They spent hours in what they referred to as his BMW but was actually a massive old Steyr 100 he had purchased in Berlin. They escaped the war and the politics and the social pressures during long drives in the countryside surrounding Budapest. During the war, Hungary remained unusually peaceful, and while there were odious and oppressive Jewish laws, there were no ghettos, no yellow stars, no deportations until April

1944. He wishes that they could be together and imagines "how nice it would be to be at your place. On Sunday evening I was looking at the moon and imagined the moon from that particular angle in your flower garden. I would like that view right now, with you beside me." Laws prohibiting intermarriage between Gentiles and Jews had already been enacted. A public liaison with my mother would have cost my father his job. Not only his livelihood but a powerful voice of opposition to the Nazis would have disappeared.

They had an unofficial—unknown to me—anniversary of September 18, 1940. They must have been on a drive and stopped at some point. Maybe he kissed her for the first time or told her that he loved her, and she must have responded in the way he longed for. Thereafter his salutations of "Dear Hanna" changed to "Hanna, my dear." He tells her that he hopes she has some good excuses for friends, who have been waiting for her. "I hope you consoled Éva and told her we had a flat tire. Or the car had to be pushed. Or why for any other serious reason you couldn't be at her place on time. . . . The weather today is almost as nice as it was yesterday, but there is a significant difference that without question makes Wednesday so much more beautiful."

As I typed these words, my translator and I sat with tears running down our faces. Each day I would impatiently wait for the next day when the letters would unfurl into English. The last letter was dated November 4, 1943, and he closed by saying, "I again have to complete some very tense work during a short period of time. The whole thing is very complicated. I hope that I will manage to make it more organized, so please think of me. Now I must finish. Goodbye, my darling." He was then in the midst of trying to negotiate a separate peace with the Allies. That effort failed and ultimately led to his arrest.

What an extraordinary new story line now unfolded before me. Two lovers severed by war and politics, triumphing over unimaginable barricades, until finally being united. How remote these people were from the sedate and deferential couple, sitting subordinate at the dinner table, hoping that their alien children would not misbehave yet again.

I can ask only now, as a divorced and remarried middle-aged woman with a daughter of my own: what would it have been like to have grown up with this as my dominant narrative of intimacy? What if, when I was a little girl, my mother had told me how much they loved each other, how handsome my father was, and how they yearned and waited during the war, when so many people did so many bad things, and so many people did so many good things, but you never knew what would happen? Finally, for them at least, they enjoyed the happiest of endings.

In his last diary entry, on December 23, 1987, his forty-second wedding anniversary, my father knew that he was going to die soon (as he did, three months later). "It won't be easy to leave my family," he wrote. "Hancsi, the children. But I am eighty-four years old, and I know that every day is a gift. But one would like to see his children in a good, married life, happily as I lived with Hanna and Puppa in unimaginable harmony and mutual care for each other."

The simple mention of Puppa explained everything: their married autonomy and centrality had been supplanted by a familial unit.

With these letters, the missing puzzle piece had been found, and the third dimension of these figures came into focus. Yes, this was a great story with real historic heft. Yes, this was one of those footnotes to the war that deserved to be the main narrative. Yes, the relationship between my parents linked two great themes of Hungarian history, the tensions and the glories between the Jews and the so-called "real" Hungarians. But I had never before realized that against that operatic backdrop, a fabulous, full-blown, twenty-four-carat love story had played itself out.

Across the years I heard their voices, speaking not in the carefully measured tones of my childhood, not with the retrospective wisdom and resignation of ten, twenty years and more, not in the alien context of America, but in real time, before all of them and the world they shaped and the world that shaped them disappeared forever. Like some precisely realized wish, I saw them not as peripheral figures but as the leading man and leading lady. The pictures on the walls of my grandparents' bedroom were brought to life as his letters animated the once-frozen images. No longer constrained by my linguistic limitations, freed by translations, I was given the vehicle to embark upon my voyage of discovery. Now all the pieces of this sprawling historical and personal puzzle were available to me. Or at least most of them. Put simply, the letters gave me the voice to tell their story.

And they gave me a completely different story to tell.

Here it is.

1940

*"In our family, as far as we are concerned, we were born
and what happened before that is a myth."*

—V. S. PRITCHETT, *A Cab at the Door*

CHAPTER 1

You See,

I Used to Live Here

In 1978 I visited Budapest for the first time. I lived in Dijon from January until June of the year between college and graduate school, and my parents met me in Zurich, where some of my mother's many relatives lived. Together the three of us toured France and Italy before arriving at our ultimate destination, Budapest.

A complete role reversal occurred when we were in Europe together. For the first time in my life, I did not mediate conversations between one of my parents and a shop clerk or a waiter or a bus driver or a flight attendant or a person on the street. Instead I was mute and inarticulate, as my parents, my incompetent immigrant parents, speaking French or German or, eventually, Hungarian, handled the quotidian minutiae that used to be my secure domain. I felt bad enough when infantilized in private conversation, but this all felt horribly, extravagantly public.

Somehow I remember our time in Hungary as being all rainy and gray, though my journal describes beautiful spring days. The city in 1978 still looked traumatized from its World War II siege and the Hungarian revolution of 1956. Bullet holes marked buildings, and dirt spewing from both factories and small Soviet cars left a haze in the air and soot on the walls and a vague headache for the first few days. And yet the grandeur of the Danube, the intricate pillars and crevices of the Parliament building rising on its left bank, the craggy hills of Buda, the flat, urban density of Pest, the sweeping bridges, and the reconstructed castle district all seemed familiar.

Images from *My First Book of Hungary* by István Csicsery-Rónay, a frequent Patterson Street guest, were now life-size and three dimensional. The book was published in 1967, and its introduction was the perfect example of the Hungarian self-involvement that I never witnessed at Patterson Street but that I grew to appreciate among some émigrés:

> Hungary, or Magyarorszag (maw-dyawr-or-sahg), as the Hungarians call their country, may well be called the land of the middle. It lies in Central Europe; it is halfway between two corners of Europe (the Strait of Gibraltar and the Ural Mountains); and it is halfway between the North Pole and the Equator.

Dispensing with latitudes and longitudes, Hungary is simply the center of the universe.

My father brightened as we approached the city of his birth, the only place on the planet where he ever felt at home, despite all its radical changes. Sitting in the front seat of the cab we took from the airport, he engaged the driver in a wide-ranging conversation about national politics and local concerns. Even though he was already seventy-five, he was vigorous and energetic. He was voraciously curious and well informed, so he knew what to ask. When I casually remarked on the presence of soldiers at the airport, he, ever vigilant, shot me a warning look that said such observations should be kept quiet.

While my parents were both from Budapest, more than the thirteen years that separated their ages divided their experiences. My mother's world of the rich but new Jewish aristocracy had once, when he was a very young man, been vividly a part of my father's middle-class resentments, class tensions, and misunderstandings. In his 1929 diary he wrote defiantly, "I always had an insensible prejudice toward the rich and powerful—maybe because I am neither of those and would like to be both. . . . I always had a sense for the social distances, especially upward, and I am proud of having that sense." It became clear to me that while my parents' two families obviously did not represent all of Hungarian society, the Szegedy-Maszáks and the Kornfelds did embody two defining elements of the myriad tensions of Hungarian identity.

My father's family—Catholic, upper middle class, intellectual Hungarian gentry—would have seen nothing unusual about locating Hungary halfway between the north pole and the equator.

My mother's Jewish, cosmopolitan, well-traveled, multilingual, and wealthy family would have smiled with just a trace of condescension at such grandiosity.

MY FATHER LED US through winding streets and away from the tourist centers into the run-down neighborhood where my aunt Lilly lived in one of the most depressing apartments I had ever seen in my life. The building smelled bad. We walked up a few flights and knocked on a very dirty door. After entering a small, dingy hall, we saw to the left a kitchen with a black iron stove, no hot water, a tiny refrigerator, and filth. The center of the apartment was the living, dining, and bedroom, with a dirty bed presiding. Each wall was covered with pictures, but the whole room was like a curio shop, so full of memorabilia as to make one gasp for air.

Lilly, my father's beloved sister—who had saved their parents during the terrible Siege of Budapest and who knocked on every official's door and called in every family favor in an effort to get my father out of Dachau—lived here. Now she was old and sick and alone except for the resentful presence of her younger sister Musi, who always believed that Lilly had things easy in comparison with her hard life. Lilly lay in this squalid lair looking at paintings that were another reminder of all that she had lost.

They were mostly painted by my father's great-grandfather, who was one of Hungary's most accomplished nineteenth-century masters, Miklós Barabás. The Maszáks came from Bohemia, and there were several army officers among them. My father's grandfather, Hugo Szegedy-Maszák, had studied art with Barabás before deciding to become a journalist, but he continued his relationship with the great painter by marrying his daughter Ilona and having ten children, one of whom was my father's father, Aladár. Strained relations existed between the father-in-law and his daughter's husband, and as impressive as Hugo's intellectual energy was, his capacity to provide for his ever-growing family was erratic at best.

Still, what Hugo lacked in financial acumen, he more than made up for in creative energy. He began a short-lived art periodical and became the secretary of the newly formed Council of Fine Arts, a position he held for eighteen years. In 1882, in the interests of freeing the Hungarian press from the pressures of the Viennese news agency, he established the Hungarian News Service, which he headed for sixteen years. In 1887 he was granted nobility. The letter explained that "as recognition of your achievements in the areas of public education and the fine arts you are most graciously granted Hungarian nobility and the use, exempt from any fees, of the 'Pesti-Szegedy' title of nobility." Much as the British confer nobility with a geographical honorific, this title indicated that he was from Pest—the two cities had not yet been united. He died in 1916.

Aladár's father, who was also named Aladár, grew up in that highly intellectual, slightly chaotic milieu aswirl with children and paint boxes and literary ambitions. One of his sisters became a portraitist and a well-known Theosophist, whose claim to fame in the family was not her religious or artistic inclinations but the small yet comprehensive library located in her bathroom. And there were suicides, three or four of them, that my father would allude to during some of his darkest moments.

Artists, Theosophists, misunderstood geniuses, chronically depressed intellectuals, all populated the extended Szegedy-Maszák family. But the twin burdens of great intellect and depressive tendencies skipped Aladár senior—who was the head of the Imperial Hungarian Court in Budapest and by all accounts enjoyed an irascible but charming personality—and landed in a highly concentrated form in his only son.

My Szegedy-Maszák grandfather, spry and dapper it seems even as a young man, his goatee trimmed with surgical precision, craved a more ordinary, or at least a more orderly, life and joined the military. There he eventually rose in the Hapsburg monarchy and was put in charge of the royal palace.

At the last coronation of a Hungarian king in December 1916, the height of my grandfather's prestige was captured in a photo that hung on Lilly's apartment wall and in my father's office. As the royal herald preceding the new king, Aladár Senior, dressed in an elaborate national costume called a *diszmagyar*, sat erect on a royal horse. It seems he peaked at that moment, as did the nation he represented, since both his career and the empire collapsed within two years. The much-longed-for ennoblement never reached him, and his wife, the formidable Sarolta Moldoványi, was deeply disappointed.

Sarolta's family was from Transylvania, so Trianon—the treaty that followed World War I and redrew the borders of Hungary so that the country lost two-thirds of its land and half of its population—was not just a geopolitical abstraction for her but a very real severing of the heart of her heritage, albeit a heritage from the eighteenth century. She was one of five children of Sándor Moldoványi, who was an industrious pharmacist in Budapest. He even established the first bandage factory in Hungary, and in 1885 he received a medal at the Hungarian Art and Trade Fair in Budapest. My grandmother Sarolta was a devout Catholic, ambitious and organized and full of hopes, first for her husband and then for her only son.

After the First World War inflation ravaged the country, and my grandfather's job disappeared with the monarchy. Following the brief intermezzo of Communism, the Horthy regime took power, and an old friend helped my grandfather secure a job, or at least the title, as the head of some economic office of the regent. His new colleagues had little respect for the old monarchist anachronism, and going to work where there was no real work, only to receive a paycheck, demoralized my grandfather.

My father as a young man saw the fortunes of the family buffeted by political storms and saw his own father descend from a kind of greatness to graceful, genteel defeat as he dressed for a pretend job with a very real salary every day. My father attended gymnasium and the University of Budapest and eventually went to the École Libre des Sciences Politiques in Paris, fulfilling the hopes of both his parents.

Yet as he sat in his sister's pitiable apartment, the guilt of all his failures as a son and brother looked like a literal burden on his back and shoulders. He had promised his parents that he would take care of her, and over and over again in his journals, he would write about the anguish of not fulfilling that promise.

ONE AFTERNOON IN BUDAPEST my mother and I visited András Belyus, who had been the head butler for her family ever since she could remember. His apartment was meticulous, the mantelpiece, bookcases, and side tables festooned with many photographs of my grandparents, my mother, her brothers, her sister, the family estate in Ireg, and their city apartment on Lendvay Street. He had begun his service to the family as a valet to my great-uncle Paul. Soon he became indispensable to the whole family.

He would become the dominant force in the Kornfeld household. At lunch or dinner, he stood at the serving table in the dining room, wearing his green or gray uniform and his white gloves, listening attentively to the conversations, and responding with silent precision to the slightest need of one of the guests or family members. His wife was a manicurist in the most prestigious barbershop in Budapest, so between the two of them, they could probably have reconstructed most of the social and political gossip of the city.

Belyus never sat down as he poured tea and reminisced with my mother about times he could share with no one in Hungary. I watched her, the hapless Scout leader, the frantic lunch mother, the Woman Who Never Wore Pants, the "bank and chauffeur" now become the gracious baroness. Not haughty and most of all not inauthentic, she was more comfortable than I had ever witnessed.

Later that day we took the little subway, the first in continental Europe, up Andrássy Avenue—although at that time it had been renamed Népköztársaság útja, or Avenue of the People's Republic—and emerged in my mother's old neighborhood. All the homes had gone through several incarnations, from private villas to chopped-up apartments, but the grandest was the former home of her grandfather, Manfred Weiss, at 114 Andrássy Avenue. Now the official Russian guesthouse, the home was spectacular, with muscular, half-naked marble men supporting the sweep of balcony. My mother told me that once tennis courts and stables had occupied the far corner of the property, but no longer. When the house was built, it was even wired with electricity. When my grandmother and her sisters had dance parties, an electrician was hired to spend the night in case any emergency repairs were needed.

Marianne Weiss lived with her parents and five brothers and sisters on the first floor of the villa, while her maternal grandparents and great-grandmother lived on the second floor. My grandmother always said that the best time to have been alive was in the early twentieth century, before World War I. Budapest was at the pinnacle of its history. No longer the shabby junior partner to Vienna in the Austro-Hungarian Empire, it blossomed with culture and new architecture and all the benefits of a world-class city.

It must have been especially nice if your father was Manfred Weiss, who did much to industrialize Hungary. He began modestly enough with a factory in the Budapest city limits that canned plum preserves.

Eventually he expanded the canning to include other food and his market to include the military. He noticed that the cans themselves were a handy shape that could be enlarged and made into little military stoves, or contracted to become bullets. Since a factory that used gunpowder near the heart of a busy city tempted fate, he bought a plot of land on an island in the middle of the Danube called Csepel and built the Manfred Weiss Works. The Austro-Hungarian army was so impressed with its work that they asked him in 1887 to manufacture shell casings, magazines, and ammunition boxes, and its German affiliate was awarded a contract by the German government to manufacture ammunition boxes for the army Mausers.

As the factory fortunes rose with war, so they fell during times of peace. Weiss then poured money into Budapest real estate: some slices of Andrássy Avenue, a hotel in the inner city, a big chunk of land in a rich agricultural region known as the Angyalföld, and a significant piece of property near the Danube, in an undeveloped area where the Margaret Bridge stood.

As with many nineteenth-century entrepreneurs, the accumulation of wealth was not Manfred Weiss's compelling need but a happy by-product of his truly compelling need, which was to make things. He was a creative genius, and his muse and motivation was the majesty of a huge factory, a new kind of factory that mass-produced a range of products in quantities undreamed of before in Hungary. But this factory would not exploit the workers strictly for profit, because a benevolent father ruled it.

There sprang up a small hospital for the workers, a day care center for smaller children, and a nursery, where mothers who were still nursing their babies could come during the day to feed them. A pediatrician was available to all the children, and other doctors were there for the workers. Weiss subsidized housing near the factory, and the workers had pensions, unheard of at the time in Hungary, rewarding their loyalty long after they were no longer able to be productive.

When he spotted the beautiful Alice de Wahl, the daughter of a leader in the European railway system, he turned to his friends and said, "Don't even look at Alice de Wahl. She is going to be my wife." They married in 1884, and quickly the children began to appear: Elsa in 1885, Eugene in 1886, my grandmother Marianne in 1888, Alfons in 1890, Daisy in 1895, and little Edith in 1899.

Weiss was a thrifty man who made sure that his children wrote down every penny that they spent in little notebooks that they were given each year. Still, the family traveled to St. Moritz, to Sils-Maria, and to Ragusa, which is now Dubrovnik. But Alice began to feel tired and weak, so ill in fact that during a summer vacation to Cortina d'Ampezzo in 1903, she had to return to Budapest. Her tongue was bright red and smooth. Her hands and feet had an almost unbearable tingling. The flush of youth and motherhood and domestic happiness was replaced with a yellow-tinged pallor. Weakness and neuropathy made it impossible for her to walk across the dining room.

Money was no object, and doctors were brought in from all over Europe—Paris, Vienna, Munich, Zurich—but in 1903 there was nothing to be done for pernicious anemia. Manfred Weiss sat at his wife's bedside for days at a time, and finally, on January 27, 1904, at the age of thirty-seven, she died. Their house went into deep mourning. A black flag was draped over the big balcony where once they had happily watched so many parades. Manfred sat shiva, and at seven every morning ten Jewish men came to the house to form a *minyan* and pray. He established two charities in his wife's memory: the Alice Weiss Maternity Hospital and Home, and an institution for the care of the incurably sick.

The family was Jewish, of course, but hardly pious; Jewish in identity but barely in practice. Indeed, it seems that the most powerful expression of their religion was when they were mourning. They supported the Dohány Street Synagogue, attended the High Holiday services, and celebrated the bar mitzvah of the older Weiss son, Eugene. Alfons never celebrated his bar mitzvah because when he came of age, his mother's illness commanded the attention of the entire household, and a celebration would have been unthinkable. Yet Christmas trees and ham for dinner made them the perfect example of highly assimilated early-twentieth-century Budapest Jews.

After the death of Alice, her mother, who lived upstairs, took over as the mother figure for the six children and the chaperone for her forty-six-year-old son-in-law. Women were eager to succeed her daughter as wife and mother, but should Manfred look twice at a maid or a governess, his mother-in-law made sure she was history.

Manfred was eager for Marianne, his second-oldest girl, to find the right husband. His oldest daughter, Elsa, had married a young seed merchant named Alfred Mauthner. Alfred was fortunate to have met Alice before she died, and she liked him and thought he would be a good match for her restless, clever oldest daughter. But Manfred had his reservations, because although born a Jew, Alfred had converted to Catholicism, along with his brother and other members of his family. For a man to change his religion was unthinkable to Manfred. It revealed a shakiness of character, a lack of the fortitude and clarity that husbands require. But the couple assured him that their children would be raised as Jews, which counted for a lot. And the fact that his late wife had liked Alfred counted for more. Finally Manfred relented.

But Marianne had not fallen in love, so Manfred brought nice young Jewish men from good families in Vienna, Munich, Zurich, Paris, and of course Budapest to balls as her potential suitors. None of them appealed to her, although two admirers in her immediate circle rose above the rest. Best friends since their university and law school days, Móric Kornfeld was the son of a prominent banker, and Ferenc Chorin was the son of another prominent industrialist.

They physically resembled each other: both were not tall, had thinning hair, and wore glasses. Chorin was a bit stockier, and as they grew older, both would worry about their weight. But their faces were vividly inscribed with their personalities: patience, introspection, gentle humor, and a Zen-like calm on Kornfeld's; humor, impatience, ambition, and curiosity on Chorin's.

Chorin was the great-grandson of a famous eighteenth-century Transylvanian rabbi who considered the Jewish dietary restrictions and the beard requirement absurd and was promptly ordered to apologize to the chief rabbi. The rabbi's son was a doctor, and *his* son became an industrialist and the father of Ferenc Chorin. Chorin's father, who was also named Ferenc, was an economic powerhouse who moved to Budapest, where he founded the Hungarian manufacturers association, known in Hungary as GYOSZ. He was the president of the Salgótarján Anthracite Mining Company, which produced 40 percent of the total brown coal for Hungary. He also served in the upper house of the Hungarian Parliament and left a legacy that his only son eventually fulfilled and surpassed.

Móric Kornfeld was the third child of Zsigmond Kornfeld, who rose from a job as a clerk in a Prague bank to become director in the Böhmischer Bankverein, where he established contact with the House of Rothschild. In 1878 the Hungarian General Credit Bank teetered on the brink of insolvency, and the Rothschilds placed twenty-six-year-old Kornfeld at the head of the Budapest branch. Before he left Vienna, he married a young Viennese woman named Betty von Frankfurter, and together they moved to Budapest. Eventually they would have five children, György, Mitzi, Móric, Pál, and Ferenc.

Zsigmond reorganized the bank completely and eventually reorganized and transformed the entire financial structure of Hungary. While he was a practicing but not devout Jew, Christianity also fascinated Zsigmond. One Saturday, when he was going to their country estate by train, he was reading *The Imitation of Christ* in the original Latin by Thomas à Kempis, a fifteenth-century Dutch theologian. He forgot the book in the train, but on his return home the following Monday, the conductor returned it to him. Kornfeld asked how he knew that it was his book, and the conductor pointed out that "on this train, only Your Honor reads Latin."

Of the children, Móric was the most serious intellectual, and Pál the charming one. Mitzi was intelligent and philosophical but constrained by her gender. Ferenc was a compulsive gambler, and the other members of the family spent a small fortune on his debts. György committed suicide when he was twenty-two. He had been in love with a young woman who was less well off than the Kornfelds. Zsigmond encouraged the relationship and told him that if he finished his university studies before they got married, Zsigmond would give her a dowry as if she were his own daughter. The reassurance didn't seem to matter. György blew his brains out with a pistol and was still holding on to his cane when he was found. Móric became the eldest son.

He was a Renaissance man. He wrote poetry and was fascinated by mathematics, physics, natural and social science, Hungarian sociology, politics and philosophy, poetry, and agrarian reform. He subsidized newspapers and periodicals and became a member of the upper house of Parliament. To his father, Zsigmond, Kornfeld confessed his love; Zsigmond asked him what color Marianne Weiss's eyes were. My grandfather admitted that he didn't know. "They are the most beautiful blue, so blue that when she enters the opera, the whole gallery lights up with her presence," his father replied. (Perhaps my grandfather was not the only Kornfeld man who was smitten.) For six years Móric and Ferenc Chorin courted Marianne Weiss, and for six years Marianne avoided making a decision. Once the two friends were so eager to impress her at a ball, they hired a waiter to sit in a tree making birdcalls.

In 1910 Marianne developed a thyroid problem, and her father took her to Bern, where a new operation that involved removing the thyroid had been created. Recuperation was brutal. She had to remain in a dark room for nearly six weeks, unable to read because her eyes had been badly weakened. Her father made sure that she was never alone, and there she lay, listening to people read her the poetry of Goethe, Schiller, Heine, Rostand, and Rilke. The poems lodged in her memory, and throughout her life she would recite them at odd moments like fragments of a catchy show tune.

She recovered, and finally, in February 1913, she accepted my grandfather's proposal. No one really ever understood why. He adored her but she never really adored him back. On June 17, 1913, twenty-six-year-old Marianne and thirty-two-year-old Móric married in the house at Andrássy Avenue. The day after the wedding the young couple, with maids and luggage and a complete entourage, arrived at the train station to go on their honeymoon in Sils-Maria. In his bliss, my grandfather garlanded the carriage and filled the inside of it with white roses. Naturally shy and sharing her father's instincts for thrift and self-abnegation, Marianne was appalled and embarrassed and probably a little bit angry at being made the center of attention as a young bride. The gesture and my grandmother's reaction to it were diagnostic; stylistically they were so profoundly incompatible that the marriage would be desperately unhappy.

World War I broke out in June 1914, and their first daughter, Mária—who quickly became Puppa—was born in September. Manfred mobilized the factory for maximum production, and he was assured that because his factory was as much a part of the defense of Hungary as the army, none of his employees would be drafted. The war was supposed to be over by Christmas, but of course it wasn't, which was terrible for millions but excellent for the Manfred Weiss Works. The factory expanded and expanded. New buildings sprang up over 570 acres on the island, and the workforce ballooned to forty thousand.

Marianne and her sister Daisy visited soldiers in the military hospitals. They saw the ravages of war, the maimed bodies, the frostbitten limbs, the horrible conditions of care. They heard stories of soldiers, officers even, only half recovered, being released back to families that were ill prepared to nurse them back to health. Their father responded to his daughters' anguish as only a wealthy man with nearly unlimited resources and good instincts could and built the Manfred Weiss Pavilion, a sanatorium where officers wounded in fighting could recover free of charge.

In contrast, his son Alfons, who was a soldier in Ukraine, lived in a villa, became friends with Russian aristocrats, and discovered a vast wine cellar that had belonged to the czar. While other Austro-Hungarian troops in Ukraine were deployed to the brutal Italian front, Manfred intervened so his son could remain on an important assignment investigating fish canneries in the region.

World War I ended in 1918, and on June 4, 1920, the Treaty of Trianon was signed. It only confirmed a reality established by military might, and the order of Britain and France in 1919. During the period of instability after the surrender but before the final treaties, Béla Kun's Republic of Soviets held power from March 21 to August 1, 1919. Communism and Judaism became linked forever in Hungarian minds, since nearly all the Communist leadership was Jewish, at least by origin if not by conviction. Members of the upper middle class and aristocrats were arrested, and some were killed. A large proportion of the victims were Jews. Manfred Weiss left his home and stayed with his daughter Elsa while a few revolutionaries ransacked his house and helped themselves to some of the family treasures, although they could not understand why a man of his wealth would have only two pairs of shoes.

Worried that his prominence would put the rest of his family at risk, Manfred hoarded sleeping pills for weeks. One night he took them all, but his daughter Daisy found him and rushed him to the hospital, where his stomach was pumped. Workers from Csepel guarded his room, and he recovered completely. He decamped to Vienna with the rest of his family and waited until the triumphant regent Miklós Horthy rode into Budapest, having quashed the revolution.

Weiss returned to Budapest to rebuild his completely robbed factory and convert it for peacetime use. Since Hungary had lost so much territory, factories for industries that had been Hungarian, like textiles, were now on Romanian or Slovak or Ukrainian soil. Csepel produced steel and aluminum products, pots and pans, cars and trucks, motorcycles and bicycles, and even textiles and spinning yarn. Ownership was transformed from a privately held company to a corporate structure, in which Manfred distributed all the stock to his children.

In December 1922 Manfred Weiss suffered a stroke, and on Christmas 1922 he died. My mother and aunt remember Móric coming into their room, wearing black, and telling them to be kind to their mother because she had suffered a terrible loss. The newspapers were filled with stories about Weiss's death and long essays describing his contributions to Hungary. One compared him to a strong and healthy oak, suddenly felled by a violent storm. The directors of the factories carried the casket on their shoulders to the funeral wagon, and a solemn procession with thousands of factory workers advanced down Andrássy Avenue. The chief rabbi led the prayers at the Kerepesi Jewish Cemetery where he was laid to rest next to Alice. He left a prosperous factory to his children and a piece of paper with the admonition: "All for one and one for all."

My grandmother and her siblings always spoke about their father with a kind of fresh grief, even decades later, living in America. They still felt an unquiet longing for his presence, as if they were incomplete because he was no longer with them. His legacy did not simply persist in protracted filial grief and loving memories—though that would have been enough; he remained an active presence in their lives every day, in the income they received, in their identity, in his paternal vigilance, and ultimately in the fact that they all survived the next war because of Csepel, his gigantic, smoking, spewing, pounding, massively productive factory.

Members of the Weiss family never moved far away from one another. Eugene Weiss moved into his father's house with his new family, and his sister Edith lived in the upstairs apartment. Ferenc Chorin married my grandmother's younger sister Daisy and bought the house next door. Behind them on Lendvay Street, their sister Elsa lived with her husband and seven children and shared a backyard with the Weiss family. Móric and Marianne moved after their marriage into an apartment on the same street and remained, though the apartment became smaller as their family grew to include four children. Only Alfons Weiss moved away with his wife, Erzsi. They took over a beautiful old villa of Manfred's in the hills of Buda.

As my mother and I turned the corner from Andrássy Avenue, we stopped at her old home on Lendvay Street. It had become the French embassy. We thought that perhaps the nice French woman with a chignon at the large front desk would be willing to indulge us in a nostalgic visit. She looked alarmed to see us.

My mother said in perfect French that she wondered if we could possibly look inside. She paused and continued, "You see, I used to live here." The answer was an unapologetic and unambivalent no. My mother was practically out the door before the answer was delivered, and we exchanged some observations about the French. Wandering up Lendvay Street, we arrived at the Museum of Fine Arts and saw some old statues and paintings that my mother grew up seeing in her now-inaccessible home. The art was taken first by the Nazis and then by the Communists. On another floor were the El Grecos that she remembered from one cousin's living room.

No wonder everything in Washington had seemed to revolve around my mother's family. There the landscape was dominated by the descendants of Manfred Weiss, the sheer number of aunts and uncles and cousins of first, second, and third degrees. Now in Budapest I was captured by the same dynamic. My father's family, distinguished as it was, left little trace beyond the Hungarian News Service, which didn't mean much to me at the time, and some beautiful nineteenth-century paintings by Barabás. But the physically majestic factories and houses and works of art, all connected to the WM of Weiss Manfred (as they called him in Budapest), were palpably imposing and impressive, overwhelming nearly everything else.

That was how we spent my first trip to Hungary, moving back and forth between the worlds that both divided and unified my parents. The symbolism was almost too precise; my aunt Lilly's grim and damaged and demeaned apartment seemed to embody all that had gone wrong for the Szegedy-Maszák family.

On our last night in Budapest, my parents and I had dinner in the vast hotel dining room. After ten days we were no longer treated like aliens, and I exchanged flirty smiles with the waiters who bustled around us. Over wine, steeped in Budapest, feeling close, I asked my parents what their romance had been like. They exchanged quick looks. I wonder if my mother would not have wanted to say something. But for once my father took charge. Smiling, he reached for another piece of bread and said with the sealed air of finality, "My dear, that is none of your business."

CHAPTER 2

The Arizona

■

■   ■

They first met at Kálmán Buday's dinner party. In his usual painstaking way, my father wrote about the evening in the memoir that he labored over for more than twenty years and that remained in thousands of pages of an unfinished draft at his death. In this memoir, safely concealed from the prying eyes of his children since it was written in Hungarian, he wrote frankly and for posterity about his life as a Hungarian diplomat. Only because my uncle Tom was kind enough to translate it for me and my brothers do I know where my father first met my mother.

It was a subordinate observation after a lengthy rundown of the notable guest list. He noted the occasion with agonizing succinctness: "It was also at [Buday's] house that I had my first long conversation with Hanna, which was the basis of our acquaintance." He then named the now-long-forgotten political and cultural subjects upon which their conversation touched.

He did not, however, mention what would most have interested me. She was twenty-four then. Did he think she was pretty? Did he like her laugh? Did he secretly admire her beautiful legs? Did she say something especially funny or charming? Was he affected by the way she touched the pearls at her throat or tilted her head to have her cigarette lit? He provided no answers, only the earnest reports of a man who felt compelled to share many unimportant details while avoiding the ones with important emotional content.

It is easy to fill in the fine points. The year was 1940, and the city was

Budapest. Everybody was smoking and dressed with understated formality, which meant pearls and lipstick and dresses and high heels for the women and dark suits and hats and handkerchiefs in the breast pocket for the men. The scene was chaotic with languages, but mostly Hungarian, German, and out of deference to their hosts (Buday's wife was British), English. Oversize cars and a few horses jockeyed for position on the streets, and beautiful bridges soared over the Danube. The war was merely a few months old, and Britain continued to fight alone. Austria had become thoroughly Nazified, but in Budapest wartime miseries were still remote. Despite the German sympathies of some of its leaders, Hungary had not yet joined the Axis. There were tensions, of course, and the Hungarian right-wing party was thriving. Still, the hard-won stability after the catastrophic losses of World War I was sustained.

My father, Aladár Szegedy-Maszák, was thirty-six then, unmarried, very handsome, and a rising star in the Foreign Ministry. His father had been forced to retire after World War I from his distinguished position in the Hapsburg Court, and his mother was a leader in the Catholic Women's League. My father shared the old family apartment with them and his oldest sister, Lilly, and some of his salary went to their support. Recently, he had returned to Budapest after spending five years as the secretary to the Hungarian embassy in Berlin, where he had watched the rise of Hitler and was appalled by the Nazis long before many of his compatriots were. He was also erudite and well respected in the Foreign Ministry, so among those most worried about Germany's ambitions, his opinions mattered. His job at the Foreign Ministry was liaison to the Vatican, but everyone knew he was destined for greater things. The position did give him the honor of playing host to Mussolini's son-in-law Ciano when he came to Budapest for an official visit.

My mother's father, Móric, already knew Aladár Szegedy-Maszák and had even invited him several times to their home on Lendvay Street—one of the bright young men summoned for weekly political discussions. Móric Kornfeld was a liberal, a member of the Upper House of Parliament, a philosopher, and a great patron of Hungary's intellectual life, all made possible by his vision and by his wife's formidable family fortune. The Kornfelds, like many highly assimilated Central European Jews, had converted to Christianity—in their case, Catholicism—in the 1920s. Hanna had no memory of any religious traditions besides Catholic mass, yet the Kornfeld and Weiss families were still considered to be Jews, albeit, like many other Jews in Budapest, Christian ones.

My mother came from a wealthy family, but she was utterly unspoiled, since the prevailing familial ethos was thrift and a determined lack of ostentation. With a prominent nose, high cheekbones, hazel eyes, dark hair, broad shoulders, truly great legs, and the posture of a dancer, she had an elegance that some might consider beautiful, if not conventionally so. Her stunning, brilliant, and talented older sister, Puppa, had a lovely singing voice and was working on her Ph.D. in medieval Hungarian history; she was as striking as her mother had been. Hanna, who was intelligent but no scholar, was bedeviled by a great sense of inadequacy. Yet people were drawn to her in friendship and intimacy in ways they never were to her much more aloof sister.

No one could have told from the fluency with which she could converse in many languages—English, German, French—or from her apparent social ease that Hanna was shy and insecure. And no one could have told from Aladár's movie-star good looks, his stellar intellect, or his résumé, which was becoming more impressive each day, that he too was shy and insecure.

In 1940 people of this class and in this region still held to some old-fashioned formalities, so when it was time to leave, Aladár Szegedy-Maszák bent over Hanna Kornfeld's hand to kiss it farewell, a gesture so embedded into Hungarian culture that it is part of the language: kezét csókolom—"I kiss your hand"—is an expression of welcome and departure.

A month later they met again at the home of the prominent Hungarian editor and literary critic József Balogh. An old friend of the Kornfeld family, and someone whose intellectual acumen Hanna's father relied upon for editing the literary journals that he supported, Balogh was a virtuoso in his talent for entertaining, matching guests with as much care as he paired the food and wine. Once more Hanna and Aladár must have gravitated toward each other, and even as they spoke to other guests, they were engaged most fully with each other. Again, on parting, Aladár bent over her hand to kiss it farewell.

Perhaps Hanna became emboldened by the unspoken recognition that it was probably the last thing that Aladár would ever do, but when she said her final goodbye—always a protracted ritual in Hungary—she suggested that he join a few people that they both knew for a drink. He met Hanna's invitation with a stumbling demurral. The invitation was repeated by Tamás de Perczel, an old friend of the Kornfeld family and a Foreign Ministry colleague of Aladár's who was escorting both Hanna and Puppa—whom he had loved for years—to the Arizona for a drink.

The allure of feather-clad women and bejeweled acrobats, the revolving-glass dance floor, and the mirror-lined walls of the Arizona was not exactly lost on Aladár, no stranger to decadence from his years in Paris and Berlin. But by then such things were far from his preferred form of postparty entertainment. He would normally have returned to the apartment he shared with his parents and his sister rather than venture across the Chain Bridge to Pest, into the neighborhood known as the "Broadway of Budapest," to 20 Nagymezö Street.

The Arizona had the kind of mystique that caused an English visitor to describe it as "the scintillating cave of the most glamorous nightclub in Europe," and four years later, its determined and naughty neutrality would allow Nazi Obersturmbannführer Adolf Eichmann to unwind there after a day of managing the two-hundred-odd transportation specialists in charge of the formidable logistics of deporting Hungary's 450,000 Jews to Auschwitz.

And yet Aladár went to the Arizona that night.

There he was, almost visibly wilting with all the noise and the music and the sheer glorious excess. There she was, radiating that kind of warmth and happiness that could immediately put someone at ease. Maybe Aladár walked to Hanna's table and she made room for him, or maybe Hanna walked to Aladár and greeted him. But years later at the dinner table at Patterson Street, my aunt Puppa would tell me, with my mother silent and smiling in her reserved way, that everyone there was astonished to see a rising star in the Foreign Ministry, a man as famously formal and old-fashioned as Aladár Szegedy-Maszák, enter a place like the Arizona late one winter night in early 1940.

My father allowed that going there that evening was memorable, even worth noting in his memoir. "It is certain," he wrote, "that at that time the political reasons for my going were at least as strong as the personal ones."

Parsing this sentence reveals so much about my father.

It is certain: Both diplomatic and passive, the "it is certain" clause never takes full responsibility for the action, but at the same time elevates it to a higher authority.

At the time: This phrase is a glancing acknowledgment that this was a distinct event and that whatever emotional state occurred was tied to that moment and might not have happened at any other time.

The political reasons for my going: Could he ever be the subject of his own sentence?

Were at least as strong as the personal ones: Was he suggesting that the tug of his emotions equaled the pull of his political obligations? No, he merely had to justify the wave of personal interest with the undertow of politics.

All those subordinate clauses. He just couldn't find it in himself to frame it differently; he could not write for posterity with ease and grace and some emotional conviction that going to the Arizona was a bold and, dare I say it, even romantic gesture.

CHAPTER 3

The Draft Board

∎

∎   ∎

My father described his world in 1940 as strangely bifurcated, and it was probably even more so than the worlds of most other Hungarians at that time. Hungary was a peacetime oasis, though dire reports of German conquest and aggression would crackle over his radio, be emblazoned across the several newspapers he read every day, and be subjected to analysis by his colleagues in the Foreign Ministry. The government was mobilized to track the conflicts and calibrate Hungary's response. Hungary carried on in relative peace and calm and even enjoyed the repatriation of some of its ethnic Hungarians as Germany conquered territories that had been lost in the aftermath of World War I.

Prior to World War I, rich Hungarian territories in present-day Slovakia, Serbia, Croatia, Austria, and Romania were all considered part of Hungary. But after the Treaty of Trianon chopped off two-thirds of Hungary, more than ten million Hungarians in these places became disliked and mistrusted national minorities, even though in some places such as Czechoslovakia they were actually a majority. The population of Hungary shrank from 18.2 million to 7.9 million. A sense of amputation and national injury would inform much of Hungarian foreign policy for years to come.

In March 1938 German troops entered Hitler's hometown of Vienna, and he declared the glorious unification of the two German-speaking countries. My mother's Viennese relatives, many of them converted Jews, bade a hasty retreat and arrived safely in Hungary, where they found apartments and something resembling employment at the factories or other businesses that the family owned.

By September of that year, with the now-notorious encouragement of the British and the rest of Europe, Germany seized the German-populated regions of Czechoslovakia. The Sudeten Germans celebrated, while the local residents either fled or kept a low profile. Poland collapsed over six autumn weeks in 1939, crushed first as the German army defeated it from the west, then by the Red Army from the east. Polish refugees flooded into Hungary. The women in Hanna's family sprang into action. My grandmother's youngest, unmarried sister, Edith, always drawn to helping anyone in need, immediately started working on behalf of the Polish refugees, finding them places to work and live. The Kornfeld family hired two young Polish women as household help. In the Foreign Ministry, my father arranged for transit visas and even Hungarian passports for many of them.

Meanwhile Hungarians waited, many of them loudly and impatiently, to see if the borders that had been disastrously redrawn after World War I—most egregiously giving the ancient Hungarian territory of Transylvania to the Romanians—might possibly be reconfigured so that at least part of the Hungarian population and land that had been lost would be regained. This was the irredentist movement, which played a large part in Horthy's loyalty to Germany.

By the time Italy declared war on France and England, Germany had already conquered Austria, Czechoslovakia, Denmark, Belgium, the Netherlands, Norway, and France. Hungary avoided any combat within its borders. Of course it supplied munitions—quite a few from the Manfred Weiss Works—and food, but there was nothing resembling real wartime mobilization.

Nonetheless, in the spring of 1940 the local draft board called up thirty-six-year-old Aladár, since he was an able-bodied man who had a driver's license. He went to the Maria Theresa Barracks, an enormous, imposing building on the way to the airport, whose ugliness was emphasized by the beauty of the building it faced: the Museum of Applied Arts, with its stunning tiled roof. At the barracks Aladár joined a large crowd of mostly professional chauffeurs, all of whom were eventually asked to strip and run naked around a dirty room, so the board could evaluate either their fitness or their willingness to obey orders.

Whichever, he passed with flying colors and was drafted to be a driver in the transportation service, a grandiose name for a fleet of horses and wagons. Much to his and his family's relief, the Foreign Ministry insisted that he could not be spared from his important work there, so he was not drafted. In fact, he actually was doing important work for the Foreign Ministry.

The prime minister at the time was Count Pál Teleki, a scholar and educator with a familiar aristocratic face who had been in public life for many years. Despite Teleki's conspiratorial nature and his terribly mixed record in responding to, or pandering to, right-wing anti-Semites, Aladár wrote that he "trusted him completely, since there was never any doubt that he had no personal ambitions." He saw in Teleki the kind of patriot who only wanted to serve and who would "never sacrifice the interests of the Hungarian nation on the altar of some ideology." Teleki had noticed Aladár when he was still a student at the University of Budapest and had followed his education at the École Libre des Sciences Politiques and his first posting to Berlin.

In 1940 Teleki wanted to appoint Aladár to be the deputy press chief in the prime minister's office, but several weeks after their discussions, one of his colleagues told my father to forget that the conversation ever took place. The right-wing Government Party elders stridently opposed him because of his well-known antipathy to Nazism. The Arrow Cross Party—Hungary's version of National Socialism—had received the second-highest number of votes in the Hungarian elections of 1939. Its incendiary leader, Ferenc Szálasi, was still in prison, but there were rumors that he would be released soon.

Those political tensions could not help but bleed into social life. As the world lost its moorings in war, "the old friendships continued or faded depending on which side of the line of demarcation the individuals took their place," Aladár wrote later. Nazism was either appealing or revolting, and this was the lens through which all else was viewed. The lines of demarcation were not restricted to politics but extended also to the friends people had and the parties they attended. Aladár wrote that he "crossed the line less and less in my private life . . . the sterile debates, right-wing slogans bothered my ears. . . . Naziphilia was a consequence or a sign of belonging to a lower social order. As usual in such situations, I began to doubt even the honest intentions and considered an inclination toward Nazism as a manifestation of a deficient national sentiment."

Aladár had had much greater exposure to the Nazis than most in the government. He had watched Hitler's rise to power and actually met him a few times when he served as the secretary in the Hungarian embassy in Berlin from 1932 until 1937. In 1933 he attended Hitler's first speech as newly elected chancellor at the Sportpalast. The legation had been given tickets, and my father and several colleagues sat in the front row. When Hitler spoke, they were stunned by the intensity of his delivery—he shrieked and emoted, and sweat poured from his face and soaked his brown uniform. The speech left Aladár cold, but he was deeply unsettled by the rhapsodic reactions of the audience. "This was my first personal experience that we were dealing with a quasi-religious mass movement," he wrote, "or perhaps more accurately, a mass psychosis."

He saw from the very beginning how devastating Nazi rule would be for the Jews. In April 1933, immediately after the Nazis came to power, universal, large-scale, organized anti-Semitic activities began. Hungarian Jews who lived and worked in Berlin lost their jobs, and many lost their property. As Aladár sat in the consular office, Hungarian Jews came in droves, begging him for advice as to what they should do and how they could help themselves. He spoke to each one "and tried hard to talk to them as an interested fellow human being and not as an official or a person in authority." He met movie directors and actresses and small-business owners. A landlord who owned a block of houses in a workers' section of Berlin had been told that if he didn't simply leave, he would be charged with molesting women. My father tried to help, but there was nothing he could do.

For Aladár, the individual human stories provided an introduction to the new system that was "much more effective than the generalities, regardless of how bloodthirsty those generalities might have been. These experiences extinguished the last, minimal remnants of anti-Semitism that I had had as a teenager during the counterrevolution. I began to experience the tragedy of fate."

As a teenager during Béla Kun's four-and-a-half-month reign, Aladár had marinated in the anti-Semitic atmosphere to which the link between Communism and Judaism gave legitimacy: to be anti-Communist inevitably meant being anti-Semitic. Aladár was not a convinced anti-Semite, but as a Christian Hungarian, from a strong family tradition supporting the monarchy, who experienced the devastation of the first Communist rule, and the devastation of the Treaty of Trianon in dismembering Hungary, he had his anti-Semitic flirtation. Among his papers was one from 1920, a journal entry from when he was seventeen years old. He was in his second-to-last year in high school. The 133-day Communist government of Béla Kun had taken place the year before and had been followed by a war with Romania and the appearance of Admiral Horthy, who became the regent for the next twenty-four years.

The young Aladár was outraged by Béla Kun and by Trianon's evisceration of Hungary and poured his resentments, his fury, and his primitive political analysis into his journal. He complained that Hungarians had inflicted no injury on those who profited, and that they even defended the war millionaires (like Manfred Weiss, though he never mentioned his name). Good Hungarians were "tattered, hungry, [and] shivering . . . while the capitalist race happily luxuriates." He complained that the Hungarian government did nothing about the Jewish issue and contrasted the Jews with forgiving Christians who were loath to "consider our Jewish so-called Hungarian brothers as enemies. . . . Those great siblings . . . liked their homeland so much that they undermined the front lines in order to assure their victory. We owe them gratitude for keeping us unemployed. They loved us so much that they wanted to send us to the other, happier world by starving us."

Appended to this entry was a note that he wrote sixty-four years later, on New Year's Eve 1984. He described how ashamed, remorseful, and guilty he felt reading this and how tempted he was to burn it and eradicate it from his past. In the end, he had decided not to. There was no more powerful repudiation of his sentiments than his subsequent personal history, but he felt that the simple fact that he wrote what he had and the way he had, was in itself a valuable, though personally humiliating, historical artifact. Here was a perfect example of "the disturbed moral sense" that arose in counterrevolutionary Hungary and endured for many Hungarians for decades.

Spending five years in Berlin proved to be a powerful antidote to any vestiges of anti-Semitism that Aladár may have harbored. He warned his superiors of the danger of the Nazis, though he could never have imagined the ultimate dimensions. He attended the Nuremberg party day in 1934, the one memorialized by Leni Riefenstahl in *Triumph of the Will*. The diplomats who had been invited to the event—including the Japanese and the Polish ambassadors—were given a special train in which they stayed and where young German Foreign Office employees entertained them. The special events included a visit to a Sturmabteilung, or SA camp, where the future terrorists of the Reich were trained. These infamous brownshirts were the paramilitary unit of the Nazi Party. The SA behaved, Aladár wrote, with "the pride of the victors and the conceit of the elect.... This was the first time that I made the observation, strengthened by subsequent experience, that people who had killed had a particular light flickering in their eyes. Maybe this was and is only imagination, but I could not get rid of it."

And then my father met Hitler for the first time. Such a strange thing to write.

Hitler entered the parlor car, and all the diplomats stood in a semicircle. He spoke directly to the ambassadors from Japan and Poland and shook the hands of all the others. Aladár could not reconcile this old-fashioned, modest, almost shy man with the "terrible mustache," who greeted them and spoke about the new era of German history, with the raving lunatic on the dais. And now the raving lunatic on the dais was taking over Europe, and Aladár was working as a midlevel officer in the political division of the Hungarian Foreign Ministry in Budapest.

Budapest was a big city, with over 1.1 million inhabitants in 1940, but it was also a small town. People in power tended to know each other, whether their locus was in the government, industry, or the intelligentsia. Ferenc Chorin was the one man in the family, in Budapest, who matched Manfred Weiss in his financial wizardry. He became the putative head of the family after his marriage to Daisy. Quick-witted, tremendously warm, and spontaneous, he certainly had his enemies, but he mostly inspired trust and loyalty and love. Short, bald, and powerfully built, he inherited the Salgótarján coal mines from his father and took over the presidency of GYOSZ, also from his father. To say that he was a friend of Regent Horthy may overstate the case, but they were good acquaintances.

As Ferenc Chorin consorted with those at the highest reaches of power, Móric, no stranger to those altitudes, was equally curious about rising younger talent. Young intellectuals, whether they were historians, literary critics, or government officials, were often summoned to Lendvay Street for discussions about current events or foreign affairs. And if the young man was especially compelling, and if it was the spring or summer or early fall, he would be invited to come visit the Kornfeld family at their country estate, which they all called Ireg, in Iregszemcse, a small town about two and a half hours southwest of Budapest.

I will never know if Móric or Hanna extended the first invitation to Aladár that spring. But after the rendezvous at the Arizona in the winter of 1940, the next trace of Hanna and Aladár's romance appeared in Ireg in May.

CHAPTER 4

Ireg

In the late 1960s a cumbersome, leather-bound book made an amazing journey from the dirt roads of a small town in Hungary to Patterson Street. It was the guest book from Ireg. Beginning in the 1920s, my grandparents owned six thousand acres there, with a grand house, tennis courts, a swimming pool, stables, and a model farm where the workers were treated with generosity and respect. Whenever anyone spoke about Ireg, they seemed transported to a lost land of perfection; expressions would soften, smiles would become tender, and stories would unfold like silk streamers in a gentle breeze.

They would talk about the swimming pool and the stables, the angora rabbits and the tennis courts, Marianne's bees and Móric's model agricultural enterprise. They would talk about the innumerable visitors who came there, some famous and exotic, like the Indian poet Rabindranath Tagore's son. My aunt Edith had met the famous poet in India when she traveled around the world, and he even came to Hungary. Several years later he sent his son to visit. Fifty girls from poor families stayed for six weeks every summer, and my grandmother gave a prize to the one who gained the most weight. When times became darker and food was being rationed, Ireg produced a bounty of fresh milk and eggs, chickens and vegetables, which it shared with friends and family in Budapest.

When Marianne married Móric in 1913, the dowry from her father provided the money to buy Ireg. While it took a few years before they finally settled there, by the mid-1920s Ireg had become an important part of everyone's life. The family would leave right after the feast of Pente-cost, which usually took place in late April or early May, and return after Marianne's birthday in October.

At the height of the summer, seeking to capture a sliver of cooler weather, Hanna and Puppa would go to the stables at six in the morning. The groom waited for them with their horses saddled and ready. They would ride through the landscape that almost vibrated with the shadowy stillness of a summer dawn, past the pool and the tennis courts, past the cherry, peach, and apricot trees heavy with fruit, past the beehives, the cows, pigs, hens, and rabbits, past the currant, raspberry, gooseberry, and strawberry bushes, deep into the heart of their land, with its rolling fields of wheat, rye, and oats. Red poppies, blue cornflowers, and fragile white daisies haphazardly punctuated the meadows. Seasonal workers who came from the poorer villages in northern Hungary for the harvest would already be in the fields. They arrived in the spring and left after the fall harvest. Men with flails in the fields threshed the grain, as women, some-times with babies on their backs, walked behind them binding up the sheaves.

Sometimes when a baby fussed, the mother would break off the flower from a poppy (the sap that ran out stained clothes with brown spots), and the baby would suck the juice and calm down. There was no roar of combines or groan of tractors, although a threshing machine left the straw in piles, smelling sweet in the dry heat.

My grandparents were still alive when the Ireg guestbook arrived, and they had not seen it for over twenty years. Apparently someone in the town had rescued it from children who were playing with it in the streets. Whoever retrieved it knew the Kornfelds (as they all did in that town) but also knew how to send it to America during those Communist times. This book began in 1925 and came to a screeching halt in 1941. On the last page, illegible Russian was scrawled over a formal photograph of my mother's younger brother György (whom I knew as George) and his new Gentile bride, Elsie. My grandmother asked a Russian-speaking friend who was over for dinner to translate the scrawl. He blushed and stam-mered and explained that it wasn't legible, he couldn't make it out. The guestbook appeared at our house like a relative who was thought to be long dead but was now, amazingly, alive. The leather looked like cherry-wood, and the cover was embossed with two small golden gothic M's flanking a large gothic K, beneath a golden crown—for Kornfeld, Marianne and Móric. The pages were thick, rich, and yellowed with age. One afternoon, shortly after it arrived, I was given my formal introduction to Ireg. Very carefully, as I sat next to my grandmother, I opened the covers as if I were opening the original folio of an old European fairy tale. In a sense I was. On the first page was a black-and-white photograph of two distinguished old men, and their two signatures. My grandmother wanted to explain how important these two men were. "Look, here is Hungary's Minister of Defense, the Baron Samuel von Hazai, and Field Marshal Alexander von Krobatin. He was the minister of war for Austria-Hungary from 1912 to 1917."

She translated von Hazai's note of gratitude for the wonderful care that he received, and then she read what Krobatin wrote. He thanked his hosts on June 30, 1925, and observed, "In these materialistic times it is wonderful to find the idealism which will show the upcoming future generation how to find comfort in their life and the reassurance to believe in a happier time for our world."

We saw pictures of rolling hills, horses, and the stag that my grandmother shot (my grandmother shot a stag with a rifle?), as well as charming colored-pencil sketches of visitors and events done by Stefan Mauthner, Marianne's cousin from Vienna, who would die, with his wife, in Auschwitz. Page after page displayed photographs, poems, drawings, fabulous flourishing signatures, and ardent expressions of gratitude and admiration in Hungarian, French, German, Italian, and English—a whole world unfolded before me. My grandmother sat quietly as I turned the pages, occasionally pointing out a photograph of my mother, but the memories that this liberated in her mind must have been far too complex and remote to share with a child.

My grandmother was long dead when I studied the guestbook more carefully, and there I discovered a prize. On a page chaotic with twenty other names—Wesselenyi, Miki; Elemer, Jancsi; Endrédy, Magda—was a careful cursive "Szegedy-Maszák, Aladár, V. 18–20." He was there from the eighteenth to the twentieth of May 1940. A few pages later I found him there again, on the weekend of June 29, 1940.

At Ireg, Aladár could see the entire Kornfeld family in ways that were never available in Budapest. He could observe Hanna's natural athleticism, for example: she would ride, swim, play tennis, and dance. Whenever there was a bridge game, she was likely to be in it. Puppa would sometimes entertain the family with Mozart arias and Schubert *Lieder*.

Aladár met their youngest brother, Tamás (Thomas), who was just six-teen, a prodigy who read Greek when he was only six and took to Latin as if he had been born in sixth-century Rome. Their other brother, György, twenty-two and already working at Csepel, would visit on week-ends. He was the fulfillment of my grandmother's fondest wish to have a boy. A beautiful child with his mother's clear blue eyes, his indifference to his studies was more than compensated for by his sheer charm and good looks. His mother loved all her children, but she *adored* György, who was tall, naturally elegant, calmly promiscuous, and effortlessly charming.

The summer of 1940 was unusually hot. Throughout the country the relentless heat and dryness that followed spring floods had accelerated the ripening of the crops. The newspaper *Magyar Nemzet* reported that the earliest harvest in living memory had already begun. It was like some middle-European version of a Shakespeare play, where nature itself re-flected the strange and unsettled state of a world in which events un-folded with unnatural, even ominous speed.

That year, on the tenth of May, the family gathered around the radio in the living room of their Budapest apartment and, as they did nearly every evening, tuned in to the BBC. There they heard that Neville Chamberlain had resigned and Winston Churchill was now the prime minister of Britain. Of course they knew of Churchill—what educated European didn't?—and were impressed by his memorable promise that he had "nothing to offer you but blood, toil, sweat, and tears."

A powerful affinity linked a whole group of Hungarians to Britain, one that grew stronger as the social divisions of war divided the popula-tion. It was not just an appreciation for British discipline and restraint—although those time-honored traits were bred in the bone of Hungarians, especially of their class and generation. But they felt an intellectual kin-ship, such that the occasional Englishman who arrived in Hungary felt unaccountably at home, even in the midst of the bizarre language and exotic Central European landscape.

The family may have clung to the reassurance of those words in Ireg a month later when, on June 5, Hitler proclaimed a war of total annihila-tion against his enemies. The moment was chilling. Yet the war's true impact was only as immediate as the radio. Daily life in Hungary, espe-cially the charmed lives of the Kornfelds and their extended family, seemed even more civilized and precious in contrast. Ireg was a small, self-sufficient kingdom, ruled over by wise and benevolent noblemen, in the midst of the increasingly violent conflict between fascism, democracy, and Communism that unfolded everywhere else.

The Nazis had already invaded France, and after the French and Germans signed an armistice on June 23, Hitler triumphantly marched into Paris and toured his newest conquest. Britain refused to recognize Marshal Pétain as the French prime minister and instead turned to Charles de Gaulle as the legitimate leader. German U-boats had attacked merchant ships in the Atlantic on the first of July, and Britain was preparing her response. One day before the French Vichy government officially broke off relations with Britain, Aladár signed the guestbook in Ireg.

Upon his return to Budapest, he wrote Hanna a thank-you note. He began with a little run-down of recent events and wondered if France would finally become part of the Axis. The conflict itself, he wrote, was "a sign of a very serious turning point." Then he asked about the weather, hoping that it was lovely in Ireg and that Hanna's summer vacation would "pass in a very pleasant manner."

As for himself, he was very busy, "since urgent and serious work was waiting for me. Today I am again deeply involved with work. The *nervouskeit*—the atmosphere of tension—persists, and I don't see any likelihood that it will change." He then became a bit more personal and said that he was facing "enormous decisions . . . I want to write certain things, and I hope that world politics will not make the realization of my twenty-year plan impossible."

I wonder what he meant by his "twenty-year plan." He was thirty-six years old—what did he imagine his life would be like as a distinguished fifty-six-year-old in the far-off summer of 1960? Nearly everyone imagined that he would one day become the foreign minister in Hungary, but was that what shaped the dreams he shared with Hanna?

He then asked her, with an eager formality, when she might be visiting Budapest again. "I hope I will get a formal notification so that I can make myself free. And," he added, to override any false modesty that she might have, "I am not telling you this to be selfless." He closed the letter by reassuring her that the lavender they had cut in Ireg had arrived safely in Budapest and that it was sitting on his desk at home. He also hoped that he might make a return visit soon. He signed the letter with the formal *kezitcsokolom*, I kiss your hands, the appropriate conclusion for any letter to a lady, conveying conventional respect, not pulsing romance.

CHAPTER 5

September 18

H anna and Aladár could not enjoy the normal, stately progression of courtship, and perhaps that discretion determined the way that they would always treat their relationship. The climate of anti-Semitism reverberated into the personal realm. And Aladár was a cautious man, perhaps even too cautious, about matters of the heart. He considered himself a confirmed bachelor, so thoughts about linking his fate to that of another were beyond his basic comfort level. A woman from a Jewish family as prominent as the Kornfelds consorting with a rising political figure as well known as Aladár Szegedy-Maszák broke no laws (yet) but certainly could attract unwanted attention.

Aladár had the most to lose. He already had been marginalized for what was seen as his extreme liberalism. If his private life catapulted into a more public sphere, his very livelihood could collapse. As compelling as stories are of men giving up everything for the woman they loved, Aladár's parents and sister depended on him for financial support. He was a deeply practical, guilty, and responsible son. Lest he forgot those virtues, his formidable mother, Sarolta, was there to remind him.

My parents never, but *never* mentioned any other romantic interests in their lives, but Aladár had written about a woman named Margit in a diary he'd kept while in Berlin. I pieced together their story from various accounts. Apparently Margit Huszár was his great love in Berlin. A chain-smoking, multilingual intellectual from a distinguished but impoverished Budapest family, Margit worked at the Hungarian embassy

in Berlin with Aladár. She resembled my mother a bit, with a long handsome face and striking elegance. When the depth of their love affair became obvious to everyone, Sarolta intervened. During a visit to Budapest,
she summoned Margit and told her that she should not expect any future
with Aladár because his basic obligation was to his family. To his lingering shame, when Margit broke off the affair, even knowing the reasons,
Aladár acquiesced. She never married, and Aladár settled into the role of
confirmed bachelor.

His job was not simply about receiving money every month. The
world was at war, and all his education and training—his studies at the
École Libre des Sciences Politiques, his late nights at the Foreign Ministry, his copious note-taking at the Hungarian embassy in Berlin—were
not merely entries on his curriculum vitae but connected to forces of
destiny. Even though he was not a central player and being liaison to the
Vatican sometimes bored and frustrated him, he knew that he was a part
of a greater purpose that involved nothing less than the survival of Hungary.

So their courtship was terribly circumscribed. He could not invite
Hanna for dinner at the Grille, or to the movies to see *The Wizard of Oz,*
or to the Circus, where a famous lion tamer named Togarek made women
swoon and lions obediently cower. They could not meet for a coffee at
the famous patisserie Gerbeaud. He could certainly not invite her to any
of the dinners that filled so many of his evenings and weekends. And yet
he wanted to see her, and the feeling was mutual.

During the summer months, guests and family members traveled
regularly between Ireg and Budapest. Now that the four Kornfeld children were adults, they would frequently return to the city for a few days
to visit friends or to attend to some business. One July day in 1940 Hanna
was in Budapest. Aladár suggested they take a drive to one of the beautiful spots outside the city. As the Hungarian poet Árpád Tóth wrote,
"Beyond the river, the hills of Buda, behold, they lead to heaven."

One of my father's favorite routes was the drive to the Danube Bend,
a gracious sweep in the river around the old seat of the first Hungarian
kings, the castle of Esztergom and the ruins of Visegrád, the castle of the
legendary King Matthias Corvinus. Together they drove in my father's
pride and joy, a Steyr 100 that he had bought in Berlin in 1935. It had
fenders like roller coasters and headlights like planets. By the time my
mother first climbed in, it might have been a bit worse for wear, but it

was still full of personality. My mother must have been delighted. She declared it his BMW, and the nickname took.

Together they left the prying eyes and whispering voices of Budapest behind and drove into the countryside. Gasoline was rationed then, and always-thrifty Hanna worried that Aladár might be wasting his precious coupons. "I received the third gasoline ticket," he later wrote to her. "You see, it would not have made any sense to spare the two liters the last time."

Thus the venue was established for their courtship. In the front seat of Aladár's "BMW," my parents courted, quarreled, laughed, complained, and permitted themselves a few dreams for the future. Despite his supremely rational mind, Aladár loved the occult. He had visited mediums and astrologers often, including a Berlin psychic whose coffee grounds were the vehicle for her clairvoyance. She bizarrely predicted that he would eventually be jailed and would die in America. In an early journal entry, he wrote, "I have the feeling that the forces of predestination, reincarnation, and free will blend with each other, that there is some sort of logic in my life, that there is some interdependence."

I can imagine Hanna, sparkling and girlish in the passenger seat, teasing Aladár a bit but enjoying the flirtatious female power of what he saw as her clairvoyance. Some of her predictions were as prosaic as where he would dine and with whom he would socialize; others were more elaborate. "After this I think I am going to turn to you for any prediction, because I heard from you for the first time that on Saturday I would have dinner at the Grille," he wrote to her at the end of July. "I would gladly risk more courageous predictions when you answer my letter," he wrote in August. "May I ask that next weekend you open your divining office?" he wrote before a visit to Ireg in September. But what did she tell him? What did she see?

Sometimes Aladár had to change their plans. On August 10 he wrote, "I am very sorry that on Thursday we did not make the usual program by car. I can honestly tell you that . . . I did not want to leave my sister alone. . . . I tried to find some other activity for her, but I wasn't successful and didn't want to hurt her feelings. You know sympathy is not always the best adviser. So instead of making an excursion with you, which would have made me very happy, I took a walk with her and was less happy listening to the same old topics of conversation."

Lilly Szegedy-Maszák, vivacious, attractive, and stylish, loved her younger brother with an intensity some might have found unsettling between siblings. The whole family cherished Aladár—so handsome and bright and hard-working and loyal. But Lilly seemed to encompass as many versions of love as one woman could possibly experience. She was both sisterly and maternal; she confided in him as she would to her best girlfriend; and she was happy to act like his wife, except in the most obvious way. She had no question that he felt the same way. The whole relationship from her side was charged with a kind of energy, that while not explicitly libidinal, certainly contained the same possessive, implicitly monogamous tension.

The collapse of Lilly's short-lived marriage came as no surprise to any member of the family and seemed to confirm her fundamental irresponsibility. It also meant that she could return home to the sprawling family apartment in Buda at the same time that Aladár returned from Berlin. So the unmarried adult siblings once more lived with their parents, and while Lilly worked as secretary to the head of Hungarian radio, she devoted herself full-time to the well-being of her aging parents and her superstar brother. She tracked Aladár's various romances with the attention of a tolerant wife who is unsettled by the distractions of her husband but is confident that in the end he will always come home to her.

Over the summer Lilly knew that Aladár and Hanna were getting to know each other, and because marriage was simply impossible, she was free to revel in the conspiracy of it all. Furthermore, the wealth and prominence of Hanna's family held vast appeal to the snob in Lilly. With reservations, she approved. So as summer eased into fall, Aladár visited Ireg and Hanna came to Budapest, and they would drive into the countryside.

Then came a turning point, when the way they related to each other shifted from something that contained almost too much room for interpretation, to something sustained by deep, resonant, mutual understanding. On Wednesday, September 18, Hanna came to Budapest to visit her good friend, Éva Balázs. Before going there, she went on a drive with Aladár.

It was a beautiful Indian summer day, and they ventured toward an old Hungarian village that had become a riverside resort. She must have looked in the owner's manual of the car and read something about the partner, the other driver, the co-owner. Who knows how this was described in the manual, but the mention of a co-owner must have unfettered Hanna's greatest anxieties that another woman could be in Aladár's life. Aladár was astonished at her insecurities. Couldn't she see how he felt? Couldn't she see how he adored her, relied upon her, thought about her, sought her out?

He wrote her a letter the very next day.

> *Hanna my dear,*
>
> *I took a look at the* Autobuch, *and I believe I have answered the question about the partner. . . . My pride was offended that for even a minute you doubted the quality of my partner or you were not immediately convinced that she was of the highest quality. I hope you consoled Éva—maybe you could write to her and say that we got a flat tire and the car had to be pushed. Or why for any other serious reason you couldn't be at her place on time. . . . The weather today, is almost as nice as it was yesterday. But there is a secret, significant difference, which without any question makes yesterday a far more beautiful day. . . . God be with you, dear Hanna. I hope that the weather will be nice in Ireg, and you will have a good time. If you have time, think about what projects we might embark upon to learn more about each other, even to sustain ourselves until the next time. Even until then, I kiss your hands many times (which maybe now are not that cold). Aladár*

The close was different this time. And now, and forever, the eighteenth of September was their anniversary.

AS THEY DID EVERY YEAR at the end of October, the Kornfelds returned to Budapest from Ireg. They settled down again in their city home and got reaccustomed to the darker rooms, the different furniture, the city rhythms. Puppa returned to her university studies. My mother went back to work at Save the Children. George appeared in the office at Csepel, and Tom continued his studies in gymnasium.

Every day, it seemed, a new political event captured their attention. In September, in the Second Vienna Award, a portion of Transylvania that had been lost in the Treaty of Trianon was returned to Hungary, and in a Faustian bargain, Hungary exchanged the glory of this prize for the danger of being even more indebted to Germany. In November, the day after Aladár's thirty-seventh birthday, this was all formalized when Teleki signed the Tripartite Act, which formally aligned Hungary with Germany, Italy, and Japan.

Aladár visited the Kornfeld household regularly. Part of the time he spent with my grandfather, discussing the affairs of the world. The other time he and my mother would retire into the salon, have a cup of tea, and share some quiet moments. The servants would press their index fingers to their lips. "The Gentleman is here having tea," they would whisper. When the couple had more time, they continued their excursions into the countryside.

The large extended family of Manfred Weiss usually celebrated the New Year at his old estate, a sweeping old mansion that towered in the almost-concave landscape of the Alföld, the Great Hungarian Plain, in the southeastern part of Hungary. The house was called Derekegyháza, or simply Derek. Ann Bridge, the wife of the former British ambassador to Hungary in 1940, had visited earlier that December for a shooting expedition; she wrote in her memoir that "something like 300 beaters turned out to drive the game and 2000 cock pheasants was a normal day's bag: the women rode out in sleighs to meet the men for lunch, which we ate sitting at tables on the snow, in the sun and out of the wind."

On December 29, the day before Móric's birthday, the extended Weiss family left Budapest to gather at Derek: Marianne and Móric and their four children; the widowed Elsa Mauthner and her seven children; Daisy and Ferenc Chorin with three children; Eugene Weiss and his wife, Annie, and their three children. The youngest daughter of Manfred Weiss, the tense and unmarried Edith, would naturally be there, as would a number of assorted family friends. Alfons Weiss would sometimes attend with his four children, but his wife, the gifted medical doctor and psychoanalyst Erzsébet Herczeg, despised the family and sought to avoid them as much as possible. The daughter of a family as rich as, perhaps richer than, the Weisses, Alfons had married her because he was confident that she had no designs on his money.

The family would play cards and go sleighing. Sometimes as they rode through the grand estate, they might be fortunate enough to see a "hare's parliament": fifty to sixty hares sitting at attention in a circle, their dark shapes silhouetted against the vast, white fields. On New Year's Eve, they would melt small divots of lead in spoons, then drop the liquid into a bowl of water, where it would splash and freeze into wild shapes. Then everyone would read fortunes that were revealed in the small, lead abstractions.

Aladár remained in Budapest with his family, and on the afternoon of December 30, 1940, he wrote to Hanna. Though they had seen each other the day before, he regretted being unable "to wish you all the good things for the new year as I would have loved." Always more at home, more relaxed in writing, he could not let "this otherwise fairly ugly 1940 . . . pass without saying thank you to you, because whatever happiness there was in 1940, whatever nice things occurred, occurred because of you."

As a special surprise, Hanna had slipped into his pocket a new cigarette case, engraved with the sentiment "Take it easy" in English. "Thank you for giving me an opportunity to think of you and be happy about you and be reassured that we love each other," he wrote. "I only wish that somehow our situation could be sustained as it is, despite the innumerable difficulties and ugliness that surround us now."

He wanted all the looming problems in their world to end, and hoped that she would have a lovely celebration on New Year's Eve and an easy return back to Budapest. "And I wish that sometimes, you would think of me. You know, dear, that if I had to make a list of all the good things that I wish for you, it would be too long. But I hope that you feel all of them, and that you know that I wish for you all the same things that you are wishing for yourself. . . . God must be with you, dear Hanna. I kiss your hands many, many times. I would very much love to go for a drive again."

1 9 4 1

"The weight of this sad time we must obey
Speak what we feel, not what we ought to say.
The eldest have borne much.
We that are young will never see so much,
Nor live so long."

—SHAKESPEARE, *King Lear*

CHAPTER 6

Never in Hungary

The Kornfeld family left Derekegyháza during the first week of January 1941 and returned to Budapest. My father's calendar notes two visits to "Kfeld," signifying the apartment on Lendvay Street. My grandparents had moved into the first-floor apartment of the three-story building after their wedding in 1913 as "temporary quarters" until they found their own home, but it was situated so close to the rest of the family that Marianne could never uproot herself from their embrace.

The entire house was furnished with Biedermeier furniture and Aubusson carpets. My grandfather's library held more than ten thousand volumes, all sealed with the ex libris of Baron Mauritius Kornfeld. The beautiful woodcarvings that my grandfather collected covered tables, mantels, and shelves. Several fifteenth- and sixteenth-century Madonnas mingled with bronze Buddhas. Saint Paul from the thirteenth century stood near Saint Margaret, who held a book. And carved Saint Egidius, a French hermit no more, forever held a shepherd's stick as a deer stood by and watched the guests of many dinner parties eat and talk, talk and eat.

There were five bedrooms and two bathrooms, a dining room, a salon, a library, some service areas, and a sewing room. Marianne and Móric each had their own room, Tom and George each had a room, even though George had already moved into his own apartment, and Puppa and Hanna shared a bedroom. The kitchen and the servants' quarters were in the basement, connected by a dumbwaiter. Their younger cousins dreaded going to the dark, formal, and somehow cheerless apartment for a visit with Aunt Marianne and Uncle Móric. But Aladár felt welcomed and at home.

On Saturday, January 18, he and Hanna went for a wintry drive, and on Tuesday Aladár went to Berlin on an official mission. Several political and economic leaders, including Móric and Ferenc Chorin, thought that he was the perfect person to take the temperature of the opposition groups in Berlin. The war had escalated over the past few months with the massive German bombing in Britain, the Italian invasion of Greece, the military alliance among Germany, Italy, and Japan, the mess in Poland, and Hungary's officially joining the Axis powers in November. Nazism or Bolshevism was a terrible choice. Geography, and historical alliances and grievances, doomed Hungary to few options. Móric would say the option was "whether you wanted to be eaten, boiled, or fried."

Aladár's official mission required that he deliver confidential mail first to the consul general in Munich, then move on to Berlin. On the evening of January 21, he traveled to Berlin. Already the inconveniences and sacrifices of the war were beginning to wear on people. The dining car was jammed and cacophonous with complaints about the small servings. In the sleeping car, his companion mumbled that he hoped the war would end soon. Aladár finally disembarked at the Friedrichstrasse Station in Berlin. Nine years before, on November 2, 1932, he had landed there for his first foreign posting, one that lasted for five years.

He had made very close friends while he was in Berlin, including a German journalist named Otto von Heydebreck and the former commander in chief of the Wehrmacht, General Kurt von Hammerstein-Equord. Aladár first met him in 1933 when Lilly was visiting, and they went to the premier of a Hungarian movie with some friends who included Hammerstein and his wife. As they were leaving, Hammerstein's wife suggested loudly that they invite Aladár's two more senior companions to dinner but then said in a stage whisper, "I suppose that we must also invite that young fellow and his sister." The conversation over schnapps and sandwiches inevitably was about the Nazis, and Hammerstein said, "Now that we have the Nazis, the question is, how are we going to get rid of them?"

Gradually the two men became friends, the Prussian general and the young Hungarian diplomat. Aladár considered him to be the most intelligent man he had met in Germany, who "saw everything clearly and without shadows." While Hammerstein could not abandon his Prussian antipathy toward the Jews, during the Nazi times he cultivated friendships with them because "it was incompatible with his moral self-respect to join those casting stones at the Jews." He was one of the first people Aladár sought out shortly after his arrival. After dinner, as they walked through the snow to the subway, Hammerstein told Aladár some astonishing news: Hitler planned to attack Russia in the spring. He was only a few months off—the Germans invaded in June.

While in Berlin, Aladár also met László Almásy, the African explorer whose life was chronicled in the novel *The English Patient*. Almásy flew over the Libyan desert performing aerial surveys for the Germans, but he seems also to have been in contact with the British armed forces. While his ultimate alliances were never completely clear, his real loyalty seemed to be to Hungary.

As much as he looked for that germ of an opposition movement in Berlin, Aladár couldn't find one. It was difficult to be hopeful, especially after he stopped off in a thoroughly Nazified Vienna. He finally returned to Hungary on January 28 and felt palpable relief to be home, away from the oppressive and debased atmospheres of Berlin and Vienna.

"It is difficult to understand today," he reflected forty years later, "but at that time we lived in a sort of euphoria." Hungary was surrounded by barbarism, yet those who talked in the cafés, at dinner parties, in Ireg, and on Lendvay Street were convinced that it would never have a Hungarian counterpart. In the fall of 1941 they observed, with the sickening fascination of protected bystanders, the Iron Guard's brutality in Romania in the wake of the power struggle between the government of Ion Antonescu and the Iron Guardists. A great Romanian historian, Nicolae Iorga, had his long beard torn out, one hair at a time, before members of the Iron Guard murdered him. Then there were mass murders of Jews in Iasi. That was typical for the Romanians, but it would never be possible in Hungary, thank God.

CHAPTER 7

Jewish Questions

.　.

My brothers both remembered when our mother told them that her family had once been Jewish. My brother Andy found it interesting, but it did not have any powerful emotional impact. My brother Peter, who was in a sensitive period of his Catholic education, was stunned. Steeped in the religious anti-Semitism of 1950s parochial schools, he worried that this implicated him in the murder of Christ, that it made him a member of a despised race, and that he might suffer consequences, if not in this life then in the next. The Irish Catholic nuns who taught him religion had taught him about Judaism in the narrowest and most anti-Semitic terms possible, and it stuck. For a little while.

As the youngest, I can't remember *not* knowing that my mother's family had been Jewish. I was told not to share this information with my cousins because, like a discussion about the facts of life, it was a subject that only parents should share with their children. I learned that her family converted not because they felt the hot breath of Nazism on their necks but earlier. By the time World War II struck, most of the family had been Catholic for nearly twenty years. The tragic experience of Hungarian Jewry was part of the monumental tragedy of the Holocaust, yet preceding that period of yellow stars, ghettos, and deportations, it was also idiosyncratic.

At the beginning of the eighteenth century, there were only a few thousand Jews in Hungary, but by 1910, when Hungary was part of the Austro-Hungarian Empire, nearly one million Jews lived in the area known as greater Hungary. There were two geographically distinct Jewish communities. The western part of the country and Budapest were the homes of modernist, assimilated Ashkenazi Jews. In the eastern part of the country, closer to Russia and Galicia, the more religious and unassimilated Hasidic Jews lived. Rather than donning the brightly embroidered clothes of provincial Hungarians, the men wore *tsitsis*—white threads hanging from their waists—and the black hats called *shtreimel*, with *peyes,* or sidelocks, dangling on either side. These Jews were foreign to the Jews of Budapest, although some lived in the predominantly Jewish neighborhood in Pest, near the Dohány Street Synagogue.

But in western Hungary as in Western Europe, from the mid-nineteenth century well into the first third of the twentieth, many Jews relinquished the traditions of their ancestors in an effort to assimilate to the dominant, Christian, national culture without actually converting to Christianity. Manfred Weiss and Zsigmond Kornfeld stopped keeping kosher and sent their children to state-run schools or good Christian schools instead of cheder or yeshiva. They began to realize that Saturday was probably not the best day to do nothing, both because it was useful to keep businesses open, and because schools at the time were running six days a week.

But for them, baptism was out of the question.

Hungarian Jews were "emancipated" in 1867, when both Manfred and Zsigmond were children. Law XVII voided other anti-Jewish laws and declared: "The Israelite inhabitants of the country are declared to possess equal rights with the Christian inhabitants in the exercise of all civic and political functions." But historians point out that while in other European countries Jews were emancipated as an expression of liberalism and political enlightenment, in Hungary their emancipation was part of a general flowering of Hungarian nationalism. This made Hungary an especially hospitable place for Jews in professions, in social influence, and in the ownership of land. Over time, of course, resentments began to fester and eventually, much to the resentment or at least discomfort of many Hungarians, Jews were prominent in early-twentieth-century Hungarian life. Assimilation and even conversion became as embedded in the Hungarian Jewish experience as it was in Austria and Germany.

Vestiges of anti-Semitism remained even after emancipation and during the "golden age." When Móric was in law school at the University of Budapest, he fought a duel to defend his religion. In May 1900, a new central building was to be dedicated. The night before the king was to appear for the ceremony, crosses that decorated the hall were broken off. Immediately the Jewish students were blamed for the vandalism, and small groups faced off, hurling accusations. Móric challenged one of the accusers to a duel, and Ferenc Chorin was his second. According to family lore, Móric, a skilled fencer, landed a quick épée to the cheek and drew blood.

A book entitled *Hungarian Duels*, however, describes the incident differently: "Aladár Toth, a law student, fought three duels in rapid succession. His opponents were Vilmos Krahl, Sandor Hay, and Mor Kornfeld and he wounded all three of them." Of course, at that time in Hungary, in anything written for posterity, a good Hungarian boy named Toth would always be victorious over a Jew named Kornfeld.

The Weiss-Kornfeld-Chorin troika alone was responsible for a huge amount of Hungary's industrial and financial infrastructure: the factory at Csepel, the stock exchange, the banking system, the coal mines in Salgótarján, and the Mauthner seed factory, not to mention all the real estate they owned and the publications they subsidized. For much of the first quarter of the twentieth century, they were responsible for 10 percent of the Hungarian GDP.

But they were hardly alone in economic achievement: 88 percent of stock market members were Jews, 91 percent of currency brokers were Jews, more than half of Hungary's industry was owned by Jews, a quarter of all university students were Jews, and over 40 percent of those in the Budapest Technical University were Jews. Budapest Jews, who comprised about 20 percent of the city's population, were among the country's most ardent patriots. Jews excelled in the world of finance, industry, and other professions, and they made up at least one-third, more often one-half, and in some cases well over one-half of the lawyers, medical doctors, journalists, printers, actors, theater directors, publishers, newspaper editors, businessmen, factory owners, gallery owners, and university students in Hungary. Before World War I, according to Randolph Braham in his book *The Politics of Genocide*, "Hungarian Jewry considered itself an integral part of the Hungarian nation and the Magyars accepted the assimilated Hungarian-speaking Jews as their equals."

And then everything changed.

The Austro-Hungarian empire was defeated in November 1918, and an era ended as well, an era when Hungary and Hungarians were part of a European power. In the new era Hungary was independent, without defendable borders or access to the sea. It entered a period of tremendous political instability, culminating in 1919, in the Communist regime of Béla Kun. The regime that promised it would "bring the bourgeoisie to its senses . . . and if necessary to suffocate its counterrevolution in blood" lasted from March 21 until August 1—133 days. Many prominent friends and relatives of the Weiss family were imprisoned. Móric and a friend hid in the countryside. Marianne fled the apartment and spent a few nights at the family barber's home, where baby George slept in a laundry basket. Puppa and Hanna had the unusual experience of playing with other children in the street. Eventually Manfred rented a villa on the Semmering for the whole family, including Elsa, whose five children had the whooping cough.

The effects of the Communist regime were devastating to the Jews of Hungary, who, despite suffering at the regime's hands and being generally opposed to it, were collectively blamed for its excesses. A period of White Terror began in August and culminated on November 16, when the imposing figure of Admiral Miklós Horthy entered Budapest. The left was crushed and the White Terror continued.

Horthy's army attacked all those remotely associated with the Kun regime, especially Jews. Since Hungary had lost nearly all of its significant national minorities when the Trianon Treaty redrew its borders, the Jews remained the single largest minority in the country and a convenient lightning rod for all the free-floating rage at the humiliation of their loss in the war, the loss of Hungarian territories, and the economic depression that followed the war, not to mention modernism, humanism, and secularism. Immediately after World War I, Jews accounted for about 6 percent of the total population of Hungary, but most Hungarians held them accountable for the nation's unhappy fate.

Communists and Socialists were marginalized, persecuted, imprisoned, and murdered. In February 1920 the National Assembly made Horthy the regent, which gave him powers that were as close to royal as one could come.

He sanctioned the burgeoning post-Kun anti-Semitism. "I have considered it intolerable that here in Hungary everything, every factory, bank, large fortune, business, theater, press, commerce, etc. should be in Jewish hands," Regent Horthy wrote to one of his ministers, "and that the Jew should be the image reflected of Hungary, especially abroad."

The economic situation in Hungary was dire following Trianon, and unemployment among professionals was high. Doctors and lawyers stood in line to see if they could shovel snow. Fueled by this "intolerable" situation, the first anti-Semitic law in twentieth-century Europe, the Numerus Clausus Act, was passed on September 22, 1920. It restricted Jewish admission to Hungary's universities to the proportion of Jews in the total population, which was 6 percent.

Jews got it from both sides: first they were despised because they were capitalists; then they were despised because they were Communists. In the end, the point was that no matter how long they had been in Hungary, no matter how deeply they themselves identified as Hungarians, no matter how perfectly they spoke Hungarian and loved the country, they were, world without end, Other. In a 1939 essay, the writer László Németh called Jews *hig magyarok,* or diluted Hungarians.

During this time many members of the Jewish upper classes or aristocracy decided to demonstrate their loyalty to Hungary, or their Hungarian-ness by becoming Christian. A few baptisms could possibly resolve the problem. Marianne and Móric baptized Puppa, Hanna, and George in 1920 but remained unbaptized themselves for several years because Marianne could not face the idea that she would not be buried with her beloved parents in the Jewish cemetery. Christianity exerted a powerful spiritual and intellectual force over Móric and even his sister Mitzi. Like their father, Zsigmond, they read Augustine, Thomas à Kempis, G. K. Chesterton, and the New Testament. Mitzi eventually became a lay nun and translated Augustine into Hungarian.

Daisy and Ferenc Chorin became Catholic on May 30, 1919, rather easily, as did Eugene, who was also married to a Gentile. But Alfons and Edith remained Jews. They were not pious, not practicing, and not prominent, but they were never baptized (though the four children of Alfons were, not as Catholics but as Protestants).

Manfred Weiss was a realist about Hungarian social and economic pressures. When he returned to Csepel in 1920, Marianne accompanied him, and the two saw an utterly ruined factory—all the machines had been stolen. Manfred Weiss started all over again, this time in peacetime production: bicycles, kitchen equipment, and cars. Horthy visited Csepel with great fanfare, but Manfred understood how profoundly life had changed in Hungary for the Jews.

The pressure to convert remained, but Marianne remembered how unhappy Manfred was that his own brother-in-law, Oszkar, had had his son and daughter baptized in the early 1900s. Oszkar didn't dare tell Manfred that he had permitted it. One day Manfred Weiss accompanied Oszkar to the train station. Oszkar boarded the train and found his compartment, and as the train pulled out of the station, he opened the window and called out, "Manfred, by the way, I had the children baptized."

In 1924, two years after Manfred's death, Marianne and the children went to a resort in northern Italy, now part of Croatia, on a vacation. Puppa was nine, Hanna was seven, and György was five—he had been sick for much of the winter. Móric remained in Budapest and was to meet them later, driven to Italy by the family chauffeur. The mountains were treacherous to cross, and Marianne became more and more worried. Distraught, she made a bargain with God: If Móric arrived in one piece, she would be baptized.

He arrived in one piece. Marianne told him of her vow, and now with Manfred dead, it was easier for her to be baptized. She had also read and was reassured by the parable of the three rings in the eighteenth-century play *Nathan the Wise* by Gotthold Ephraim Lessing. Nathan was modeled after Moses Mendelssohn, the father of assimilation, and the parable explained that in the eyes of God, the three monotheistic religions were equal. When they returned to Hungary, Móric and Marianne were christened.

It astonishes me how quickly the family assimilated.

In 1932, when little Daisy Chorin was about to enter Catholic elementary school, her mother decided that it was time to tell her a bit about her background. The great-granddaughter of a famous Transylvanian rabbi, and the daughter of two baptized Jews, the little girl had grown up as a Roman Catholic. Nonetheless, as the youngest daughter in the prominent Chorin family, now thrust into a protected yet more public arena than ever before, she was vulnerable to the simmering and often explicit anti-Semitism of the time. It was more than likely that some anti-Semitic comments would come her way, and her mother, Daisy senior, wanted to make sure that she had some context, if not some preparation.

Daisy took her daughter to her room, sat down, and explained that the family had a Jewish background and that this was especially important for her to know, now that she was going to school. She continued that it didn't matter if someone was a Jew or a Christian because in the end religion was not what was most important. What was most important was to be a good and an honest person, no matter what religion you were. Satisfied, Daisy looked at her daughter and asked, "Do you understand?" And the young Daisy said emphatically, "Yes I do." Her mother then asked, "Well please, do you have any questions." The seven-year-old nodded. "Mama," she said, "have you ever seen a Jew in your life?"

At this time Puppa was already in college studying history. In the spring some racist thugs planned anti-Semitic demonstrations. One of her professors suggested that Jewish students should probably stay home for the week until the unpleasantness passed. Not only did Puppa not stay home, she made sure that she took notes and took them to the students who stayed home. It simply didn't occur to her that she fell into the category of Jew. "It didn't involve me," she said. "I was Catholic." Perhaps, but more important, she was a Kornfeld and in an altogether separate category.

Yet, Puppa wrote many years later, "Holy water or not, the family was Jewish, and in a country where anti-Semitism was always there, baptism did not make much of a difference." It was one of the reasons that as children, they had few playmates outside the family. Marianne had few female friends, but with so many sisters and cousins, she didn't feel their absence. When Puppa and Hanna were adolescents, they went to some parties at the homes of Gentile girls, but they always felt like outsiders.

AFTER THE NUREMBERG LAWS of 1935 codified racial discrimination against German Jews, the time-honored tradition of anti-Semitism throughout Central Europe was given greater legitimacy. Even for many moderate Hungarians, the question had never been whether to accept Jews or annihilate them but how best to diminish or eliminate the prominent Jewish presence in Hungarian life. The Jews of the Weiss family were fundamentally untouchable. There could be anti-Semitism, nasty slogans, and unemployment among Jewish professionals during the Depression and after, but this family was insulated from much unpleasantness by its wealth and social status.

In 1938, with the *Anschluss*, Hitler's Third Reich became the neighboring regime. The Hungarian Parliament decided it was time to pass what was known as the "First Anti-Jewish Law" (even though technically the first one had already been passed in 1920). Carrying the logic of the *numerus clausus* into civic life, Law XV of 1938 limited the number of Jews to 20 percent in law, medicine, engineering, finance, and commerce. In order to achieve that golden ratio, Jews could not exceed 5 percent of the newly admitted professionals. Some Hungarians were acutely aware of the worsening situation for Jews in the Reich. Manfred Weiss's in-laws quickly slipped into Hungary after the *Anschluss*. Many Jews genuinely believed that this law was just a "mildly restrictive" measure, the kind of concession that was necessary for fending off attacks against Jewish interests or the fundamental rights of Jews. Once this law was passed, Jews and converts believed, the anti-Semites would be satisfied, and the Jews could live in peace.

But one Jewish law is never enough. Another one, entitled "Concerning the Restriction of the Participation of the Jews in Public and Economic Life," followed quickly and passed on May 4, 1939, Hanna's twenty-third birthday. It defined a Jew as someone who had anywhere from two to four Jewish grandparents. The law was agonizingly baroque: Jews who had converted to Christianity before August 1, 1919 (the last day of Béla Kun's regime), were exempt from the law, provided their ancestors had resided in Hungary since January 1, 1849. Jews could not obtain Hungarian citizenship either by naturalization or by marriage. Therefore 150,000 Jews who lived in the Trianon territories that had now been restored to Hungary were not permitted to become Hungarian citizens. Jews could not hold any government position.

The law also limited how many Jews a business could employ. As a result, an estimated 250,000 Jews lost their jobs. Many Jewish small business owners hired a nice Gentile to be a *Strohmann*, or straw man, to appear as a front man while the Jew was in the background working, thus giving the impression that the firm was a Christian enterprise. Aladár's father was a *Strohmann* for a small Jewish business that made typewriter ribbons. At Csepel, the board of directors was restructured giving the appearance that Christian "partners" played a more prominent role.

Chorin was outraged by these actions. In his role as a leader of industry, and as a member of the upper house of Hungary's Parliament, he wrote a memorandum that condemned the law. "Today, under the influence of German ideas," he wrote, "agitation against the bank, the factory, and capital are just instruments of racism, according to the German model. Today the problem of protectionism, tax policies, and price policies become insignificant when compared with the true purpose of the agitation, which is the elimination of the Jewish influence from economic life and from Hungarian public life in general."

Kornfeld and Chorin worked behind the scenes to support anti-Nazi causes and to mount an anti-Nazi campaign directed at the massive Hungarian middle and working classes, many of whom inhaled Nazi ideology like oxygen. They funded newspapers and writers, and Móric even commissioned a cartoonist to draw grand anti-Nazi cartoons and posted them on prominent kiosks in the city. Jewish organizations—some funded by Edith Weiss and other family members—tried to help those who were impoverished by the Jewish laws. Unemployed actors and singers formed a theater company that was subsidized by rich Jews. But again the Weiss family was relatively unaffected: you could lay off a machine operator, but you could not lay off such a prominent owner. At least until the time came when even prominent owners could lose their jobs.

After the second Jewish law, Jewishness became a strictly racial definition, which meant that post-1919 converts to Catholicism were considered legally to be Jews. Móric wrote to the prince primate of the Catholic Church to ask for a special consideration of this particular group of people because the Jewish law "affects them emotionally," since they are not sure "whether there is a refuge for them on the rock that the Church represents." Many were going to lose their jobs, but the Jewish organizations that were in place to help unemployed Jews would exclude the Catholic converts.

Móric asked the prince primate to let these Catholic converts "know that they were not alone in a hostile world and could count on the support of the leaders of the Church ... and those members who were not contaminated by the spirit of the times." In order to create this moral support, Móric established an organization called the Holy Cross Society, and gradually it gained support from the Central Catholic Seminary and others. Móric was acting as a benefactor to a marginalized class; that he was also a member of that class was nearly irrelevant. The swirling currents of emotion, ideology, and political will were too strong. Again and again the more moderate parts of government rationalized the law as a way to finally satisfy the anti-Semites once and for all.

And of course it didn't.

Military forced labor had already been established in late 1919, when Horthy and his military advisers decided that Jews were unfit for military service, especially since being in the military involved carrying weapons. They established labor battalions, in which Jewish men were forced to serve their country outside of the regular army. The institution was not relevant until the war, but in 1939 the government decided that a Jew should not be a military officer or a soldier yet should not be exempt from serving in the military. It created the Labor Service, in which Jewish males from the age of twenty-five to sixty were called up to serve. During the first years of service, they were allowed to wear a uniform, but by 1941 the image of a Jew in a uniform was so offensive both to the military and to the German allies that they were told to wear civilian clothes, a yellow armband, and a neutral cap. By December 1941, fourteen thousand Jewish men were in the Labor Service. Eventually thousands more would be brought in, and the institution bore closer and closer resemblance to slave labor. The young men of the Kornfeld and Weiss families avoided service. Perhaps their work at Csepel was deemed sufficient.

The previous Jewish laws were autographed by the prime ministers of the time. Prime Ministers Kálmán Darányi and Béla Imrédy were the sponsors of the first law—ironically, the ardent Catholic Imrédy had a Jewish grandparent and was forced to resign. Prime Minister Pál Teleki championed the second law. Some of his supporters argued that he thought that once he dispensed with the annoying Jewish problem, he could move on to the more serious business of protecting Hungarian interests in the face of German pressures. His detractors saw this as proof of how deeply anti-Semitic he truly was and how, once in power, he seized the opportunity to exercise it.

Hungarian Jewish leaders knew what the Nazis were capable of and understood some of what they were actually doing to Jews in the European countries they dominated. But they did not want to assert Jewish nationalistic interests in Hungary because they hoped that the Horthy government would protect them. According to Braham, "Practically until the beginning of the deportations, the Jewish leadership continued to believe that the Hungarian Jewish community, unlike all other large European Jewish communities, would emerge from the war physically relatively intact even if economically generally ruined."

In March 1941 Germany wanted to use Hungary as a transit point for troops entering Yugoslavia. Only months before, in December 1940, Prime Minister Teleki had signed an Eternal Friendship Pact with Yugoslavia. Teleki believed that Hungary should resist being used by the Germans and believed that the nation's honor depended on maintaining its integrity. But Horthy and his other advisers were convinced that the alliance with the Germans was the only way to restore Hungary's ancient territories and protect Hungary itself against the Bolshevik surge.

One of the leaders of the opposition in Hungary, a friend of Móric's, was in Teleki's office on the afternoon of April 2 when the telephone rang. In the midst of the conversation Teleki turned beet red and told him, "This is dreadful. The Germans have entered Hungary, and I didn't know about it." Teleki knew that if Hungary did not resist the German transit to Yugoslavia, Great Britain would sever diplomatic relations, the sacred trust between the two countries would be violated, and a declaration of war would follow. Teleki saw the end of his neutrality policy and the loss of his nation's honor. That night he committed suicide.

Shortly afterward, Admiral Horthy appointed László Bárdossy prime minister, a man who, my father said, was, like one of his predecessors Imrédy, "both unlucky and bad." On the other hand, Aladár had enjoyed working with him when he became foreign minister in January 1941 and described him as "a brilliant man, perhaps more brilliant than gifted. His judgment was lacking, and he was very quickly affected by emotional considerations." He was an ultra anti-Bolshevik anti-Semite and believed that harmonious cooperation with Germany was a historical necessity.

Almost immediately after assuming office, Bárdossy announced that the Jewish question was one of the most pressing problems in Hungary and suggested that there should be laws prohibiting marriage between Jews and Gentiles. Signed into law on August 2, 1941, part four of the legislation focused on "the prohibition of marriage between Jews and non-Jews."

> Mixed marriages had a definitely detrimental effect upon the evolution of our national soul; they brought into a position of influence that Jewish spirit whose harmful effect we have seen. There is no doubt about the failure of the experiment in assimilation. We now want to exchange this for disassimilation.

Móric wrote in his memoirs, "The 1941 anti-Jewish racial purity legislation was the clearest violation of the sacrament of marriage when it forbade the marriage between two Catholics one of whom was considered to be a Jew under the law."

Móric and Ferenc Chorin despised Parliament's weakness in the face of this legislation. The upper house introduced some amendments that tried to mitigate the legislation, but not only did it finally reject these amendments, the lower house went on to forbid sexual contact between males of Jewish extraction and Christian females. No limitations were placed on Christian males.

In July and August of that year, nearly 20,000 Jews who were considered "aliens"—mostly Jewish refugees who had fled Poland and Austria and settled in Hungary—were forced out of the country. Some were Jewish refugees from Galicia, whose families lived in Hungary for generations, but never bothered to obtain documentation of their Hungarian citizenship. They were rounded up and forcibly deported to Kamenyec-Podolszk in Western Ukraine where most of them were murdered.

And yet, everyday life in Budapest, indeed in much of Hungary, was an island of tranquillity compared with much of the rest of Europe. The garden-variety Hungarian anti-Semite belonged to one club, and the Jews belonged to another club. The Gentiles didn't want to join their club and didn't want them to join his club. The Kornfeld, Chorin, and Weiss families had each other. They occupied a privileged separate category, at least for the time being.

The Reason the World
Looks So Lovely

▪   ▪

So far the Kornfelds had been mostly insulated from effects of the Jewish laws, such as the restrictions on professions. Even the accommodations they had to make, such as changes to the board of directors at Csepel, were far removed from their daily life, and they were still able to channel their wealth to good causes. But a law prohibiting the intermarriage between Jews and Gentiles collapsed barriers of class. The family was riddled with intermarriages, and Hanna's younger brother George had just fallen in love with an Austrian Gentile girl named Elsie Kavalski.

In 1938 George had been in England, perfecting his English and working in the factory business there, when he was called back to Hungary. He flew back to Budapest on November 2, 1938. This was the day of the First Vienna Award, when Hitler forced Czechoslovakia to return the southern parts of Slovakia and Ruthenia that Hungary had lost in the Treaty of Trianon. Hitler made one of his interminable speeches that were broadcast on the Hungarian radio. As Puppa and her mother drove out to pick up George, the airport was strangely dark, and Hitler's voice blasted from a loudspeaker.

George lived a comfortable life in Budapest. He had his own apartment and valet and a variety of lady friends who were drawn to his grace and charm and the fact that he clearly loved women. At a dance he met Elsie Kavalski, who had just moved to Budapest from Vienna to escape having to become a member of one of the obligatory Nazi organizations for young women. Blond and vivacious, she was living with prominent friends of her family. George was instantly smitten, and Elsie seemed to feel the same way. Eventually they were inseparable.

Every day the news pointed to the inexorable fact that they would not only be forbidden to marry, but even their relationship would be illegal. By the spring of 1941 it became clear that as far as marriage to Elsie was concerned, as Macbeth said, "If it were done when 'tis done, then 'twere well it were done quickly."

For Hanna and Aladár, in the late spring and early summer of 1941, the pace of life quickened both personally and politically. Little circled H's appear on Aladár's calendar throughout May and June. Pentecost was early that year, and it was time to return to Ireg once more. Aladár was with the family in Ireg that first weekend in May, celebrating Hanna's twenty-fifth birthday. It must have seemed momentous at the time. Her mother married at twenty-five, and that was considered long overdue.

Then several weeks later, at three-fifteen in the morning of June 22, more than three million German troops attacked the Soviet Union. Aladár and most Hungarians were pleased. They hated and feared the Russians and were morbidly afraid of a Pan-Slav deluge and of the Russian steamroller. With no knowledge of Auschwitz or Treblinka, they considered Bolshevism an even greater menace than Nazism. They knew about the destruction of the kulaks, the forced collectivizations, the Stalin purges. How could Nazism possibly be worse than that? It never occurred to them that the Germans might be defeated in the Soviet Union, but some entertained the possibility that in the course of battling the Soviets, Nazism could be so severely weakened that a new German leadership could be constituted. Or so they hoped.

The very next day Aladár went to Berlin as a courier, and while he was there, Hungary joined Germany in declaring war against the Soviet Union. When he returned to Budapest, a letter from Hanna awaited him, to which he replied immediately. "The period of not seeing each other is much, much too long," he wrote. "It will be so nice to see each other again and tell each other everything that has accumulated in the time we were apart."

Soon afterward he visited Ireg with his sister Lilly. The place was already astir with wedding plans for George, concerns about the newest Jewish law, and the war with the Soviet Union. A whole host of political worries collided with personal worries and enveloped them. But at least

Aladár and Hanna were together and had come to a happy modus vivendi. Lilly and Hanna liked each other, and Lilly fit into the social scene at Ireg easily. Hanna and Aladár took walks in the beautiful countryside; they sat in their chairs by the swimming pool and looked at the moon. There were so many people there that summer weekend that Lilly was happily entertained and the couple could capture some solitude together. "It was very difficult for me to leave," Aladár wrote the next day, "and so difficult to get used to life in Pest without you. . . . I am not going to make any commitments for Monday, and unless I hear from you, I will be waiting for you in the usual place at 4:30."

Hanna came to Budapest, and they drove into the countryside, toward Gödöllő, one of their favorite retreats. Most Hungarians had visited Gödöllő, but Aladár provided a special perspective on the tour of the estate, which had been the emperor's chateau and a vacation spot for the Szegedy-Maszák family when Aladár was a child. As a child he had wandered through the Park of the Palace, the beautiful linden tree avenue that led to the statue of Queen Elizabeth. Verdant forests surrounded Gödöllő, and my parents meandered through them, stopping at the local wine cellar or the Blaha Lujza swimming bath, luxuriating in being normal, public lovers.

But Hanna was tormented. Their love affair was unsustainable, given the political climate. The more beautiful a time that they had, the more fearful she became of the enemies who surrounded them. She experienced a kind of existential stage fright, rehearsing the words in her mind before saying something important, much as she wrote first drafts of her letters. She sat silently on the drive home, deep in thought. Finally she gave voice to her worries.

With the Jewish laws only days from passage, what was going to happen to them? How could they possibly maintain a relationship? Any plans for the future were impossible. What was the point of staying together at all?

Aladár did not know what to say.

Hanna would become so isolated when she was hurt and vulnerable that she took shelter in brittle anger. She longed for comfort, but Aladár was unable to summon any comforting words. Her raw emotion disorganized him, and he stuttered and fumbled and stammered and only further isolated Hanna in her anguish and in the certainty that she was right.

They parted with terrible tension and sadness between them.

Late the next afternoon Aladár wrote her a letter. He never mentioned the Jewish laws, ever the diplomat, but he obviously didn't have to.

He apologized for his awkwardness and acknowledged that of course he had thought about this "topic of conversation." But with completely uncharacteristic optimism, he wrote that he simply didn't see the "problem" as insurmountable because it was "inseparably connected with you and everything that you mean to me, therefore I cannot see it as a dead end street."

He acknowledged that their lives were likely to become more complicated in the near future, and there would be times when they would feel as if there was no way out. But he knew with a conviction that was as pure and unambivalent as any in his life that no edict or legislation would prevent them from being together. They belonged together. In the end, whatever barriers were in the way would diminish by the sheer force of the goodness of their love. "If that weren't the case," he wrote, "I would not write to you, I would not look for opportunities to be with you. Instead I would accept everything as a reality and manage alone, no matter how difficult and painful that would be."

He begged her to put aside the dark thoughts and instead see how many obstacles they had already surmounted. He had tried to tell her the day before, though probably not as clearly or as eloquently as when, undistracted, he could write and think, that his biggest worry, and his most powerfully protective instincts, were directed toward her. "For more than a year, I have been standing next to you like a scarecrow and made your life confused," he wrote. "Believe me, this only increases the responsibility that I feel toward you."

The reason he had been so awkward the day before was not because Hanna had expressed the ambivalence that he felt. Quite the reverse—he just needed to think about all they had discussed. He had needed some time to reconcile the beauties of the afternoon with the darkness of their conversation. "Please don't be angry with me. It was not so simple to switch from the mood of happiness and the harmony of being together, to the mood of problems and worries and difficulties. I do not want to diminish my responsibility, but you must understand, your presence is the reason that the world looks so lovely."

The third Jewish law passed on August 2, 1941.

George married Elsie, in Ireg, on August 11, 1941.

Hanna and Aladár celebrated their first anniversary on September 18. In Aladár's somber little diary, the entries on the seventeenth, eighteenth, and nineteenth are all festively written in red pencil, with several circled H's like streamers on the dates. His letter on the nineteenth seemed to reveal that their time together in Budapest was golden. "If the next two years pass in the same way, if we can be so happy with each other in the future too, then we can truly be satisfied."

In December, Hungary reluctantly joined Germany in declaring war against the United States and Great Britain, but the Americans did not see it as being legally valid since Parliament had not voted on the measure. The United States would acknowledge the state of war only months later, in the summer of 1942. But for the Hungarian leadership, especially Bárdossy, the most important goal was to avoid German occupation, even as he believed in the common fate of Germany and Hungary.

Aladár remained in Budapest for the Christmas and New Year's holidays as he always did. And Hanna went with her family to Derekegyháza as she always did. As he sat at home on the night of December 29, he wrote his New Year's letter to Hanna. He dined with friends but felt irritated during the evening. He got a haircut and visited with an old Benedictine monk who was somehow related to his family. But he admitted to feeling terribly tense and a bit nervous, and he needed the solitude that could come when sitting peacefully and writing to the woman he loved.

Without you, this year would have been another year of war, both better and worse than the previous one, but I cannot possibly judge because we were together. If I had to spend the previous year without you, it only would have been a relief that it is now over. But I cannot say that about 1941 because tonight, as I see its end, I feel melancholy. I regret the passing of everything that brought us such lovely times and so much happiness. I hope that the New Year will be even better, and certainly not worse, and that it will bring peace and happiness, more human solidarity, cleaner and healthier air to breathe. We two have many things to wish for, and we both know so well what they are. God bless you, my darling. Don't catch a cold. Be very happy in the New Year.

I kiss your hands many times,
Aladár

1942

I have dared to sing the song of Bernadette, although I am not a Catholic but a Jew; and I drew courage for this undertaking from a far older and far more unconscious vow of mine. Even in the days when I wrote my first verses I vowed that I would evermore and everywhere in all I wrote magnify the divine mystery and the holiness of man—careless of a period that has turned away with scorn and rage and indifference from these ultimate values of our mortal lot.

—FRANZ WERFEL, *Los Angeles, May 1941*

CHAPTER 9

The Satanic Nature of His Character

. .

The year had a bloody beginning. After the invasion of Yugoslavia in 1941, Hungary reclaimed portions of the territory that it had lost after World War I. This multiethnic region rebelled at the imposition of Hungarian military rule, and during two appalling days in January, Hungarian military units massacred over 3,300 people in Újvidék (now the Serbian town of Novi Sad), including one thousand Jews. Refugees who had escaped from the area brought news of the event to Budapest, and most Hungarians were horrified.

On January 5, during a military meeting with some top Wehrmacht officers, the Hungarian major general József Heszlényi announced that Hungary would be interested in transferring 12,000 "alien" Jews to Russia. This was consistent with Hitler's visions of ridding Europe of its Jews by deporting them east. But on January 20, the Nazi leadership adopted a more comprehensive approach at the Wannsee Conference: the utter destruction of European Jewry. It started to make the necessary arrangements for the "complete" resolution of the Jewish question in the areas of Europe under the German sphere of interest, since thus far, according to the head of the Reich Security Office, Reinhard Heydrich, who chaired the conference, only 537,000 Jews had emigrated from the Reich, from Austria, and from the Protectorate between the time the Nazis came to power and October 31, 1941.

In March, after a series of missteps, Prime Minister Bárdossy resigned and was replaced by the old aristocrat Miklós Kállay. Kállay was already an anachronism in Hungary. He belonged to the world before 1914 and was immune to the spirit of the times, especially the spirit embodied by the Nazi Party. Calm and rational, a man determined not to be surprised by anything, he could waver between the British and the Germans but never between the Germans and the Russians.

On the day Kállay was sworn in, Chorin gave him an astonishingly prescient memorandum. It said that Germany had already lost the war and that Hungary should reach out to the Allies to make peace and soften the ordinances enacted against the Jews. Soon afterward Kállay presented Regent Horthy with a memo containing a five-point program to maintain Hungary's independence and regain more of the lands lost in Trianon.

He suggested that they resist German demands but only to the extent that they could avoid occupation; maintain the independence of the military; and emphasize anti-Communism and make pro-German gestures and declarations in order to allay German suspicions. He also believed that Hungary should seek contact with the British. In some of his speeches he could be passionately anti-Semitic, but instead of acting radically, he would merely speak radically. He hoped to dispel the suspicions of the Hungarian right wing and the Germans.

Kállay was given a relatively free hand to pursue this strategy, but he knew that he had bigger and more intractable constraints. A friend congratulated him on his appointment saying, "Miklós, you are now in the saddle."

"Yes," Kállay replied, "but there is no horse under me."

Kállay was invited on an official visit to Hitler's headquarters in East Prussia on June 6 to 8, and he asked Aladár to go with him. My father had been promoted to deputy head of the political division in the Foreign Ministry, tasked with negotiating the alliance with Germany—a remarkable appointment given his widely known anti-Nazi stance. The trip meant Aladár had to postpone yet another rendezvous with Hanna. He had been much less reliable in his trips to Ireg that summer. Hanna was hurt and gave him the silent treatment, but it eventually, inevitably thawed. My father wrote, "I believe that we have created a new indoor game called 'I-am-angry-at-you-don't-be-angry-with-me.' . . . But there is a very important result of the game. I love you even more than before, and I am much more optimistic regarding the future despite the entire range of your doubts."

Days later he boarded the train with his boss, Andor Szentmiklóssy, and the prime minister to go to East Prussia. There they were met by the Hungarian ambassador to Germany and some of his staff, as well as the staff of Germany's foreign minister, Joachim von Ribbentrop. My father and Szentmiklóssy were given precise instructions as to which door the prime minister was to exit and where on the platform they were to line up. "The new protocol is a martial one and leaves nothing to the individual's manners or tact," my father observed. The German military attaché in Budapest who accompanied them said with no irony at all, "How nice it is when they tell you exactly what you have to do, and thus you don't have to do any thinking." My father found himself in a "Prussian paradise where the angels do nothing but issue orders and make sure that the souls of the blessed do nothing but obey."

They ate in the Führer's dining car, and during most of the evening meals, the curtains were drawn, a protocol amazingly called *Kameradschaftsverdunkelung* (roughly translated as "comradeship blackout"), so that poor, hungry Germans would not have to see the lavish meals that the dignitaries were served. My father's conscience was immune to *Kameradschaftsverdunkelung,* and he could not ignore the hungry eyes of Germans peering into their car. At the first social gathering of the evening, "the loquacious General Bodenschatz put six hot dogs on his plate."

Then they went to have lunch with Hitler. The Hungarians entered the compound, a little city of bunkers surrounded by fresh, early summer forests, blooming springtime lilac trees, and barbed-wire fences. Hitler lived in two low-ceilinged bunker rooms and the dining room doubled as a conference room for eight months during the bitter winter of 1941. Maps covered one set of walls; General Enno von Rintelen, now military attaché in Rome, rather incautiously observed that the maps did not show how much larger Asia was than Europe. A woodcut on another wall depicted a knight in armor with a swastika on his shield.

In this convivial setting Aladár was reminded of the first time he saw Hitler, in 1933 at the Sportpalast, where he experienced his extraordinary personality and the "suggestive power of his eyes." The Hitler now eating an enormous salad for lunch before him had gained weight, and his face was pale and swollen. General Jodl had a nervous rash, and Keitel and von Ribbentrop were also heavier. All the men looked tired, showing the strain of the less-than-successful Russian campaign.

Hitler was calm during their meal and talked freely, his mind running on its own paranoid associative tracks that Aladár remembered vividly:

Roosevelt is as crazy as Wilson and would soon be committed to an insane asylum.

This serves the Americans right since they too are insane for having entrusted their future to a lunatic *for the second time.*

The entire Russian economy is based on everyone cheating each other, most of all the Jews, who cheat everybody.

Large estates are of enormous importance to the local economies. A system of land redistribution would be disastrous, and a system of smaller properties would never be endorsed.

In fact, rural men should be compelled to move to the cities unless they marry a peasant girl, in which case they would be compelled to remain in the country. Having the marriage to a peasant girl as an incentive, small farmers could go far, and the stability of the peasantry would be increased.

Aladár listened and watched and wrote dispassionately about the events, recording the flow of the conversation. During Hitler's monologue, Aladár experienced a powerful internal shift. He had not ignored the dangers of Hitler—indeed, he had given one of the earliest warnings about him in the Foreign Ministry; he had been anti-Nazi for nearly as long as the Nazis were in power—but he had never before apprehended the Satanic nature of Hitler's character.

Aladár was shaken out of his inertia during that visit. He could no longer watch and wait and do his job while rhetorically opposing too close an alliance with Germany. There was a moral urgency to the opposition. This was a moment in history that required men of decency and integrity to act with courage. He knew that he must do something to help extricate Hungary from the Axis embrace.

The Führer disappeared after lunch, and the rest of the party went outside to smoke. And then it occurred to Aladár that even though he had seen Hitler now for the third time at close quarters, he still could not remember the color of his eyes. (They were blue.) East Prussia bloomed with spring that June; the scent of lilacs saturated the air, and the forest surrounding them glowed pale green. The beauty of the landscape was so jarring in comparison to the context. With subtle, irrevocable vehemence, the trip radicalized my father.

Aladár returned to Budapest even more pessimistic than before and went immediately to Ireg, seizing some time to talk about what he had seen and experienced. He and Hanna spent three days together, looking at the moon, walking in the park, sitting on the steps near the swimming pool, and regaining a sense of equilibrium that the times challenged.

Aladár brought her the new book by Franz Werfel, *The Song of Bernadette,* the story of Bernadette of Lourdes and her visits by the Virgin Mary. While Aladár's mother was an ardent Catholic, according to Hungarian custom he had been raised in the religion of his father, which was Calvinist. But the mysticism of Catholicism exerted a powerful tug on him, and this story of the simple peasant girl moved him deeply. "I am happy to see that *Bernadette* had the same effect on you as it did on me," he wrote in July. "So together we should go to Lourdes."

Thirty-one years later, they would.

CHAPTER 10

Inertia and a Decisive Mindset

■ ■

In 1942 most Hungarians still managed to sustain a kind of normal life. Coffee was a thing of the past, gasoline was rationed, and often the bread was sour. A poor harvest and other shortages occurred, but Hungarians were much better off than the rest of Europe. The war appeared in newspapers, in cinemas, in the urgent radio broadcasts with fraught references to the Axis and the Allies, and in the haunted faces of Polish and Austrian refugees. War was not an abstraction, but one could ignore its devastating concreteness.

Many years later my father observed: "It was one of the major anomalies of 1942, how little the great events affected one's private life. The burden of the war grew in every way: the second army and the forced labor battalions were in a certain sense sacrifices to pacify Hitler and to buy the relative tranquillity and peace for the majority of the country."

The bounty of Ireg cushioned them from even the minor inconveniences of the shortages. Hanna and Aladár continued their meandering drives to small towns outside Budapest, to little forests with forgiving paths, to easy mountains that were not much more than hills. If there was something unreal and cosseted about the lives that they led, there was also something defiant about their determination to sustain that existence as long as possible. If there was something culpable about their ease and privilege, there was also something noble in their refusal to emigrate.

Opportunities to emigrate presented themselves in 1942. Marianne and Móric made a brief trip to Switzerland, and Hanna and Puppa received an urgent call from the writer and editor József Balogh. Tell your parents to stay in Switzerland, he warned them, because something dreadful is happening, and it could get much, much worse.

Could Balogh, with his extensive web of Western friends and contacts, have heard some grisly strand of news about Auschwitz, once the mass murders of Jews officially began in June? Was his worry provoked by the attack on Reinhard Heydrich in Prague? Five months after Wannsee, when Heydrich had triumphantly presented meticulous and practical plans to obliterate the Jewish population of Europe, he was so brutally attacked that he died a week later on June 4. Five days later the Nazis literally liquidated Lidice in a reprisal, and perhaps from this, Balogh believed that Switzerland was far safer than Budapest.

His warning only made my grandparents return home more quickly. They had many opportunities to emigrate during those early years, but a combination of what Móric described as "inertia and also . . . a decisive mindset" kept them in Hungary. So many fine but inviolable threads linked all the family members and wove them together in such a way that they were all immobilized. In a brief memoir, Móric wrote, "Leaving behind our customary environment, which not only provided our comfort but also provided us with a function, would have affected not only our way of life but our vanity as well. Our life abroad would have necessarily been a modest, restricted, and anonymous one."

But it was not just vanity that held them there, or the greedy desire to continue an indulgent life; these my grandfather referred to as "uninspiring reasons." They had other reasons that were more elevated.

All of those with whom we had collaborated politically, with whom we lived and planned and who would have an important role to play abroad, remained at their posts, although they clearly saw the inevitable approach of the confrontation. If they, rightly or wrongly, chose to act in this fashion, I could not seriously entertain the thought of a temporary emigration. Acting alone would have meant that I abandoned a situation in which my friends continued to fight and in which, in a modest way, I might have been able to make a contribution.

And so the patterns of life continued much as they had the previous year. Right after the feast of Pentecost, the family packed up to go to

Ireg. Hanna and Aladár met as often as they could. They captured some time to go on long drives, though the gas rationing made those journeys less predictable. Aladár became thoroughly integrated into the life of the Kornfeld family, dining with Móric even when Hanna was still in Ireg.

Aladár's parents and Lilly were invited to visit Ireg, a trip that must have caused my mother great agonies. She had charmed Lilly completely, and the two of them had even fashioned a kind of friendship. But the ambitions and the prejudices of Aladár's parents, especially Sarolta, were no secret, and as confident as Hanna might have been in his love, she also knew the enormous power his mother possessed over him. The visit went beautifully, despite one painful moment at the beginning when Aladár Senior asked his son, thinking Hanna was out of earshot or perhaps not, "If you are so enamored with this family, why didn't you fall in love with the pretty one?"

My mother told me this story once or twice, forty years later, as if it were funny, even though we both knew it was awful.

Had Aladár's father known about Puppa's romantic inclinations, he might not have been so enthusiastic. Puppa's intimate life was complicated. Marianne's first cousin Vera was married to János Zwack, who, with his brother, owned a large family distillery that manufactured one of Hungary's most famous digestives, Unicum. János, who was also known as Coko (Tso-ko), was immensely charming, confidently promiscuous, and twenty-one years older than Puppa. He became mesmerized by her languid voluptuousness when she was just eighteen. They fell in love, maintaining a discreet but intense love affair for nearly twelve years.

With his wife and young son, Peter, Coko was thoroughly integrated into the family activities, spending most of their vacation time in Derekegyháza but visiting Ireg as well. Puppa loved her independence and her privacy and often said that the only way she would ever marry would be if she and her husband had separate apartments. A number of different, more appropriate suitors courted her, and several regularly asked her to marry, but she was content in her affair with Coko.

But in 1942 she was getting older, and the affair had lost all secrecy. One day Vera invited Puppa for afternoon tea. They sat in the Zwacks' beautiful house in the Castle District of Buda. A maid served them tea. After the exchange of some pleasantries, Vera, who was an efficient woman, got down to business.

She told Puppa that Coko was her husband and would never leave his family to marry her. How easy this was going to be.

"Let me assure you, Vera, I have no interest in marrying him," Puppa replied. "I never want to marry, and I certainly wouldn't dream of disrupting your household. Your life is perfectly safe, I promise."

What could have been a classic, even caricatured confrontation between mistress and wife became a decorous tea party. Neither of them experienced a tremor of apprehension or a surge of jealousy. Perhaps because the affair had been going on for such a long time, both women had accommodated themselves to the situation. For a certain portion of upper-class society during this period, fidelity was a flexible concept.

But during this time my mother and my aunt, whose lives were mirror images of each other, who grew up wearing identical clothes and walking in unison and traveling together and sleeping together and giggling about the same elderly guest at dinner, shared yet another parallel experience. For very different reasons, they were both in illicit relationships.

Hanna could not share her relationship with nearly anyone outside the family because of politics and anti-Semitism and insensible prejudices. But at least she could enjoy the luxury of her family's very public acceptance of Aladár. And in private she could enjoy his confiding, intimate letters that appeared nearly every week that summer. She had become his "darling Hancsi," about whom he was "thinking constantly." He described everything he did, everyone he saw, what they discussed, and how he loathed the heat. They had reached the point of such tranquil affinity that the period immediately after parting was disorienting.

"For the time being I am trying to get used to life without Hancsi, and it doesn't come easily," he wrote. "Because it was so very good to be with you, to know that you were always within reach and in the evening later to sneak out to the bench and be only with you. Thank you so much, my darling, for so much kindness and just for being with me. For a while, again, one can live off the experience, knowing that it will be repeated. You know, my darling, all this is so natural, the rightness of our being together is so self-evident, it is almost impossible to write about, impossible to describe. It is like breathing."

CHAPTER 11

A Christian Enterprise

■
■   ■

The Manfred Weiss Works had to be considered a Christian enterprise, and the only way to achieve that fiction was through 51 percent ownership by Gentiles. Fortunately the family had a large number of spouses—like George's new wife, Elsie—and in-laws and friends who qualified. They were given stock in the holding company of the factory to reach the 51 percent level without diluting the family's governing stake.

The factory had expanded enormously over the previous decade, and its line of production included cars called WM (for Weiss Manfred). In the 1930s the Manfred Weiss Airplane and Motor Factory had been founded. The plant manufactured passenger cars for the taxi fleet, trucks, tanks, and most recently, airplanes.

As the war progressed, both the German air force and the Hungarian government increased their demand for the airplanes, but the name of the product did not sit well with German consumers. The Manfred Weiss Airplane and Motor Factory reeked of suspect Jewish industry, so the subcompany was renamed the neutral Danube Aircraft Manufacturing Company.

Vilmos Billitz, a lawyer and executive of the factory, developed close ties to the ministries of defense and treasury in both Hungary and Germany. The enterprise was so confidential that Eugene and Alfons, the two sons of Manfred Weiss, were not permitted to enter the area where this manufacturing took place.

In every aspect of society the line of demarcation between Jews and

Gentiles grew sharper. Men of Jewish descent could not serve in the regular army but were called upon to serve in the Labor Service—the work details in forced labor battalions that toiled under terrible conditions. Even Jewish officers were stripped of their rank. By February 1942, when members of the Jewish battalion prepared to go to the Soviet Union, the government required that Jews wear civilian clothes with a white armband emblazoned with a yellow Star of David.

Conscription for the brigades increased at the beginning of 1942 under a notice called the SAS, or Hurry Immediately Urgent. Nearly all the grandsons of Manfred Weiss were employed at the factory. Its important wartime role was a useful insurance policy against their being placed in a labor battalion.

George was actually called up to serve in a battalion that was being sent, ill equipped, to the Russian front. This was very different from his military service in the 1930s, a more carefree time when he once summoned a chauffeur from Ireg to bring his battalion a small feast—venison and salads and chicken and fabulous sweets, accompanied by fine wines. But this assignment was deadly, and while the family didn't know exactly how deadly, their connections in the government were better informed.

The summer of 1942 was dreadfully hot, and the winter was homicidally cold. Jewish doctors, lawyers, and businessmen were sent to Russia to serve with no weapons, wearing suits and city shoes and little caps and their armbands. These were disposable people, and sending them to the front achieved two objectives: to exhaust some Russian firepower without draining the military, and to exterminate Jews camouflaged as military men. In April the commanders were ordered to make sure that 10 to 15 percent of the field labor companies were composed of Jews, and they especially wanted those Jews to be prominent, "well known by their wealth or reputation."

As a young, able-bodied man, George was called up. But a prominent figure in the department of war named István Oláh loved George's mother, Marianne. He had visited Ireg and had spent time on Lendvay Street and was charmed by her. Could he possibly intervene? It was a great deal to ask, and of course she would understand if the circumstances made it impossible, but just a word from him would make such a difference.

Of course, of course, he would see what he could do.

George had already said his goodbyes to the family and was literally on the train to go to the front when Oláh found him and explained to his platoon leader that George worked at the Manfred Weiss factory and was far too indispensable for wartime production to be absent. He returned home that afternoon.

The group to which he had been assigned was slaughtered in the Battle of Voronezh, on the river Don.

Remarkably, many Hungarians who were not Jewish and were not worried about being dragged into combat were able to ignore the war. Budapest was never blacked out, and many of the air raid sirens were either rusted or clogged, so they didn't sound. All that changed on Friday night, September 4, 1942, when Soviet planes bombed Budapest. Hungary's long period of illuminated innocence ended.

Hanna was still in Ireg when the bombs fell, as was Aladár's mother, Sarolta, who had been suffering from heart problems all summer and found the atmosphere of Ireg especially healing. Aladár and his father had just returned home from their visit and spent a peaceful afternoon together, playing solitaire and reading the papers, the father filling cigarettes with tobacco for the son and complaining about getting old.

In the evening, the quiet routine was interrupted by the blaring of one of the functioning air raid sirens. They looked at each other, shrugged, and decided to remain in their apartment. They heard only an occasional distant explosion. My father went to the window, with its beautiful view of the Danube, and saw "Stalin's candle"—the nickname for Russian artillery—nicely illuminated over the river. Over the Pest side of the city, the explosions cast a crimson, smoky light. "In the first few minutes we were a bit scared," he wrote Hanna the next day. "But then we did not feel any deeper emotions and waited for an hour. By that time we became tired and went to bed. But before falling asleep, I could still hear the explosions. . . . Today the Danube shore looks so peaceful, it is hard to believe that it wasn't always like that."

The bombs in Budapest were only a small part of a massive coordinated air raid by American, British, and Russian bombers throughout Europe. American pilots attacked the le Havre port and the Rouen railway yards, while hundreds of British aircraft bombed Bremen. The Russians attacked Vienna, some German cities, and Budapest.

This was the first time that the two great cities of the old Austro-

Hungarian Empire had been bombed. *The New York Times* reported, "A note of hysteria in Axis lands over the Russian raids, combined with the Anglo American air attacks from the west, was reflected in reports coming via neutral capitals." But, the reporter explained, "the most unusually effective of the air attacks, in the opinion of the authorities here, was the Russian Friday night bombing of Budapest where Moscow reported thirty-three vast fires were started." Eight people died directly from the bombs, and twenty-one were wounded.

C. A. Macartney, a British friend of both the Kornfelds and Aladár, was a historian who lived in Budapest but worked on the side for British intelligence. He wrote that the event evoked "from the Hungarian press an amazingly comic exhibition of injured innocence."

This air raid jolted the country out of its complacency. The Hungarian government instituted the policy of blackouts every night. While Budapest would not be bombed again until later in the war, the air raids continued. On the day that Sarolta returned "in extraordinary condition," Aladár reported, the now-repaired air raid sirens blared once more. "She became very frightened of the sirens, and we became frightened along with her. Her heart went pit-a-pat like a machine that went bad." This time the family descended into the air raid shelter, where they all calmed down; but Aladár's most pressing worry was the health and well-being of his mother.

He then inquired about Hanna. "Darling, how did you spend the critical night? Did you hear anything at all? Or did you find out that something like this happened only later? I hope that you were not scared and that you are not afraid of coming to Budapest. If it would cause even the slightest worry, then don't come. It really doesn't make any sense to expose yourself to such anxieties. I don't have to tell you that it does not mean that I don't want to see you. Quite the reverse. But it is most important that you are not afraid."

How could she possibly not have been afraid? The bombs were only the most recent reason. She was afraid they would never get married. She was afraid that her parents would die. She was afraid of the Germans and even more afraid of the Russians. She was afraid that my father might get hurt, lose his job, or be killed in his travels. She was afraid that eventually he might get bored with her. She was afraid that the air raids meant there would be more bombs and they would be killed or injured.

She was less afraid in Ireg because Ireg was such a timeless and secure world.

But she was always afraid and hated herself for it. She was the only member of the family who indulged in such a weak emotion. She summoned her courage and visited Budapest, bombs or no bombs, because Aladár, once more, was preparing for a trip—this time to Lisbon.

CHAPTER 12

What About Hungary?

A ladár accompanied Brazilian ambassador Freitas and his wife to Portugal and met the Hungarian minister to Rio de Janeiro. Billed as an "official exchange of diplomats," the trip occurred because the Pact of Rio de Janeiro that Brazil had signed with its new ally the United States in effect severed relations between Brazil and its former Axis friends. Hungary was the last country to cease relations for many reasons, not the least of which was that the Hungarian minister to Brazil was Miklós Horthy, Jr., son of the regent, and he frankly liked the country. Eventually it grew impossible to maintain these relations, so my father and a small entourage traveled across Europe to Lisbon.

He was happy to go to the west and to see the Atlantic Ocean. In a vague and indistinct way, the wild, stray thought of defecting occurred to him. But he was trapped by the same sense of duty and inertia from which the Kornfelds suffered. At the French-Spanish border they had to transfer to a Spanish train, since the Spanish system used a wider-gauge track. The Spanish stationmaster shrugged and said that the train was broken down, there was no spare engine, he had no idea when one would appear, and all of them should prepare for a long, long wait.

Another reflex in Aladár was triggered—the diplomatic reflex—and he confronted the stationmaster. Negotiations for this journey had already taken place with the Spanish government. They had been going on for weeks. The Hungarians had been given full assurances that every-thing at the border would proceed smoothly. Another shrug of indifference. Aladár wanted to telephone the Hungarian legation in Madrid. Could he please have a telephone? Another shrug, this one with contempt. Then the Brazilian ambassador intervened and said, "I have a thousand cigarettes and need two engines. If you give us the engines, you may have the cigarettes."

They were under way in less than an hour.

Aladár was shocked by the scenes flashing past his window. The Spanish Civil War had been over for three years, and yet everywhere they passed starving children, ruined buildings, and staggering poverty. At the Portuguese border, the station was cheerful, clean, and well supplied with newspapers, cigarettes, and chocolates. As the train snaked through the placid Portuguese countryside with its hills and olive groves, Aladár took stock of Salazar's country, which was so important in the thinking of Hungarian conservatives and Catholics. The benign authoritarian who ruled over a country that enjoyed prosperous and comfortable neutrality— this was a dream that could be realized only by the blessings of geography.

They remained in Lisbon for nearly two weeks, enjoying the freedom, the coffee, and the socializing with expat Hungarians. The *Yankee Clipper*, an airplane that in a mere twenty-six and a half hours flew from New York to Southampton, stopped several times in Lisbon when they were there, bringing mail and *The New York Times*. Eventually they returned to Budapest, crawling from the tip of Western Europe back to the heart of the Axis, bringing with them the regent's son as well as a huge amount of coffee and tea for the Foreign Ministry and of course for the Kornfeld household. How fascinated the family was to hear about Lisbon. None of them had ever visited Portugal, but it must have seemed so exotic and interesting.

Among all the countries under the German sphere of influence, Hungary was considered the most unreliable in its willingness to dispose of its Jews. Kállay was known to find the whole notion abhorrent. Despite his strong words after the time of Béla Kun, Horthy appreciated the importance of Jews in Hungary and was not eager to align himself with the strident anti-Semites, both within Hungary and in Germany. But in the summer of 1942, months after the Wannsee Conference, the specific plans of the conference for Hungary were outlined. By regaining some of the territories that were lost in Trianon, Hungary had also regained the Jewish population of those territories, so the "Jewish problem" in Hungary had expanded as well.

The head of Germany's Department D (which stood for Deutsch-
land or Internal Affairs) was Martin Luther, who had attended the
Wannsee Conference. He was also the head of a section that was one of
the most important offices to implement the final solution, which aimed
at the total eradication of European Jewry in other countries. He outlined the steps that the Hungarian government should take in order to
comply more fully with the Reich's approach. It should allow Germans
to resettle Hungarian Jews, it should make wearing the yellow star mandatory for Jews, and it should develop a strategy to eliminate the Jewish
presence from the country's economic and cultural landscape. It should
seize the property of Jewish citizens so that Jewish capital would be eliminated from Hungary.

Kállay despised these demands but was enough of a realist to recognize that outright refusal would make him too unreliable to continue as
prime minister. He tried to explain to the Germans that the situation of
the Jews in Hungary was different from what it was in other countries,
and therefore their treatment should also be different. A huge number of
Hungarian Jews actually lived in the countryside, so they were far from
contaminating urban life. Hungarian Jews were enormously important
economically—far more so than in other countries. The Weiss, Chorin,
and Kornfeld families were only a part—though a considerable part—of
the powerful Jewish financial and industrial base, and that base was
working for the Reich. Moreover Hungarian Jews were so isolated, they
had no international influence and thus were far less dangerous than the
French, Swiss, or American Jews.

On October 22 Kállay gave a speech to a Government Party conference in which he walked a fine line between demonstrating some fealty
to Nazi anti-Semitism and distancing his government from an anti-
Semitic program. "I must contradict those people who can see no other
problem in this country except the Jewish problem," Kállay said. "Our
country has many problems beside which the Jewish problem pales into
insignificance. Those who can see Hungary only through such spectacles
are degraded men who must be eliminated from our community. I shall
do my utmost, I shall go to the utmost limits everywhere in the country's
interest, but I cannot and will not allow anyone to soil the national honor
and reputation of Hungary, nor to obstruct the great aim of concentrating the nation's forces by political extremism and base propaganda."

Even with the obvious excesses of the Nazis, the inhumanity of the concentration camps and the extermination camps were simply not in the realm of the possible; quite literally they were unimaginable. Auschwitz had begun its horrific extermination enterprise in June 1942.

A friend from the Foreign Ministry, Andor Gellért, worked in Berlin and had heard the details of "the final solution." At first he could not believe it, but the stories kept repeating. He didn't know if his acquaintances were trying to warn him or frighten the recalcitrant Hungarians. Indeed, it was not even clear what "the final solution" actually involved. He told Aladár and his colleagues, but they thought he was exaggerating. They knew that deportations to the east were occurring, but they simply could not fathom that there was going to be a systematic eradication and that organized mass murders were already taking place.

My father had heard from Polish refugees that the *Einsatzgruppen*—the SS detachments for special services, populated by some of the most sadistic Nazis—murdered groups of Jews. Returning soldiers from the Eastern Front also described Jewish carnage. But every war has its unspeakable isolated crimes, and as abhorrent as these were, the mind could not make the leap from what seemed like isolated, despicable incidents to an efficient, massive government program to exterminate millions of human beings.

The Foreign Ministry was preoccupied with more immediate concerns. A German victory was not to be taken for granted, and discomfort with the alliance troubled several members of the Hungarian government. Aladár did not believe in a German victory, he considered it to be a huge danger to Hungary, and he was outspoken in saying this.

He submitted an essay entitled "Some Elements of Hungarian Policy" to the intellectual journal *Hungarian Studies* under the transparent pseudonym Pál Szegedi. In it he suggested the importance of having a foreign policy that was completely independent of that of the Germans. The Germans saw the essay as a public airing of the unreliable philosophy of the Kállay government and further confirmation that Hungary was an untrustworthy ally.

After his moral awakening with Hitler, Aladár realized that he had to act boldly within the constraints of the Foreign Ministry. He was one of a number of men there who believed that it might be possible to approach the Allies and attempt parallel and separate peace negotiations. They believed that in comparison with its neighbors, Hungary's position was a positive one: its treatment of the Jews was relatively humane, its society was relatively stable, and its government was cautious and careful in its relationship with Germany.

These officials tried to set up contacts, with threads he recalled were "as fine as spiderwebs," to gain information from the Allies and to get their advice. They considered the establishment of contacts a triumph, though perhaps they exaggerated their initial significance. They extended feelers to contacts in Istanbul and Bern, Stockholm and Lisbon.

And then at the beginning of December, Berlin told the Hungarian government that it would tolerate no orientation toward the West. Certainly Pál Szegedi's essay contributed to this ultimatum, but others in the Kállay government were considered equally unreliable. Furthermore Hungary's relatively benign treatment of its Jewish population was additional evidence of its unreliability. This admonition only increased Aladár's determination to reach out to the West and craft a separate peace with the Allies.

As the year drew to a close, he wrote his year-end meditations in his journal: "What about Hungary? The war approaches its end. . . . This last phase will also determine the place that Hungary will have at the peace negotiations and in postwar Europe. There is no doubt about it, we are the least weakened among the Axis countries and have been the least exposed to the weight and the ravages of war. It is also evident that we have been partners in the crimes of Nazism much less than the others and that in the eyes of the American and perhaps English leading circles we are judged favorably." For pages and pages he ruminated on various scenarios that could play out. The Foreign Ministry, he wrote, had "ceased to be a ministry and has become an assembly of three or four groups working partly together and partly against each other."

The greatest hope for Hungary, he believed, was the United States, which "thanks to the genius of Roosevelt, wishes to organize Central Europe from a practical point of view, without resentment, and without falling into yet another ideological captivity." But even as he wrote to clarify his thinking, the path of his analysis brought him to still another hopeless corner, another dead end.

The choices are between extremes, and the only certainty is that we are facing very hard times. We could be faced with the worst scenario: becoming a battleground. . . . Nothing represents as great a danger than being forced for many months to continue to dance on eggshells and to exhaust our already-meager reserves. At the very least aerial bombings will begin in the spring. They may or may not destroy us with bombs. . . . The prospects are often apocalyptic, but hope and faith whisper to us that we may reach the far shore without a serious crisis. How the final resolution will come cannot be predicted. It will probably be much simpler or more complicated than I can put down on paper, since life is always either simpler or more complicated than the image we try to conjure up.

While my father collected his annual reflections, and my mother prepared for Christmas in Budapest, a meeting took place between Adolf Hitler and Heinrich Himmler, Reichsführer-SS, chief of all German security forces, criminal and political police, head of the SS, and the organizer of the concentration camp system. With the war in Russia taking an enormous toll on Germany, the faint anxiety that perhaps Germany might not actually win the war began to gnaw on Himmler's unstable mind. Exterminations were taking place at an appalling rate in concentration camps, but Himmler decided to talk with his Führer about exploring other options with the Jews. He wrote a brief description of this conversation, dated December 12, 1942: "I have asked the Führer with regard to letting Jews go in return for ransom. He gave me full powers to approve cases like that, if they really bring in foreign currency in appreciable quantities from abroad."

1943

I can fight without hope.
My resolve is based on my sense of duty.

—FERENC DÉAK

CHAPTER 13

Spiderwebs

■

■   ■

Aladár was not a romantic hero and had an instinctive mistrust of people who played that role. His need to see all sides of the story, while useful for a diplomat or a historian, often left him mired in an elaborately rationalized and elegantly intellectualized swamp of inaction. It always seemed to me that he liked it that way, that he could do nothing else— that he was one of Hungary's many Hamlets.

But that was the father I knew, not the father I have come to know. In falling in love with my mother, he had already taken an uncharacteristically bold stand. Other, more socially and politically acceptable women would eagerly have welcomed his interest, but he followed his very inconvenient heart. That he chose and loved and became committed to my mother was a brave act for him that carried some very real professional risks. His anti-Nazism, his friendships that ranged throughout the political spectrum, and his philo-Semitism were well known, and many of his colleagues found him dangerously unreliable.

At the end of 1942 and throughout 1943, he embarked on an even riskier enterprise. He remembered Hitler's demonic presence and knew that other options had to be explored, even acted upon.

Aladár was not alone in this conviction. Meeting at the Kornfelds', Chorin and others eagerly expressed their desire to help and to support efforts to reach out to the Allies. They offered strategic advice, foreign contacts, and financial support for travel that might not appropriately appear on the government ledgers. The contacts Aladár had made with

Western diplomats when he went to Lisbon expanded to include others in other countries, and he was hard at work on a long memorandum that would eventually be passed along to the Allies that analyzed Hungary's larger political situation and explained in great detail how it ended up more prisoner than ally of the Germans. He also envisioned eventual Soviet domination of the region and wanted to alert the Allies to this danger.

The combination of these two powerful images—the present difficulties in the German alliance and the future image of Soviet domination—made it clear to Aladár that his beloved country was in a no-win situation, fenced in with practically no good option for escaping. On the other hand, sustaining this carefully calibrated but precarious relationship with Berlin could perhaps help Hungary survive World War II and even spare its 800,000 Jews the fate of their neighbors.

He was working terribly hard and also spending a great deal of time with Hanna. But the fact that a courtship of this length was not leading to a clear wedding date was enervating. Despite the war, others in their circle were exchanging vows and rings, celebrating the creation of new families, embarking on an uncertain life together.

Hanna and Aladár were stuck. They could not get married for the usual reasons, and she could not exert any pressure. She was nothing if not realistic, so she accommodated herself to the circumstances. And yet all the reassuring words he had written nearly two years ago, after that fateful drive from Mogyoród when the final Jewish law was passed, now seemed so naïve, so idealistic.

Looking at her many cousins and close friends who now had babies (even her brother George was about to be a father!), she must have felt impatient to begin her own family. She was going to turn twenty-seven in May, a natural point to begin a married life and start having children, who could then play with and befriend their cousins.

I can't know the pangs of regret or worry or yearning or envy she felt, but she must have experienced them, even as much as she adored my father. She could certainly not share any of those feelings with Puppa, who was flatly uninterested in marriage and children and quite content in her quiet affair with János Zwack. But Hanna's life hummed with activity.

Her favorite cousin had given her a thick leather-bound diary. It spanned five years from 1943 to 1948. Hanna began the year attending

mass, playing innumerable games of bridge, and traveling to Derekegyháza for the traditional New Year's trip, where there was "wonderful
weather, shooting, afternoon conversation, and good spirits." She returned to Budapest the following week and on January 8 met Aladár for
dinner with some other family friends. Every other day his name appears, in the midst of snowfalls and bridge games, days at work and evenings with friends, and regular news reports on the war.

"It is amazing," Hanna wrote on January 8, "that such a carefree
peaceful life still exists in 1943."

Or at least it was peaceful in Budapest. In Russia one of the greatest
battles of World War II was just ending. Since September, German and
Soviet troops had fought at Stalingrad, a central spot for Russian communications and industry. The two great armies were eventually reduced
to hand-to-hand combat in single streets, like a horrifying neighborhood
gang war backed by superpowers. At one point over a million Russian
soldiers surrounded the city, strangling the German troops who were
initially desperate for munitions. Ordered not to retreat, the Germans
were trapped for months. Their desperation for something to fight with
was replaced by the more elemental desperation for something to eat and
drink. The carnage was simply unbelievable in the brutal Russian winter,
and eventually 400,000 Germans who did not die from injuries in battle,
starved or froze or did both. By the beginning of February, the Germans
had no choice but to surrender.

But for Hungarians, the German loss was eclipsed by their own
blood-drenched tragedy on the Russian front. In order to do their part to
support the Axis assault on the Soviet Union, the Hungarian army had
been charged with defending a part of the river Don on the front lines.
While the Germans lost ground in Stalingrad, in their push west the
Russians had to cross this area near the city of Voronezh.

Waiting for them were more than 200,000 Hungarian soldiers as well
as 40,000 Jews in labor battalions—a pathetic challenge to three times
the number of Soviet troops. The assault began on January 12, and within
a week 130,000 men had been killed, wounded, or captured and 36,000
Jews perished. Horthy had tried to forestall the catastrophe weeks before,
on Christmas Eve, when he sent a telegram to Hitler begging him to
send the weapons and equipment he had promised in exchange for the
troops going on this mission. Nothing was sent.

Ill-equipped and ill-trained, the Hungarian troops panicked. The commander of the second army, General Gusztáv Jány, wrote that losing a battle was no disgrace, but there was a disgrace at Voronezh "in the panic stricken cowardly flight of the troops on account of which the German allies and our fatherland bear us in contempt. . . . Characteristic of the events of the last few days is that the Jewish labor service companies march in close order and in good discipline, whereas the so-called regulars give the impression of a horde sunk to the level of brutes." So the Jews acquitted themselves admirably before they were slaughtered. But their courage did not affect the sensibilities of the anti-Semites in the Hungarian government, who were more determined than ever to shape their government's very restrained hand into a fist.

Prime Minister Kállay, looking at the German defeats and the Allied victories, appeared to become even more committed to trying to extricate Hungary from its alliance with Germany, indeed to extricate Hungary from the war, while still hanging on to the territories it had regained. But he was trapped by his own indecision. His largely pro-German, anti-Semitic cabinet was determined to continue Hungary's alliance with Germany. Most Hungarians—except for Jews and those who apprehended the sheer evil in the Nazis—saw the Soviet Union as a far greater threat than the Nazis. Indeed, they viewed the alliance with Germany as a protection against Bolshevism.

Nonetheless, several in the Foreign Ministry thought the time was right to make overtures to the West. Aladár was central to those plans and activities. The first order of business was to communicate to the Allies that Hungary would not resist an Allied invasion, especially by American, British, or Polish regular forces. They all agreed that the Russians were horrifying. They also wanted it to be known that if Hungary received some assurance that it would be supported, that it would not be left twisting in German hands, it was willing to fight the Germans.

This was the simplest and most basic part of the plan, but to enact it was far more complicated. The plan was christened Operation Spiderweb for its intricacy and delicacy. Elaborate secrecy was essential because if the Germans had any idea—and of course they had ideas—then the consequences could be dire.

On January 26, a secret memorandum was transmitted to the British political intelligence department from a source in Stockholm who reported, "The Hungarian reader in this bureau saw a telegram from the Hungarian Ministry of Foreign Affairs to the Hungarian Minister in

Stockholm drawing his attention to the article in *Pester Lloyd* of January 3rd. . . . One may conclude that the Russian threat is causing panic in Budapest. According to the same source an attempt is to be made to send Szegedy-Maszák to Stockholm for a short visit."

He left on February 20 and spent the first night in Berlin. He had enough time to be visited by one of his most trusted psychics, Várady, who predicted that there would be many Russian victories and that the Russians would occupy Berlin. His predictions about my father are lost forever. Aladár left the next day for Sweden. Arriving in Stockholm, he was struck by how, "as in every neutral location, there is a flourishing spy exchange . . . partly under the aegis of that peculiar, secret, Freemason-like solidarity that somehow seems to link people engaged in information gathering."

He first checked in with the Americans. A Harvard professor named Bruce Hopper was the chief of the OSS group in Stockholm. He was supposed to have been Roosevelt's personal representative, and since Aladár had received English lessons from Hanna's old British governess Miss Thompson, he could speak English with relative fluency. He told Hopper that Hungary was eager to find a way out of its alliance with Germany but was constrained by the fact that the only Allied troops in Europe were the Russians. Hopper acknowledged that "one can only make a choice if one has two options" and "understood we wished to avoid chaos and that this was their goal as well." He made no false promises, no suggestions for future approaches to the Americans, but after the conversation, "I felt that our opinion was reinforced and that we would find more understanding in the United States than in England."

Aladár's next contact was with Vilmos Böhm, who tracked Hungarian newspapers and activities for the British embassy in Sweden. An older man who had served in the government during World War I, he had briefly worked in the Béla Kun government before escaping to Sweden. There he crafted a life, eventually working with the British. During the war he became the point man in Stockholm for Hungarian contacts with the British Foreign Office.

When Böhm was a young boy living in a Jewish orphanage, he was one of the children who had been invited for Sunday lunch to the house of Baron Zsigmond Kornfeld; after lunch they would play with little Móric and his brothers and sister. Now, working for the British, his position gave him a resurgence of prestige and importance that he hadn't enjoyed for decades. He was seen, mistakenly, as a crucial connection to the British Foreign Office. Böhm arrived at the apartment of a friend of Aladár's for their first meeting. As Böhm entered the apartment, Aladár extended greetings from Móric.

Aladár recited the parameters of Hungary's diplomatic situation that he had described so many times, in so many ways. "We had no choice but to stay with the Axis to try to preserve our present, relative independence," he said. "German occupation had to be avoided because of its disastrous consequences to the Jews and to left-wing politicians and refugees. It is critical that American troops appear on the continent as soon as possible," he continued. "We would not resist them or Polish troops, but we would resist Soviet, Romanian, or Yugoslav troops."

He stated his concern that the Russians would dominate the region after the war, while Böhm assured him that Hungary would be under the Anglo-Saxon sphere of influence.

While Aladár talked with Böhm in Stockholm, others in the spider-web were working in Lisbon, Bern, Stockholm, and Istanbul, all trying to break Hungary's isolation and somehow convince the West that it was worth saving—not an easy task. The Allies were suspicious of Hungarian motivations and preoccupied by their own advancement in the war.

Trust was in short supply everywhere. Aladár and others provided a great deal of information to Böhm, and he initially responded as if he were the mouthpiece of the British Foreign Office. As cooperative as he was during the early part of 1943, by the end of the year he had soured. Whether because of jealousy, a Hungarian tendency to lack solidarity, or a need to shore up his own importance in the eyes of the British at the expense of others, he wanted to completely eliminate Aladár and his colleagues from any involvement in British-Hungarian matters. When he reported to his British contact, he suggested that Aladár was not an honest broker.

While in Sweden, Aladár went to an English bookstore and bought presents to bring home. He bought Jan Struther's *Mrs. Miniver; Grey Eminence,* Aldous Huxley's book about Père Joseph; *The Moon Is Down* by John Steinbeck; and Eric Knight's *This Above All,* which had been recommended by his friend, the writer Sándor Márai.

This Above All is set during World War I, when a young working-class soldier meets and falls in love with an upper-class girl. The romance may have been interesting, but Aladár was captured by the sociological insight. When the working-class hero of the book threw himself into fighting the war to the finish, it was not for the sake of the empire or the fate of the world but to settle old scores. When Aladár read this, he realized that Britain would never support the Hungarians. Britain's rigid social structure, especially as it was reflected in its Foreign and Home Office bureaucracies, would make them utterly mistrust and misunderstand the social nuances of Hungary. Hungarians were unlikely to throw themselves into any war in order to settle old social scores. He realized then that were there to be any hope for negotiations, they must be held with America.

After Stockholm, on March 1, he returned to Berlin. Flying at low altitude, a powerful wind buffeted the plane mercilessly. The wind persisted, and when he arrived at Tempelhof, the sheer force of it nearly toppled him as he walked to the terminal. That evening he visited his old friend the journalist Otto von Heydebreck, and together they talked about Stockholm and about Budapest acquaintances. Heydebreck's son was in the army, and Heydebreck described the appalling shortages throughout Germany that winter. The stores were generally closed except for grocery stores; no shoes, underwear, stockings, needles, combs, brushes, or paper (not even toilet paper) was available. Trams and trains were scarce. Of course, butter, coffee, and cigarettes were impossible to find. There was a flourishing black market, but the bread was awful and the beer watered down. Germans' diet consisted mostly of beans and misery.

Then the air raid sirens blared.

Aladár and von Heydebreck went down to the air raid shelter, with many others who were calm and resigned, as if this were an inconvenient fire drill rather than the precursor to seven hundred tons of bombs dropped by 302 British bombers. It was the most massive British bombing raid to hit Berlin, Churchill proudly cabled Stalin.

In the well-furnished shelter, Aladár and Otto found their places with the other adults, who sat calmly, their exhausted faces resigned and expressionless, as children lay on couches and beds and slept through all the noise. It had become a part of daily life. A bomb fell in the neighboring Bayrischer Platz, and the door of the shelter blew open. Several men scurried to seal the shelter again. For two hours they talked quietly until the all-clear sounded.

My father walked to his hotel, the Eden, which years ago would have been an unimaginable luxury. The wind was still strong, and the fires that blazed in all directions provided the only light to illuminate his walk. When he turned down the street to the hotel, a policeman shouted, "Light! Light!" A dangerous sliver of light had seeped through a curtain not yet fully drawn.

CHAPTER 14

The Usual
Boundless Optimism

■   ■   ■

Back in Budapest, as the Kornfelds gathered around the radio for the news, they heard reports of the bombing in Berlin. Hanna wrote in her journal on March 1, "Great English air-raid in Berlin. Afternoon shorthand. Later with Eszter. In the evening a great rehearsal for Uncle Feri's birthday play: a newspaper and pertinent 'articles.'" She learned only later that Aladár had been in Berlin at the time of the raid. Ferenc Chorin was going to celebrate his sixty-fourth birthday that year, and as he was the recognized head of the family, a big celebration was planned. As always, the "children," now mostly in their twenties, would perform a play in honor of the birthday.

Chorin, one of the stalwarts of the manufacturing industry, one of the financial leaders of the country, and a good acquaintance of the regent, had been fired from the presidency of GYOSZ, the manufacturers association that his own father had founded. He had also been forced to resign from the vice presidency of the bank. He continued to wield influence behind the scenes, attempting to advise Prime Minister Kállay on maintaining a healthy distance from the Germans and even warning Regent Horthy that the Germans were likely to occupy Hungary. As Chorin later recalled, "The regent, with his usual boundless optimism, ignored my warning."

The Germans were pressuring all the publications that Móric and

Chorin founded and subsidized but especially the newspaper *Magyar Nemzet*. They objected to the paper's political orientation and its anti-German stance, and demanded that it cease publication. Prime Minister Kállay generally protected the paper, but it was made clear that the editorial stance had to be softened even as the editors remained strongly anti-Nazi.

There was also the Csepel factory, the crown jewel of Hungarian industry, whose board of directors had become Aryanized. A quiet tug-of-war was taking place between those in the government who assumed the factory would be taken over and nationalized, and others who still appreciated that this was private property. At one point Marianne's brother Alfons was even charged with espionage, though the charge was later dropped. Intermittently, visiting German delegations would go to the Manfred Weiss Works and insist that the war production shift into still-higher gear.

As they celebrated Uncle Feri's birthday, their lives seemed to be continuing largely undisturbed—family celebrations, trips to various country estates, work, and concerts. However, Móric and Ferenc Chorin were preoccupied with trying to steer the political ship in a different direction. Every Monday night, at either the Kornfelds' or the Chorins' home, a group of men involved in opposition work gathered to discuss the progress of the war and plan for Hungary's future after the inevitable German defeat.

Puppa was buried in the library, working on her dissertation about medieval Hungarian cities. George was preparing for the birth of his first child and worked at the factory. Tom had enrolled at the University of Pécs Medical School with the dream of opening a clinic at Ireg and providing medical services to the community there. The Pécs medical school had been generously endowed by Móric and had even awarded him an honorary degree.

Hanna worked in the Save the Children office and assisted her mother and aunt Edith with their various charitable activities, especially helping the innumerable Polish refugees who had arrived in Hungary. She maintained a wonderfully busy social life. Nearly every day of her calendar was marked by some social event—card games and dinners, trips to movies and walks with friends. Several times a week, sometimes nearly every day, Aladár's name would appear in her diary: "Office, afternoon with Aladár, who was in Berlin when it was bombed. His journey was not as useful or interesting as he had hoped. Only one thing is for sure . . . In the evening with Mami and Puppa to see a French film."

Toward the end of March, the Reich's discomfort with Hungary's behavior had finally reached the point where it concluded intervention was necessary. It summoned the regent to meet Hitler in Klessheim on April 16.

Hitler was clear about his dissatisfaction with the Hungarians. He told Horthy that Kállay had to be fired and that the Hungarians could no longer prevaricate about the Jews but needed to begin implementing their own final solution. The Germans were well informed about Hungarian overtures toward the West and presented the regent with a memorandum of the "list of sins" committed by the Hungarians. Hitler "simply could not understand" Hungary's friendship with the Jews. The Duce and the Romanian president Antonescu both realized that without the elimination of the Jews, the events of 1918 could repeat themselves. In the end the Jews were responsible for everything that was wrong, Hitler argued. In fact, there would not be a war right now if it weren't for the Jews.

Horthy knew that he could not mount a spirited defense of the Jews and blamed them for much of the gossip in Budapest. He said that Hungary was the first country in the world to take a stand against the Jews with the *numerus clausus* and racial laws. Horthy would do everything he could against the Jews by civilized means, but he would not murder them or eliminate them in any other way. Besides, economically they were tremendously important.

Hitler allowed that completely eliminating the Jews was not necessary—they could just be isolated in concentration camps, the way the Slovaks handled the problem. But the day after the meeting Hitler was more florid, comparing the Jews to the tuberculosis bacillus, and he asked why Hungary spared the wild beasts that wanted to bring Bolshevism on the world.

After this meeting the right-wing parties in Hungary became more outspoken and active. Aladár had already spent a great deal of time working on what later became known as the Szegedy-Maszák Memorandum, and during the first months of 1943, one of his co-conspirators who worked closely with the British reported that the British would be interested in learning about the concrete plans that Hungary had for the future. The meeting between Horthy and Hitler only increased the urgency of their work.

In the memorandum, Aladár articulated official Hungarian policy and ultimate goals not as a political statement but as a national one. "We were thinking in terms of the country, not the regime," he wrote later. "We were clear about the omissions and mistakes, but did not believe that the only method of approaching the problem was masochistic self-criticism."

In this manifesto he completely and decisively rejected any connection with Germany and Nazi ideology. He outlined the position of Hungary since 1919 and the devastating effects of the Treaty of Trianon on the Hungarian nation. For twenty-three densely typed pages written in English, he took each segment of Hungarian life—political, military, social, economic, cultural—and argued for its autonomy and for its fundamental independence from the German alliance. His proposal for the future was not to regain the lost territories but to form a new Carpathian alliance that would be democratic and Western in its orientation, respecting the national interests of each of the small countries while engaging in some mutual support so that they would not be obliterated by the threat of the Soviet Union.

He presented the memorandum to his boss in June, and it was approved by all of his superiors without any changes, then passed along to the prime minister. Kállay and Aladár went through the text together, and only minor changes were inserted. The memorandum was then circulated to select Hungarian ministers in neutral countries—those who had already been a part of the Spiderweb conspiracy. They emphasized in the transmittal letter that it was not to be shared but that it should serve only as a kind of baseline for future discussions.

Once released into the world, Aladár lost control of the document and its consequences. Either because of an indiscretion by one of the Hungarians or a provocation by the Germans, a rumor spread that a Hungarian peace offer had been made in Madrid. Aladár quickly moved to quash the rumor, emphasizing in a letter that the memorandum had not been written to be transmitted, that it was not an attempt for a separate peace, and that a single glance at any map would convince anyone that such a thing was impossible.

Then he discovered that one of his colleagues, Andor Gellért, who had been working in Sweden, had shared some information from that letter, which was supposed to be private, with Böhm. "It never occurred to me that in order to enhance their own credibility, my correspondents would quote my letters verbatim, or even hand over the entire letter. . . . All this contributed to the fact that on the other side they attributed much more importance to my person than what was indicated or appropriate."

Aladár had no idea what the impact of his work would be. He did not know that the British regarded it with contempt. C. A. Macartney, the British historian of Hungary and Aladár's eventual close friend, considered that it was at best untimely, since it came from a Hungary against which Britain had already declared war and that, on its own, had declared war against the United States and the Soviet Union. "The complete failure to appreciate the realities of the situation" was the basic criticism of this work. Some Hungarians considered it an apology for the Horthy system, while others thought it was completely unrealistic, even offensive to the Allies.

Several months after the memorandum was transmitted, a Swedish journalist asked Aladár if he could visit the Jewish quarter personally to confirm the claims made in the memorandum. Aladár had many friends who were Jews, including Zionists, so the visit was easy to arrange. In his first job, as the officer in charge of religious matters in the political division of the Foreign Ministry, Aladár had become friendly with Dr. Miklós Buk, who was the secretary of the Hungarian Zionist organization. Through him he had gradually met other Zionist leaders and begun to understand the tensions and the fissures in the Budapest Jewish community. Influential members of the Jewish establishment were strongly anti-Zionist since they too connected the movement with leftist politics. Aladár was struck with how disunited, competitive, and antagonistic the Jewish community was.

He knew where to go. The most important Jewish neighborhood in the city was in the seventh district in Pest, around the Dohány Street Synagogue. Small two- or three-story buildings, built in the early nineteenth century, had apartments on the upper floors and small businesses on the street level. An occasional Hasid would walk in the neighborhood, where you could see people going to synagogue on Friday nights and on Saturdays. This was not a Jewish ghetto, where Jews were forced to locate. Only much later did it serve that purpose. Instead it was a vibrant neighborhood populated largely by Jews. The journalist left Hungary concluding that the statements made in the memorandum were true and that the Jews in Hungary lived much better than in any other country fighting with Germany. Aladár harbored hope that what he had written was gaining attention.

In Britain the Foreign Office reviewed the document. On the front page of the dossier were comments from the research department responsible for vetting the information. "This is the most authoritative account of Hungarian hopes and fears that has so far reached us. The author, Szegedy-Maszák, as well as Kállay himself, was one of the four inspirers of the recent approach which we have received."

The reviewer then decimated the document, saying that the argument attempts to present Hungary as "the unwilling and ultimately innocent victim of circumstances but the impression remains that she has been guided throughout by the most blatant opportunism." This tone continues until the final conclusion: "If these are the ideas informing the basis of which the Hungarian govt [*sic*] hopes to enter into discussions with us, they still have a lot to learn."

For the British, the only acceptable Hungarian option was unconditional surrender. But how could Hungary surrender when it was not being attacked? Prime Minister Kállay allegedly said with some exasperation, "I can't surrender unconditionally over the long-distance telephone."

The Allies could not appreciate how alienated the Hungarians had become from the Germans because the Nazis thought that Hungarian leadership was shockingly soft on the Jews. The Jewish laws that had been passed, however humiliating and unjust, were merely symbolic compared with the mass deportations and the mass murder that had been organized in other parts of the Reich. Hungary had done nothing to eliminate the Jews—it only inconvenienced and humiliated them. Aladár noted many years later, "In spite of some excesses and some legal restrictions, our handling of this issue was a clear and unmistakable rejection of the Hitlerian policy and it also became increasingly mentioned, visible and convincing evidence of our 'resistance.' In this respect, Hungary was still an island in Axis Europe."

That was one of the reasons Aladár believed—naïvely, of course, but still with some fragile hope—that what he wrote might, somehow, present the Hungarian case persuasively. Hungary and Finland continued to be the least Nazified countries in Axis Europe, which gave Aladár and his colleagues the kind of moral and political confidence that was both understandable and excessive. They did not understand exactly how uninterested the Western powers were in their neighborhood, the Carpathian basin. Still, he was pleased with what he had done. Reflecting on the memorandum, he later wrote in Latin—the classical language of nineteenth-century diplomacy—"*dixi et salvavi animam meam.*"

I spoke and thus I have saved my soul.

CHAPTER 15

A Promotion
into the Abyss

■
■　　■

On June 17, 1943, my grandparents celebrated their thirtieth wedding anniversary. Marianne was now an elegant but matronly fifty-five, and Móric was a distinguished gentleman of sixty-two. The family had already spent some of their summer in Ireg, but the celebration was back in Budapest. It was likely a modest event, a great contrast to the beautiful wedding thirty years before that had taken place just around the corner, in a house that was now occupied by Eugene Weiss and his family.

In some ways, it was miraculous that their marriage had lasted so long. The stylistic differences between them were initially corrosive, in the way that small but symbolic disagreements can become in a marriage. In the Weiss household no one cared about food. In fact, excessive concern about the preparation of food was seen as unseemly. Not so in the Kornfeld household, where Móric's mother painstakingly wrote menus for the week, and cooks were hired and fired routinely. Móric enjoyed playing cards and socializing at his men's club. Marianne's life centered on the family, in a way that her husband found oppressive.

When they married, Móric sent his shirts to Vienna to be laundered and starched, an excess that Marianne found unfathomable. At the same time, while Móric wrote beautiful poetry, he could be acerbic and cutting in ways that Marianne had never experienced. At one point, after George was born, her family urged her to divorce, but she refused. Finally, as they celebrated their thirtieth year together, they had learned to appreciate each other. When Marianne played roulette, which she loved to do when they traveled, her lucky number was seventeen, their wedding date.

There were already shortages in the countryside, but the bounty of the estate still provided food. They would sometimes bring cherished gifts of butter, eggs, or a chicken back to Budapest for friends. While his parents and his sister Lilly spent time there, Aladár could not. He was consumed by work. Early in June, Hanna observed, "Aladár looks terribly pale."

She visited Budapest frequently that summer, so there were hardly any letters from 1943. Aladár did write the day after the Allies invaded Sicily. Budapest vibrated with rumors about what this might mean for Hungary. Perhaps the Americans and British would move up through Italy and liberate Hungary!

An atmosphere of uncertainty and paranoia had insinuated itself into their lives. The previous ease with which he shared his thoughts had disappeared because "it is definitely uncomfortable to think that a letter is read not only by the person to whom it is addressed. One feels that as we enter summer, the decisive period slowly will arrive. Of course it will not be pleasant, because the time of decisions in historical eras is generally not pleasant."

Only two weeks later Prime Minister Kállay shook up his cabinet. Nazi foreign minister von Ribbentrop had marginalized Kállay to the point that any instructions that he sent to Hungary pointedly excluded the prime minister. In response, Kállay did not bring in German sympathizers but instead rearranged the trusted inner circle, replacing the head of the Foreign Ministry with the previous secretary general of the Foreign Ministry, Jenő Ghyczy. Szentmiklóssy, who had been Aladár's boss as head of the political division, then became the first deputy of the Minister of Foreign Affairs, and Aladár took his place as the head of the political division. Hanna wrote from Budapest on July 20, "In the morning a special breakfast, Mami came in to say that Aladár will become head of the political division."

Becoming head of the political division gave Aladár far more power. It was the third-highest position in the Foreign Ministry, an incredible accomplishment for a thirty-nine-year-old with only fifteen years of experience.

If there were only some way he could refuse.

His promotion was premature, and he was uncomfortable participating in matters that were against his convictions. Especially when there was no chance for success. But he accepted the job, realizing that his psychological and professional equilibrium would come only if he kept one foot still in the former monarchy and the other in the distant, dreamed-of, and hoped-for free Hungary

His parents were naturally proud and thrilled. After his mother's life of social disappointments—the loss of stature in 1919 and the near-miss at nobility—the public recognition and political ascent of her beloved son was gratifying beyond words. Aladár's father could also see a kind of personal redemption in his son's accomplishments, and as much as he loved knowing the inner workings of government activities, he must have imagined that the new position would promise even more inside information. The disappointment came later when he realized that Aladár had become even more circumspect.

Other friends and supporters, including Móric and Ferenc Chorin, crowded around, celebrating the promotion of one whose strong moral compass they trusted. Even diplomats from other countries expressed their pleasure at the news. After the official announcement, the exclusive men's club the Nemzeti Kaszino—a club that my grandfather and Chorin were excluded from since they were Jews—invited him to become a member. He had entered a social realm that held little allure, indeed one that he had long viewed with suspicion and even a bit of contempt. But now he had officially become an "Excellency."

Given the circumstances, he never enjoyed any of the perquisites that accompanied his rise to power. His friend István Bede was promoted to lead the press division, and the two of them commiserated on the futility of their new positions. Aladár was much, much too aware of the hopelessness of their situation. In August he wrote a letter to Böhm in Stockholm (which Böhm duly passed along to British intelligence) expressing the way he and Bede felt about their rise to power:

> In normal times it would have been the fulfillment of our dearest
> wishes, the threshold of a brilliant career exceeding all our hopes. But
> today it is like jumping on a carriage when it is galloping: we have to
> seize the abandoned reins. It is not enough that the horses carry us
> with them down into the abyss. We shall have to bear direct responsi-
> bility for that disaster. We can only comfort ourselves with the thought

that millions in this unfortunate war have lost legs, arms, and eyes, or have sacrificed their lives for their country. We, too, must comply with the demands of duty.

He officially assumed his new job on Friday, July 23, and by Sunday he was faced with a crisis. Mussolini had fallen.

This development meant that Italy might defect from the German alliance and perhaps welcome Allied troops, who could then appear on Hungary's southern borders, where Hungary could surrender without the misery of a German occupation. The news was a crucible for the wildest and most optimistic conjectures. The Hungarian government was consumed with weighing the options. Perhaps the fall of Mussolini could trigger a decisive Hungarian split-off from Germany. Kállay received a memorandum from Endre Bajcsy-Zsilinszky, the editor of the anti-Nazi newspaper *Szabad Szó,* and Zoltán Tildy, the head of the Smallholders Party, that demanded that Hungary withdraw from the war, bring its troops back from the Russian front, and become a neutral nation. The government should repeal all Jewish laws, reestablish full constitutional rights, dismiss officers and officials who collaborated with the Germans or who had committed atrocities, and establish self-government in Transylvania and Ruthenia. They were audacious suggestions, but in retrospect, if they had done all these things, maybe the greater cataclysm could have been avoided.

Some of their contacts in the West were caught by the contagion of these events, sending messages to Kállay, urging him to take some decisive action that could at last set Hungary apart and demonstrate to the Allies that it could act independently of the Germans. The suggestion was made that Hungary should even turn to the Russians and present its willingness to withdraw from its alliance with Germany. But all was hopeless. Even in his weakened state, Hitler soon became the most powerful presence on Italian soil. It was crushing to see that even the British and American troops, more powerful in every respect, could not overcome the weakened Wehrmacht and SS formations.

No one could fathom how this had happened, except to realize belatedly that only second-tier Allied troops had been sent to what was seen as a second-rate war zone. Churchill had hoped that the Allies would invade "the soft underbelly" of Europe and make their advance through the south. But Stalin and Roosevelt were determined to drive in from the east and the west. The Americans saved their real firepower for a northern European invasion, not for Italy. Early euphoria about Mussolini's fall collapsed under the realities of the military situation.

As the summer ended and the fall began, the other depressing fact that the events in Italy revealed was that anything that added to the Wehrmacht's burden—even the occupation of a country like Hungary—would be good for the Allies. Hungary's strategic importance was as a costly distraction, a drain into which German resources could pour, diverting them from far more important goals like winning against the Russians or mounting an effective defense against the Allied invasion.

Germany was weakened and drifting toward defeat, and in a more rational world one would imagine that Germany would husband scarce resources for greater battles than one against a less significant, disobedient ally. But a divided, weak, and vulnerable Hungary did not know how to respond to the increasing pressure that Germany was exerting. It did not realize that in September Hitler's patience had reached a breaking point and that the tantalizing allure of liquidating the last, relatively intact Jewish community in Europe impelled him to order plans for the occupation of Hungary, codenamed Operation Margarethe.

Now more than ever, Aladár suffered. The stress and hopelessness of each day battered his nerves, and every morning the latest bad news assaulted him. On October 7 Hanna wrote, "Aladár looks terrible and is in a bad mood." Despite knowing how futile it all was, he still hoped that another yet-untried option would reveal itself as in some spiritual vision. When he met with the foreign minister, they took turns quoting the great Hungarian patriot Ferenc Deák to each other: "I can fight without hope, my firmness is based on my sense of duty."

The fall was rainy and cool that year. The BBC warned that Hungary was about to be bombed, and while it happened only much later, the threat was never far from anyone's mind. "Cooked or broiled," Hanna wrote that September. Cooked by the Germans or broiled by the Russians. This was the option that hung over their lives.

Aladár's friend Otto von Heydebreck visited from Germany. His wife and daughter were dead from bombs, and his son was dead on a battlefield. He had faced these monumental losses while watching his country collapse under the weight of war. In September he visited Ireg, sharing as much grim news as he could about life in Berlin. Hanna and Aladár were apart on their third anniversary, September 18. She wrote in her journal, "Riding in the morning. In the afternoon four Chorins arrived with Edith. The weather is perfect. The Allies came out on top at Salerno. This is the third anniversary. What will the fourth be like?"

The Italian campaign bled into more Russian triumphs as the Soviet troops drew closer and closer. The abbot of the Cistercian Abbey of Zirc became a regular guest at Ireg and even invited Hanna and the Chorins to a grape harvest in a region called the Badacsony. Both Ferenc Chorin and Móric Kornfeld had spoken with him about possibly hiding in his monastery should the need arise, but the request was only theoretical.

Just as a precaution, in case of an air raid, everyone in the family had a small bag packed under their bed. But in the back of their minds, they were concerned about what to do should the Germans arrive. As prominent Jews, they could hardly remain in their homes. Having a large group of friends scattered throughout Budapest, they each knew someone who might hide them, if only for a little while.

In November Aladár's mood became bleaker. He was approaching his fortieth birthday "disgusted and depressed," as Hanna observed, and the political situation was becoming more desperate every day. At the beginning of the month, while Hanna was in Ireg for her mother's birthday, Aladár wrote to her. He recounted his activities, visits with friends, and dinners with others, but his letter did not include all that weighed on him—he could not put it down on paper anymore.

On All Souls' Day, an important feast in Hungary, he went to the cemetery with his father and lit candles on the graves of his great-grandparents. He was so busy, he said, "I cannot get to my work." He was impatient for her return, and they met again on November 11. Hanna wrote, "Aladár at dinner. Depressed. Very bad times are coming. It would be a miracle if we could escape it. It is better not to know what the next months will bring." The next week they celebrated his fortieth birthday.

Occasionally Aladár worried about his personal safety in case of a German occupation. Once some members of the right-wing party that detested him and all he stood for anonymously sent him a copy of the right-wing paper *Nemzeti Figyelő* (National Observer) in which paragraphs about loyalty to one's allies and national honor were ominously underlined in red. A Greek diplomat sent word to Aladár via a friend that for his own safety's sake it would be prudent for him to go abroad.

"This had occurred to me as well," Aladár wrote. "But it was my feeling that in the wide range of cowardly acts, this would have been the most despicable."

The Christmas season came, and Marianne's room became more and more crowded with wrapped gifts for family and friends. On the morning of Christmas Eve, Hanna, Puppa, Marianne, and various other family members headed out to Csepel, where as always gifts and food were distributed to the workers and their children.

That evening the various families of the descendants of Manfred Weiss went to the Chorins for dinner and to exchange presents. There they all gathered, Móric and Marianne, their four children, their daughter-in-law, and their first grandchild, little Stevie; the five Chorins, Daisy and Ferenc and their three children, Erzsébet, Daisy, and Ferenc Junior; and most but not all of Elsa's seven children. Eugene appeared with his three children and beautiful wife, Annie. Edith was there, but Alfons and his four children, respecting the strong feelings of his wife Erzsi, did not attend.

Ferenc Chorin presided with ebullience. There were many gifts, and the tree was radiant with candles and ornaments. The sheer relief at having made it through another year, the simple happiness of being together, eclipsed the more potent anxieties.

Aladár and Lilly went to midnight mass in Buda, while Hanna and her cousins pulled on their coats and hats and walked into the cold night to the Mission Sisters for mass in Pest. For once, one can imagine that most of the prayers centered on the same themes. *Protect us. Protect everyone we love. Deliver us from evil. Amen.* The miracle of the Christmas story, the sheer beauty of the night, the peace and the brief respite from the turmoil of the world must have touched each of them. In their separate corners of Buda and Pest, each with their own families, Hanna and Aladár celebrated their last, miraculously conventional Christmas.

A few days after Christmas, the Kornfelds and many friends of the family, including Hungary's ministers of the interior, justice, and commerce, decamped to Derekegyháza for hunting and the New Year's celebration. More than forty people filled the old mansion, some waking at dawn to shoot pheasants, others remaining in the house for their customary five meals a day—breakfast, second breakfast, lunch, tea, and dinner. In the midst of all this plenty, the Russian advance continued inexorably.

At one point, after the hunting and sleigh rides, card games and fabulous meals, the interior minister, Ferenc Keresztes-Fischer, asked Ferenc Chorin to talk with him and the commerce minister, Felix Bornemissza, in the privacy of his room. The three men gathered; perhaps cigars were lit, perhaps Cognacs were in their hands. The big ceramic stove in the room radiated warmth. Keresztes-Fischer then began to talk.

He revealed that the situation with the Germans had become even more serious. The Germans were aware of the Spiderweb plot, maybe not in all its intricacies, but they certainly knew that members of the Kállay government had tried to contact the British and the Americans on several occasions. Keresztes-Fischer warned them that they should all be prepared for a catastrophe.

Chorin listened gravely. He had already weighed and dismissed the possibility of emigration. It would have been difficult for them anyway, since the Germans would never have given a man of his stature a transit visa. But he also worried that if he left, the Germans would interpret his departure as another governmental attempt to open negotiations with the West and as concrete evidence that the situation for the Jews of Hungary was hopeless. This would not only undermine the government, it would put his remaining family members at terrible risk. Besides, several months earlier, Prime Minister Kállay had asked him not to leave the country, and he kept his word.

Political reasons aside, the practical reasons alone would have made emigration impossible. This was not just a family of five figuring out how to get to Switzerland but a herd of at least forty people.

"At the time we did not think that the Germans would occupy Hungary (!)," Chorin wrote years later, "but rather that they would demand a more manageable government than Kállay's." What that would mean was difficult to divine, but clearly it did not bode well for any of those gathered at Derekegyháza as 1943 turned into 1944.

"Very good shooting weather, good spirits," Hanna wrote on New Year's Eve. "The Russians advance well around Kiev, and on the other Russian fronts they slowly advance. One would not believe that all around us there is so much trouble. One has to hope that the coming year will be as good for everyone as the last one was for us."

1944

You who will emerge from the
flood
In which we have gone under
Remember
When you speak of our failings
The dark time too
Which you have escaped

—BERTOLT BRECHT, *"To Those Born Later"*

CHAPTER 16

March 19

O
n March 19, 1977, my father sat in his small home office on Patterson Street, a room that had once been Móric's study, smothered by books, papers, piles of newspaper clippings, and letters in many languages. A watercolor of his young father in uniform faced him, and photographs of his mother and sisters covered the walls. Aladár was seventy-three years old, and a gentle Washington spring was on the other side of his second-story window. Huddled over his notebook, gripping a ballpoint, he quoted the Hungarian poet János Arany to describe this day as "*vegzetes evi nap*," the day of the fatal anniversary. He wrote, "I am writing the same on the thirty-third anniversary of March 19, the humiliating and shameful memory of the great collapse, of disintegration, of national impotence and decomposition, the gaping precipice. The devastating and frightening way it happened. We counted on possibilities, which is why we wanted to resist. But no other preparations were made, not even in symbolic form."

The Nazis invaded Hungary on March 19, 1944.

After a week of cold rain, beautiful mild weather appeared unexpectedly on the weekend of March 17, 1944. Such a Saturday would have offered Hanna and Aladár the chance to escape Budapest for the Hungarian countryside. But that particular Saturday was Aladár's mother's seventy-fifth birthday.

Hanna was the only guest for the evening, but Lilly dusted the finest china, pulled out the stiff lace tablecloth, and closed the blackout curtains. The fate of Hungary preoccupied all of them, but a close second was the fate of Aladár, who was drawn and tense; the weight of months of anxiety seemed to burden him physically. In his ruminations on the world and politics at the end of 1943, my father presented Hungary's stark options: apocalypse or miracle.

Even as Germany suffered some important defeats and the Allies advanced and Russian troops marched toward the Hungarian border, my father grew more anxious, more depressed. Perhaps Hungary could avoid the worst of the war, as it had for nearly five years. During the first three months of 1944, it seemed as if a miracle might be remotely possible. Not a deus ex machina kind of miracle but a quieter, more incremental one, like the unanticipated recovery from a fatal illness.

The week of March 12 had been especially tense. On Wednesday, March 15, at the Opera Ball, the German ambassador invited Admiral Horthy to visit Hitler at his estate in Klessheim, Austria. On March 18 he met with Hitler. Budapest seethed with rumors that German troops were gathering in Vienna, but in fact they were encircling Hungary.

Oddly, the city's mood seemed to lift a bit by the end of the week. "The tension is a little better, the uncertainty is still great," Hanna wrote in her journal on March 18. Life carried on: birthdays were celebrated, church was attended, bridge was played, work was done. Some even saw the regent's visit with Hitler as a sign of détente. The Weiss family's good friend, the chief of police, had called on Saturday afternoon to say that he thought things were improving and the family could relax.

That same night the Chorins hosted a "dinner for gentlemen" at their house on Andrássy Avenue. Minister of Commerce Bornemissza and Minister of Justice Andor Lázár; the former vice president of the House of Representatives Zénó Bessenyei (who was now president of the Budapest Public Works Council); Richard Rapaich, one of the oldest generals of the army; Károly Széchenyi and Lajos Erdőhegyi, members of Kállay's most intimate circle; and some other bankers and politically prominent men all traveled through the dark city—the lights were out because of the air raids even though no other bombs had been dropped—and arrived at the Chorins' darkened house.

Upstairs, curtains drawn, eighteen-year-old Daisy, her twenty-year-old sister, Erzsébet, and their younger brother little Ferenc—who was sick with the measles and pneumonia—listened to the rise and fall of conversations. The guests were worried because Horthy had not yet returned from Germany. Minister Lázár recalled that they were all aware that Hitler's impossible demands were escalating, yet they were "all convinced that the regent would be able to make the Hungarian point of view prevail and that the heavy losses suffered by Germany would bring Hitler to a more sober position." The last guest left at one in the morning.

At five o'clock Sunday morning the telephone rang in Ferenc Chorin's apartment. Lajos Erdőhegyi, who had left the Chorins' home as his guest, called several hours later as his sentry. The Germans had crossed the Hungarian border and prevented Horthy's return to Hungary. They held his train for several hours at Klessheim so that he could not issue orders to resist the German occupation. After the prime minister heard that the German troops had crossed Hungary's border, he asked Erdőhegyi to contact his old friend, who was also one of the most vulnerable men in Hungary.

The apocalypse officially began.

Chorin called Marianne at the apartment on Lendvay Street. Immediately she woke Móric. Other family members in other houses got the news. After all these years of war, they had only the most rudimentary and hastily contrived plans, but they knew that when the Germans crossed the borders, any immunity they might have once enjoyed was over. They were rich Jews and were certain to be arrested. They had known that fact for years, but as long as they were not threatened, they had been able to carry on a normal life.

Now the threat arrived. Móric and Marianne knew they would go their separate ways; Móric would go with Ferenc to the monastery at Zirc, while Marianne would join her sister Daisy and hide with friends. Hanna and Puppa had already contacted Gentile friends to ask if they could stay with them. Tom was at medical school in Pécs, and George would leave Elsie and little Stevie and hide as well. The entire family had made similar plans. They all understood that both as Jews in the eyes of the law and as prominent citizens, their lives were at stake. No one knew about extermination camps, but certainly they all knew that Jews had been taken to terrible concentration camps. The family members scurried around in their gracious homes, servants offering some assistance, depite their own mix of anxieties and uncertainty about their own fate.

As dawn broke, Operation Margarethe, the German occupation of Hungary, was proceeding with chilling, even elegant efficiency. Hitler devised a concentric invasion of Hungary, a four-directional attack that eventually encircled the prize, Budapest. The government was paralyzed; the prime minister, the minister of foreign affairs, and the various generals in the army had been instructed to greet the German troops as allies not as adversaries. Any resistance would be "ruthlessly crushed."

Marianne, Puppa, and Hanna unearthed the little bags they kept packed for air raids and looked around for whatever else they might want to take. My grandmother brought out some jewelry she had purchased for bribery: a pair of diamond chandelier earrings, for example, a gold bracelet that weighed a few ounces, and a tiara. She made sure that Móric had all that he would need during the time when they were not together. To his little bag she added books, warm clothes, and a few extra handkerchiefs. What were they actually packing for? A long period of hiding, or a brief intermezzo, after which the Allies would sweep in to save the day? Her favorite piece of advice for travelers was to bring fewer clothes and more money than they thought they would need. Under these circumstances that advice never seemed wiser.

Puppa was haunted by the fragment of a dream that lingered. All that she could recall was the Greek word *ananke,* or fate. Hanna was terrified but disciplined and determined to maintain the family stoicism. She took the cache of Aladár's letters and the journal that was her cousin's gift. Neither could be left behind, for both sentimental and practical reasons: if their house should be taken over by Germans, the list of names and places would endanger others. And then she packed some clothes, of course. Despite the beautiful mild spring weather, she brought her winter coat. She was always so cold.

She and Puppa walked out of the room they had shared for twenty-eight years and went with their parents to the Chorins, where they found the same combination of packing, turmoil, and indecision but on a much larger scale, with many more people. Across the Danube, the Alfons Weiss family had been alerted. Alfons initially expressed skepticism, but since his house was on Gellért Hill, the panorama before him revealed that the Germans had arrived. He and his son Gábor immediately left their villa, while his wife, their German shepherds, and their nine-year-old son, János, and daughter Marika remained behind to pack. Their daughter Márta was on a ski trip.

Every family member had some provisional place to hide, some destination that would suffice until it became too unsafe. Marianne and

Daisy went to the apartment that the Chorins had purchased for their old governess, and they took with them young Ferenc, who was seriously ill. Their husbands had arranged with the abbot of Zirc to go to his monastery north of Lake Balaton. Móric was apprehensive about the plan; it required a three-hour drive from Budapest, only to hide in a place that was so isolated, it offered no natural option for escape. At sixty-three and sixty-five, he and Ferenc were already distinguished older gentlemen, accustomed to walking slowly and having others carry their bags.

As they prepared to leave their wives and children, the questions—when or even if they would see each other again—remained unspoken. When Móric embraced Puppa, she told him about her dream. No other member of the family would understand so completely the weight of the word, or the significance that it was in Greek, another ancient civilization that had disappeared forever.

As the sun rose, they could hear the thrum of German airplanes roaming over Budapest. German troops had encircled the city, and by seven that morning the bridges, the wireless station, the police headquarters, and other targeted buildings had been taken over. No Hungarian soldier broke ranks to try and stop the German advance.

Móric and Ferenc had taken off to meet the abbot of Zirc, who was serving mass at the Cistercian monastery in Budapest, and Marianne, Daisy, and her son were driven to the governess's apartment. Hanna and Puppa walked to the little subway stop around the corner at Heroes' Square. As they left, Chorin's cook stood in the doorway crying, "I will never see you again."

Cousin Hansi Mauthner, one of Elsa's most audacious and courageous children, mounted a Red Cross emblem on his car and chauffeured his mother and sisters and some cousins to their hiding places. Two of Hansi's sisters were married to Gentiles, so their homes were thought to be safe. He took his mother to the home of her-son-in-law Ferenc Borbély. There she sat with her two young grandchildren.

It seemed quite impossible that something so unalterably terrible could happen on such a radiant Sunday. Hanna and Puppa silently sat in the gleaming, familiar little subway cars and looked at their fellow passengers, who were probably unaware of the cataclysm that had occurred. Finally they reached the stop on the main shopping square at Váci Street. They walked toward the Danube. Around them families walked to church, bachelors stopped for a coffee, and couples blinked at the early

morning sunshine and planned their day to take advantage of the be-
neficent weather.

When they arrived at the Chain Bridge, the two magnificent, imper-
turbable lions guarding it as they always had, the sisters said goodbye.
Puppa crossed the bridge to Buda, to her friends the Oberschalls, who
lived in the Castle District, while Hanna went to her friend, the historian
Éva Balázs's house in Pest. There she wrote the last entry in her old journal, on March 19. "The most exciting day of my life," she wrote. "*Minden
prius.*" Everything that once was, is over.

The Weiss relatives scattered throughout the city, and their speed
that morning saved their lives. Shortly after Alfons Weiss and his oldest
son Gábor fled the beautiful house with the magnificent garden in the
hills of Buda, the Gestapo arrived. Erzsi, imperious and brilliant and terrified and unconverted, faced them with her young son János and her
daughter Marika. The Gestapo lined up the family and asked them
where Alfons had gone. What was he doing? Did they know where he
was? Erzsi told them a sufficiently convincing story so they left. But still
needing to demonstrate their dominance over a woman and her two children, the Gestapo shot the two family dogs.

This was how the end began.

CHAPTER 17

At the Foreign Ministry

■

■   ■

Shortly after midnight on the nineteenth, news began to come in from some of the border stations that Germans were crossing the frontier. Keresztes-Fischer, the minister of the interior, notified the prime minister of "ominous reports," and a governmental meeting was convened. Aladár was summoned to the Foreign Ministry early that Sunday morning and was part of the group that attempted to figure out how to respond to the invasion.

He did not call Hanna, did not warn her, did not make any contact when he still could. Surrounded as they now were by enemies, he must have worried that a call from him would only further complicate their lives. He regretted this omission for decades. When they said goodbye after his mother's birthday party, he had had no idea that it might be their final parting.

Horthy's train finally arrived at the Kelenföld station in Budapest at ten on Monday morning. A German honor guard accompanied Prime Minister Kállay to greet the regent. At noon that same day, the entire cabinet offered their resignations, which the regent accepted. The Nazis wanted a regime change because they saw the sitting government and cabinet as not sympathetic or trustworthy. The Germans demanded that the ever-loyal Nazi Béla Imrédy become the new prime minister. "That Jew?" Horthy countered, reminding them of the former prime minister's pedigree that had led to his stepping down in 1941. Horthy refused to nominate him under any circumstances.

In the Foreign Ministry, Count István Bethlen, who had been summoned by Prime Minister Kállay as an elder statesman and wise counsel, told Aladár to write a proclamation, like the one that worked so well with the Danes, announcing the regent's refusal to nominate a Quisling government. The regent should lead the highest Hungarian officials to continue the business of government, while he remained as regent. Aladár saw little feasibility in such a plan and did not believe that Horthy had a prayer to remain in charge.

THE NIGHT OF MARCH 19, after everyone had left the ministry, Aladár remained, and Lilly joined him. Together they went through his files and made a small bonfire in the large ceramic stove in his office. Documents about Operation Spiderweb turned to ash. His reflections on 1943 went up in smoke. Correspondence to other legations, ambassadors, friends, coconspirators, sympathizers, Jews, foreigners, and contacts in the Allies were all destroyed. Hanna's letters to him, the carefully crafted second or third drafts, drifted into the flames. This was not a panicked inferno but a prolonged and patient farewell to his life and to his past, so that when the inevitable search of his files by the Nazis took place, they would be disappointed.

The next day Regent Horthy asked Aladár whether he had begun the draft that Bethlen had suggested. He hadn't, he explained, because he was convinced that the top priority of the regent was to save what could still be saved. Horthy agreed and told him about the German's suggestion of Imrédy and his response. On March 21, Horthy nominated as prime minister Döme Sztójay, the former Hungarian ambassador in Berlin, whom my father had long disliked and mistrusted. Inevitably and inexorably a new cabinet was established in which Imrédy became the economics minister. Kállay sought protection in the Turkish embassy, while other members of his cabinet were either arrested—like Interior Minister Keresztes-Fischer—or remained in Budapest awaiting their fate, like my father.

Many around him, especially former prime minister Kállay, begged Horthy to resign or to assert some power in order to establish his independence from these choices, but he refused. He wrote, "I am still an admiral. The captain cannot leave his sinking ship; he must remain on the bridge to the last.... Who will defend the honorable men and women in this country who have trusted me blindly? Who will defend the Jews or our refugees if I leave my post? I may not be able to defend everything but I believe that I can still be of great, very great help to our people. I can do more than anyone else could."

On March 22, Sztójay took over the government and personally approved the immediate deportation to Auschwitz of 100,000 Jews who were in the Jewish labor force. Adolf Eichmann and his special, murderous SS detachment, the *Sondereinsatzkommando,* had arrived in Budapest with the first German troops on March 19 and immediately started to tackle Hungary's Jewish "problem." Russian forces had already reached Romania, and relentless American bombing had considerably weakened Germany itself. All of a sudden, Germany's Hungarian alliance gained some vital strategic importance. German military supplies destined for the already-weakened German armies fighting multiple fronts in Romania, Yugoslavia, Greece, Albania, and Bulgaria could travel only through Hungary to get to their destinations. Hungary could offer factories and valuable assets. The Germans were suspicious that the approach of Russian troops, and the presence of the Allies nearby, might encourage Horthy and Kállay to switch sides, either by surrender, a proclamation of neutrality, or an emphatic declaration of support for the Allies.

No matter how assiduously my father and others involved in the Spiderweb plans attempted to engage the Western allies, the Allies had no interest in intervening after the German invasion. In fact, the United States and Britain were eager to let the Germans exhaust themselves in Hungary, then have the Russian army finally defeat them there.

Soon after the Sztójay government took power, my father was put on "suspended status," official limbo between employment and arrest. He couldn't consider fleeing or hiding because his parents and sisters would be vulnerable if he did. There were already too many stories of family members held hostage as their relatives, the real quarry, hid. "I wandered around Budapest," Aladár wrote, "oppressed by the feeling of personal and national bankruptcy."

He worried about air raids, about being arrested, about the English lessons he had taken from Miss Thompson, about Hanna (especially about Hanna), and about his family. He also worried about being followed, stopping every once in a while during his walks to look to see if someone behind him also stopped. Embarrassed by his own desperation but still unable to control himself, he repeatedly asked his successor, the new head of the political division, László Csöpey, if he knew what the Germans planned to do with him. But he got no answers.

"I ran into Aladár, whom I find very depressed," wrote Countess Éva Dessewffy, the hostess of innumerable dinners he enjoyed with her and her husband, Gyula, who edited the newspaper *Kis Újság* (and who also worried about being arrested). With the German invasion, she began a journal recounting the events of those days. It was nearly six inches thick by the end, neatly typed and bound together with some string. (I found it buried among the detritus at Patterson Street, a meticulous record of a treacherous time, by a long-forgotten woman, who had no children and suffered the cliché of a humiliating divorce from Gyula after the war, because of his infatuation with a much younger woman.)

During one of Aladár's walks, they met. He said to her, "I have failed twice: once as a human being, and once politically."

"No," she protested with as much vehemence as the circumstances would allow. "In our eyes the picture is so very different." She reminded him that she and her husband were eyewitnesses. They had accompanied him in his thinking and listened to his analysis, his spiritual struggles. "It is absolutely irrelevant what light the traitors shed on your work," she concluded. My father nodded silently. Éva walked away and wrote after their meeting, "Our dear, clever friend, he was wounded for life in his heart, in his soul."

CHAPTER 18

Saying Goodbye All Over Again

. . .

Shortly after they arrived at the monastery in Zirc, Chorin was unable to restrain himself from calling Budapest. The first time he phoned Erdőhegyi to find out exactly how the occupation was unfolding in the city. The second call was to Daisy. He realized how vulnerable she was and what an obvious place it would be to search. He told her to leave with Marianne, but they could not move their son, who was still so sick. Early in the afternoon the Germans arrived looking for her and wanted to arrest his son. The old family nanny persuaded them that a young, sick child would be more trouble than he was worth and it would be much simpler just to leave him there.

But Chorin was not so effective in protecting himself. Perhaps the Germans tapped Erdőhegyi's telephone and thus immediately knew where he was hiding. Or perhaps Nazi sympathizers lived in Zirc, and the news of some "dignitaries" who had arrived at the monastery spread rapidly among them. Early Tuesday policemen surrounded the abbey searching for Chorin. Móric was still hiding, and the police had not yet made the connection that the two had escaped together. Chorin knew that once he left the monastery, his life would be over. Maybe not in a shower of bullets, but the death sentence was inevitable. My uncle went to another part of the abbey for the sacrament of confession.

Ever the pragmatist, even in the midst of his confession, Chorin asked for some poison to take if the circumstances became impossible. The abbot refused, but Chorin said that without the poison, he would not leave, thereby placing the entire monastery in jeopardy. The abbot brought him two tablets. After writing a farewell letter to his wife and children, Chorin left with the policemen, and they drove to Budapest.

En route a young Hungarian gendarme berated him and told him that he would be hanged as soon as the Gestapo arrived. They took Chorin to the Astoria Hotel in Pest, which had become the headquarters for the Gestapo. "This is Chorin," the gendarme said, presenting him to the German officer in charge. "He was the president of the manufacturers association and a member of the Upper House." The officer knew Chorin, greeted him, and went over to shake his hand. "How can you shake hands with that Jew?" the Hungarian gendarme screamed.

The formal transfer of Ferenc Chorin, senator, president of GYOSZ, president of the Salgótarján Anthracite Mining Company, philanthropist, and civic leader, from the Hungarians to the Germans took place on March 21, 1944, at the Astoria Hotel.

Two days later Móric was also arrested. He knew there was no place that he could really escape to and had hoped that the authorities might have gone elsewhere to find him. He only took his briefcase and left his suitcase behind, he later wrote, "because the items in the suitcase represented the all-encompassing loving attention of my wife, and was such an accurate representation of her entire being, that saying goodbye to the suitcase was like saying goodbye to her one more time." The two men who arrested him were Hungarian gendarmerie detectives but young and decent. They spent much of the drive to Budapest begging Móric not to hold this arrest against them and apologetically asking him to remember that they had performed their unpleasant duties with consideration, even thoughtfulness.

Unlike so many of their comrades in the gendarmerie, who took to the persecution of Jews with the enthusiasm of long-pent-up attack dogs, these young men were still not used to their powerful new roles. Some vestigial sense of deference to age and social standing remained. One could only wonder for how long.

NO ONE IN THE family knew where the others were hiding. The Kornfelds' loyal chauffeur Schaffer somehow managed to keep track of all the travels of the various family members, evade German notice, and inform members of the family at least about the safety of the others. He got word to Marianne and Daisy that their husbands had been arrested, as well as their brother Eugene, and that they were all in the Budapest jail.

Marianne moved from one friend's home to another, briefly settling with a family who disguised her as a peasant servant. They called her Mária Néni, or Aunt Maria. One day Marianne, who was restless and assumed she was anonymous, wearing her black head scarf and servant's long skirt, ran into Béla Imrédy's wife. Long ago the couples had dined together in the splendor of Lendvay utca. Marianne approached her, asking her if there was anything she could do to save her husband and the rest of her family. After all, her husband was now in the new government. Mrs. Imrédy replied with anodyne regrets. But as they parted, she turned to my grandmother and said, "Now it is *our* turn."

Sometimes family members ended up at the same friend's house. Hanna and Marianne spent several days with Puppa at the Oberschalls'. Another day in May, Hanna ended up with her aunt Elsa and her uncle Alfons at the Gyarmatis' who were Elsa's Gentile in-laws. My mother's cousin Hansi, one of Elsa's seven children, was utterly fearless. His cousin Daisy recalled many years later that Hansi "would move around during the German occupation as if it were nothing." Putting a red cross on his car, he drove around the city with utter impunity. He ate at the Ritz, surrounded by Nazis. Like a carrier pigeon, he joined Schaffer in visiting family members and telling each one how the others were doing.

Márta, who was called Juci by the family, the twenty-year-old daughter of Alfons Weiss, had left Budapest by train very early on the morning of March 19 to go skiing in Transylvania with some friends. Hours later the train stopped and was held for some time. Finally the engines fired and the train started moving again, but the direction was wrong. It was returning to Budapest.

Her friends appreciated her vulnerability as the granddaughter of Manfred Weiss and the daughter of Alfons Weiss. They urged her to get off at the next stop. She should go to a hospital, they said, and complain of various symptoms that needed immediate attention. Once they got back to Budapest, they assured her, they would let others know where she was, and those influential friends would ensure her safe return to the city. She got off the train at the next station and found the local hospital. A few days later a very high-ranking officer who was connected to the factory at Csepel appeared at the hospital to discharge her. The nurses in the hospital were nuns and in all likelihood knew that this strapping, athletic, beautiful, twenty-year-old woman was far from ill, but they treated her well. The officer took her back to Budapest and on the drive told her that the family was in hiding and she would not be able to return to her home. She found a friend, the first of several with whom she would stay.

Chorin's two daughters, Erzsébet and Daisy, ended up at their alma mater, the English Sisters' School, and hid in the basement. "That was incredible," Daisy remembered, "because first of all, you saw all of these nuns, who were your teachers, in the evening, when they looked totally different." Massive Allied air raids began on April 2, and many houses and apartments were destroyed. Most of those in the Weiss family, and others who were in hiding, were not permitted to go into the bomb shelters during the air raids for fear that they and their protectors would be discovered. My mother hid in an upstairs closet at the Gyarmatis' as the sirens wailed and bombs fell.

The first evening after Erzsébet and Daisy arrived at the convent, an air raid took place. They sat with the nuns at a long table after dinner. The nuns prayed loudly, over the thunderous sound of the air raid, and sang religious songs as they knit thick short socks, like booties for adults. The girls sat there quietly, absorbing the utter surrealism of the scene. Suddenly Erzsébet put her head on the table, and her shoulders began to shake. "Oh my God, she is hysterical," Daisy thought. So she put her arm around her older sister and attempted to console her. Immediately she felt a sharp kick in her shins. Daisy looked closer and saw that her sister was laughing uncontrollably. The praying and the singing, the knitting, the air raid—it was unbearably absurd.

The bombing also signaled the beginning of the more systematic drive to eliminate Jews from Budapest. One plan proposed that Jews immediately vacate their houses and apartments, so as to give Christian victims of the bombing places to stay. Another plan called for rounding up prominent Jewish professionals and relocating them to areas around strategically important sites like industrial or military compounds. These Jews would serve as deterrents to the bombers, or if they did not, then at least the Jews would perish in the process.

"The Royal Hungarian Government will cleanse the country of Jews within a short space of time," read an order from the Ministry of the Interior directed to senior police officers. Bank accounts were frozen, and

Jews were forbidden to purchase certain food items like sugar and lard that were in short supply. In a smaller, pocket-size calendar, Hanna noted on April 5, "From today, the yellow star." The star was to be sewn on a yellow patch measuring six by four inches and was to be worn by all Jews over the age of six.

The youngest Kornfeld child, Tom, was hiding in Ireg, translating a medical text from German to Hungarian. He asked his former nurse if she could possibly sew the star. He wore it to mass in the church next door, the church that his father supported so generously. One day two gendarmes arrived with orders to take him to Budapest. They handcuffed him and went by train to a police station somewhere in the city. "Nobody said word one to me about anything," Tom recalled. "Nobody asked me anything or told me anything." And then it was over. They told him it was time to return to Ireg, again escorted by the two gendarmes.

Because it was late in the day, there were no trains, so they would have to spend the night. Tom called his sister-in-law Elsie, who was Austrian and Aryan, and asked if they could possibly stay with her and her infant son, Stevie. Her husband, George, was in hiding as well. She agreed, and the two gendarmes and Tom spent a cozy evening, sleeping in the living room on couches and settees. The next morning they apologetically handcuffed my uncle again and took him back to Ireg.

The Germans took over Budapest with assembly-line efficiency. An April report from the American consulate in Istanbul to Secretary of State Cordell Hull described Hungary: "The German occupation forces are on their good behavior. . . . With minor exceptions, few German troops have been seen in the streets of Budapest. . . . This arrangement has apparently been made by the occupation authorities in view of the unfriendly attitude of the inhabitants of Budapest. . . . While there is no doubt of German control, the occupation authorities are trying to cover the iron hand with a velvet glove. . . . [But] if German troops in Budapest were conspicuous by their absence, the same could certainly not be said for Gestapo agents. The latter . . . are usually in plain clothes, but stand out on the landscape of Budapest like a handful of sore thumbs."

Long lists of Hungarian politicians, civic leaders, civil servants, businessmen, aristocrats, artists, journalists, policemen, Jews, industrialists, and financial and economic leaders provided the road map for mass arrests. When the Hungarian Parliament met for the first time after the occupation on March 22, one member of the lower house suggested that the arrests violated the Hungarian constitution. He was immediately shouted down by his colleagues and ruled out of order by the speaker.

As the reactions in Parliament so vividly show, many Hungarians did not consider the arrival of the Germans a disaster. Much as they appreciated and protected their national autonomy, the more alien, menacing Russians were of greater concern than their longtime German allies. Even without the rabid anti-Semitism, which was an asset for some and an inconvenience for others, they felt some relief that the irritating prevarications of Kállay's leadership were finally over.

My father once described this society as having been fragmented by the war. Like one of those globes from which a wedge has been removed, revealing layers of the earth teeming beneath the surface, the layers of life in Budapest became powerfully stratified. For a little while, the external world carried on with an exaggerated normalcy. The trams ran on time. Restaurants still served diners. Shops still sold shoes and dresses, books, and rationed food. But at the same time, at the Astoria and in the Fő Street jail, leaders of Hungary's political, economic, and civic life were interrogated, starved, imprisoned, and tortured.

Hanna recorded her days in a tiny calendar, marking each entry with the name of the saint whose feast it was. On March 20, Saint Benedek's day, she wrote, "Awful mood, many people arrested, Germans are already in our apartments." On March 21, Saint Katalin's day: "General confusion." On Saint Victorian's day, March 23, she began her wandering. She had to leave the home of Éva Balázs because the maid appeared to be unreliable. Sometimes Hanna intersected with her mother or Puppa. Other times she was alone with friends, occasionally getting messages about the family's whereabouts. She never heard from Aladár and never tried to get in touch with him. It was much too dangerous for both of them. She was alone in ways that she had never been before. On March 24 she wrote, "Father arrested, we do not know where he is." March 25: "Anti-Jewish laws." And Sunday, March 26, the week after the invasion, was also the last Sunday of Lent, before Palm Sunday. This day is known in Hungary as *Fekete Vasárnap* or Black Sunday. Hanna underlined the name with three sharp lines. I could see her impatience, her desperation.

Her twenty-eighth birthday came and went. She knew that their homes had been ransacked and that her father's precious library, their art, and their personal belongings were being handled, evaluated, and stolen. She knew that her father and uncles were in prison. There was no mention of Aladár.

ON A SHELF IN the closet in my parents' bedroom at Patterson Street was an old, disintegrating, brown-leather overnight bag. It was my mother's repository of important papers: report cards from the three of us, some bank statements, birthday cards, a few carefully crayoned masterpieces from elementary school, paperwork from car purchases, old official papers, and some house and car keys that had long ago been separated from their locks. The intimate time capsule was mostly filled with things that had to do with our growing up, I thought.

When my mother died, all the objects in their room that had once been shielded from our curious eyes by the simple life force of my parents being parents were no longer private property. At first tentatively and then boldly, I opened drawers, pulled things from shelves, and plunged into the bag. After separating the stuff of our childhood into three neat piles, and throwing away papers that had been useless even long ago when they were first put there, I came upon a relic from that time: a crumpled six-pointed yellow piece of fabric, carefully hemmed around the edges, no larger than my palm. It was my mother's yellow star. I flattened it on the dresser. I had always imagined that yellow stars would be made of fine, crisp cotton, not this oily material.

My mother's yellow star. It felt so personal, yet so illicit there, shoved at the bottom of the Bag of Precious Things. She just couldn't throw it away. I took it downstairs where Puppa sat and read and smoked. "Look what I found," I said.

She took it and raised her eyebrows, as a curious and slightly ironic expression played on her face. What memories did this trigger for her? "Is this Mom's Jewish star?" I asked the obvious.

"Yes, it is," she said with a mild smile.

"Why would she keep it?"

My aunt shrugged, sighed, and stamped out her cigarette. "A souvenir," she said.

Enough Pride and Enough Humility

•

After Móric's arrest at the abbey, he was driven through Budapest. He was "struck by how normally life was going on without me. I am a living dead." His destination was the Astoria Hotel, and after his name and personal effects were taken, he was led to the basement, into what had once been a bar and dance floor and now was the holding pen for some of Budapest's most honorable men and women. The first person Móric saw, after his eyes grew accustomed to the light, was Ferenc Chorin.

With a forty-eight-hour head start, Chorin was already a seasoned veteran of Nazi hospitality having been deprived of food and sleep and sanitary conditions. In another corner he saw the former head of the intelligence service, Ferenc Keresztes-Fischer. Móric squeezed next to him on a bench. "At this point," my grandfather wrote, "I ceased to be somebody and became something. A thinking reed—according to Pascal—but without roots. . . . We realized with deep consternation how deeply we had sunk, how the country cannot, or perhaps did not want to, protect its citizens, nor the army one of its general officers, against a foreign power."

Many people arrived and departed, all the new arrivals bringing with them word of arrests, the formation of a government, and the progress of the war. Much of it, Móric noted, later turned out to be wrong. Both my grandfather and my great-uncle wrote about their experiences during these days, and their temperaments and personalities emerge powerfully in their narratives, like photographs of the highest possible resolution.

Móric Kornfeld was philosophical and detached, subordinating whatever fear he most certainly must have felt with curiosity, perhaps religious faith, and the view of this particular historical moment as only the most recent event in a dynamic as old as civilization, invasion and domination, submission and the end of the ancien régime.

Ferenc Chorin was a man of action and intensity. He described his time imprisoned by the Nazis with journalistic attention to detail. For his entire life, he could accomplish things for himself and others. For the first time, he was helpless. "I cannot forget, even today," he wrote, "what a humiliating experience it is to stand quietly while being slapped and not to be able to hit back."

After a sleepless night, the interrogations began. Móric and Ferenc were taken outside onto busy Kossuth Lajos Street, where the traffic and lunchtime crowds went about their business as if nothing unusual had happened. They were put into a truck that had a lattice of boards at shoulder height so that all the men stood with their heads poking out from a small wooden frame, making any thought of escape impossible. The intention, Móric observed, "was not security but humiliation."

At the Pest area prison, they were placed in individual cells. Móric managed to keep his copy of Thomas à Kempis, which he read quietly. It was a peaceful evening, and the next day he and Chorin were taken back to the Astoria. They were interrogated in adjacent rooms.

Two members of the Gestapo greeted Móric and even offered him a chair. He sat down and was asked about his family and his education, and lengthy and detailed questions about his financial status. They wanted to know about the Manfred Weiss Works, of course, and how much it was worth, and how much his share was worth. After the first hour of relatively civilized questioning, it took a more aggressive turn. Upon finding out that this was the "Jew Kornfeld," a younger officer ordered Móric to stand up.

He showed him a briefcase and asked if he was familiar with it. When Móric said he wasn't, the officer began to shout in fury, literally foaming at the mouth, that Roosevelt and the Jews around him were responsible for the cream of German youth dying on the battlefield. He hit Móric across the head with the briefcase with such force that his glasses fell off.

Móric staggered, picked up his glasses, and said quietly, with his characteristic ability to frame the essence of the problem, "I did not start this war."

Later in the afternoon the interrogators discovered that the briefcase belonged to Móric's son Tamás. Clearly the apartment had been searched. Móric was forced to translate every piece of paper it contained, and on one page was a quotation, "Every woman makes her man unhappy, whether because she is beautiful with her unfaithfulness or ugly with her faithfulness." The officer so enjoyed this, he asked Móric to repeat it, then took him to another room. "In one of the corners sat a higher ranking, bemedaled officer with an expressionless face like some carved eastern deity, who never made a single move during the entire time that I was in the room. Two large, ungainly louts stood in the room. One of them, the more despicable one with glasses (you can't even trust glasses anymore), screamed at me: 'Where is your wife?'"

Móric was relieved that they hadn't found her. His love for Marianne gave him the strength to endure the next hour. Over and over again he was slapped and kicked, harder and harder each time he responded that he did not know where she was. He was surprised at what little real physical pain the blows caused. "Perhaps because I considered them as the forerunner of something much worse, but mainly because I considered them as the manifestation of some elemental disaster, which has nothing to do with self-respect. In the final analysis only those can be humiliated who have neither enough pride nor enough humility."

Next door the German officer asked Chorin for the details of how the Jews sabotaged the war effort. Chorin, as the president of the Salgótarján Anthracite Mining Company, was accused of making sure that there were no coal deliveries to the Manfred Weiss Works at Csepel. Chorin responded that the deliveries might have been slowed down because there was severe flooding in the mines. The officer said that Chorin was responsible for the flooding. Then he wanted to know about the briefcase. When Chorin said that it was not his, the officer hit him over the head with it repeatedly, saying he would hit him with it until his ears fell off. When Chorin refused to admit that he had sabotaged the German war effort, the officer hit him so hard, he fell to the ground. The hectoring and the blows continued all afternoon. My uncle collapsed, then struggled to his feet and was struck again.

When he was asked where his wife and the rest of the family were,

Chorin honestly had no idea. This was too much for the Gestapo. A large man stood on his feet and shook him violently. After asking him about his relationship with Horthy, the interrogation was over, but not before he was given a transcript to sign. "I had no opportunity to read it, but thought that it would be better to sign," he wrote. "It didn't matter anyway."

Bleeding, exhausted, brutalized, Ferenc and Móric were returned to the Astoria.

For nearly a week they were shuttled between the Astoria and the jail. They saw some old friends and heard rumors about others. They were fed very little and slept badly. Their identification caromed between "political prisoner" and the debased rank of Jew. There were moments of indelible kindness. Bauer, the chief bookkeeper from Csepel, was there with his son. When he heard that Móric's watch had been taken by one of the guards, he slipped his son's watch into Móric's side pocket. Another day Chorin saw some old friends who had just been arrested. One of them gave him three lumps of sugar—a luxury.

The friends were eventually separated. Chorin was taken with a group to the Eastern Railway terminal. No one knew where they were going. He was bruised, aching, sick with worry, and thoroughly defeated by circumstances for the first time in his long and successful life. The two cyanide pills in his pocket offered little consolation.

Honorable Confinement

For twenty-six days Aladár walked around Budapest feeling both anxious and paralyzed. He watched the transports and heard news of friends and colleagues who had already disappeared into Nazi oblivion. Once he ran into his old friend, the writer Sándor Márai, who embraced him and offered him his second apartment, money, and every possible assistance imaginable. Aladár was grateful, even as he had to decline the generous offers.

Never knowing when his inevitable arrest would occur, he was a man on a wire, teetering, unable to make a single move of self-protection. He heard about women who were taken by the Gestapo instead of their husbands as "sibling hostages" and dreaded the possibility that the same fate was in store for Lilly. Every time a car stopped in front of the family apartment, he panicked, once even climbing up on the windowsill to see if the car was one of the dreaded yellow military vehicles.

He was ashamed of himself, even thirty years later, when he wrote about the events. "Thinking back to these times, I must say that I did not stand up well under these trials. I demonstrated nothing but weakness, nervousness, and passivity. My self-discipline was poor, and I awaited my fate with trepidation but also with apathy and made no attempt to avoid it." He consoled himself that he no longer had any responsibility for the terrible decisions that the government was making. "The thought that oppressed me more than any other was my feeling that I had abandoned Hanna."

On April 13 there was a spectacular air raid. As they did every night when the sirens began, Aladár and Lilly carried their mother in a chair to their basement air raid shelter. It was very late when they emerged and went to bed.

At six o'clock the next morning the doorbell rang, and the family's manservant Pali came into my father's bedroom. He told him that some Germans had arrived and wanted to talk to him. My father was in his bed, still warm under the sheets, when the four Gestapo men entered with drawn pistols. They watched as he got dressed. He picked up the cigarette case Hanna had given him for Christmas many years ago. "Take it easy," it advised in English. He looked questioningly at their leader, who nodded that my father should take the cigarette case with him.

His parents and Lilly stood by. "My God, what will happen now?" his mother asked. "God has always helped me," Aladár replied. As he said goodbye to his mother, she made the sign of the cross on his forehead with her thumb, as she had every night when he was a child. The yellow police car was parked a few doors away. Aladár walked solemnly down Lánchíd Street. He would never see his childhood home again.

He arrived at the Pest area prison and was taken to a room on the third floor, where there were several American aviators who had been shot down during the air raid the night before. One had bad burns, and his face glistened with some ointment. The commander of the prison entered and turned to Aladár.

"Are you a Jew?"

"No."

"Are you a Pole?"

"No."

"Are you French?"

"No."

"Well, what are you?"

"I am a Royal Hungarian Counselor of the Legation."

They told him to stand with his face against the wall and his hands above his head until he was taken to his cell. The door was marked 1-A, which meant that he was an Aryan and had to be in solitary confinement. The guards took his suspenders, shoelaces, necktie, watch, and wallet but let him keep his money. "For a while you won't be needing this," the commander said as he took the cigarette case. Meanwhile the Gestapo returned to his family home and, in "a manifestation of selective terrorism, which the Germans understood so well," thoroughly searched his two rooms while leaving Lilly's and his parents' rooms alone. They found nothing incriminating. They took his decorations, his briefcase, and a bottle of very good whiskey that he had once received as a gift from the old friend, the editor József Balogh. Both a homosexual and a Jew, Balogh likely had already been arrested and murdered in Szeged.

Aladár's fluency in German helped the interrogation along. He kept repeating that he was just a government official as they were and always acted under instruction, just as they did. They reassured him with empty promises that there were no serious charges against him and that he would likely be freed in just a few days. Once one interrogation was over, he began worrying about the next one. What would they ask? Would they ask about Stockholm, about his personal relationships? What means of torture would they use? How would he be able to "say nothing sincerely and credibly"?

About a week after his arrest, he heard that several of his colleagues, including his former boss Andor Szentmiklóssy, had also been arrested. The guards became more and more interested in the American parachutists and a possible connection that my father might have had with them. Their suspicions were not completely far-fetched. During their attempts to reach out to the Allies, the Hungarian minister in Switzerland, György Bakách-Bessenyey, and the Americans had crafted an agreement. The two sides agreed that some American fliers would be permitted to land in Hungary so as to get a better sense about potential aerial attacks against Hungary, especially against Budapest.

Aladár told his interrogators that the only reason the government had allowed them to land was that they wanted to figure out some response to potential Allied air raids. He emphasized that they didn't talk about military questions because there was no espionage. Otto Klages, the head of the SS intelligence and counterintelligence agency in Budapest, ran the interrogation and kept pushing him to disclose more, but he stuck to his story.

When he got back to his cell after midnight, his guard gave him something to eat and then said that Klages was not satisfied with the results of their conversation. Aladár was put in a dark, windowless basement cubicle where he remained for ten days. The only light allowed in was when he was examined or fed and a door was opened. He slept on bare boards, comforted by the fact that there were at least fewer lice and fleas here than in his other cell. He was already covered with bites. Occasionally an SS man sat on the other side of a grating that divided the cell and pointed a rifle at him.

He wrote nothing about his reactions to the circumstances, nothing about what went through his mind as he lost track of days and nights. "It was here that I observed the first signs of humanity on the part of the young guards," he later wrote. One of them frequently asked him if he wanted more fresh water and would leave the door open while he got it, permitting him to enjoy the light for a little while.

The time in the dark did not break him. It ended without much fanfare, and then other interrogations occurred, each with its own moments of fear, but never with the kind of brutality that he witnessed across the courtyard in the Jewish cells.

Aladár also noticed a change in himself. The anxiety that had dominated his feelings immediately after March 19 slowly abated in the prison. He was reminded of final exams in school, when he would be tormented by dread, only to have it disappear when he sat down and began to write. He knew why he was there, and he was willing to accept the consequences, able to "cope with prison, much better than when I was waiting for something to happen."

One day an older investigator in an SA uniform arrived to interrogate him. My father noticed his singsong German accent and asked if he hailed from Saxony. The officer was pleased—indeed he did. Somehow this personal exchange shifted the dynamic between them from prisoner and guard to something more nuanced, more human.

Almost immediately after this exchange, the officer became very belligerent, asking my father about a very sensitive issue—a radio that had been used to transmit information among the participants in Spiderweb. Aladár mumbled that he wasn't feeling very well, and the Saxon began to shout at him in a furious and threatening way. He said that they had means to break my father and make him talk. He then leaned over to my father and whispered, "The Hungarian government used the radio as a means with which to communicate with its own people." My father immediately repeated the sentence in a loud voice, and even added a few embellishments. The interrogation continued on these two levels: belligerent exchanges between victim and perpetrator, then conspiracy and comity.

Aladár suffered as much for what he witnessed as for what he personally experienced. A happy young Polish boy was taken away one morning, "and when he was returned in the evening he was trembling all over," my father wrote. The boy would reveal nothing about what had happened, "but said only that it had been terrible." When the deportations of the Jews began, one of the first who was taken away was another Pole, an orthodox Jewish baker and father of nine children who had once cleaned out the cells of the other prisoners just as a gesture of kindness. He was assigned to an Auschwitz transport. Before he left, he said farewell to each of the prisoners on his block. Aladár embraced him and, as his mother had done when he was arrested, marked his forehead with a cross. He wanted to extend some gesture of tenderness and affection and protection no matter how technically inappropriate. "God will help me," the baker said. In fact, he survived, but his entire family, with one exception, was killed.

Aladár's solitary confinement was occasionally interrupted by roommates. One was a shop assistant from a small town who was arrested while helping his Jewish boss escape to a hiding place. Aladár comforted him by telling him that he had some status as a political prisoner. Political prisoners were the aristocrats of the prison and received privileged treatment. He explained the concept of "honorable confinement" and told him that it was only in recent times that political prisoners were treated worse than common criminals.

In contrast to Móric and Ferenc, Aladár enjoyed special treatment as a political prisoner in solitary confinement. The food was a bit better. He was surrounded by many of his friends and colleagues from the Foreign Ministry. He received packages from home with food, books, and clean underwear. The packages were not only reassuring reminders of home; they also proved that everyone was still safe, despite the almost nightly air raids.

A secret memorandum to the political intelligence department of the British intelligence service, dated May 21, 1944, described a number of arrests of prominent people in Hungary. After describing Horthy's fate, the fifth entry of the memo is about my father:

The former chief of the Political Department in the Ministry of Foreign Affairs, M Szegedy-Maszák has not been taken to Germany. He is still detained in Hungary and will be brought before the Hungar-

ian military tribunal for his activity under the Kállay regime. His
prospects are black.

While he was in prison, his sister Lilly became consumed with trying
to secure his release. She went to the son of the regent, Nikki Horthy,
and begged him to intervene. She visited Sztójay, the new prime minister, whom she had known in Berlin, and asked him to help. He suggested
that she go to Edmund Veesenmayer, the representative of the Reich in
Hungary. When she asked him to set her brother free, he wouldn't hear
of it, saying that he was a dangerous man. She even spoke with Péter
Hain, who had worked in the political division of the Foreign Ministry
since 1937 as the head of the unit that was in charge of ensuring the safety
of state leaders. He became a paid German agent in 1938, but when Lilly
went to visit him, he had been put in charge of reorganizing the political
division for the new government. After saying there was nothing to be
done, he whispered to her, "Why didn't he go into hiding?"

To hide would have been to abandon his colleagues and his principles. Aladár was even relieved to be in prison—it was far better than "to
be free in the Pest of those days," which was dominated by "moral dissolution and decay." In prison, the inmates found the basic human solidarity that had collapsed in Budapest under German rule.

Spring turned into summer. The cells became so hot, the inmates
washed the floors every day and let them stay wet, hoping that the evap-
oration might cool things off. Aladár tried to maintain his spirits and
later wrote about the time with equanimity, but he was deteriorating.

Lilly wrote Hanna a letter in July. (I have so many questions about
this letter: How did she get it to my mother? How did it survive? How
did I manage to find it? By July my mother was no longer in Budapest,
which makes it even more extraordinary.)

> *Aladár as yet is not with us and I do not know if he ever will be, al-*
> *though I hope to get him out soon. I have tried everything and am*
> *waiting now for the results. . . . We met two weeks ago. He looks well,*
> *although pale, and he has put on a little weight. But he is nervous and*
> *is not able to bear this situation. The most awful fact is that the little*
> *room where he is kept is full of insects. He is alone. He asked me to do*
> *all that I can to get him home as soon as possible.*

The composure Aladár tenuously maintained throughout the summer collapsed in the autumn. His health, both mental and physical, deteriorated. Lilly became more and more frantic. In her journal, Éva Dessewffy wrote about my father's despondency, about his life, "the constant darkness, solitary existence, tension, when is the deportation coming." His friends and sister had discussed audacious and impossible schemes to help him escape—"liberation plans," Éva called them. "Aladár would not agree, if we could not liberate the others, too. And if it would not succeed, the results would be catastrophic."

CHAPTER 21

Enter Becher

■

■　　　　■

Móric arrived a few days after his brother-in-law at a camp called Oberlanzendorf in Austria. After the *Anschluss,* the Nazis established it as a juvenile detention facility for the youthful dregs of Europe. Truants, scofflaws, and the most marginal slivers of society were sentenced by a military tribunal to several weeks or months of hard labor. The facility eventually expanded to include others who had been arrested, before they could be moved to various other concentration camps.

The wooden barracks lined an elongated yard. On one side was a two-story command building; on the other was a wall with a large gate that led to another courtyard. There the kitchen and the administrative offices of the camp were located. Móric and Chorin were assigned to the same barracks and greeted about fifteen other old friends from the higher reaches of government and finance. They were warned not to drink the water from the well, which might have been contaminated by the latrines.

They had already established a governing system and a routine. Chorin, of course, was elected president. He appreciated that having held so many presidencies in his long career, he would end his life with the same title. His major role was to mediate disagreements and act as an arbiter of disputes. An attorney named Bálint was elected room commander since once he had held a high military rank. The men entertained each other by telling jokes. Chorin and another inmate debated the past and the future. Móric discussed various aspects of religion with one of the other inmates, and two others repeated the same old fights that they fought during meetings of GYOSZ, the manufacturers association.

Móric observed that one of the characteristics of this kind of existence is that every small thing, a smile or a frown, a rainy day or cold coffee, had powerful symbolic value as some sort of foreboding for good or evil. The days passed monotonously but hardly happily. They were not called upon to perform any manual labor, and occasionally someone was called in to be interrogated. Ferenc suffered from horrible boils and a case of dysentery. But even more disturbing to those who knew him, his ebullient personality disappeared; he was mired in deep, almost existential pessimism and despair.

Móric slept between Ferenc and Leo Goldberger, who owned a textile empire in Hungary and regarded Chorin as the only reliable source of wisdom. Their conversations were often conducted over Móric's supine body and would begin with an observation by Goldberger that contained the phrase "If I get home again." To which my uncle would reply, "Why do you think that you will ever get home?" Once Goldberger asked Móric if he should take some poison that he had secreted in his pocket. He was the wrong person to ask. While Móric had resigned himself to dying in prison, for him life was a right and an obligation. Móric replied, quoting Nietzsche's aphorism, "Through how many sleepless nights has the possibility of suicide sustained me."

April 17 was Daisy's birthday. It was a mild spring day at the camp, and Chorin thought longingly of his wife and children, certain that they would never see each other again. He shifted his focus to birthdays of the past. These tender thoughts disintegrated when he was summoned to a room that was set aside for special punishments. Already so thoroughly weakened and demoralized, sick with dysentery and in pain from the boils that were blistering his skin, Chorin braced himself for an even more brutal series of interrogations.

Instead, he was greeted, with unusual civility, by Obersturmbannführer Kurt Becher.

Becher, who was thirty-three years old, was a close confidant of Heinrich Himmler and was in charge, at least on paper, of the Commission for the Registration of Remount Horses, Armament Staff. In April 1943 he had received the Nazi Gold Cross for distinguished service. Puppa once said that one would only need Kurt Becher and his female counterpart to create the German race dreamed of by Adolf Hitler. Blond, pale, blue-eyed, tall, and handsome, with meticulous grooming and impeccable manners, he exuded power and authority. Born in Hamburg, Becher was the son of a merchant and was eager to make his own mark in the business world. As a young man, he became an avid equestrian. His proficiency on horseback had introduced him into a new and prestigious social circle.

After Hitler took power, Becher entered the military and became a loyal and enthusiastic Nazi. When the war broke out, he served in Poland and back in Germany, including a tour of duty at the concentration camp Dachau. He was part of the Reiter SS, a unit of the elite corps that rode on horseback. Because he knew both horses and commerce, one of his duties was to acquire (also known as stealing) horses from any of the recent, vulnerable conquests. While at Dachau, he observed transactions between desperate Jews and guards and was astonished at the amount of gold, jewelry, and money the Jews had managed to hide. Incredible as well, they willingly parted with their riches in exchange for a little more bread, meat, or cigarettes.

When the Germans invaded Hungary, Becher was one of the first officials to arrive, and with his arrival came his promotion to SS colonel. When he was interviewed after the war, he said that his task in Hungary was to procure "horses and equipment for the Wehrmacht and Waffen-SS, horse-drawn and mounted units, both new and reinforced." But in fact, his ambition was far higher and his cunning more dangerous. He was sufficiently canny to realize that things were not going well for the Germans at this point in the war, so he was presented with the dual challenge of taking as much advantage of his position as possible and hedging his bets for the future.

He had already summoned his mistress, and together they moved into Chorin's home. He helped himself to some of the family's possessions, lived in luxury, and gained an understanding of the man, a feel for him that was almost too intimate. As he thought about the future, Becher faced two goals that were ostensibly mutually exclusive: securing an industrial base for the Reich, and saving his own skin should the Reich collapse. Conveniently, Chorin offered the key to both.

After presenting Chorin with some clean underwear, Becher invited him to sit down. To be asked to sit down under these circumstances could only mean that things were not so bad. And to be asked to sit down on his wife's birthday might even portend a small miracle.

Becher told him that his wife and children and the rest of the family were alive and well. He permitted Chorin to write Daisy a letter and assured him that she would receive it. They had sought him out, Becher said, because they had been told that he was the most informed man in Hungary about economic matters. After a lengthy interrogation, Becher asked him if he would be willing to provide them with further information. Chorin agreed and concluded, "There was never any question of cooperation."

Becher was not just talking economic generalities. He knew what the Manfred Weiss empire represented. Anyone involved in industry in central Europe at the time knew about this industrial giant. While he was in Budapest, Becher summoned Vilmos Billitz, the trusted director at Csepel, who told him that the only person who could possibly provide the *ordentlichkeit*—the orderliness—that he required was Ferenc Chorin, who had been arrested.

Chorin returned to his barracks, bringing with him some canned goods that Becher had given him, probably taken from his own kitchen. Several days passed without any further contact from the SS colonel, but Chorin probably could not have managed an encounter even if he had been summoned because his diarrhea was so severe that one evening he passed out. When he regained consciousness, Móric had somehow found a doctor from the Pécs medical school, in another barracks, to help. Not only was he suffering from severe dysentery, his boils were horrible.

Nonetheless, the next day he was interrogated again—not by Becher but by others, who asked him a range of pointless questions about his relationships with prominent politicians. They wanted to know who went to the hunts at Derekegyháza, and what was discussed at those events. If they didn't like his reply, they hit him. One of the regular interrogators, a tall man with a bloodhound, stood with a gun in his hands, and Chorin had to stand facing the wall. At one point, the interrogator had sex with his secretary, as Chorin stood quietly by: disgusted, physically sick, motionless. His bowels had turned to bloody liquid. His boils burned with pain. The next day he was too ill to be interrogated.

After Becher went back to Germany, one of his assistants appeared with the news that Chorin was going to be taken back to Budapest. Once the hierarchy noted his slight shift in status, the interrogations involved less slapping, less standing. He was told to prepare to leave the camp.

But what did that mean? Under what circumstances was he returning to Budapest? He knew that he had no chance of becoming a free man, being reinstated into his previous life. During a single month of captivity, he had plummeted a great distance from that secure existence. The other prisoners crowded around him begging him to give messages to their loved ones, wondering if Chorin really was going to go back to Budapest, or if he was going to yet another prison.

My uncle traveled the same route that had brought him to Oberlanzendorf. His heart lifted to see Budapest again. They stopped at a café, where his captors had a drink and where Chorin saw, and was seen by, a Budapest newspaperman. The once-great magnate was now shabby, sick, and shockingly diminished, holding two ragged paper bags with all his earthly possessions. They then took him to his home on 114 Andrássy Avenue. The grand villa, with its lovely gardens and generous porches, its sun-drenched rooms and fine appointments, had undergone a change; it was now the headquarters of the economic branch of the SS. Becher slept in his bedroom, ate from his china, sat at his desk, and appreciated his art and fine wines.

Only two of the household staff remained: Chorin's father's secretary, who was visibly shocked by Chorin's appearance, and one of the maids. After he took a bath in the unaccustomed luxury of his own bathtub, the next round of interrogations began. They took place next door, in the old home of Manfred Weiss. Chorin entered the familiar library, now dominated by fifteen high-ranking German officers who had been assembled by Becher. Among the many reasons the Germans invaded Hungary was their need to exploit its industrial strength. Both Himmler and Hermann Göring were intensely interested in Hungary's manufacturing base, and the Manfred Weiss Works on Csepel Island, with its twenty thousand workers, the munitions, and Messerschmitt engine plants, was the greatest prize of all.

What Chorin did not know, but Becher certainly must have, was that several powerful German interests were vying for both the Manfred Weiss Works and the Danube Aircraft Manufacturing Company. Göring, the head of the Luftwaffe and Hitler's designated successor, had already established his massive industrial complex, the Göring Works, that included gravel pits, coal fields, lime deposits, steel factories, arms and munitions manufacturing, shipping lines, and other industrial enterprises. The Manfred Weiss Works would expand his empire to the next logical geographical region. Göring had already conducted talks with the Hungarian government about it and was given provisional approval to proceed with the transfer of ownership in early May. Göring was unaware that secret discussions between Chorin and Becher were under way.

Randolph Braham, in his monumental two-volume book on the Holocaust in Hungary, *The Politics of Genocide,* placed the discussions about the Manfred Weiss Works within the historical context. During the recent meeting with Horthy, the Germans agreed that their presence would not formally violate Hungary's sovereignty. They would occupy the country, but economically, politically, and socially it would remain autonomous. Implicit in these discussions was that Hungary would be able to maintain its own industrial base and to control the Manfred Weiss Works, the coal mines, and all other industries. The Nazi agenda would focus on eliminating the Jewish population.

This last was a demanding job, but Adolf Eichmann eagerly took it on. In less than two months after the invasion, 8,225 leading members of Hungary's Jewish community had been arrested, and throughout Hungary Jewish populations had been herded into ghettos. Eichmann and his entourage had decided to eliminate the Jewish population in the countryside before taking on the Jews of Budapest. That disaster would only happen several months later. Mass deporations to Auschwitz began in the countryside on May 15. About 170,000 Jews of Budapest were moved into 1,900 "yellow star" apartment houses, thereby concentrating the Jewish population and opening up their former apartments for Christians who had been left homeless because of bombing or who just wanted a nicer place in which to live. More than 120,000 other Jews hid with Christian friends or protectors.

After his first interrogation, Chorin was moved to his sister-in-law Edith's apartment, which was on the second floor of the Manfred Weiss home. There he lived under constant guard by two soldiers, but he was so ill, he was visited by a doctor.

The gossipy world of Budapest flourished, and word leaked out that Ferenc Chorin, the capitalist supreme, had reentered the city after being freed from a concentration camp. Repeatedly during Council of Ministers meetings, Béla Imrédy, who was the new finance minister, objected to my uncle's presence in Budapest and suggested that he would be better off in Mauthausen. But Becher reassured Chorin; he told him that he had "promised [Imrédy] to do this but had no intention of keeping his promise."

Under house arrest, Chorin asked to talk with various people who retained their professional positions, if not their previous power and authority. He concluded that the notion of fleeing to Switzerland or liberating some funds from Hungarian banks was pointless. The most powerful bargaining chip that they had was the factory at Csepel, damaged a bit by Allied bombing but formidable nonetheless.

Becher seized on the idea and urged Chorin to include not just the factory at Csepel but all the holdings of the family: the anthracite mines, the homes, and the other factories. In exchange, he said, he would guarantee that all members of the family would be taken safely to a neutral country. Becher would later describe the negotiations during his testimony at the trial of Adolf Eichmann: "In the course of these *convivial* conversations which Dr. Chorin and I had back then, he one day made the suggestion to me that Germany might take over the Manfred Weiss Group—that is to say, the shares that were formally in non-Jewish hands—but in return permit the members of the Manfred Weiss family to leave the country. On my suggestion Himmler gave his permission for the conclusion of a trustee contract and ordered that Obersturmbannführer Bobermin and I be appointed to the management of the group."

It was all quite elegant, really—a basic financial transaction that Chorin could have done in his sleep. Except that in this case the power differential between the negotiating parties was extreme. It's unclear exactly what leverage Chorin had. He was a prisoner of the SS. His family was in hiding. The Germans could have simply taken what they wanted and murdered the family. They certainly had done that before.

The negotiations went on for weeks. Chorin wanted the agreement to be a short-term lease. Becher wanted a long-term lease. German and Hungarian attorneys were involved, all sworn to secrecy. Keeping the Hungarian government out of the discussions was essential, as was keeping the information from leaking to Göring. If Chorin had any real power in this negotiation, it was only because the Germans themselves were divided. Becher cleared every part of the arrangement with Himmler, especially since this agreement involved the SS actually sparing a handful of Jews, a notion that was abhorrent to his boss, the head of the SS and organizational genius of the concentration camp system.

The 51 percent of the shares held by the Aryan part of the family would be transferred immediately to a new corporation that was Becher's holding company, while the 49 percent that was still owned by the Jewish members had already been seized by the Hungarian government. But Becher didn't just want the Manfred Weiss Works—he wanted their entire fortune. The family members who left would be permitted to take some of their valuables and some foreign currency. They would also be paid about $600,000 and nearly 250,000 German marks. Becher also made sure that he and others in the SS involved in the transaction would personally earn 5 percent of the gross income of the factories in payment for their services as trustees.

Everything required Himmler's approval. It was thought that the document even reached Hitler, although there is no record of it. A week of complete uncertainty passed. Chorin cleaned his apartment, being careful to avoid the window, since he was warned that he could be spotted. During air raids he was the last person permitted in the cellar, and once he was there, he was sequestered in a single room, from which he could hear the servants and the German soldiers entertaining each other.

Finally Becher returned from Berlin. He had good news. Initially Himmler had balked at the idea of permitting the richest Hungarian family of Jewish extraction to escape to a neutral country, but that was before Becher used his formidable powers of persuasion. Eventually Himmler accepted the basic premise of their proposal and made it his own, with a few strategic changes. One was that the contract should be set up on a trusteeship basis. Becher, without a trace of irony, considered this a more "morally" acceptable solution since the works would remain "a part of the Hungarian National Patrimony."

The trust arrangement was to last for thirty-three years, and the family was bound, under the terms of the contract, not to discuss this arrangement with anyone. Chorin protested—he asked for a twenty-five-year agreement. During a rare private conversation with Becher, the two men agreed that there was little point in arguing about the length of the agreement. As Chorin later wrote, it soon became apparent that "either the Germans would win the war, in which case Csepel would be gone and what we would gain from the agreement would be our only profit; or the Germans would lose the war, in which case the agreement reached under duress would be null and void anyway. At this point I was already convinced that the Germans had lost the war, and I think that Becher also began to see the situation more clearly." The final agreement was for twenty-five years. The shares were to be held by the trustee, but the family retained full ownership of the works—not that this technicality made much difference.

In order to ensure their discretion, five members of the family were to remain as hostages and live in a predetermined city as "guests" of the Third Reich. Chorin assumed that he would be one of them, but Becher insisted that given his political prominence, this was impossible. Vilmos Billitz, the manager of Csepel, who had been instrumental in initiating the contact between Becher and Chorin, told him that his brother-in-law Alfons Weiss was willing to remain a hostage, provided that his wife and four children could escape. Billitz also agreed to remain behind, since his expertise in the factory was essential. They also decided that Elsa's son Hansi Mauthner and Móric's son George and his wife, Elsie (who was an Aryan and Viennese), would remain. Most of the other members of the family were permitted to go to Portugal, and a few others were granted passage to Switzerland.

Chorin wanted to know how their escape would be organized. They would need Swiss and Portuguese visas. Furthermore, signing all the papers required to make this a full and binding contract would involve gathering all the shareholders—the children and grandchildren of Manfred Weiss—together in one place, tempting quarry for Eichmann or other members of the SS. Yet, he wrote, "I always relied on my insight into character, a talent on which I have always prided myself, and I trusted Becher. We agreed to a day on which to gather the family at a site outside Budapest and to depart from there to Austria."

Could the empire built by Manfred Weiss and sustained by his children save their lives?

CHAPTER 22

A Family Reunion

. . .

Several days after Chorin left, Móric was transported to Mauthausen, the concentration camp built around a stone quarry, where tens of thousands of prisoners had died working under brutal conditions. His few remaining possessions were taken, his body was shaved, and he was given nothing to eat or drink. He was taken to a communal shower, where an SS guard painted a large red J on the left side of his chest. Alarming as it was, as soon as the water hit the J, it began to dissolve; its very impermanence transformed a threatening gesture into one of unpleasant bullying. My grandfather was berated for not knowing how to make his bed with military precision and was told not to feign stupidity. "I did not admit to him that, on the contrary," Móric would write, "all my life I had been feigning wisdom."

In previous winters, inmates by the thousands had to stand for hours in the freezing cold. When one collapsed, the guards threw water on him so that he froze to the ground and died. Thousands more were swallowed up by the quarry. The director of the camp had two skulls on his desk—the remains of Dutch Jews whose teeth he particularly admired. Beatings were regular occurrences. Often, with little provocation, a prisoner would be pinned against a wall, and every SS man who passed would hit him. One of the most notorious SS officers would walk through the camp with his equally notorious dog that was trained to jump on an inmate and rip out his throat on command.

By the spring of 1944 the extreme misery and torture had abated, and no one could explain why. One theory was that the wives of the SS men were recently permitted to live with their husbands at the camp, and their domestic presence may have had a calming effect on the otherwise sadistic men. Others, like my grandfather, believed that the change was due to the faltering German war effort and its impact on the guards' entire attitude toward the war. They may have known that the end was near. Móric said that the days "passed more pleasantly than in Oberlanzendorf." A loudspeaker played censored news from a centrally controlled radio. When it played music, the barracks commander turned the volume up to a deafening level. A library lent out novels, and a seven-member brass and vocal ensemble made up of prisoners sometimes played in the central living area of their barracks.

Móric Kornfeld, prisoner number 65369, had been in Mauthausen for two weeks when, on Saturday, May 20, after the prisoners had just finished their twice-weekly exchange of underwear and were sunning themselves in the yard, one of the camp managers told him to gather his things—it was time for him to leave. Did this mean more interrogations? Or did it portend a fate similar to Chorin's, whatever that had been? Móric was stunned, overwhelmed by the feeling of unreality that had really never left him since March 19. It was not that he wanted to stay, but he had completely resigned himself to the fact that he would end his days in prison with his fellow inmates.

He could barely say goodbye to his comrades, and it felt almost indecent to be unfettered while they remained in shackles. Their lives had been reduced to the barest, most inadequate of essentials, but from that meager economy had flourished unexpected riches of kindness and affection. No one who did not share in that experience could possibly have understood its significance, nor how difficult it was to go away.

ACROSS BUDAPEST, IN VARIOUS hiding places, family members were summoned. Hanna had moved about ten different times. Sometimes she was reunited with members of her family. Other times she was alone with friends. During the frequent air raids, she could not take shelter with her protectors in the basement. Occasionally, in some apartment buildings, a resident was assigned to go through all the apartments after people went to the basement, to make sure that no one remained behind, so Hanna would hide in a closet. One of her protectors was a high-ranking military official who was so ashamed of these events, he felt compelled to show that not all Hungarians were indecent. Because their cleaning lady was untrustworthy, they introduced Hanna as a relative from Transylvania. My mother told me that she was petrified that she would be asked anything about Transylvania, since she didn't know a thing about it. Finally, during the second week of May, she moved with her mother and her aunt Elsa (who was going stir crazy) to the home of Elsa's Gentile son-in-law.

On May 16 Hanna wrote in her calendar, "Great excitement, they speak about one departure for the entire family." On the afternoon of May 17, Elsa's son Hansi arrived and told them to gather their things. He confirmed that they would be leaving the country. The three of them had no idea what this could possibly mean, but they were soon packed and ready. Hansi drove them to another villa, also one of the Mauthners', in the hills of Buda.

In Ireg, at seven in the morning, Tom was just waking up when his former nurse Liesl came into his room and told him that two German soldiers were there to pick him up. Briefly he considered jumping out the back window. He didn't, fortunately, because the execution of the deal required every member of the family to be accounted for and sign the agreement. He was brought back to Budapest in a surreal drive, where he chatted with his Gestapo guards, one of whom even let him examine his gun. When he arrived at the Mauthner villa, the first person he saw was his aunt Annie, the wife of his uncle Eugene Weiss. Tom was wearing his big green loden coat with the yellow star that his nurse had made for him. "Take it off," Annie told him. She handed him a small silver star to put in its place.

What a reunion it must have been: sisters and brothers and parents and children and cousins—nearly forty of them—together at last. Some other families were also there; relatives of key Csepel employees like Billitz were included in the escape.

But the excitement was compromised by the weight of uncertainty. Alfons's wife, Erzsi, repeated over and over, "Now they are going to take us to Auschwitz." Edith, who had helped scores of Polish Jews, was also convinced that deportation was inevitable. Hanna and Puppa, though worried, had some faith that things would work out. Their mother watched the various reunions, wondering if her husband would appear at some point, trying to accept the idea that he wouldn't. Every face was etched with resignation and relief, worry and happiness, anxiety and fatigue.

Chorin was the last to arrive. He was escorted to the villa by Becher late that night. When they crossed the majestic Chain Bridge, Chorin had the powerful sense that he was seeing his country for the last time. Memories overwhelmed him at that moment—the lives of his parents, his childhood, his great friendships with men who mattered. Power and influence were his birthright, a fundamental, almost physical element of his persona, but they had been erased by the last two months of the German occupation. The experience had weakened his spirit as much as his body. Even though he fervently believed that the Germans would lose the war, at that moment in the car with his SS protector, he had the soul-deep recognition that he would never again cross the Chain Bridge, would never again see the great city on the Danube, would never again go home. The recognition was an example of his profoundly demoralized state of mind, but it also had the quality of prophecy.

The car entered Buda and finally reached the Mauthner villa.

Daisy and the children rushed to embrace him. Young Daisy noticed the immense change in her father. He had been horribly ill. While the dysentery had been treated, the boils continued to plague him. Not only was he thin and pale, but a more fundamental transformation had occurred. No longer did he radiate confidence, humor, and well-being. Daisy could only describe that his eyes no longer looked forward, but were cast down at the floor. While he had saved the family, he was defeated. For others, the presence of Chorin had, as it always did, a reassuring effect.

Becher immediately presented the broad outlines of the transaction. He then asked Chorin to continue. Surrounded by his captors, he explained to his family that in exchange for their holdings, they would be permitted to leave for a neutral country. Some of them—Alfons, George and his wife and son, and Elsa's son Hansi—would remain behind as hostages. They were assured that these family members would be treated well. Chorin read the seventeen-page agreement, read the long list of their holdings and belongings—the factory, Ireg, Derekegyháza, the anthracite coal mines, on and on. At one point Elsa, whose indifference to the realities of money was exceeded only by her pleasure in spending it, said that if she had known they had this much, she would have spent more.

When it was Daisy's turn, she protested. She would not sign the document as long as the hostages had to remain behind. She could not bear to leave her older brother and split up the family. This arrangement flouted her father's most important commandment: "All for one and one for all." How could they sacrifice five for the sake of thirty-six? But if she didn't sign, the deal would not go through. Without her signature, they could all be deported. They had no choice, there was no alternative. Surrounded by the SS, only recently out of hiding, no one could speak about any discomfort or reluctance they might have felt.

And so Daisy reluctantly signed. It was well past midnight when all the documents were completed.

A fleet of little yellow Gestapo cars waited for them outside, fifteen in all, and the family split into groups of two and three. A large armed truck led the way, and on either side of the cars were motorcycle escorts. They were leaving Hungary. Their first stop would be Vienna, and then they would split up; most would go to Portugal, others to Switzerland. At the border between Austria and Hungary the convoy only slowed down as the German guards waved them through.

They arrived in Vienna early in the morning and were taken to the train station. They boarded a special train to Hütteldorf-Hacking, just outside Vienna, then were shuttled a few hours later to Purkersdorf, a small hamlet near Vienna. Several railroad wagon-lit cars awaited their arrival. The family settled among the cars, their temporary home until visas to Portugal and Switzerland were secured and various other aspects of the deal were finalized.

Marianne had written Móric a letter and asked Becher to make sure that he received it. She also wrote to George, who had moved in with his in-laws in Vienna, and mentioned how much she would miss them when she was in Portugal. Elsa wrote to her daughter, who was also living with Viennese in-laws, and asked for a Portuguese dictionary. Somehow the letters got mixed up.

Not twenty-four hours passed before news of the deal reached the government. Prime Minister Sztójay convened a special Council of Ministers meeting. There was outrage, especially vented by Finance Minister

Imrédy, that the crown jewel of Hungarian industry had been pocketed by the Germans.

IN MAUTHAUSEN A GUARD entered the room and asked, "Where is the stinking Jew?" When Móric identified himself, he was told to put on the clothes—now much too big—that he had been wearing when he had been arrested. He was then introduced to a young SS man who would escort him to the Mauthausen train station. Móric had no idea where the train they were catching was headed.

During his stay at Mauthausen, the early buds of spring had burst into the beauties of summer. Each tree was cloaked in rich green leaves, every shrub and flower seemed especially vivid. Móric, old and frail, lost in his clothes, his legs and feet horribly swollen, must have seemed especially vulnerable. Once out of sight of the camp, the young guard offered to carry his small package of belongings. After they walked a little while longer, the guard handed him a letter from his wife. But it was a letter she had written to their son George. At that moment Móric realized that the family was together in Vienna and that they would soon be going to Portugal.

Vienna first. Then Portugal. So the train that he was boarding was bound not for Budapest but for Vienna. Móric was so relieved to see Marianne's handwriting, he felt that his "soul had been refreshed." Slowly he pieced together at least some fragments of what had brought him to this point. Clearly Chorin's departure from the camp the month before was somehow connected to the reunion in Vienna and their ultimate destination of neutral Portugal. Worries about the fate of Hungary came later. At this point he simply enjoyed each detail of his walk: the sun on the green grass, the light shimmering on the red roof tile of the farm-house, the smell of spring, the fact that his wife and family were alive and safe. The SS officer apologized for rushing him but said he was concerned that they might miss their train. He apologized again that they were traveling third class.

They boarded the train. By the time they arrived in Vienna, it was dark. Móric had had nothing to eat or drink all day, and when they walked into the Westbahnhof station, the loudspeaker instructed his escort to report to the station commander. There was no car available to pick them up, as planned, so they raced outside and managed to catch the last streetcar. The young SS man did not know his way around Vienna and unsuccessfully asked several people on the street for directions to the Hotel Metropole. The happiness with which the Viennese had greeted the Germans five years earlier had soured, and they refused to give an SS man any information. The hotel, which was Gestapo headquarters in Vienna and the site of legendary brutality, was notorious. Finally a woman guided them from the streetcar stop.

When they arrived at the Metropole, Móric was led to a room on the second floor, where two lawyers—one from Vienna and the other from Berlin—welcomed him. They asked if he wanted to see his wife before they talked business. A veil is drawn over their reunion in my grandfather's recollection, but he did write, "I could take her in my arms and thus the great uncertainties of the past weeks and of the future lost their importance. I have come home." Home was not Hungary; home was with Marianne.

She must have been shocked by his appearance. He was thinner and grayer, his mustache was gone, and his head was shaved. His ankles were grotesquely swollen. But he was alive. Marianne, always practical, always a bit shy about the intensity of her emotions, always so formal, quickly brought him up to date. All six Weiss siblings and their families, as well as the families of Vilmos Billitz and one of their lawyers, György Hoff, had been brought to Vienna. They were all going to be taken to a neutral country, in exchange for which they had to give up their fortune.

When the couple returned to the other room, Ferenc and Daisy Chorin were there, and Ferenc explained the situation in greater detail. The long contract was waiting only for Móric's signature. He read it, and "even though the contents were of no import since all of us were in the hands of the Gestapo: I signed." They were taken by car to Purkersdorf, where the rest of the family waited for him.

Services Rendered to the Country for Decades

■   ■

■   ■

The train from Munich to Vienna passed Purkersdorf, a nondescript suburban Austrian town. I traveled past the station on my way from Munich to Vienna—a trip that my father took many times, once in a cattle car. It was an early October day when I went, and brilliantly sunny. Close to the tracks are open fields, where still some wildflowers bloomed. This became the family home for several weeks, on three sleeping cars, plus a dining car, as they waited for the deal to be finalized and to receive their visas to Switzerland and Portugal.

While Chorin maintained a brave front, each passing day increased his worry that the Germans were not going to keep their side of this elaborately constructed bargain. He lay awake wondering if his usually infallible instincts for people, the instincts that had served him so well for sixty-five years, had at last betrayed him and led him to trust Becher when he should not have. The most important transaction of his life might actually have been collateralized only by wishful thinking and desperation. If so, then the railway cars in which forty-one of the people closest to him in the world were gathered could conveniently transport them to the camps, as his sisters-in-law kept insisting.

Edith especially could not imagine any happy ending to their ordeal. The high-strung youngest daughter of Manfred Weiss, she worked closely with Jewish refugee organizations in Hungary, providing generous financial and moral support. She had heard countless stories from Polish refugees describing the horrors of the camps and had no illusions about the civility of the Nazis. "She suffered a nervous breakdown," her niece Memi once told me. "She was completely undone by the events. And of course she was the intelligent one. She knew what could happen while the members of my generation were so stupid. We just weren't frightened."

Chorin did not share his concerns with other members of the family. Instead, the older generation imposed order even in this bizarre circumstance. Chorin and Móric gave lectures to the young people, educating them on history and literature and politics and economics. Hanna, Puppa, and some of their female cousins would help out in the kitchen, peeling potatoes or cutting vegetables. The railroad cars occasionally shuttled back and forth between Purkersdorf and Hütteldorf, two small adjacent stations. Eugene, an engineer who was always a bit eccentric, sat with a pen and a pot of ink, graphing complex equations and plans.

When the air raids came, their guards would usher the family into a gully in a nearby field, where they would crouch and wait until the drones of the engines passed. During the raids, Eugene would make sure to bring his pot of ink and notebook. During the peaceful days, their SS guards, many of whom were genial and bored to tears with this assignment, would sometimes bounce Alfons and Erzsi's youngest son, nine-year-old János, on a big blanket. Horrified parents watched the rambunctious little boy shouting with pleasure as strapping young Nazis tossed him into the air, catching him always as he tumbled down.

Many days Elsa would gather her black bag and go off to pick wildflowers in the fields. The SS lieutenant was so fed up with trying to corral her back into the compound that he said that he would rather be sent to the Russian front than guard these Jews. His wish, apparently, was granted a few months later.

Once a week their guards took them to the Diana Baths in Vienna, where they could either take a steam bath or swim in a pool. Hanna, Puppa, and their mother opted for the pool where they could also wash some of their clothes. Elsa had never seen a steam bath before, so this was an opportunity to explore its humid mysteries. Already a bit bent, always clad in voluminous black dresses and shawls and carrying a big black purse, Elsa entered the steam bath fully clothed and looked around.

Once their captors even took them to a movie in Vienna. Bridge games popped up now and then, and anyone who had anything to read would pass it along. Food had been taken from Ireg and from the various family houses in Budapest, so early in their stay they ate fairly well, but the food got worse and worse. And the days passed.

Becher appeared at the train to confer with Chorin, Móric, Eugene, and Alfons. Following his visit, he tried to demonstrate his goodwill by arranging for two shipments of suitcases from Budapest containing clothes and other belongings. No one really knew who made the choices, but among the items they received were Móric's *diszmagyar,* an extravagant formal imperial uniform perfect for coronations or other high-level state events, and his ceremonial saber. Marianne was reunited with her entire white-lace wedding trousseau, all handmade a mere thirty years before, as well as a few lovely nineteenth-century ball gowns, one in rich blue velvet. These items found their way to Patterson Street, where they moldered in the basement, bereft relics both of eradicated worlds and of the mordant senses of humor of the SS or those left behind in Hungary.

The deal had ignited tremendous conflicts between Germany and Hungary. Himmler informed Veesenmayer, the Reich's representative in Hungary, of the deal and made it his unhappy responsibility to give the news to the Hungarians. The Germans had tried to impress upon the Hungarians that they were not going to be intrusive in their domestic affairs. Veesenmayer attempted to rationalize the deal by emphasizing Horthy's friendship with Chorin, hoping that this would make it more palatable or divert responsibility from the Germans and toward the inner workings of Hungarian society.

In Berlin, Foreign Minister von Ribbentrop was furious that the transaction had taken place in such secrecy, without even a whisper of cooperation, much less requests for permission. Von Ribbentrop and Himmler had always been rivals, and this deal further escalated that rivalry—especially after von Ribbentrop discovered that Hitler supported Himmler and approved of the deal. No wonder it took several weeks for the final agreement to be concluded.

On June 6, Chorin was summoned to the Hotel Imperial in Vienna. The hotel was full of memories from family visits there when he was a child. Ironically, the old corner room where Chorin had stayed with his father had now become Becher's Vienna office. Other SS men accompanied Becher, who seemed to need to revisit long-resolved issues yet again in front of his colleagues. They wanted to further consolidate their economic power in Hungary—now that they owned so many of the family assets—and Chorin was the man to provide the road map.

Chorin gave them some suggestions and then asked about the Jewish employees at Csepel. He finally felt free enough to make the request. Becher assured him that they would be protected from harm, at least from the Germans. (He couldn't have predicted the actions of the Hungarian gendarmerie.) Outside the window, written on a chalkboard that hung outside a house across the street, was the news that the Allies had landed in Normandy and that all steps had been taken to expel them. In other words, Chorin realized with some relief, the landings had been a success. D-day had officially begun, and with it the final turning points of the war. Becher was unmoved by the news; he was more concerned that the additional assets that had been uncovered be included in the agreement. Chorin was in no position to argue.

On Friday, June 23, the family was told that the visas had been arranged and they would be leaving the next day. "Now they are taking us to the camps," Erzsi said. Whatever anxieties the others felt were lost in the packing. The group was taken by train to Stuttgart, where three German airplanes waited for them. The one bound for Switzerland left first: Elsa's two daughters—my mother's cousin and best friend, Mopi, and her sister Baby—and their new babies and husbands, fourteen in all.

According to the agreement, they were supposed to receive $600,000 (roughly $7.5 million today), which would be paid in installments, plus 250,000 German Reichsmarks (approximately $320,000 today). The group that went to Portugal, headed by Chorin, received $170,000 (about $2.1 million) once they arrived in Lisbon, and the group that went to Switzerland was given $30,000. In a Viennese bank was placed the 250,000 Reichsmarks, for the hostages. The $400,000 balance was to be paid in installments, but the SS defaulted on its payments.

With their suitcases full of ball gowns, damask tablecloths, clothes, heraldic uniforms, sabers, riding boots, and, in Hanna's, a protected file of letters from my father, it was now time for the other two groups to leave. They said goodbye to Alfons, George, Hansi, and the other hostages. The family signed additional papers empowering Alfons to act on their behalf. This last signature was the most difficult, since they all worried that they were putting Alfons in an impossible situation. They had little time for tender goodbyes, as German guards hurried the remaining thirty-two people onto the two waiting German civilian aircraft, piloted by Göring's very own Luftwaffe pilots. For many of them, this was their first flight.

And a rocky introduction to flying it was. Since D-day, German planes had had to fly at a very low altitude even over the mountains. The Chorins' youngest child, Ferenc Junior, "vomited like Vesuvius," according to his sister Erzsébet's diary. They refueled in Lyons, a city under active bombardment, and then went on directly to Lisbon. The other plane, which carried the Kornfelds, Elsa, and her daughters, stopped in Madrid overnight before proceeding on to Portugal.

They had been given an orange to share when they refueled in Barcelona, and Tom noticed a banana peel discarded on a windowsill. He had not seen a banana for five years, he recalled, "and suddenly realized there was another world out there somewhere." They were free.

Newspapers. Chocolate. Real coffee. Baths. Cigarettes. Light. Color. Open windows and doors. Loud conversations on streets. Cars everywhere. That night when Hanna and Puppa settled into their hotel room, Hanna raced to the windows to draw the blinds, so accustomed was she to having to black out rooms, and then stopped. For the first time in years she and Puppa looked outside and saw the city lights glinting in the darkness. The next morning the indomitable Aunt Elsa asked their SS guard what time the flight to Portugal was scheduled to depart. He told her that it would leave in the afternoon. She asked his permission to go to the Prado, since who knew when she would be in Madrid again. The guard must have thought they were all crazy but permitted a small contingent from the family, including Hanna and Puppa, to go to the museum. As soon as they returned, they were told to pack quickly. There was some problem with their visas, and they had to go to Portugal immediately.

After the family was in Lisbon for a day, the Portuguese police detained the male members of the entourage for having submitted forged visas. Chorin was appalled. The idea that these visas were forged was incomprehensible to him. How could they have managed to make it this far only to have the entire elaborately constructed transaction collapse over this stupid bureaucratic technicality? Chorin appealed to the German officer who had accompanied them, but there was nothing he could do. The Portuguese police captain shrugged and adhered to the letter of the law.

Depsite the bureaucratic limbo, they had somehow regained some of their previous status. Chorin's older daughter, Erzsébet, wrote in her diary, "We were very pleased that on the first afternoon the biggest American news agency and another writer from another newspaper arrived to interview Father. Of course because of [the hostages] we had to send them away. But it is such a wonderful feeling that one is somebody again."

With this reinstatement of their standing, they were able to enlist the help of two old friends from Hungary who were in some position of power in Lisbon: Andor Wodianer, the former Hungarian minister in Lisbon who had resigned when the Sztójay government took power in Hungary; and Sir Owen O'Malley, the British ambassador in Hungary in the late 1930s who had been reassigned as ambassador to Portugal. O'Malley had spent many happy hours at Ireg and Derekegyháza when he was ambassador, and now he was able to vouch for the family.

The men were released but were told that the family could not stay in Lisbon. By now the second group had arrived. Edith realized that she had once met the daughter of President Carmona of Portugal. She managed to reach her on the telephone, and the daughter intervened. Carmona spared the family the displaced persons camp but placed them under police guard in a summer resort called Curia that was about six hours by train from Lisbon. They finally arrived at the tiny station at the end of a tree-lined road leading to the resort, about half a mile away. A police officer in mufti who was with them called the hotel to send porters with handcarts.

The Chorin and Weiss families stayed at the more elegant Palace Hotel, while the Kornfelds and a few other cousins stayed at the more modest Hotel Curia. They were restricted to a three-mile radius around the spa and were guarded all the time.

News of their arrival had already hit the papers. On June 29, 1944, a three-paragraph article appeared in *The Times of London*, dateline Lisbon:

> Thirty-two members of wealthy business families in Hungary, mainly Jewish industrialists, have arrived in Lisbon this week traveling in German aircraft, and hope to go to America. A huge financial and material deal with German interests made it possible for them to leave Hungary.
>
> Among those who have arrived are Choren [*sic*] and Weiss, reputed to be the richest men in Hungary, who have a virtual monopoly of the coun-

try's heavy steel and munitions industries. They were arrested on March 19 and taken to Vienna, but after intercessions by the Hungarian government they were released and returned to Budapest. There, without the knowledge of the Hungarian government they made an important deal with a German financial group, and were consequently permitted to leave Hungary with their families—but each family has had to leave a hostage behind to guarantee their discretion abroad.

A special train took them from Hungary to Stuttgart where three special airplanes awaited them. They were allowed to bring out cash, jewels and gold, which have been deposited with the Portuguese customs authorities. The first group arrived here on Sunday and the last group yesterday.

"Millionaire Chorin Buys Nazi Freedom" read the bold headline in the *Syracuse Herald American*. Paul Ghali, the correspondent in Bern, wrote, "It was by selling to the Hermann Goering [sic] crowd all his shares of the Salgo mines and the Manfred Weiss Armament works that the Hungarian Jewish multi-millionaire Francis Chorin and his family were able to escape to Lisbon a few days ago."

Ghali reported that Chorin planned to go to America, "convinced that there is nothing in this world that money cannot buy. Meanwhile, his fellow Jews in Hungary, not being millionaires, must continue to submit to Nazi tortures. . . . Recent estimates speak of 300,000 Israelites as being earmarked for deportation. . . . Reports reaching here indicate that 100,000 Hungarian Jews have been gassed in the Auschwitz camp, Silesia."

British and American intelligence services in Portugal assumed that the family must be German spies. O'Malley suggested to the Foreign Office that, given the enormity of the transaction that took place in Hungary, Ferenc Chorin and Eugene Weiss be taken to Britain for interrogation, but the Foreign Office was not interested. A declassified U.S. State Department analysis asserts that the transaction looked like "a German move to plant suspicion in Soviet minds of the attitude and actions of the United States Government and His Majesty's government." The logic, tortured as it was, was that the deal implied that Germany had engaged in special negotiations, possibly peace talks, with the United States and the United Kingdom and that one part of those discussions involved the protection of these prominent Jews. The Russians could not help but feel cut out of those arrangements, and their suspicion would corrode the alliance.

I have a thick file of these reports from the OSS, the U.S. State Department, the British Foreign Office, and the British embassy in Portugal. Each one contains fragments of the truth. Telegrams that my uncle sent to Switzerland congratulating his niece on the birth of her child are also included. A July 1 memo from the OSS with SECRET stamped across the top announces, "Prominent Jews Escape. A reliable source has informed the OSS representative in Bern that a number of upper class Jews have managed to escape from Hungary by buying their way out."

The communications finally reached Winston Churchill, who was being asked from all directions for permission to pursue the family. The Russians insisted that these rich German spies should at least be interrogated, if not apprehended. Finally, on the eighth of August, Churchill wrote in his special minutes, "This seems to be a rather doubtful business. These unhappy families, mainly women and children, have purchased their lives probably with nine-tenths of their wealth. I should not like England to seem to be wanting to hunt them down. By all means tell the Russians anything that is necessary, but please do not let us prevent them from escaping. I cannot see how any suspicion of peace negotiations can be fixed on this miserable affair."

CHAPTER 24

A New Era of Captivity

B y July, Eichmann had deported 458,000 Hungarian Jews from the countryside. He found the Hungarian gendarmerie to be enthusiastic partners. These resentful, unappreciated Hungarian thugs relished cramming generations of Jews into stifling freight cars bound for Auschwitz. The extermination was so ambitious, so systematic, that the Western Allies could no longer divert their attention from the enormity of this catastrophe. In July the kings of England and Sweden, the pope, and the International Red Cross all asked Horthy to intervene, and Roosevelt suggested that the Americans would bomb Budapest.

Horthy finally acted. Especially since the Russian forces were nearing the Hungarian border.

At the end of June, the Crown Council decreed that the deportations would end, and briefly they did. Of course no train turned back, no prisoner was released, but the Jews of Budapest were spared for the last time. The summer of 1944 was the last brief moment when the regent could have seized some control over events. Horthy sanitized his cabinet and attempted to rid it of the most aggressively pro-Nazi elements, beginning at the top with Sztójay. He replaced him with an army officer he trusted, Gen. Géza Lakatos, who took over for a very brief tenure as prime minister on August 29.

Only four days before the change of command, Germany's loyal Romanian ally made an abrupt about-face when Russian troops crossed its border and declared war on both Germany and Hungary. Horthy could not accept that the Americans and the British genuinely considered the Russians to be equal allies; he believed that the Western Allies would somehow prevent Russian troops from crossing Hungary's southeastern border. On August 31 Horthy's government decided that Hungarian troops, with German reinforcements, would attack Russia in southern Transylvania, while at the same time Hungary would ask Britain and the United States to occupy the country to free it of German control.

Aladár remained in the Fő utca Prison, as sensitive as a Geiger counter to the reverberations from the political events. The Gestapo guards were twitchy. When Lakatos became prime minister, there was a glimmer of hope among the inmates. Then the talk of deporting the prisoners sank everyone's mood—until the rumors morphed again into discussions about a possible release. Aladár considered this "a new era of our captivity" characterized first by hope, "then nervous waiting, and finally disappointment." He and other prisoners who had worked in the Foreign Ministry learned that their release had been discussed during a Council of Ministers meeting, but their hopes evaporated in a matter of days when the rumor simply disappeared. They were even more bitterly disappointed when prisoners who were members of the upper house of Parliament, who had been the subject of other rumors, were in fact released.

Finally it was time for Horthy to do what many had hoped he would do years before; he told his council on September 7 that his government would be embarking on peace discussions with the Allies. But with incredible innocence, or naïveté, or sheer stupidity, he announced as much to the Germans. The council saw some obvious problems with this approach and advised that the country continue to rely on Germany as a protective ally and ask it to send in troops to protect Hungary against the Russian invasion.

One of the janitors in the Fő utca Prison was a Jewish journalist named Pál Fodor who had worked for the *Kis Újság,* Dessewffy's newspaper. Fodor helped all the inmates and was a valuable source of information because he could walk nearly everywhere, carrying his mop and his pail. The story was that Fodor began his career as a very young man, by calling a newspaper and asking them if they were interested in "two cadavers," who happened to be his parents, who had just committed suicide. The newspaper was so impressed, they hired him on the spot. My father never knew if the story was true.

In prison Fodor managed to get newspaper delivery for the prisoners,

passed along bits of gossip and important information, and even persuaded the guards to release the prisoners from their cells during the days
so they could relax and socialize. When they heard an authority figure
approach, the inmates would immediately return to their cells and close
the doors, while the guards fumbled for their keys, to keep up the ruse of
their confinement. Many mornings the prisoners would stand in their
doorways, chatting among themselves. Aladár surveyed the scene and
thought they looked like maidens in a small-town whorehouse.

Politically, the situation in Hungary was deteriorating. The Russians
had broken through the eastern border. On the highway to Vienna, rows
and rows of trucks were lined up, with Germans securing booty and carrying it west. In the Castle District, near the Foreign Ministry, the streets
were full of ash. People were burning any evidence they thought might
be incriminating, either for the Germans or for the Russians. By October
10, the city was overrun by refugees from the countryside, small bundles
of their belongings beside them. "They sit at the most improbable places,"
Éva Dessewffy wrote in her journal, "at the tramway stop of the Szent
Rókus Hospital, at the City Hall Street. They just sit there with expressionless faces, without hope, wordless."

Horse-drawn carriages from the southern cities and small towns of
Hungary clattered through the streets. The carts were overburdened
with packages and blankets, the small and big belongings that anyone
could fathom wanting to save, both to have them and to prevent the
Russians from taking them. Automobiles, similarly overburdened, idled
in traffic. Dessewffy saw one such car with packages piled high on the
roof: "On top of them, almost lost, are two containers with pink flowers."
Throughout the city the Nazi leadership who had appropriated family
houses was now emptying them of their contents. The major who had
been living in János Zwack's home was seen loading his possessions onto
a waiting truck. Becher remained in comfort at Chorin's home, sending
out inconspicuous packages of the finest silver, linens, and antiques to his
address in Germany.

Horthy persisted in seeking an armistice and turned to Finland as an
example of how one could be achieved. He suggested that German troops
could retreat from Hungary, and the Hungarian army would remain
armed but no longer engaged in combat. Meanwhile the Allies could rely
on Hungary. No one could imagine negotiating with the Russians except, eventually, Horthy, who embarked on secret negotiations with

them. In the second week of October, Molotov agreed to a preliminary armistice with Hungary. Hungary would have to break relations with and declare war on Germany, withdraw troops from the very areas it had reclaimed after Trianon, and resign itself to the Trianon borders.

The country had no choice. As unpalatable as these terms were, being destroyed by the Germans and the Russians would be even worse. So Horthy accepted them, asking for a brief undeclared truce, during which the Soviet army stopped fighting the Hungarians in Hungary. Horthy was supposed to announce this great news only after he put into place the actual logistical requirements. But he was so worried that his government would be overthrown by the Arrow Cross, he announced the armistice before anything had been done to make it a reality.

In prison, Pál Fodor whispered an ongoing commentary on the political situation that he gleaned from the guards' radios and from the newspapers that he managed to glimpse. Fodor suggested that the only thing that could save the country would be if the Russians reached Budapest rapidly. Aladár knew that even if the Russians did arrive in Hungary, he was personally doomed because of his work with the Americans and the British.

On October 14 Fodor reported that Horthy had issued a declaration on the radio that he planned to seek an armistice with the Allies. Hitler had lost patience with Hungary for many reasons, but the fact that Jewish deportations had been stopped was especially galling to him. Horthy had to be replaced by a loyal Nazi government, and Szálasi and his comrades in the Arrow Cross stood at the ready. On October 15 Horthy's son, thirty-seven-year-old Nikki, was attacked and abducted by the SS. At that time the Crown Council was meeting with Horthy, who told them that he had "called together the members of the cabinet in this darkest hour of Hungary's history. Our situation is gravely critical. That Germany is on the verge of collapse is no longer in doubt. Should that collapse occur now, the Allies would find that Hungary is Germany's only remaining ally. In that case Hungary might cease to exist as a state. Hence I must issue an armistice."

In the midst of that meeting, Horthy was told that his son had been kidnapped. He continued the meeting, which then meandered into agonizing discussions of various recondite legal issues. Eventually the prime minister told Horthy that since Parliament had not been included or consulted in efforts to negotiate with the Allies, he and his cabinet had to resign. Horthy responded that while he accepted their resignations, because he was the supreme commander, he could both conduct an armistice and request that the cabinet be reappointed.

Horthy then met with Veesenmayer, the German representative in Hungary, and told him of the plans to seek the separate armistice. He was furious at the German treatment of Hungary, including the gangland abduction of his son. It might have been a great moment if it had not been so pitifully overdue. The game was lost. Horthy's radio announcement of the armistice and his order for Hungarian troops to lay down their arms was shortly contradicted by the Germans, who enlisted the help of pro-German officers in mobilizing the troops against Horthy.

Within hours the Germans had organized the deposition of Horthy and the installation of Ferenc Szálasi and his Arrow Cross followers as the new government. With his son held hostage, Horthy was forced to recognize Szálasi and then resign, placing himself under German protection. Nikki Horthy was not reunited with his family; he was sent first to Mauthausen and then to Dachau. Horthy and his family were exiled to Bavaria and eventually to Portugal.

With Horthy gone, the Szálasi regime took power, and any vestiges of civility and decency in Hungary disappeared. Some believe that the Arrow Cross regime surpassed the Nazis in sheer brutality. The SS and the Hungarian gendarmerie zealously embraced the destruction of the Hungarian Jews. The police were given free rein by Eichmann to terrorize the Jews, which they did both arbitrarily and systematically.

Szálasi ordered the creation of a ghetto near the synagogue where Manfred Weiss and Zsigmond Kornfeld had once prayed. One hundred fifty thousand of Budapest's Jews were initially crammed into it and deprived of sanitation, food, and shelter. Soon 80,000 were shipped out to concentration camps. Another 20,000 Jews were taken in by so-called "safe houses," houses that were under the protection of embassies like Sweden and Switzerland and were considered neutral territory; they were referred to later as the "international ghetto." Finally, sympathetic Gentiles hid roughly another 20,000 Jews.

By the evening of October 16, those being held at the Fő Street Prison knew that they were doomed. "The guards were just as depressed as the prisoners," Aladár noted. The prisoners knew that they faced either butchery by Arrow Cross Hungarians who hated them, or deportation to German prison camps. The guards knew that they would not stay in

Hungary under this new regime that was, if possible, even more extreme than the one for which they worked. The complete breakdown of society that the Arrow Cross represented had begun. That evening several Arrow Cross men appeared at the prison, announcing their intention to guard the prisoners, but the Gestapo guards would not let these drunken, belligerent, and primitive thugs near "their" prisoners.

Two days later, at the Foreign Ministry, the new foreign policy representatives of the Arrow Cross regime gathered all the employees in an auditorium so they could take an oath of loyalty to the new government. Those who refused were told to leave and wait in one of the offices. Only two people refused, both of them women, and one was Katalin Máriássy, who many years later would become my godmother. Graceful and elegant, she had just returned from serving in the Hungarian legation in Greece. She said that when she sat in the office awaiting her fate, she wanted to demonstrate that she was unafraid of her new bosses. It was lunchtime, so she took out her sandwich and began to eat it. Unfortunately, her hands were shaking so uncontrollably, they contradicted what she had hoped to convey. The two women were threatened with prison but were then released.

More prisoners appeared at Fő Street—Aladár spotted old friends from the army and the Foreign Ministry in the yard. But he realized that their days there were coming to an end. He hoped to be deported, "since in Germany I became only a number, while for the Arrow Crossists I would have remained the personification of everything they hated and wanted to destroy." Fodor reported to Aladár that deportations had resumed. He had found his own escape hatch, he said, pointing to a small window without a grating that overlooked a courtyard. "If I am signed up for Auschwitz, I will jump," he said.

"Lilly tells us that seeing Aladár breaks her heart," Éva Dessewffy wrote on October 7. "The constant darkness, loneliness, tension, the waiting for when they will deport him, just adds to his depression." Lilly and her father were still able to visit Aladár, but they were shocked to see how much he had deteriorated emotionally. He was utterly distraught from the uncertainty, the air raids, the months in prison, and the horrible period of waiting for the unknown had left him tearful, in a state beyond hope or reason. "I was very happy to see them but considered it a farewell, and cried throughout their visit, mumbling that we would never see each other again," he wrote. He was terrified that his parents and sister would be exposed to even more air raids and street fighting. After half an hour the visit was over, and my father cried openly when they said good-bye, convinced that he would be dead in the coming months, or they would all be.

The steady roar of cannon fire was a new addition to the cacophony outside the prison walls. On the afternoon of November 4, an enormous explosion convulsed the entire prison building, rattling windows and the nerves of prisoners and guards alike. Across town Éva Dessewffy waited for her husband. She too heard the explosion. The Margaret Bridge, linking Buda to Pest, had disappeared, she discovered, hurling hundreds of pedestrians, packed streetcars, and buses into the icy waters of the Danube. The Germans had attached dynamite to the bridge, and by some mistake, the explosives had detonated. Aladár observed that the only good to come out of it was that the explosion made it possible for the Germans to lose track of a number of people they had been following.

Éva raced outside to the Fisherman's Bastion in the cobblestone Castle District of Buda, to see the burning bridge in the distance. "The distant torn bridge is an apocalyptic scene," she wrote. "The bridge posts rise out in the Danube, with a train hanging on parts of it. Something falls, a piece of stone or a human being. A hopeless bitterness engulfs me. Again, something we have to thank the Germans for and the power intoxicated Arrow Crossists."

That evening the SS guards were gloomy. Many had not had news from their families for weeks. Some strange, harmonious community of interests had emerged among the men. Aladár would write, "At times we felt that these Germans had more affinity to us than to their own uniform." Two days later, through his closed door, he heard Pál Fodor making his usual morning rounds. But this time was different. "Aladár, they put me on the list for Auschwitz. God be with you, pray for me," he said. "For heaven's sake, don't do it!" Aladár cried through the closed door of his cell. But almost immediately he heard the shattering of glass, and then a thud. For a brief moment the entire prison was like an agitated beehive with frenzied activity. Guards and prisoners shouted.

Then silence.

Aladár stood in his cell, staring at the blank wall, too shocked to grieve. He took inventory of the multiple failings, *his* innumerable personal failures that had led to Fodor leaping from the window. His guilt expanded beyond all reasonable proportion, like a flood of water that filled his cell and threatened to drown him. "What could I have done to prevent it? Had I omitted doing anything? To this day I cannot give a satisfactory answer," he would write thirty years later. Even then he still thought of "the Little Fodor" with respect, friendship, and gratitude. "I can still see his large sad eyes and his cheerful and proud smile as he stood with us in front of the cells on Sundays, listening to mass, in a shining white shirt." The train he was supposed to be on never reached Auschwitz. Most of that group of deportees survived, a fact that only further emphasized how unnecessary his suicide was.

What existential curse had been visited on my father to make his guilt so consuming and indiscriminate and indelible? During mass, thirty years later, I remember how powerfully he pounded his chest during the *confiteor*, the confession. He muttered, "*Mea culpa, mea culpa, mea maxima culpa*"—through my fault, through my fault, through my most grievous fault.

After Fodor's death, after the takeover by the Arrow Cross, Aladár disintegrated into despair. He read constantly but could not remember what he read. He felt that he had been "granted the privilege of complete passivity" and could comfort himself that he was no longer responsible for anyone, even himself. He worried about his parents and sister and Hanna as well as himself. But he had completely surrendered to events, had become merely an insignificant bit player in a real-life Götterdäm-merung. Nonetheless, he prayed constantly.

When, on November 8, a young SS guard told him to pack his things and get ready to go to the Reich, Aladár felt a certain relief. At least he would not have to face Szálasi's sadistic executioners. He clung to his cardinal rule: avoid being noticed. Cooperate as best as he could. Avoid excess zeal, mingle among others as much as possible, and show a united front with his fellow prisoners.

Aladár boarded the train, designed for eight horses or forty-eight men. He was one of forty political prisoners, journalists, and military men who had proved unreliable. There were no Jews on this transport; the Jews were packed in cattle cars going to Auschwitz. These men were all in the category of political prisoners.

On the floor was a three-inch layer of dried cattle droppings and dirt. Aladár carried with him a yellow comforter from home and a few be-longings. He wore a heavy wool suit so as not to get cold. Some old friends greeted him, including his former boss from the Foreign Ministry, Szentmiklóssy. Once they were lined up on the edge of a ditch to empty their bowels as a line of SS men, pistols drawn, faced them. "It was a pity that there was no photographer," Aladár wrote. "Since the whole scene was extraordinarily grotesque."

The train continued on its journey west. The prisoners tried to figure out where they were headed. Aladár had heard terrible stories about the concentration camps and was afraid of where they might end up. He and Szentmiklóssy concluded that Mauthausen would be the best spot, since they had heard from some prisoners who were returned to the Fő Street Prison that they had enjoyed certain privileges in Mauthausen, like letters and parcels from home. An Austrian who had been interned in a number of places overheard them and said, "Anything but that."

After crossing the frontier into Austria, the train rolled on more rapidly, through the bleak November countryside. Soon they were in Vienna, where a few prisoners were removed from the car. Then, on November 14, 1944, a week after leaving the Fő Street Prison, the train arrived at its destination.

CHAPTER 25

Dachau

■
■   ■

Created in 1933 by Heinrich Himmler, Munich's newly installed police chief, Dachau was Germany's first state concentration camp. It was situated on the site of a neglected World War I munitions factory in a small village about fifteen kilometers outside Munich. The intimidation, punishment, and torture of political unreliables, social misfits, and Jews was no longer an ad hoc, case-by-case endeavor. It was now systematized. The Bavarian state police initially were in charge of the camp, but within a month an SS unit took over.

Days after new management was installed, after evening roll call, the SS summoned four Jewish prisoners. They led them outside the camp-grounds and shot them, for attempting to escape. The message was clear: nothing rational would govern what was going to happen there. A prison within the prison was set up in what had once been a lavatory. Wooden planks were laid across the floor as beds, and the area was christened the "bunker" but should have been called the torture chamber. After spending time in the bunker, most inmates either committed suicide or were murdered. All new prisoners, especially Jews and anti-Nazi public figures, were greeted with immediate brutality. New arrivals were initiated with twenty-five lashes from a bullwhip.

When Aladár arrived on November 14, 1944, feverish and parched, his head aching and his throat raw with strep, he became prisoner number 125739, a *Schutzhaftling*, or protective custody prisoner. Seasoned inmates assured him that, compared to the past, Dachau was a sanatorium. Since many of the prisoners were sent out on work details to German factories, they were not harassed with all-night roll calls, interminable calisthenics, and other forms of abuse that had once been a form of entertainment for the guards. The food was still execrable, the lice were pervasive, and the accommodations were subhuman. Aladár had heard of Dachau, since it had been written about extensively in the German press as the humane repository for the dregs of society: Jews, political dissidents, homosexuals, and common criminals. But as he wrote later, "When I thought about all the things that I had heard, ever since Berlin, about these camps, it made my flesh creep. As always, I was praying a lot, perhaps even more than usual."

His prayers were as much a devotion to his mother as to God; she had taught him how to pray. "Even today I pray the same way as she, with the difference that I pray less from the prayer book and more with my own text that has evolved over the years," he wrote when he was seventy-five years old. "It is certain that without God, I cannot live, just as I couldn't live without air."

When he arrived, Aladár was sent with the other prisoners to the showers, where he was stripped bare, shaved from head to toe, and given threadbare clothes reeking of chlorine. When he was taken to their cell-block, he found a bunk near his former boss Szentmiklóssy. He felt awful, feverish and thirsty, with a terrible sore throat. He felt even worse when he was told that he could not drink the water since it was probably contaminated. Another prisoner asked him what was wrong and returned a few minutes later with something for him to drink.

Within the first week of his imprisonment, he learned a number of strategies for survival. Don't drink the water. Eat your food slowly. And most important: Avoid transports at any cost. In November 1944 Dachau had become a kind of hub for sorting prisoners. The healthiest and those who appeared able to work remained in Dachau. Others were sent to Auschwitz or other extermination camps.

Other prisoners gave him the prisoner number of someone who had already been sent away, so when they were all lined up, naked in the snowy yard before the "selection committee," and found to be suitable for transport, he gave the phony number, which assured that he could remain in place for a while longer. Staying alive, or at least prolonging life, was the dream of every prisoner, but death was everywhere. The Gypsy who died in their cellblock was laid out in the toilet until his body was removed. The seventy-year-old secretary from a Budapest Greek Ortho-dox church who had been accused of hiding gold died after the guards punished him. A wise old, chain-smoking man, who traded his meager food for cigarettes, starved to death.

Aladár willingly took on the first assignment that he was given, which was to be a subject in a medical experiment on blood clotting. He re-ported to work at the hospital, where they drew his blood, gave him some medication, and a few hours later drew more blood. He didn't realize that he was part of an experiment that had begun in 1939 under one of the craziest Nazi doctors, Sigmund Rascher. In one, seventy prisoners died a horrible death after they were placed in an altitude simulator to see how they would react to crushing pressure and then drastic drops in pressure. Ninety others died in a series of hypothermia experiments in which they were strapped in freezing water and died while doctors timed how long it took. Prisoners were infected with malaria and left to die. Two thou-sand Gypsies were recruited from Buchenwald for a devastating inquiry into the potability of sea water.

The blood-clotting experiment in which Aladár took part tested the effectiveness of a substance called polygal, invented by a Jewish chemist who had been imprisoned at Dachau. Polygal could speed up the time it took for blood to coagulate. On the battlefield alone, this material could potentially save many lives. In order to test its effectiveness, Dr. Rascher at first would murder prisoners and then inject them with the serum to see how quickly their blood clotted.

By the time Aladár became one of the subjects, Rascher had retired from his debased research. Perhaps that was why Aladár wrote of his good fortune in being assigned to the "only decent experimental unit in Dachau, where a good and honest physician tried to find some medica-tion to hasten blood clotting." The experiments began on his forty-first birthday, an event he remembered with gratitude since he was not "in overcrowded, unheated, filthy cattle cars, with very little food and water, perhaps surrounded by dead bodies. Dreadful things happened on these transports. Drinking urine, mass deaths, and even some forms of canni-balism. I was fully aware of this, but it still took some time before I re-signed myself to Dachau."

His health in Dachau was faltering; he was weak, and his nerves were shot. When it started to get cold, one of his fellow prisoners, a Dutch physician named Jan Droste, who had taken a liking to Aladár, gave him a threadbare sweater, and later a woolen cap. Aladár was so overwhelmed with gratitude he began to cry. One day he and his fellow prisoners were all herded to the showers because their beds were being disinfected. The water was freezing, so the prisoners hesitated before going in. One of the prisoners, a kapo whose job it was to supervise others, became enraged and began to beat the people around him. His anger was contagious, and "an otherwise friendly, good-natured Rotterdam dock worker also got mad, took off his belt, and started to thrash prisoners with it."

Eventually they went into the showers and even enjoyed a little bit of warm water, but there were no towels to dry off. There they stood, naked, shoulder to shoulder. Aladár noted the bruises and blood from beatings on the bodies around him.

One of the kapos ordered him to go with a Gypsy prisoner to fetch a kettle of soup for dinner and bring it to the bathhouse. The two of them went to the kitchen, but the kettle was too heavy for my father to lift. When they returned to the bathhouse empty-handed, Aladár confessed his weakness to the kapo. Furious, the guard cursed him and used the ladle he was holding for the soup to beat him. Aladár felt the blows of the ladle across his shoulders and head. Another prisoner was sent to get soup with the Gypsy, and Aladár sat with the other prisoners, now with fresh bruises on his body as well. They all remained in the bathhouse, naked, freezing, until the next morning. As they got up to go back to their barracks Aladár looked around and saw pale, motionless bodies. A few men hadn't survived the night.

They were all obsessed with how much the others ate. Hungry eyes darted from pots to plates, each of them worried about who received more than their share of meat fragments, watery broth, and slabs of old bread. No matter who got what, each of them was always positive that the room elder and his assistants got more. The veteran prisoners, the ones who had survived for years and enjoyed an elevated status in the prison hierarchy, ate very slowly and chewed whatever might be chewable as carefully as possible to extract every fraction of nourishment from the bits of food.

In mid-December Aladár was assigned a new job: making buttonholes in tent canvases. His coworkers included the entire former Ljubljana railway management team, "a group of old Slovenians who dated back to the monarchy." Somehow they were skilled at this kind of work and helped him as if he were a young apprentice in the railroad business. In the freezing weather, without a thimble, he had a hard time pushing the needle through the thick canvas. But every morning the promise of receiving some bread with meat on it provided an incentive for his work.

Then it was Christmas. Even as other days blurred, a few remained uncontaminated by the circumstances—his parents' birthdays, September 18, All Saints' Day. He missed his family with even greater intensity and longed to have some word that they were safe. Only vague information of how the war was progressing had reached the prisoners.

He remembered his Christmas in Dachau as "an exceptionally good day for me." There were some scraps of meat in the stew that was served. One of his Hungarian friends recited poems by the great Hungarian poet Endre Ady, while a few prisoners sang "The Marseillaise." A friend brought him a jar of Maggi, a highly concentrated stock that he added to his soup and smeared on a piece of bread. Suddenly the long-forgotten flavors awoke a cascade of associations to happier, easier, more convivial times that made the whole day somehow benign. One of his friends in the cellblock was a Polish priest; with him he took long meditative walks in the prison yard where they discussed theology and Aladár's desire to convert from the Protestant religion of his father to the Catholicism of his mother. On that "exceptionally good day," this priest gave him a large piece of bread with margarine on it. My father wrote over forty years later, "I am ashamed even today that I did not share it with my fellow sufferers."

Shortly after the New Year, a quarantine was imposed on the camp because of an outbreak of typhus. The disease had appeared earlier, when thousands of new prisoners had arrived from the Eastern Front: some of the concentration camps there had been evacuated, and men and women who were already ill were transferred to Dachau. Typhus is wildly infectious, transmitted by lice or fleas. A louse bites, a prisoner scratches, a small cut develops, and the excrement of the bug works its way into the bloodstream. The infection is rapacious and deadly. Fevers soar, heads split with pain, an awful rash spreads over the body, and usually the victim dies.

The first cases of typhus had been confirmed in Dachau weeks before the New Year, but the medical leadership in the camp refused to establish a quarantine since they did not want the authorities in Berlin and Munich to see Dachau in a lesser light. Typhus was the disease of a lower-order camp, like Bergen-Belsen or Auschwitz, not one that was a steady and reliable source of labor. No one in the leadership wanted to be responsible for compromising the flow of workers to the factories. Instead, they put up posters that were supposed to educate the prisoners that "*eine Laus, dein Tod,*" one louse and you're dead.

On December 21, in an effort to contain an infection that was already beginning to sweep the camp, fourteen hundred "invalids"—prisoners suffering mostly from typhus but from other illnesses as well—were transported from Dachau to Bergen-Belsen, the storage facility for terminal illness. In the next four months, typhus would claim more than thirty thousand prisoners there.

Shortly after Christmas, several members of the SS became ill, and it was no longer possible to maintain the illusion that all was well. Berlin ordered that the camp be put under quarantine, transports were canceled, and morning and evening roll call ceased. Delousing became an obsession among the guards. Aladár learned how to look for lice, even enjoying the discipline of his twice-daily delousing ritual. He realized that delousing had become a diagnostic tool as well. "Those who were unwilling or unable to do it," he wrote, "were lying quietly in their bunks . . . on the road to death."

He awoke to an agonizing headache unlike any he had ever before experienced. Within a day or two, he could no longer stay conscious; at one point he fainted when he went to the toilet. Typhus is named from the Greek word *typhus*, which means "smoky" or "blurred," an apt description of the state of mind of those infected with the disease. Aladár lived in a blur; he lost his precious hat. He vaguely remembered being taken by a Hungarian friend to another cellblock, where a French doctor took his temperature several times. He must have looked so ill that other prisoners assumed he wouldn't survive. An elderly Hungarian kept pressing him for his ration of bread. But Aladár emerged from his fog long enough to firmly refuse.

His Dutch friend Droste, who had given him the sweater, spoke to the kapo in charge of the hospital and asked him to admit Aladár. The kapo agreed on condition that Aladár walk to the hospital on his own two feet. Had he stumbled, fallen, or been unable to manage the two hundred yards from cellblock to infirmary, the guards would have picked up his body and dragged him back to his cellblock, where he would have died. Miraculously, on February 1, he was able to stagger to the prison hospital and arrive in the lobby, where he promptly fainted.

1 9 4 5

And may her bridegroom bring her to a house
Where all's accustomed, ceremonious:
For arrogance and hatred are the wares
Peddled in the thoroughfares,
How but in custom and in ceremony
Are innocence and beauty born?
Ceremony's a name for the rich horn,
And custom for the spreading laurel tree.

—W. B. YEATS, *"A Prayer for My Daughter," June 1919*

CHAPTER 26

The Siege

· ▪ ▪

The Arrow Cross regime, described by historian John Lukacs as comprising "not only fanatics but criminals," embarked on an anti-Semitic reign of terror that rivaled the worst of the Nazis in sheer brutality. The Hungarian gendarmerie were so ruthless that stories circulated of SS officers intervening on behalf of Jews whom they attacked. At the same time, the cool, systematic murder of Hungarian Jewry by Eichmann was given free rein. He and his henchmen finished the job that he had begun in the countryside the previous spring. Everything seemed to be unfolding at warp speed: the advance of the Russians, the extermination of the Jews, the hopeless and sadistic destruction of a once-great European city, all consistent with and a rebuke to Germany's endgame.

Since the railways were no longer running as efficiently as they had, Eichmann dispensed with the transportation technicalities and forced the remaining Jews from the ghetto to march to their death. At a rate of two thousand a day, women carrying babies or pregnant themselves, men who had not been swept up by work brigades or prison, children, the old and the young were forced to march two hundred kilometers to a border checkpoint, where those who survived were presented for work details in various concentration camps. .

An American intelligence report from March 1945, called "Relief and Rescue Work for Jewish Refugees," noted that "12,000 Hungarian Jews were now in Vienna, 16,000 in surrounding districts, besides 8,500 mostly women, who had arrived in mid-January under the worst conditions by foot from Budapest and were transported to Bergenbelsen [*sic*] under bad conditions." Many who survived the journey did so only to be murdered in a concentration camp.

In November the Soviet army moved closer to Budapest. The Germans assured Szálasi that they had no intention of permitting Budapest to fall—they were far too dependent on the factories, especially Csepel, and other natural resources. Stalin had his own reasons for wanting to capture and occupy Budapest, reasons beyond defeating Germany. If Soviet troops took over Budapest, it would be much easier, in the not-so-distant future, to force Hungary under the Soviet sphere of influence. On October 28 Stalin ordered his army to conquer and capture Budapest. As if the only impediment to Nazi victory were attitude, posters appeared on walls in Budapest exhorting citizens in bold letters: PERSEVERE! COURAGE! FIGHT!

Adding to the misery was the weather. The winter of 1944–45 was bitterly cold, and there were shortages of everything—fuel, food, bread, water. Lilly continued to work as a secretary for Victor Oberschall at the Kammer Company. Oberschall was the head of the family where Puppa hid before she escaped. He had previously attempted to bribe the Gestapo to release Aladár and now was just intent on keeping his wife and new baby safe. Lilly was grateful for the job and poured her considerable energies into working for him and caring for her frail and anxious parents.

On December 1 Hitler decided that Budapest was going to be a fortress for the Reich, the ultimate bulwark against the advance of the Soviet army. Meanwhile the Soviet army, replicating Germany's tactics in March 1944, encircled the city. Points of confrontation emerged in what was called the "phony war": a series of skirmishes between German, Hungarian, and Russian soldiers that were more like neighborhood gang fights than battles between trained soldiers. Soldiers actually took public transportation to get to their next encounter, while the citizens of Budapest were often caught in the crossfire. British historian C. A. Macartney wrote that the Soviet army's arrival was so surreal and unexpected that some parents who left Buda in the morning to shop in Pest for Christmas presents for their children could not return home later in the day.

On Christmas Day all public transportation was halted, and the run-ins that had characterized the phony war metastasized into bloodier, more violent combat, still in houses and movie theaters, subways and sewers, cemeteries and city parks, basements and streets. The battlefield was everywhere, in public spaces and intimate rooms. The 1.1 million residents of Budapest were caught in a vise, completely encircled by the Soviet army, while the 80,000 Hungarian and German soldiers in the city refused to surrender.

In the city park, a few blocks away from Lendvay Street and the great houses of the Weiss family, Budapest policemen attempted to fight the Soviet army. The Budapest Zoo, with its 2,500 birds and monkeys and zebras and bears and snakes and giraffes, became a battlefield. "In the confusion of the deadly peril," the zoo director wrote, "large groups of men armed with axes, hatchets, and knives swarmed all over." If the weapons didn't kill the animals, the bitter cold and starvation did. Only the hippos, luxuriating in the warm water, survived.

Rubble and glass from shattered buildings were everywhere, surrounding the corpses of human beings and horses that were now on every street corner. Even now, even when all was lost, the extermination of the Jews continued, and they were led out of the safe houses and shot as they stood by the Danube. The scenes from the apocalypse were varied and surreal as the frozen city became a place of anarchy. Several Catholic priests wearing Nazi armbands over their cassocks murdered patients in a Jewish hospital; bloodred ice floated on the Danube; soldiers fought in a movie theater.

Several bombs hit the Szegedy-Maszák home, and while the damage was not irreparable, the apartments became uninhabitable. Lilly managed to move her parents to one of the cellars in the hills of Buda, which then became flooded. A friend of theirs helped Lilly extinguish fires on the roof of the shelter. Sarolta became seriously ill at the end of the siege with a viral infection called the "Ukrainian disease." Lilly walked to Pest via Csepel Island in an attempt to avoid the marauding Russians to go to a clinic where a family friend admitted her mother. Sarolta recovered sufficiently to go to her cousins in the village of Pomáz, outside the city.

And then on February 11, 1945, the siege was over. What remained of the celebrated German army escaped to the castle district, blowing up the bridges over the Danube, partly in an act of sheer, gratuitous destruction, the final mutilation of an already-vanquished city. The castle district was then bombarded and the victorious Soviet army unleashed itself on the civilian population. The soldiers raped and murdered and robbed and drank with the abandon of juvenile delinquents on a rampage. Primitive pontoon bridges appeared over the Danube. Aladár's cousin Maria Steller told me that once she was walking behind a trio of drunk Russian soldiers who pushed one of their comrades into the freezing river, to his death. That was their sense of what life was worth, she said bitterly.

One war in Hungary was nearly over. Another one was just beginning.

CHAPTER 27

Displaced Persons

There were thirty-three of them, now even closer and more intertwined than they had been in their interlocking compounds on Andrássy Avenue and Lendvay Street. The youngest, Alfons and Erzsi's son János, was only nine, and the oldest was Ferenc Chorin, who celebrated his sixty-seventh birthday in Curia. They worried about the hostages who remained in Vienna. In Portugal Marianne fretted over her son George and his wife, Elsie, and her first grandson, Stevie, whom she barely had an opportunity to know. But Móric's safe return led to a kind of honeymoon between them. All the years of tension disappeared, and they were at last, when they celebrated their belated thirty-first wedding anniversary, a happily married couple.

Erzsi Weiss had never enjoyed a happy marriage with her husband, Alfons, and heartily disliked his entire family. She had availed herself of an extremely independent, even liberated life as a medical doctor and a psychiatrist in Budapest and had never renounced her Judaism. Alfons remained in Vienna as a hostage—they had no news of him. Apparently he gave Becher a letter to send to his family that Becher threw in the trash.

Now that they were far away from the ovens that she had been convinced were their fate, now that she was secure with her two daughters and two sons, she plunged into a serious depression. Replicating their lives in Budapest, albeit on a vastly reduced scale, she decided to live apart from the rest of the family. While the Chorin, Kornfeld, and Weiss families lived in a hotel on a hill, she and her four children settled into a pension in the valley. Soon little János was enrolled in a military school, and Marika was enrolled in a Catholic Dominican school in Coimbra, not far from the rest of the family.

To Hanna's worries about her uncle and cousins and brother must be added her very lonely anguish about Aladár. She knew that he had been arrested, but that was her last point of certainty. She carried her well-worn collection of his letters like talismans. Each one contained powerful reminders of the world that had once so securely anchored her: the tranquillity of Ireg, the secret drives into the countryside, the absolutely inconsequential spats and disagreements, and the unforgettable moments of sweetness. Some days she imagined that he would survive and they would be together when the war was over. Other days she knew that he had died alone at the hands of the Germans and could not fathom what life would be like once this was confirmed.

The family was guarded around the clock and they were not permitted to travel beyond a two-kilometer radius. If a toothache struck or a doctor's appointment was necessary, they had to get permission to visit Coimbra, the nearest city, about a forty-five-minute train ride away, and had to check in with the police there. That is not to say that they suffered under house arrest. To live in Curia in the summer was to enjoy some of the nicest aspects of Portuguese hospitality. Still, during a few awkward days, a large group of Germans who were being repatriated from Argentina were temporarily domiciled in the same hotel and entertained anyone within the two-kilometer radius with robust interpretations of Nazi songs.

The family celebrated a grateful Christmas in Curia, and in January 1945 they were told that their assignment there had been canceled, and they were free to move to Lisbon or anywhere else in Portugal. However, they were still required to report to the police station once a month. Most of the family decided to remain in Curia for a while longer, but Tom decided to move to Lisbon and stay with a Hungarian friend. He was determined to finish his medical education and became an assistant in the physiology lab at the medical school. He and his cousin Márta Weiss applied for American visas.

Eventually the family left Curia and moved first to Lisbon and then to Estoril, a beautiful resort by the Tagus estuary, where they met the

Gábor family. Back in Budapest, the Gábors had been a nice, socially aggressive Jewish family with a matriarch whose ambitions were limitless. Her daughters Zsa Zsa and Éva had already fled to Hollywood, where they joined some other Hungarian Jewish émigrés in the movie business. Zsa Zsa went on to marry Conrad Hilton, the hotel magnate. But the eldest daughter, Magda—whom the Kornfeld, Weiss, and Chorin families agreed was the nicest one of the lot—stayed behind and enjoyed a pleasant romance with the last Portuguese minister to Hungary, Sampaio Garrido.

Garrido had left Hungary as soon as the Nazis took over and returned home to his wife and many children and grandchildren. As reports reached him about the siege in Hungary, he grew concerned about his former love and her parents. In January 1945 he arranged for the Gábor family to come to Estoril. Lest this trio of Hungarian Jews raise any untoward suspicions about his relationship to them, Garrido arranged for the thirty-two members of the Weiss family to join them there.

Jolie Gábor, the matriarch, would complain to Marianne that she had not slept with her husband for the last twenty years and now was stuck sharing a room with him. Looking at the modest and aristocratic girls of the younger generation—Hanna, Puppa, and their cousins—Jolie would shake her head sadly at all the wasted youth and virginity and assure Marianne that if she would permit her to tutor these girls for a month, "they would be married within a week."

One night Ferenc was awakened by an emergency call from the Gábors. Jolie was dying. Whatever felled her came on suddenly, and the end was near. Her last wish was to bid adieu to one of the richest and most powerful men that Hungary had once known. Ferenc ventured into her room, from which she had managed to jettison her husband. There she lay, wan and appealing against the sheets. "Dear little Feri," she said, "I am dying, and I have my shabbiest nightgown on." Whether this was an invitation to remove it or provide her with the means for a nicer nightgown was never to be known since Ferenc immediately returned to his bedroom. The next morning Mama Gábor was miraculously much improved.

Their natural sense of order and discipline almost immediately asserted itself in the Weiss family, as did the need to start making some money. This was not so easy because no one had a work permit. The female cousins did various odd jobs: babysitting, knitting, doing embroidery, teaching languages to the children of affluent Portuguese families. Some of the cousins studied Russian in preparation for their return to Hungary. Memi Mauthner taught French, while her sister taught English. All the cousins were occupied with some means to bring in a few escudos.

In the spring of 1945, a tennis tournament took place at the hotel. Some of the cousins, like Márta and her brother Gábor Weiss, were accomplished tennis players and joined in the fun. Other cousins were better at the socializing and dancing that took place after the tournament. The cacophony of nationalities was impressive—Portuguese, French, German, Spanish, and a few Slavs in the mix. "All of Estoril was full of refugees," Hanna would later recall, "but very, very good society." The son of the deposed king of Spain was there, and eventually would share whiskey sours with Puppa in the afternoons at a bar near the beach.

One of the men who played tennis was a Catalan painter named Luis Alsina. He had fled from Franco's Spain and had been living in Portugal for a number of years. Márta and young Daisy met him on the tennis court, and both were struck by how much he reminded them of János Zwack, Puppa's great love, who had remained in Budapest. Something about the angularity of his face, the way he held his cigarette, a certain meticulous quality in his bearing impressed them. Eventually Luis and Puppa met and soon became romantically involved.

The intelligence services of the United States and Great Britain were, if not preoccupied with, still extremely interested in the family. The Ministry of Economic Warfare in London tracked the flow of their assets. Chorin had been in touch with Jacques Kanitz, a cousin who lived in Switzerland and was managing some of their affairs there. Kanitz informed the British consulate in Bern of what was going on and received guidance from them as to the transfer of assets from Switzerland to Portugal and back again.

Edith Weiss, who had been so active in the Red Cross, visited a delegate of the International Red Cross in Lisbon. He sent a letter to Geneva in which he wrote, "This lady is very interested to know the actual situation in Hungary and would be willing to return to her homeland and resume her former activities." He attached a letter that Edith had written to the head of the Red Cross.

Dear Colonel,

*Up to the time of German occupation I have worked in the Jewish
Bureau of Assistance. I was especially occupied with the problems concerning refugees, their placement, liberation out of internment camps,
the placement of children etc. My nieces Anna de Mauthner and Baroness Hanna Kornfeld worked for years at the Union International
Save the Children in administrative work in Hungarian, German,
English and French. . . . We had to leave our homeland and are refugees ourselves here in Portugal. For months we have not had any news
from home. We would love to know what happened to our former coworkers and to the institutions we had ties to. . . . I would also like to
know if the CICR has the intention to send a commission to our so
cruelly hit country and to make an investigation and to help. I would
be happy, if given a chance, to join that commission. There is nothing
I wish more fervently than to be able to work again—preferring to do
so in my own homeland.*

She had no answer to the letter. The family waited. Edith, who had
always managed somehow to get things done even when circumstances
seemed impossible, was suffocated by her impotence. Her migraines returned. Her mood deteriorated. She had become one of the displaced
people she had so often tried to help.

On January 2, 1945, after describing some of the news about the siege
in Budapest, Hanna wrote in her journal, "We have settled back into our
previous lives." The observation was borne out for the next six months,
as she jotted down daily activities: morning excursions, visits to various
relatives or friends for lunch or dinner or tea, bridge in the evening, mass
on Sunday. While the melody was her quotidian life, the counterpoint
was the stuff of headlines and history books: "The Russians advance
strongly." "Warsaw falls." "Armistice is signed." "Pouring rain." "Mami
felt her appendix but thank God it was nothing." "Turks declared war on
Germany." "Go to dentist." "Allies cross the Rhine."

CHAPTER 28

The Day of Deliverance

Dachau had turned into a floating island, and Aladár was one of the passengers. The island was destined to float to Switzerland, where he would say goodbye to his fellow passengers, then disembark and luxuriate in the freedom and the neutrality. Sometimes castles appeared, two of them, on opposite sides of a verdant Bavarian valley—or perhaps it was a Hungarian valley—and he would stand between them, trying to decide whether to stay in the castle on the right or the castle on the left.

For days Aladár hallucinated as he lay in Dachau's hospital. As he turned onto his right side, he entered the castle on the right; when he rolled over, he entered the castle on his left.

His doctor friend Jan Droste was determined to keep him alive. They had first met when Aladár was involved in the medical experiments and Droste was one of the doctors who took his blood. After three years Droste was a seasoned veteran of the camps, and somehow was one of those people whom others recognized as a figure of authority. Even SS doctors would sometimes turn to him for advice. The threadbare sweater and woolen cap Droste gave Aladár were gifts of immeasurable value during that punishing winter but that were lost in the delirium of his fevers. After he collapsed at the hospital entrance, Aladár was roused to appear before the hospital board, a panel consisting of prisoners who were also doctors. Somehow he managed to answer their questions, and the panel diagnosed typhus. Once on the wards, he went into a coma for several days.

"You are now saved," announced a man in a white coat. His eyes still closed, Aladár left whatever castle or island or other surrealistic place he then occupied. He sensed that he was lying in a real bed and was surrounded by others, also lying in beds. He was actually alive. He was weak. He was, as he wrote later, "apathetic and anorexic" and not consistently clear about his whereabouts. At one point he apologized to a doctor for the bad timing of his illness but assured him that he would be ready to leave soon.

In one of the few observations he would share about Dachau, Aladár said later that if he hadn't gotten typhus, he would never have survived. Droste and a Harvard-trained, English-speaking Slovenian doctor were determined that he should live. When he refused to eat, or could not eat, or simply did not eat, Droste managed to make a plate of sandwiches with cheese, hard-boiled eggs, and even a bit of anchovy paste to stimulate his appetite. Aladár was stunned at the luxury but still could only pick at the feast. He was given two blood transfusions, one from a Dutch dockworker. The fevers and the dehydration had made his pulse erratic, and his Slovenian doctor managed to find a glucose solution that he administered to him regularly over two or three weeks.

But psychologically Aladár had run out of reserves. During the early months of 1945, he was in a concentration camp hospital. The German army was nearing its defeat, supplies everywhere were running low, the winter was freezing, and the influx of prisoners from other camps and from the Eastern Front brought harrowing overcrowding and terrible illness. Except for the doctors and nurses and other hospital staff, everywhere you looked, you saw nearly unendurable suffering.

He tried to nurture a small bit of optimism that perhaps Hungary had pulled out of the fight. He hoped that it had capitulated or found a way out and would so be spared combat. One afternoon, when he was in the toilet, he heard several inmates singing a Hungarian military song. Stunned, he realized that he had completely deluded himself. The Hungarians hadn't laid down their arms and abandoned the Germans. Far from it—they were still allies. All his hopes had been futile. He was crushed.

After gaining a bit of strength, Aladár was moved to a different ward, where there was less medical supervision, perhaps because the patients were nearly all suffering the final days, or weeks, of starvation. These prisoners came to the hospital, Aladár wrote, "as skin-covered skeletons, having lost most of their human traits. They were in a daze with a vacant wandering stare, giving the impression that they did not know where they were or what was happening. They were incontinent, soiling their bed. They were then taken to the toilet, where they threw water over them but did not really clean them." After months and years of starvation, they now suffered from a kind of malignant diarrhea that the prisoners called *Scheisserei*, which can only be translated as "shittiness."

They would only last a few days in this condition, but their final days were wretched—no longer able to leave their beds, they would initially cry out loud and then quietly complain until, in a diminuendo, the moans rattled in their throats, any strength that remained expended by thrashing. The cacophony of sound slowly evolved into a scale of agony, which indicated how close to death they were. Aladár wrote:

> Observing the process made me forget that in every case it was a human being that perished and suffered an undignified death. It bothered me more that the noise kept me from sleeping, consoling my protesting conscience with the thought that it would be better if a rapid death would put an end to their hopeless suffering. In other words, I became used to the fact that human beings were dying all around me. I became an expert in the agony of death.

The ward was crowded, and once, to Aladár's horror, the doctors were going to double up the beds and make him share a bed with one of these men. Fortunately, he was spared. To share a bed, all day, with one of these men would have been more than he could bear. The propinquity of death began to terrify him. Nothing frightened him more than the thought that he would become one of those men, writhing and moaning on a cot, hours away from death. The suffering, the lack of dignity—could this be his future, too?

He became so weak and depressed that he stopped washing himself in the mornings. Dirty and disconsolate, he muttered in German that he was giving up, the end was near. But a French nurse, who worked for a risqué Parisian weekly called *Vie Parisienne*, would not let him give up and, in a hectoring but kind way, forced him to keep himself clean and disciplined. Droste made him some bitter teas that also helped a bit. But in retrospect, what really saved him was a friendship.

François Fauré, a French member of the de Gaulle underground, ended up in the cot next to Aladár, and the two men began talking. When life was normal, Fauré had been an architect from a distinguished French family of intellectuals. When the war began, he had joined the de Gaulle information service and often went to London. He was dropped behind enemy lines by parachute to gain information, and several times he managed to complete his mission without being caught.

Inevitably his luck ran out. After his arrest he was taken to one of the most horrible concentration camps, a quarry in Alsace-Lorraine called Natzweiler-Struthof, run by criminals who subjected prisoners to beatings and torture and medical experiments with mustard gas—that toxic relic from the First World War. Every morning they worked at the quarry, and even those who were too sick or weak to move were carried there and left to lie there all day. In the evening, dead or alive, they were carried back to camp. Many prisoners committed suicide, while others were pushed into the quarry by sadistic kapos. When that camp was disbanded, Fauré was transported to Dachau.

For some reason French prisoners received Red Cross parcels that were a virtual piñata of fantasy foods—chocolate, fruit, sardines, cheese, dried fruit. Fauré shared his portion with Aladár and others on the ward as if they were family. Unable to move around freely, confined to their beds, surrounded by the sick and dying, unaware of much that was going on outside the hospital or the barbed-wire walls, during that February and March 1945 their friendship deepened.

My father retained his French from his student days at the École Libre des Sciences Politiques, so they could exchange more intimate details and worries: Aladár about Hanna and his family; Fauré about his son, who during the war enjoyed a thriving black market business—not a career with much of a future after the war was over. Fauré spoke tenderly about his wife and his mistress, both of whom offered him quite different forms of succor. (Curiously, the mistress provided the intellectual stimulation.) Aladár confided his hopes to one day have a small country house in Badacsony, and Fauré drew him a plan for the house. A country house for him and Hanna, not far from Ireg but very modest, of course—a perfect place for them to take the children they hoped to have. His sisters, Lilly and Musi, and his parents could visit. They could spend a few weeks in the summer there, all together.

When he later wrote about what Fauré did for him, he was grateful for the food and respectful of the person. But the conversations with this civilized man not only changed his grim assessment of the French; they gave him the chance to think about a future. It was a very real talking cure. Fauré was discharged before Aladár and as a parting gift gave him a pair of boots.

Aladár's kidneys were giving out, and he developed a high fever and even more bowel problems. He was transferred to another ward, and his temperature shot up to 103. A Catalan Trotskyite doctor took care of him and suspected that he had a serious kidney infection. Aladár felt wretched and could not eat or drink much. He lay in bed and prayed, and while he knew that the end of the war was very near, he worried that he would die before the gates of the camp were opened.

His illness both psychologically and logistically insulated him from the chaos in Dachau as the war neared its end. He collected fragments of information: Roosevelt had died. Buchenwald had been liberated by the Americans. He didn't know that Hitler had told Himmler to be sure that no other camp could be liberated. Himmler decided that the way to avoid that was to murder all the prisoners and then destroy as much evidence as possible. One plan suggested that as the Americans approached, the thirty thousand prisoners in Dachau should be shot. Another plan called for them to be bombed by German planes. Still another proposed that they be poisoned.

On April 26, as American troops neared Dachau, the SS started to organize the prisoners for evacuation by nationality. Germans and Russians were the first groups to leave—about seven thousand men gathered for a long march to an unknown destination. They left in the middle of the night but didn't get far. Prisoners from other camps were arriving in Dachau, adding to the general confusion. The atmosphere was thick with anticipation that the Americans and liberation were only moments away. But another day passed. The Red Cross arrived and promised to deliver food to the camp. A committee of twelve prisoners, told about this, decided that the food should not be distributed until after the Americans came. No one wanted to share it with the SS.

Another day passed.

On Saturday morning, April 28, the air raid sirens wailed; the enemy was approaching, but the enemy was now the liberators. Again they waited, and again nothing happened. Rumors festered that the SS hierarchy were sneaking away, and the committee of prisoners was going to be in charge of the thirty thousand inmates of the camp. My father heard that white flags were now fluttering in place of the Nazi flags and that many of the SS had departed peacefully. But in the watchtowers, SS guards remained. When the Americans were spotted, those in the watch towers opened fire. One Polish prisoner raced to the gates and was officially the last man murdered in Dachau. Finally, at around three in the afternoon, three American tanks appeared at the gates.

Aladár heard that the guards in the SS towers had been killed and that the Americans caught about 150 other SS men, whom they lined up against the wall and shot. There was a prisoner uprising, and Aladár's former Armenian block elder died. The sudden change, what he called the "decompression," caused many deaths. The kitchen was ransacked, and much of the SS food supply was stolen. The Americans were not prepared to feed the inmates, and the Red Cross supplies did not last long. During the first week the Americans managed to maintain some order and distributed the SS canned meat, warning everyone that eating too much would be dangerous. During the following week, more prisoners died from overeating than had died from the typhus epidemic. In the latrines the stinking mess was several inches deep.

Aladár was moved to the former SS hospital. One of his "fellow sufferers" claimed that he had spent several days in an "El Dorado staffed by nurses," which was the American hospital, and there was orange juice and soups and chocolate. Aladár wondered if he hadn't just imagined it all. An elderly Polish doctor in street clothes was in charge, assisted by a German prisoner-of-war doctor, and they disagreed about how to treat Aladár's kidney disease. The Polish doctor prescribed limiting food and liquids; the German doctor urged more fluids. Former prisoners, now patients, shared their disappointment in the Americans. "This was the first time after the war that I encountered the evanescence of American hopes," Aladár wrote. "It was partly our fault for irrationally and unrealistically magnifying our hopes instead of rationally and realistically reducing them."

Gradually he regained his strength. His friend Gyuri Pallavicini represented the Hungarian prisoners committee and asked that Aladár be released from the hospital so that he could take over the job and Pallavicini could leave. With some reservations, the Americans agreed.

IN THE SAME BAG where I found my mother's yellow star were three crumpled pieces of brittle yellowed paper. Two were no bigger than index cards, while the third was double the size. Nothing indicated their importance. On the large piece of paper was typewritten, in English:

I held these documents with a kind of reverence. How indifferently they had been tucked away. In a way they were a perfect metaphor for the way that, in this cathedral to the past that was Patterson Street, my parents had had to protect the bits and pieces that were theirs alone, distinct from the grand legends. In protecting them, they concealed them from our sight and left them to crumble with time and neglect.

My father had no passport, no visas, no *carte d'identité*. These scraps of paper, at one time, were all that constituted his official existence.

Aladár took over the Hungarian prisoners committee, which in May 1945 consisted of two priests, two medical doctors, and a Csepel machinist who had finished high school and had been an active leader of a small but ardent group of Communists when he was arrested. As president,

Aladár was responsible for the repatriation of the several hundred Hungarians who were once Dachau inmates. Figuring out how to get them back to Hungary and provide them with the basics of food and clothing, not to mention identification, was a huge job.

A "pleasant, social democrat know-it-all" named Gerő published a little newspaper. But the *only* organized group after liberation were the Communists, and because they were organized, they enjoyed much greater influence in the camp than their actual numbers would have justified. When something concrete had to be done, the collective took care of it, especially if there was money to be made. Money wasn't the only incentive; the Communists decided that if someone did useful work, they got larger servings of food. Aladár opposed this principle but confessed that he took advantage of it because he was hungry.

From May until the beginning of August, Aladár lived in the netherworld between imprisonment and freedom. He slept most nights in Dachau, sharing a room with other leaders of the Hungarian prisoners committee. All around him he saw the effects of "decompression," the behavior of people who had once been "compressed" by imprisonment—what we would call PTSD today. The trauma of imprisonment was complicated by the other trauma of liberation. The prisoners were recovering physically—gaining weight and getting stronger. Aladár also saw evidence of the psychological damage. When the American commander of the camp asked the prisoners committees to clean up their living areas, the Hungarian committee recruited about sixty people to help out. They formed a long line to pick up the trash, but less than an hour later only the committee organizers remained.

After the Russian prisoners were taken away, the biggest building became vacant, and Colonel Roy, the American commander, offered it to the Hungarians, provided that they cleaned it up. It seemed like an ideal opportunity for larger space, and Aladár went with a few others from the committee to evaluate it. Even a year in the concentration camp had not prepared them for what they saw. Pillows had been ripped open, and white down feathers were everywhere. Every sheet and blanket had been ripped into pieces. Long frayed pieces of what men once coveted for warmth were now filthy and scattered. Every piece of furniture was broken, the legs from chairs snapped in two, tabletops smashed. And all of it—the feathers, the blankets, the floors, the furniture—was covered with shit. It was impossible to clean up, impossible to know where to begin. The job was finally, fittingly, given to the SS prisoners, but after it was cleaned, the Hungarians never got the building.

When Aladár wrote about this time of decompression, the images are as impressionistic as a dream. An American congressman toured Dachau and refused to believe any stories about crematoria, or Auschwitz, or the torture and unspeakable brutality. A handsome blond American, Captain Heinz, walked around Dachau with a riding crop, surveying his new domain. My father observed that the difference between SS Dachau and GI Dachau could be illustrated by the difference between the smoke from the crematoria and the smoke from American cigarettes. A young American military rabbi attempted to sequester all the Jewish prisoners and keep them in a separate area. A Hungarian Jewish friend of Aladár's told him that if this became mandatory, he would immediately get baptized.

Some shirts that were supposed to be distributed as part of an aid parcel were stolen. After a few days the thief was caught, although he denied everything. He was given a few powerful slaps, then confessed. Aladár reminded the interrogators that this was just the kind of behavior they had loathed under the Nazis. They agreed but replied that the man would never have confessed if they had not hit him. When bedbugs or fleas or lice appeared, GIs holding dust blowers were positioned throughout the camp. Every time someone passed them, the soldiers sprayed DDT under their shirts and down their pants.

Later on, to his horror, Aladár got scabies, "perhaps the most humiliating event of the period after my liberation." Scabies had always been associated with "dirt, the complete absence of cleanliness, and a sort of moral disintegration." He got some tar ointment and covered himself with it from his neck to his feet. He left it on for two days, then stood under a warm shower, soaping himself over and over. He thought they were gone, but then he got scabies again and had to repeat the treatment. This time it worked, but he was haunted by fear of scabies for months afterward.

On July 4 all the prisoners gathered, and Aladár gave a speech about the signing of the Declaration of Independence, the beginning of modern democracy.

And so the months after liberation passed.

Dachau is practically a suburb of Munich, so Aladár occasionally went into the city on some official activity or another. He visited the former Hungarian consulate, where a young man who had served in Berlin was in charge. He lent Aladár some money but was arrested by the Americans before my father could repay him. Once Aladár was stopped by some American soldiers because he was wearing an old SS jacket. At the Hungarian consulate Aladár met a pretty young woman officer who was shocked that a "gentleman" like my father would have been put in a concentration camp by the Nazis.

Slowly he gained some weight and physically recovered. Emotionally he continued to live in the cocoon of the camp and not in the real world. He still felt the lingering effects of his illness, of the coma, and he still didn't know if his parents or sisters were alive. As he thought about it, he was amazed at how passive he had become, how strangely detached, almost indifferent. He did what was required and even took some small initiatives within the narrow constraints of what was possible, but on a deep level he felt that his life progressed on the path set by circumstances rather than with any volition. He lived "very much like my time in the hospital when I became an expert on death among the dying. This approach makes life easier, but it is also frightening since it shows a degree of adaptability of which we saw many frightening and revolting examples during the war. At any rate, I wanted to go home to see my mother and father. But then I had my doubts. I wondered for what purpose I should be going home."

CHAPTER 29

Broken and Without a Job

■ ■
■

After the war in Europe ended on May 8, 1945, the OSS section in charge of Hungary started to look for my father. Because of his efforts to reach out to the Allies, they saw him as one of the potential leaders in postwar Hungary. On July 19 Zsolt Aradi, who had been the press attaché at the Hungarian legation at the Vatican, appeared at Dachau wearing an American uniform. He brought a stack of Hungarian papers with him, and the Hungarians who remained there because of illness or inertia or some job in the camp, or some difficulty with paperwork, eagerly devoured the news. The Communists in the group joyfully acknowledged every acquaintance whose name appeared in the stories.

Aradi told Aladár that Márton Himler, one of the leaders of the Hungarian section of the OSS, wanted to see him in Salzburg. Budapest, he reported, had been nearly destroyed by the fighting between the Germans and the Russians. The bridges, the electricity, the food supply, over half of its factories, and 40 percent of the railways had been destroyed. Aradi didn't need to explain that the fighting had nearly wiped out the political and intellectual infrastructure as well. Many of the leading members of the intelligentsia and the democratic opposition to Nazism had been arrested and tortured and either died in prison, or were murdered en route; the seeds of freedom landed on rather shallow soil. As the Americans surveyed the country—the dominance of the Soviet occupiers did not make that easy—they realized that they had to find some of the former political and intellectual leaders and restore them to leadership positions so that they could influence the future of the country.

More than 900,000 Hungarians—including 650,000 Jews—had died in the war. Another 600,000 Hungarians were captured by the Soviets, and while most of them were in the military, 120,000 were civilians. Of the group taken prisoner by the Soviets, 300,000 never returned to Hungary. Over 1.2 million people out of a total population of 11 million were gone. It was as if another Trianon had occurred, with the added dimension of a physically ruined capital. The Russian victors and liberators staked their claim on the country, but the Hungarians' already-low opinion of the Soviets sank even lower after marauding soldiers finished raping, pillaging, and plundering the capital and the countryside.

On the other hand, as Aladár could see even in the prisoners committee at Dachau, the Communists in Hungary were well organized, and possessed greater influence than their numbers would deserve. Aradi told them that a new provisional government had been formed and that one of its first acts had been to enact radical land reform. The large estates once owned by people like the Weisses and the Chorins were nationalized and broken into smaller holdings, the smallest of which were distributed to previously landless peasants. Aradi got Aladár a pass, and together they got into his jeep to drive the 110 miles to Salzburg, where he would meet with some of the OSS leaders.

This fragile Hungarian coalition government consisted of members of the Smallholders Party, by far the most popular of the parties, the Social Democrats, and the Communists. But the Communists recruited as many people as possible, including some former Arrow Cross goons, who eagerly exchanged their black swastikas for red stars. Their ideology was neither left nor right but the starkly nonpartisan quest for power and domination. Democracy had no robust tradition in Hungary, yet it certainly was not a country predisposed to Communism. Those who remembered Béla Kun's brief reign of terror after World War I were loath to replicate it. In the postsiege chaos and power vacuum, nearly anything could happen and did. One consequence was that many Hungarians—former prisoners like Aladár and refugees like the Weiss family—were afraid to return to Hungary.

Yet the Americans and others knew that Hungary desperately needed people who could offer stability and professionalism and who could communicate to the war-weary citizens that after one oppressive regime had been defeated, another one did not have to take its place.

When my father arrived in Salzburg, he was immediately taken to meet with Márton Himler. Himler worked with a few Hungarian officers and some noncommissioned officers. Aladár met the commander of the group, Lt. Col. Gillmore Flues, whom he described as "an extremely pleasant lawyer from Toledo who had a good fund of political information and who had some connections to Hungarians in the United States." They became friends for life.

Salzburg had become a Mecca for Hungarians who were unwilling to return to Hungary but were ambivalent about where they were ultimately going to end up. Aladár met old friends, including Hanna's brother George, who had left Vienna with Elsie and their son, Stevie, as soon as the Russians approached. It was only then that he learned about the deal and that Hanna was safe in Portugal. What did he think of this deal? What did he feel? Was the distance, the not knowing, excruciating or comforting because of her safety?

During a long conversation, in which Himler described the overwhelming Russian influence, Aladár asked him if it made any sense at all for him to return to Hungary, since under these circumstances it was not likely to pursue an independent foreign policy. Quite the reverse, Himler responded—Hungary needed people who were knowledgeable in foreign policy more than ever. At the end of July Aladár returned to Dachau, where he was told that an American captain, Muller, from Munich had been asking for him. He had orders to take Aladár to Paris, orders from the chief of U.S. intelligence in Paris, General Betz.

This did not suit Aladár's plans at all, since his trip to Salzburg had shaken off a bit of the torpor that had surrounded him and he was eager to return to Budapest. But he had no choice. "When the jeep came on August 2, I climbed in like a good boy and got out in the intact villa with a large garden of the OSS," he wrote. The next day he flew to Paris with Muller and two young French women who had attached themselves to Muller in Paris for household work and complained during the whole trip that the captain, who had been born in Switzerland, was too lenient with the Germans. Aladár was shocked when they were taken to a two-bedroom suite in the Hotel Bristol on the Rue de Rivoli; during his student days he had seen the elegant facade as the ultimate symbol of the unattainable.

Once ensconced in his luxurious room in Paris, he took out a fountain pen and scrawled at the top of the page, "Parizs augusztus 3." Having been liberated for just over three months, his penmanship was shaky, and the words seemed to cascade downhill on the page. The letter began:

My dear Hancsi,

This is the first opportunity to write you, to ask you: do you still love me and to tell you that I love you. In my case, there is no change, and I wish that you would be my wife as soon as possible. That is, unfortunately, one thing that did change. I became a bit worn out, physically and maybe even emotionally. I had typhus, myocarditis, prison diarrhea, and nephritis. I almost perished, but I had a Dutch medical doctor friend who saved me at the last minute. Now I am in general okay, but I still move around with difficulty and have to watch my heart. This is the physical part. The emotional one, of course, I cannot judge myself, but sometimes I feel as if I have problems there too. I am even more indecisive and helpless than before. Consequently, I feel that it is irresponsible to want to tie your fate to mine, yet broken and without a job, I am asking you to be my wife.

On the back and front of each page, and on the back of the fourth page, his writing even crawling up the margin, he wrote about the uncertainty of his situation. He described the prisoners committee and his presidency of it, the utterly disorganized approach to dealing with the prisoners, and his confusion about what would actually happen to him. He described meeting her brother George in Salzburg—"he looks well, a little skinnier, but in good spirits and sprightly"—and their discussion about family affairs. Could they all return to Hungary? What should Móric do? He was writing to her from Paris but had no idea why he was there. He told her that he was staying at a lovely hotel, even as he remembered that "in Dachau, in the winter, I was totally infested with lice and we slept three in a bed. You can imagine that it is very enjoyable for me to show off, and in my only but ill-fitting civilian suit and borrowed underwear, what a distinguished figure I must cut."

Several pages into the letter, he returned to the days after March 19 and asked her forgiveness for having been "so cowardly that I walked out on you and did not come to see you. I was in a horrible state of mind. I was watched, and I expected to be arrested. This, of course, is not an excuse, only a mitigating circumstance, because nothing can excuse that I left you. But I have been punished a little, and maybe I can atone by never leaving you again. Supposing, of course, that you want this too. Think about this profoundly, my Hancsi, because we will not have an easy life. I may have to repeat, in a different direction, the path that I have taken since April 14, with the only difference that I cannot get typhus anymore because you can only get it once."

All he wanted was "to go home and to live at home. I know that this will not be easy or very comfortable, but I cannot imagine things otherwise. For emigration I have neither the desire, nor talent, nor a material basis. I am forty-two years old, and at this time, even at home, it will be difficult to start a new life; abroad it would be even more difficult, even hopeless." He kept returning to his confusion about being in Paris and the frustration of having "X or Y who wants to talk to me, wants to 'help me.'" On top of this, he had no identification, so he was imprisoned in his very nice hotel room: "You know, I am still the old helpless guy who can only live under legal conditions." He finished the letter expressing his "terrible impatience to know when we can finally and definitely get together. God bless you! Innumerable kisses and hand kisses, Aladár."

I have no idea how my mother got the letter. I remember asking her once when she had heard from him, and she told me that he "wrote from Paris somehow. I don't know." What an anodyne, passionless, boring thing to say! I thought. I figured she was talking about a telegram. "Am Alive. Stop. Love. Aladár."

But even then . . .

"He wrote from Paris somehow. I don't know." How could she not know? She hadn't heard from this man for over a year. She hadn't known if the love of her life was dead or alive.

Maybe the evening after I asked her, she went upstairs, and safe in their bedroom, away from her intrusive daughter, she pulled out the drawer of her bedside table, and took out the letter to reread it. I will never know. But when she was dead, I found this letter in the drawer that contained the others. There was no envelope to reveal whether it had been mailed or hand-delivered by someone they both knew who was going to Estoril.

"Consequently, I feel that it is irresponsible to want to tie your fate to mine, yet broken and without a job, I am asking you to be my wife."

Yes. The answer was yes.

The Ice of Mistrust

■　　　■

After the German defeat, the family in Portugal could at last think about the future in ways that were not entirely theoretical. Communicating from a functioning country to a ravaged one had never been so difficult, especially since the old addresses were no longer reliable. Who knew if a building was still occupied by those who lived there before the war, or if it was even still standing? In many cases, an old-fashioned courier system was used, where friends took letters from other friends or friends of friends who might be traveling to France or Switzerland or Austria or Hungary.

Through this sophisticated grapevine, somehow, the family in Portugal heard that all of the hostages had survived and were healthy. This was an enormous relief for Móric and Marianne, who were unhappily preoccupied by the new romance in Puppa's life. She and Luis Alsina were deeply involved in an affair, much to the dismay of her parents, who would refer to him in letters not by his name, but as "the painter."

The family's version of the "decompression" that Aladár observed among liberated prisoners was that their congenital indecisiveness became even more pronounced. Where should they go? Switzerland? America? Some of the younger members of the family, like Tom and Márta, were keen to go to the United States. Tom was twenty-one years old, still had his medical studies to complete, and figured that he could finish medical school there. After all that had happened, Hungary held no appeal for many of the young people. Indeed, Tom would not return for almost forty years.

Others wanted to return to Hungary, perhaps deluded about what awaited them there—comfort, ease, and familiar if not equally prosperous or influential circumstances. If life were literature, or if they had been Italians, they would have stayed for a while in exile and then returned home, in much-reduced circumstances, and played a role in the reconstruction of their country, commensurate with their previous social stature.

But Budapest offered no such haven. Hungary was in a terrible state, in total physical devastation—the Red Army had left a mess similar to the one they had left in the Dachau barracks and that was on top of the destruction by the Germans during the siege. A State Department brief about the situation in Hungary in the spring of 1945 painted a grim picture. British and American members of the Allied Control Commission visited Hungary and "raised hopes that the Soviet pressures would be relaxed," according to a State Department report.

> The main topics were inevitably the activities of the Red Army soldiers and the Communist Party. The cattle had almost totally disappeared from the countryside, driven off by the Russians; the peasants' homes had been stripped by bands of foraging soldiers and their daughters raped; the foodstuffs the government sent for relief of starving Budapest disappeared on the way and were later found to have been diverted by the local Red Army division commanders; . . . every movable object of value from watches and clothes to furniture and motorcars had been seized.

The political and social situation in Hungary was impossibly complicated. On the one hand, the Soviets had relinquished some control in a coalition government, but the Communists were well organized and supported by the Soviet Union. Since the time of Béla Kun, the Communist Party had been associated with Jews, and certainly a number of the leaders of the Hungarian Communist Party in 1945 were in fact Jews, who channeled some of their rage at the Nazis and the Arrow Cross regime into Hungarian political life.

Ferenc Chorin was in a terrible position. In Hungary he was seen not only as an extremely conservative ally of Horthy but as a Jewish capitalist and industrialist who had saved his and his family's collective and individual skins by selling the crown jewel of Hungarian industry to the

Nazis *and* living in luxury on the sunny beaches of Portugal while Budapest burned. He could become a lightning rod for all sorts of free-floating Hungarian resentment and rage, either as a Quisling or as a Jew, as someone too close to the ancien régime of Horthy, or as a selfish capitalist whose deal was almost indecent given what Hungarian Jews had suffered.

Was it possible somehow to set the record straight? To communicate at least to the Allies that Chorin and Kornfeld and the others had hardly had a choice in the matter; that not only had their backs been against the wall but they too had suffered at the hands of the Nazis?

The British ambassador to Portugal, Sir Owen O'Malley, had been the British ambassador to Budapest before the war. Marianne and Lady O'Malley—a writer who wrote under the name Ann Bridge—would sometimes meet for tea. Lady O'Malley was gracious and warm, in contrast to her husband's rather chilly Foreign Office persona. Years later, every once in a while, my mother or my aunt or my grandmother would fondly mention Lady O'Malley, recalling her with affection.

The women had their domain, and the men occupied theirs. Ferenc and Móric trusted and felt a kind of kinship with Sir Owen. He had hunted with them at Derekegyháza and had dined with them on Lendvay Street. He had known them before they were tainted refugees, when they were at the center of politics, business, and culture in Hungary. That meant something to them, if not to him.

In the declassified papers of the British Public Records Office was a file: "1945, HUNGARY, *M Kornfeld and F Chorin: possible source of information on course of events in Hungary.* Enclosed letter from Kornfeld and Chorin, Hungarian Jews, states the facts about their pro-Allied leanings and their treatment at the hands of the Nazis. Suggest that these two men, if handled carefully, could be successfully used to add to information already known about the course of events in Hungary."

The last third of the nine-page report consisted of an earnest, obsequious letter that Móric and Ferenc had written to O'Malley on April 23, 1945. They hoped an endorsement from him could erase the unfavorable regard that the deal had created. O'Malley knew of their long-standing pro-British sympathies, and thus they were alarmed by the propaganda that existed "even in England, [that] tells its readers and hearers that in Hungary the Conservatives and the capitalists were pro-Nazi: the contrary is the truth. In the great struggle between liberty and equality . . . the

Hungarian land owners and industrialists in general were on the side of liberty and their political and economical extermination will fatally weaken the democracy in Hungary."

They described how hard they had worked inside Hungary in opposition to the pro-Nazi forces that had gripped the country. The most convincing proof of their position was what they suffered after the Nazis invaded: "we were taken—after having been physically maltreated— . . . to Austrian concentration camps, the second of which is one of the most ill-famed. Our families, who were sought by the Gestapo, had to seek refuge with friends because their [lives were] in danger. Our lodgings were sacked. . . . We had to sacrifice all our fortune inside Hungary for being transported to Portugal." The letter continued:

> You can imagine, dear Sir Owen, our amazement when arriving in Portugal we read in some English papers a very critical account of our liberation, and when we heard of the very unfriendly atmosphere in the English and American circles in Lisbon. We are averse to gain sympathy in showing our wounds received in battle, but we thought—erroneously as we now know—that in escaping the consequences of our anti-Nazi politics, we would have, if not the assistance, at least the sympathy of Western powers, even if with regard to the hostages we could not reveal some very few details of the arrangements made, though with regard to the changing situation we could do so now in a very short time.

The gap between their experience and the way they were perceived was great. How little the Allies knew about what they had endured: the interrogations, the indignities, the illness and the desperation at Oberlanzendorf and Mauthausen, the fear that stalked all the family members who had to hide. Only the grace of God had saved them as air raids screamed overhead and members of the family were not permitted to enter basement shelters.

They hoped that "the ice of mistrust" was beginning to melt from the United States, but they knew the British still viewed them with suspicion. Only a few days ago someone told them that the embassy was asked about the family, and "we were still not cleared entirely from suspicion." They wrote: "We cannot suppose that the fact that our family had also armament works should have to do with this attitude. In times of war the rights of the owners of all factories are suspended and we do not think that even in England the government would tolerate conscientious objectors between the great industrialists."

They explained that the Hungarian government had had complete control over the output of the factory, and the pressure by the German government on Hungary increased this pressure as well. At that time their brothers-in-law Eugene and Alfons had been managers at the factory, but they were completely marginalized and not even able to gain access to the area where the munitions were manufactured. When Germans and members of Parliament toured the plants on the invitation of the Hungarian government, the two owners had not even been invited.

Móric and Ferenc wanted only that "dear Sir Owen" would set the record straight and provide an introduction to those at the embassy. There were many reasons, but perhaps the most compelling was simple justice, "because to try to make the best [efforts] you can in a cause and then to be misjudged by those in whose cause—which we identified with in the interests of Hungary—you fought is really very bitter."

O'Malley passed this letter on to a man identified only as "Mr. Williams" in the Foreign Office and sent it on with the cover note that began, "With reference to our conversation of this morning, I enclose herewith a copy of the letter to me from Konfeld [sic] and Chorin which ought, I should say, to be on your files, as I do not suppose we have heard the last of this bunch of people."

O'Malley did not plan to send a reply to this letter, but he did have the temerity to suggest that there was "a discrepancy of view between myself and the Foreign Office in regard to Hungarian personalities and politics, and I still think, as I have thought all along, that these Jews ought to be pumped by some agent of yours whom they trust with a view to filling out our present information about the course of events in Hungary, if for no other reason." He acknowledged that these two men "have always been and still are on our side." But that was not to suggest that they were fully trustworthy: "Like most Jews they would need to be handled carefully as they might use any association with ourselves for more extensive purposes than suited us, but I should not have thought that for this reason we need to keep clear of them altogether."

Perhaps this was actually an official, carefully compromised expression of friendship and loyalty. O'Malley disguised his willingness to extend himself for them with a canny mix of innuendo and contempt. Still, lines such as "Like most Jews" startle. Didn't they know each other well enough to be free from some stereotypes? The recipients of his letter were far less inclined to think positively of the family. A Mr. Addis wrote in crisp cursive: "Sir O. O'Malley's correspondents want a gesture of friendship from England. There seems no reason for us to comply. The 'ice of mistrust' has not melted yet."

So where were they to go? It was clearly not safe to return to Hungary. The deal they had made with the Germans was viewed as Nazi collaboration. Other parts of Europe were possible, but the only reasonable country would be Switzerland, where three of Elsa's children had settled. George and Elsie were possibly heading there from Austria. America exerted a powerful attraction, but Chorin's sights were set in Europe, and that was where they would stay.

In August, Chorin wrote a letter to Ferenc Marosy, an old friend who had become the head of the "Royal Hungarian Legation" in Madrid. Chorin had already written several letters to the American embassy outlining the situation in Hungary and strategies for rebuilding the country. That summer the Hungarian government declared the agreement that the family had made with the Germans invalid and returned their assets to the original prewar holding company. Csepel had a new board of directors, composed of old family friends, including Péter Domony, Móric's nephew. In Chorin's letter to Marosy he wrote, "The number of surviving Jews is estimated at 150,000. . . . For the entire country the survivors represent approximately 30 percent. This is still a major difference compared to Slovakia, Moravia and other countries, where only a small percent survived. It is my hope and my greatest pride that the high rate of survival was to some extent due to my activities."

Then came the central question: "What do you think I should do? Would it be reasonable for me to go there for financial reasons? Do you believe the time has come for you to get involved in the postwar problems?. . . Koszti Takácsy, who is at the Manfred Weiss Works, . . . is very optimistic about the developments in Hungary and thinks that most members of the family could go home soon. The young ones right away. He is the first of our people to arrive in Switzerland, and hence his opinion is very interesting."

Takácsy might have been optimistic, but in November a full-page, front-page article about the family appeared in the right-wing newspa-

per *Haladás,* which means "progress." Trials of the Hungarian war criminals had begun, and that of Béla Imrédy had riveted the public's attention.
The disgraced anti-Semitic prime minister had found a brief second career—despite the misfortune of the public discovery of a Jewish grandmother—as the minister of finance while Horthy was still in power but
after the Germans had invaded. He resigned in August 1944 and insisted
in defense testimony that the reason he resigned was that he was so dis-
tressed about the Manfred Weiss deal.

Imrédy's friend Béla Zsolt argued, in an article entitled "The Manfred Weiss Case," that the family should not be maligned because in 1944
"with the Gestapo guns in their ribs they made a deal with German fascism." His argument focused on their behavior long before the Germans
took over: they had permitted Germany to take over the factory, enjoyed
the profits, and in fact used those profits for anti-Semitic activities,
maybe siphoning off a few pengős for the opposition, instead of quietly
emigrating and letting Hungary manage the assets. Zsolt described them
as "voluntary coworkers with and profit makers from the German war
machinery." Zsolt accused Chorin, "the grandson of the chief rabbi of
Arad," of being a war criminal whose money "reeks of blood."

One can only imagine how potent his message must have been for
impoverished Hungarians who just had emerged from the devastation of
the siege, the sadism of the Russian troops, and the losses and destruction all around them. These readers regarded the new democratic government, still in its embryonic stages, warily. Masquerading as a patriot,
Zsolt appealed to Hungarian readers' lowest instincts when he descended
into obscenity, writing, "There is no money in a democracy of decent
people where it can buy moral resurrection for the morally dead."

Imrédy was found guilty and executed by a firing squad in February
1946.

Zsolt's rabid accusations festered. The family was obviously in no position to provide a rebuttal, but Chorin's successor as president of
GYOSZ, the Hungarian manufacturers association, was. Miksa Fenyő—
a friend of the family, to be sure—wrote with the controlled outrage of a
man armed with the facts who simply wanted to set the record straight.
He pointed out that after the *Anschluss* in 1938 and for the rest of the war,
Germans had controlled the entire Manfred Weiss Works, as they controlled all Hungarian industry, and Chorin's capacity to negotiate had

been nonexistent. Fenyő had warned Chorin that the British had targeted the factory for bombing, to which Chorin had replied grimly, "I wish that they would." These were not the words of a man working in prosperous cooperation with the Nazi oppressors.

Fenyő's argument may have been true; it was just less believable.

You Looked for People You Knew

The end of the war revealed the fault lines between guilt and innocence, between perpetrators and victims. All of a sudden moral concepts of right and wrong were inadequate to characterize what was ultimately revealed to be the battle between good and evil. But in such a dichotomized world, the category occupied by the Manfred Weiss family because of what they did and how they survived became ever murkier. Were they victims? Yes, of course they were. They had been targeted and terrorized. They hid. Their lives had been in jeopardy.

But on the continuum of suffering, the family had no illusions about where they fit. Obviously they had survived, yet they were not in the indisputable postwar category of survivors. That was for others, for those who had endured unimaginable agonies. Once when one of my brothers was struggling with depression, he told my mother and aunt during a family therapy session that his psychiatrist had observed how commonly depression occurred in children of survivors. My mother nodded sympathetically. Later, I said, "That was an interesting point about the children of survivors and depression." My mother replied, with complete empathy for everyone but my brother, "Well, of course they would be depressed, the poor wretches." I tried to remind her that for much of the world, our father's experience in Dachau and hers in fleeing Nazis put us at least in the periphery of the category of "children of survivors." But it was almost unseemly for me (and that psychiatrist and my brother) to suggest that they were linked.

Part of me understood this perfectly: her natural modesty and reticence, and the dominant family ethos, made it impossible for her to appropriate the monumental human suffering of innocents targeted for extermination as her own. Her family's good fortune and my father's survival separated all of us completely from those with numbers tattooed on their arms. But the interstices between these radically different experiences remained unexplored.

Early in the summer of 1945, photographs from the camps, taken by the Allies, were exhibited in Lisbon. Strangely, in the well-worn narrative told me by my mother and aunt, this fact was mentioned to me only once, when my aunt Puppa came to visit me. I am not sure why she stopped by that day in February 1997, but my husband and I had just split up. I had moved out with my four-year-old daughter, Joia, and had rented a new house. Perhaps Puppa was just curious about the transition—she was always protective of Joia—but there was something more to that visit. She seemed to want to talk to me without my mother's presence.

She sat, smoking cigarettes, as a cup of coffee grew cold in front of her. As relaxed and calm as a Zen master, she meandered through some of the cherished stories of the past. The horses and fields of Ireg. The trips with her parents. The flight to Portugal. The tedium of the days in Portugal. But that day for some reason we were going a bit deeper, into the recesses of less immediately accessible memory. She spoke in a way that I had never heard her speak before or since about a gossamer sliver of time, that dividing line between one way of looking at the world and another. One could call it a loss of innocence, or more accurately, the shock of actually waking up in reality after a long period of oblivion. She described the moment when the reports of the murders and the atrocities that she and the family had been spared became graphic images. That moment occurred at the photography exhibit, of images from the camps, that she had visited with her lover, Luis.

"It was really a shock," she said softly. "You knew people were hungry and people were needed to work in these camps. But then to see all the skeletons as high as that"—her arm raised above her head—"you saw the actual pictures."

As I listened, snapshots from dog-eared history books flashed through my consciousness: the stacks of starved, disembodied naked limbs, the tangled piles of hair, the pyramid of eyeglasses. My aunt remembered a time when people had not yet seen such things, when these photographs had been revelations, when they still had the power of propinquity to shock.

There was more: "You see, these were pictures where you looked to see if you knew anyone."

Years later I visited Dachau, some twenty years after my father's death. Before I went, I fantasized about some mystical communion with him, hoped that I would be captured by a momentary frisson, the synapse between memory and encounter, in which the absence of death is eclipsed by a fleeting, powerful presence. In the main exhibit hall I looked for my father's gaunt face in every terrible photograph that I passed. Then I began to appreciate what my aunt meant. I looked for only one familiar face. She looked for faces that had populated the life she left behind. I asked if she had recognized anyone. She shrugged and paused.

"And then came letters," she said. "This one had died and that one died. And then you heard about the march. The Russians almost had closed around Budapest, and still they marched the rest of the Jews, as many as could survive, on to Vienna. There was a very nice laboratory doctor at Csepel. She was head of the laboratory and almost deaf because she had had scarlet fever as a child. And she couldn't be a doctor, because she couldn't hear the heartbeat or anything. So she became a very good technician. They made her march. She died on the march. . . .

"And then you heard these things. Somebody knew somebody who didn't come back. Someone else let you know someone died. Then the Russians came, and that wasn't much different. Some people who had barely survived the Nazis were killed by the Communists. Or people returned from Auschwitz and were sent to Siberia."

Studies of the Holocaust brought the term *survivor guilt* into popular consciousness. In the 1960s, after Holocaust survivors began suffering the longer-term effects of their horrific experiences and turned to therapists for help, the similarity of their symptoms—the inexplicable mood swings, the suffocating burden of guilt, the paralyzing depression, the pervasive anxiety—gained attention in the psychiatric community as a full-fledged syndrome. In various colloquies among the psychoanalysts who dominated the profession—many of them guilt-ridden European Jews—the nature of the disorder and the treatment options filled volumes.

I would ask my mother and my aunt about feeling guilty. There we would be, in the tranquillity of Patterson Street, talking about old times, and the question would come up: "Did you feel guilty?" The answer would always be the same: "Yes and no." Or rather: "Yes, but." Of course they felt guilty, but they would then shrug and say, "What could we do?"

Having survived left an uncomfortable hangover. The emotional tugs were almost less psychological than existential.

In the summer of 2007 a Portuguese television film crew arrived in Washington because they were making a documentary about the Weiss family. It was to be called *Chorin's List.* The historian and filmmaker António Louçã had happened upon the story many years before when he was doing research in Germany on the Portuguese dictator Salazar's wartime experiences. During that research he came across the story of Kurt Becher and then, inevitably, the story of Ferenc Chorin and the family. So Louçã decided to make a movie about this famous deal. In his synopsis were all the familiar points of reference: the March 19 invasion by Germany, the deportation of hundreds of thousands of Hungarian Jews, the importance of the Manfred Weiss Works, the deal that was crafted by Chorin and Becher, the way the SS deceived the German Foreign Office about the whole operation and informed von Ribbentrop only shortly before the family arrived in Portugal. Salazar had known about the arrival of these Hungarian Jews before the German officials did.

Together with his producer, Sofia Almeida Leite, Louçã interviewed family members. They went to Budapest with Daisy von Strasser—the daughter of Ferenc Chorin—and walked through the factory and their gracious old home. They went to Connecticut and New York, where they spoke with the children of Alfons and Elsa Weiss—Martha (Márta, Juci) Nierenberg, John (János) de Csepel, Mary (Marika) Radcliffe, and Gabriella (Memi) Mauthner. My mother was already dead, and Puppa and Tom refused to talk to them, for their usual complicated reasons of privacy and disdain.

Chorin's List was shown in Portugal and even won some prizes. Near the end of it, the camera fixes on the beautiful and patrician figure of Martha Nierenberg. Well into her eighties, her back was ramrod straight, her mind perfectly clear. While she had studied chemistry after her arrival in the United States, she eventually met and fell in love with an American named Ted Nierenberg, and together they went on to anticipate the American desire for inexpensive home style and created the company Dansk. She is a brisk, no-nonsense woman, the mother of four overachievers and grandmother of ten. Composed and regal, near the end of their interview, she looks into the camera and says with the candor and self-revelation that are sometimes so much easier with strangers, even strangers with cameras, "We could have ended up in Auschwitz. Why didn't we? It was a miracle. But I must tell you in retrospect—I never talk about this when I am in America, I never want to touch this subject—because somehow I feel guilty. Here I am, and so many people perished, and why I, and not them? So this is a recurring feeling, I think, with survivors."

I listen to my aunts, reflect on old conversations with my mother and aunt, and wonder about the thoughts of my grandparents, of Ferenc Chorin, of his wife and her sisters and brothers and their children, all of whom lived in that time, now long dead. What conflicting emotions must they have experienced? How could they not have been relieved at their good fortune? How could they not have felt ashamed of it as well? There was no resolving the dilemma, no escaping from the circular thinking.

Yes, my mother and aunt would say, of course they felt guilty. For years.

Then the quick turn, so elegantly articulated by my aunt, as she sat in my new kitchen, near the end of our conversation. She was retreating now from the immediacy of the past and putting to rest the conflicting emotions that might have bubbled to the surface. "Yes, I felt guilty," she said, "which is stupid. It wouldn't have helped anybody if we ended up in Auschwitz."

No, I agreed. It certainly wouldn't. She then talked about the time of transition in 1945 when everything was opening up and no one knew where he or she would go, except my mother. She was going to be leaving to marry my father.

An opening! Given how freely she had just spoken, perhaps she could talk about my mother. Perhaps just as she described that exhibit, she could pull the curtain of privacy back on the day my mother heard from my father for the first time.

"When the cable arrived in Portugal saying that Dad was still alive"— back then I thought it had been a cable—"what did Mom do?"

I could almost hear the click of the lock. "You have to talk to *her* about this," she said.

"Yes, of course I will, but you are her sister. You shared a room," I persisted. "I mean, she must have talked to you about what she felt . . . or how happy she was, or how worried she was when she waited."

"No. We never talked much about things."

"That's so strange to me," I said, truly bewildered.

"No, we never talked much. Everyone's affair was their own business."

Going Home

After Aladár left Paris, he returned to Dachau, which had turned into a "beehive in turmoil," as he put it. The former prisoners had no sense of where to go, how to get papers, or what options they had and were becoming more and more agitated. In his absence, the Hungarians had been moved to a vastly inferior building and told him that it never would have happened had he remained there. Everyone was eager to return home, and they could not understand why repatriation took so long. So the group decided that Aladár and two others would return to Budapest and attempt to expedite the process.

On August 12 Aladár left Dachau, planning to return in a month or so. He stuffed a GI duffel bag with some underwear, his raincoat, and his writings on the lost generation that he had been working on since he got out of the hospital. He first stopped in Salzburg to meet with some official representatives from the Hungarian government and with Márton Himler from the OSS. The point of the meeting was to get organized to return to Hungary and begin the formal repatriation of the Hungarian prisoners of war. The three from Dachau were given the keys to a small Mercedes that had once belonged to a sports reporter from the Hungarian News Service, and another Hungarian named Zoltán Friedman joined them. The men created travel documents that they signed for each other as members of the prisoners committee. A letter from a Catholic priest was supposed to serve as a formal letter of transit. The only hard currency they possessed was a few cartons of American cigarettes, and they had enough gasoline to make the trip.

Aladár drove.

My father, whom I would never see behind the wheel of a car, was chosen to drive his three fellow Hungarians the 281 miles back to Budapest.

The Allies had chopped up this part of Europe and divided it haphazardly into Russian and American zones. Each zone became a self-contained entity, with its own border crossing and, as it turned out, its own rule of law. As they approached Linz, which was in the American zone, their trip became slower and slower, the result of a crazy traffic jam: American jeeps, trucks, and private cars, and men, women, and children everywhere, holding bags, walking, and hitchhiking. When cars went through various checkpoints, the American guard saw to it that the pedestrians had right-of-way and forced any vehicle with an empty seat to pick up some people. As my father drove through the villages, children played in the streets, and the local villagers and the refugees who were passing through chatted with American soldiers.

Then they reached the Russian zone, and the difference in mood was stunning. Suddenly all the traffic seemed to have evaporated. They saw an occasional farm wagon or a small herd of cattle driven to the east, but there were no people in the streets, and the windows and doors of all the houses were tightly shut, even in the warmth of August.

Zoltán Friedman had some rudimentary Russian and was in charge of talking to the guards at the Russian control posts. At the first one, he walked into the primitive checkpoint with several packs of American cigarettes. The others remained in the car, tense and silent. After a few minutes Zoltán appeared, beaming and cigarette-less. The Russian guard waved them on with a friendly grin. The routine was repeated several times during the course of their journey. Zoltán convinced the guards that they were Communists returning from German captivity. One of them even waved goodbye to the car, affectionately calling, *"Communisti!"*

After every checkpoint, their spirits rose incrementally. They were soon going to be home, they would soon see their families and learn what had happened in the ten months since they left. Looking around, they saw the ruins left by the war. Vienna was desperate and sad, a defeated city where wreckage from the fighting still littered the streets.

When they crossed the border from Austria into Hungary, they were overwhelmed. They cried. They embraced each other. They kissed the ground.

When they reached the city of Győr, Aladár believed that the Benedictine monastery there would shelter them for the night. He was sure that his mother's prominence as the leader of the Catholic Women's League still carried some weight, and he only had to tell them who he was and they would be welcomed. No such luck. The priest who stood outside the church firmly refused. One of Aladár's companions remembered that one of his former classmates worked in the office of the Episcopal church for Bishop Apor. He found his friend, and they were invited to have dinner and spend the night. An atmosphere of sadness and worry was palpable; Bishop Apor had been shot and killed by the Russians a few months before when he had tried to defend some women who fled to him for protection.

They set off the next day for Budapest. Aladár's heart tightened as he drove the same routes that, many years before, he had driven with Hanna. He had no idea if she had received his letter, much less what her answer would be. Looking at all the destruction and detritus on the sides of the road, he found himself searching for evidence of his old car. Perhaps the license plate A3272 would be there, peeking through the wreckage.

On August 17 they arrived in Budapest.

The city was in ruins but alive with activity. Uniformed Russian women directed traffic. Streetcars were running. Much of the rubble had been cleared away. When he saw the Danube denuded of bridges, Aladár's first thought was about the murders that it represented. Before going in search of friends and family, the men had to report to the offices of the Ministry of the Interior, at the infamous address 60 Andrássy Avenue, which would be the scene of more death and torture in the coming years. But now it was merely the office where they had to check in, in order to begin repatriating the other Hungarian prisoners in Dachau.

When they parted, Zoltán told Aladár that he wanted to change his family name to one that sounded more Hungarian than Friedman. Aladár had been dazzled by this young man's performance. His audacity and his confidence and his psychological acuity had made their incredibly dangerous transit possible. On the basis of their travels, Aladár suggested that *Merszei* would be most appropriate—loosely translated, the word means "one who dares." Incredibly, he took the name and moved to the United States, where Geoffery Merszei became president of Dow Chemical Company.

Unchangeably, Hanna

Aladár went to the offices of the Kammer Company, where he was sure Lilly still worked. The family manservant, Pali, was there. This was the first moment Aladár realized that he was home, that his family was safe, and that he had a link to what once had been. The two men had last seen each other on the morning of Aladár's arrest sixteen months ago, and they embraced and began to cry. Lilly emerged, stunned, and she too began crying. Her boss Victor Oberschall, who had sheltered Puppa when the family was hiding, also appeared. He told Aladár that he had tried to bribe the Gestapo for his release, obviously to no avail.

Lilly could hardly speak quickly enough, telling him all that had happened since they last had seen each other, ten months ago. Their parents were alive and healthy. Several bombs had struck their house, and while the damage was reparable, the apartments were uninhabitable. They never were able to go back. One of their former neighbors, a man named Jóska Mel, still lived in the house, and as my father later wrote, he "compensated for his Nazi past by becoming an enthusiastic Communist." He organized some of his like-minded comrades and filed an official petition that stated that my father, "who voluntarily escaped to the West"—at the spa in Dachau—should not be permitted to keep apartments away from the workers who so richly deserved them.

Aladár and Lilly then got into a horse-drawn carriage and went to the house of the Catholic Women's League, where the director generously let the family stay. Aladár Senior had been certain that his son was still alive, despite the rumors of his death that had circulated in Budapest. Still, he must have been astonished when Aladár and Lilly entered the room. He walked toward his son and began to cry. Aladár could no longer contain his emotions, and he too sobbed. They were finally together. They had survived.

As they sat in their single room and tried to bring each other up to date on what had transpired over the past year, the conversation focused on the horrors of the Russian occupation. Lilly, who in October 1944 had impatiently waited for the Russians to arrive, could not speak about them without a shudder. Each time she met a Russian soldier on the street, she felt sick with worry. "There was no end to the dreadful and ludicrous stories," Aladár wrote. "The Soviet trauma had already replaced the memory of the Nazi trauma. "

Aladár wrote Hanna a second letter after he arrived in Budapest. He still had no idea if she had received the first, if she still loved him, if she wanted to marry him. But for his own sanity, he proceeded as if she did. He needed to write to her, to talk to her and make up for the eighteen months of silence. A coalition government had formed, and while he knew and even liked some of its members, he also knew that any fragments of the old life were gone forever. He walked through the city, dumbfounded by the destruction everywhere but heartened by the enterprise that he saw. Compared to defeated and passive Vienna, Hungary was vital, even entrepreneurial. He wandered up to Lendvay Street to pass by Hanna's old house. It was badly damaged but still standing.

As relieved as he was to be home and know that his family and Hanna had survived, he was tormented by guilt, his very Catholic version of post-traumatic stress disorder. "I somehow felt responsible for everything," he wrote. "This was not just a masochistic interpretation of collective responsibility or a gross overestimation of my role. It was probably the result of the fact that everything we tried to avoid actually did happen and as Hungarians we were not able to prevent these things from happening." His walk through Budapest was so reminiscent of those weeks after March 19, though now he ruminated on the mortal sins of his country and on his own personal failures. He would repeat, over and over again, that Hungary was "the retarded student of democracy." He searched his soul seeking a national and personal reckoning of all the "errors, omissions, and sins during the past twenty-five years."

Aladár remembered, before the war, going to a play by his friend Sándor Márai called *The Citizens of Kassa*. When an actor exclaimed, "One cannot live without laws," the audience, Aladár included, burst into applause. After Dachau and after the entire experience with Nazism, Aladár thought of that moment and altered the line to make it his own: "One cannot live without principles."

Hungarians are not known for their aversion to argument, and after the war Budapest immediately was electric with accusations hurled from left to right and back again. The dominance of the Communist Party in the popular discourse short-circuited the kind of national examination of conscience that Aladár felt was essential. Because the Russian troops had behaved so badly, the moral high ground that could have been staked out by the left wing was easily assailed. In the grand tradition that the best defense is a good offense, the Communists were unapologetic for the behavior of their Soviet comrades during the siege and began a barrage of accusations against the Hungarians for their Nazi alliance.

Such accusations triggered neither penitence nor a thoughtful postmortem that examined the various forces that had led the country to its ruin. Instead, the new national mood was predominantly defensive. Aladár toyed with the idea of establishing a Hungarian human rights organization, but his most pressing concern was figuring out how to repatriate those Hungarians who remained in Dachau, and how to prevent a "brain drain," where those who might have chosen to return to Hungary were so discouraged by the delays that they fled west instead. As he reflected on the need for national atonement, he wrote Hanna a third letter in which he made his own intimate confession.

He described his long drive and the way her presence haunted him as he passed by the familiar routes of their "educational excursions." He wrote about Lilly's heroism and the horrors of the siege. He told her that he had walked by "Lendvay ut 27, [and] it was so strange and hard to believe that the house was not there anymore, that you are not living there anymore, that one cannot go there and that you are not here."

The letter had momentum that seemed to gather in speed and urgency. Aladár had to tell her everything before she consented to marry him. He had no job. He did not know what he was going to do with himself, how he was going to make a living as a forty-two-year-old man who had spent his entire adult life in a profession that no longer seemed to have any room for him. Perhaps he would go into business. But that was also difficult to imagine. When he read some of his earlier writings, he realized that he was dogged by another problem as well: "I became very worried because today I would not be able to write those things."

Dachau, which was not "what you would call a finishing school," had left its indelible mark on what Aladár called "vulgar habits," both in language and behavior. He assured her that being home had improved things, but he noticed that his language had coarsened. Yet "there is still one positive effect based on the captivity and camp life: I realized that many things that I had considered important until now, like ambition, success, manners, and so on and so forth, are not important. What is *really* important are human relations, goodness, and readiness to help."

He could not have been speaking to a more receptive audience. Because if there were three qualities Hanna understood, possessed, and embodied, it was a deep capacity to connect, an innate goodness, and a reflexive eagerness to help. As a result of this insight, "the last remains of my social prejudices more or less have disappeared. . . . I think that I can bear being poor more easily than I did until now, and this is a great advantage." He knew he would have to work, he assured her, and worried that he would not be able to offer her "that standard of living that you have gotten used to." He was so frustrated in having this one-sided conversation—he needed to talk with her, to hear what she would say. He needed her presence. "Goodbye, my darling. I wish you everything the best, and if it is possible, write to me please. I would very much like to know something certain and to get some sort of direct news from you. . . . Countless hand kisses, Aladár."

In her daybook Hanna noted that on August 18, many letters arrived, and one of them was from Aladár. I longed to at least see an exclamation point, but there was none. She immediately sent him a three-word telegram: "Hanna voyage Paris." Her telegram and his next letter may have passed each other. She knew that Aladár was returning to Budapest, so she sent the telegram to János Zwack, their dear friend and Puppa's old lover. He had survived the siege with his wife, Vera, and their son Péter, through sheer wits and generous friends. Hanna knew that if anyone could find Aladár, the man they all knew as Coko could.

He succeeded on September 14—he found Aladár celebrating his parents' fiftieth wedding anniversary. Aladár's mother Sarolta had returned to Budapest from Pomáz, and his sister Musi had come from Diósgyőr after an adventurous journey. The family was still staying at the Catholic Women's League apartment, and the head of the organization managed to cook a festive dinner for all of them after they attended a private mass. My father had earlier remembered their silver anniversary in 1918, when his father had just lost his job, and their forty-ninth anniversary, when he was in the Budapest jail—he had asked his SS guard if he could stop in the chapel after his walk in the yard to pray for his parents.

In his memoir, Aladár wrote almost as an afterthought: "As a peculiar coincidence that same day a telegram came from Hanna, saying that she was ready to go to Paris, which I took as an affirmative answer to my two letters. I told my father and mother that I was getting married, and Mother said that this was the best possible anniversary present." His mother was not just speaking rhetorically. She was desperate for her only son to be married. Many years later Aladár wrote in his diary that as a student and young diplomat, he had been incapable of finding "joy, entertainment, or potential wives" in his social circles. He wrote, "I believe my mother feared that I would have the reputation of being an eccentric, or she may have feared something worse."

Years and depressions and history and regret and his father's resolute Calvinist sense of privacy all conspired to ensure that he would not write anything more fulsome. And yet in a letter to Hanna a few days later, he described his reaction to her "affirmative answer":

> My dear Hancsi, it is incredibly difficult to write now, so I will only write very briefly so I can be sure to send it to you. One sentence in the cable made me extremely happy. Hanna voyage Paris. Coko was very charming because he brought it to the golden anniversary. When I saw it, I couldn't control my emotions, and I wept through the entire ceremony. This short sentence assured me that you too haven't changed your intentions. Finally, what I had been only hoping for became certain. . . . Now however I have only one ambition: to tie my life together with yours.

He longed for her to come to Budapest but worried that he was being selfish in calling her back "to this very sad city in this very terrible winter. Therefore please give a great deal of consideration to your decision. Are you going to come now, if it is possible? Or should we wait until spring, when maybe you would come home with your entire family? I am very

very much longing for you, I don't deny it. But if one has to wait, I still can do it."

Hanna had already written him. At some point in October he finally received it. She knew the letter was likely to be read by others, so she carefully avoided being too expressive. First she thanked him for his letters, "which took a heavy load off of me. It was horrible to know that someone who is very, very close to my heart was in such a terrible danger and that I could do nothing to help, and even now it is horrible to think of what you went through."

Then she could hold back no longer.

> *But now only one thing is important, and that is that you exist. . . . I can't comprehend everything that has happened to us since we last saw each other. I only know that since we left, despite the enormous relief that the whole family escaped all that danger, we lived in constant fear for those who stayed home. And it always hurt that we could not be with them during all those ordeals and that we were so powerless. One only lived in the present. Looking back on the past, one didn't have the courage to look ahead. And then two letters came, and the future opened up again. Anywhere. Any way. Just let's be together again. I am sure that time didn't pass us without leaving its mark. I cannot be a judge of that. But I know that in one thing, nothing changed. I am always ashamed that I lived in such security while you——. Even imagining it is horrible. But alas, we cannot change these things anymore. Now the only thing that is important is that you take care of yourself. The good Lord should bless the Dutch doctor. If I knew his address, I would have written to him. I now feel as if I were sitting in a railway station and the train is late, they can't tell me when it is coming, and I am waiting impatiently and even more impatiently. Every day I wait to get some news and directions for the future. Many loving hand kisses to the whole family. Always and unchangeably, Hanna*

It took five years, but finally they were getting married.

CHAPTER 34

The Love That Makes Life
Beautiful and Happy

In the middle of September two men from the Foreign Ministry visited Aladár and told him that an interparty group had decided that he should be the next minister to Washington. There was no embassy there yet, so he could not be an ambassador, but minister would be tantamount to the same role. The previous spring the United States had announced that it was willing to receive quasi-diplomatic political missions from Hungary, Romania, and Bulgaria. Out of deference to the Soviet Union, it didn't happen.

But now, in the early autumn of 1945, the Soviet diplomat in Hungary, Georgiy Maksimovich Pushkin, had announced that the Soviet Union would recognize the autonomous Hungarian government and would establish diplomatic relations with it. He became the Soviet ambassador. At that point it was possible for the Americans to do the same. A number of candidates had been suggested, but Pushkin vetoed each one, until Aladár's name was raised. Perhaps the Communists from Dachau who liked him had given good reports.

For his part, Aladár was stunned, and his first reaction was to politely decline. He wanted to remain in Budapest, to be married to Hanna, to help in the preparations for the peace conference. Besides, he did not feel he could speak English well enough for the job. He told some friends that if he were appointed, it would be a very expensive English lesson for

Hungary. But before rejecting the offer outright, he said that he wanted a few days to think it over and talk about it with two trusted friends from the Foreign Ministry. They both said he should accept the job. It was not a lifetime appointment, and he would be better off outside Hungary. Besides, he needed to think about Hanna, and he owed this to her. He remembered that a fortune teller whom he had seen in Heidelberg told him, "*Sie müssen an Ihren Stern glauben und werden durchkommen.*" You must trust your star and you will succeed.

He was mulling over the decision when he wrote to Hanna, who was still in Portugal awaiting her Hungarian visa, about how frustrated he was in his inability to get to the American zone so they could marry. "You know, my darling, I am extremely angry at myself for my powerlessness, but I am unable to be pushy. Self-promotion might be more practical, but for me it is terribly offensive. Don't be angry, you have always known how impractical I am. Now however, I have only one ambition: to tie my life together with yours. Otherwise I am absolutely uninterested in all the competitive and unscrupulous ambitions surrounding me."

Ambition was not the reason he decided to take the job. It was simple patriotism. He was asked yet again to serve his country, and he heeded the call. He would have preferred to go to London—it was so much easier, still reassuringly European. But they wanted him for America, so that was his destination.

Once he made the decision, he threw himself into this new project. His top priority was to figure out what America's interest was in Hungary. He understood how fragile democracy was in Hungary, and he knew that the agreements in Yalta were putting Hungary squarely in the Soviet sphere of influence. The country needed to be protected from a Communist takeover. At the same time, the looming Paris peace conference was going to be extremely complicated for Hungary as a former German ally and now as a pawn in the burgeoning Cold War. Domestically Hungary could not become a Communist satellite, and internationally, it could not afford the kind of dismemberment it had experienced at Trianon. Not that it had any territory left to lose, but the potential war reparations could cripple any chance of recovery. Economic assistance was essential, and the United States was the only country capable of providing it.

On October 8, 1945, Aladár's appointment became official in a document from the Hungarian Foreign Ministry. It "presents its compliments to the mission of the United States of America and wishes to communicate the following: The Provisional National Government of Hungary intends to appoint Mr. Aladár de Szegedy-Maszák, Counsellor [sic] of Legation, as head of the Mission to be sent to the United States of America and as minister designate. Mr. Szegedy-Maszák's short biographical sketch is enclosed. The Hungarian Ministry for Foreign Affairs would be greatly obliged for an early reply of the Government of the United States of America."

The biographical sketch was one page and covered all the important points of his career, his education, and his imprisonment. And at the end were two sentences:

"Mr. Szegedy-Maszák has been appointed member of the Committee entrusted with the task to prepare the peace negociations [sic] of Hungary. Mr. Szegedy-Maszák is engaged and about to get married."

Their engagement had become an international affair.

To have the bride in Portugal and the groom in Budapest, even under normal circumstances, was problematic. But in the fall of 1945, when the entire continent seemed to be in flux—trains not running on time, flights impossible to get on, exit visas difficult to come by, borders further complicated by the American, British, and Russian zones—figuring out not just when but where and how to tie the knot was a full-time job. My parents had thought that perhaps they would meet in Paris and marry there, but Aladár wanted Hanna once more to see the country that she was about to represent. The Hungarian Foreign Ministry raised another impediment by refusing to give her an entry permit. Some bureaucratic misunderstanding, or more likely the petty action of someone familiar with the deal, didn't like it, and wanted to exact some revenge on someone in the family.

Hanna wrote to Aladár at the beginning of November: "Unfortunately the possibilities for travel are still miserable. You have to wait weeks to get a visa, and then it is difficult to get space on a plane or a train. It would have been impossible to arrive in Budapest or even Naples in three weeks. You can imagine how impatiently I am waiting to see you. Now I have started the process for the American visa. They were very nice and promised that maybe in two weeks I will be able to receive a visitor's visa."

There were cables from France suggesting some transportation possibilities. A ragged dog-eared cable that had gone through London read, "Szegedy just wired permit delayed Hanna should stay Lisbon love."

After his appointment was announced, Aladár went on a round of introductory visits that included Soviet ambassador Pushkin. Pushkin said he remembered him from Berlin. Aladár did not recall such a meeting and asked him where they might have met. There was no reply, but Pushkin asked him about a number of Soviet diplomats who had been in Berlin at the time. At the end of the conversation, Aladár mentioned that his fiancée was having a difficult time getting an entry permit to Hungary. They wanted to marry in Budapest. "They had to leave because of their anti-Nazi activities, didn't they?" Pushkin asked. My father told him that her family had owned Csepel and that after the occupation, because of the fight between the SS and the Göring Werke, the family was able to go to Portugal. The very next day Pushkin sent my mother's entry permit, which the Foreign Ministry had refused.

THE NEWS OF HANNA'S engagement traveled fast. By the beginning of November, she was getting letters from Switzerland, Vienna, Budapest, and Paris, from friends and relatives who had heard the news: Hanna and Aladár were getting married and moving to Washington, where Aladár was going to be the Hungarian ambassador. Against the backdrop of so many deaths and disappearances, the triumph of this romance, the happy ending after such enormous hardship, offered the broader reassurance that life, which had been so arbitrary and evil, could also sometimes be gentle and good and just.

"My sweet Hancsi," a letter from her cousin Baby in Zurich began, "I would like to congratulate you and find only clichés about lots and lots of happiness that do not express what I so deeply feel. I wish that life would bring to you and Aladár only beauty, warmth, joy, and a great mutual understanding. Now, writing these words, do I realize that with all my heart that I wish you the same things that I obtained from fate." Her favorite cousin, Mopi, a regular and energetic correspondent, was living in Basel. Hanna had apparently written to her confessing that she looked to her new life with "mixed feelings" because she was so worried about her new status both as wife and as Mrs. Ambassador. Mopi reassured her: "I am convinced that once you are over there, Aladár will help you over every problem.... You know how much I hate sentimental gush, and now I am mad at myself for being unable to tell you how happy I am because of this good news and how terribly I will miss you."

Hanna's aunt Edith was tense, prickly, and prone to migraines, yet Hanna occupied a special, protected place in her heart. "My darling Hancsi, how much I would give to be able to hug and kiss you now, how full my heart is with love, with best wishes, intense deep prayers for you. The sufferings and worries of the last years formed you into a complete person, but even more, you carried these years in such a way that the sunshine of your dear smile illuminated our sometimes despairing souls."

Marianne and Móric both wrote to my father. "A big stone fell off our hearts when we heard about your being set free," Móric wrote. He congratulated Aladár on his new job and on the advancements that he made in his career and reassured him that "the scale of the task is worthy of you and your talents."

He then went on:

> By the time you get this letter we will know where and when you will meet Hanna. That your old wish—which was also my old hope—will be now fulfilled is comforting to me, even though I have had to resign myself to many things. I imagined that this would be different. Yes, the last years have taught me to differentiate between the essential and the unimportant. How many things that we thought to be essential in life have turned out to be unimportant. Know that the road on which you are now embarking will be accompanied by our warmest wishes. . . . The ideal union is the one in which one person's wish for happiness is sustained by the other's happiness. I deeply trust that your wedded life will be an ideal marriage, just as it is on its start. You can imagine how painful it is for us that we cannot embrace you before your wedding. That you will not be blessed in the church in the well-loved surroundings of Ireg. We will put all these wishes in the multicolored past, the return to which we have to give up. . . . May the heavens bless you, my dear Aladár. God be with you. In the hope of a not-too-distant encounter, I embrace you. Your old friend, Móci

Then, a week later in November, shortly before Hanna left Portugal, Marianne wrote the purely protective letter of a mother whose daughter was at the brink of leaving home for the first time in her life.

Dear Aladár,

I don't know when and where these lines will get to you—I just know that they bring with them my love, my confidence, my anxious and happy thoughts. It cannot be expressed with words what I feel now that I have to separate from Hanna. Only heaven knows for how long. It hurts very much that I cannot see you together and cannot be happy with your happiness, but all this is secondary. What is important is that you be together and find in each other everything that makes this complicated life more beautiful, sunnier, and easier to endure. What Hanna meant to us in these difficult times, her radiant and sweet disposition, how much strength she gave us and how happy she made our lives, I cannot talk about right now. May God give you the chance to find in her all that is not readily apparent. Her intelligence, her goodness, her good instincts as far as people are concerned, her cleverness, her gift of insight about others, and her gentleness will make her a real help for you, and in these difficult times she may be your real better half. I do not want to give you any advice; I just want to ask you to please take very good care of her and surround her with the love that makes life beautiful and happy. God bless you, dear Aladár, and I hope that we will soon have the opportunity to take part in your happiness. With warm love, I embrace you. I am very proud of my new son. Marianne.

Hanna's last days in Estoril were full of packing and official uncertainties, needing to be prepared to leave and never being sure of when that was actually going to happen. Finally, on December 4, she had her ticket to Paris. Then on the fifth she wrote, "Packing, horrible mood." The anxiety, the uncertainty, the wrenching separation from her family must have worn terribly on Hanna. On December 6 it was time to go. "In the morning I start. At the border I am almost thrown out. Exit visa not in order. After that everything goes right."

When Hanna finally arrived in Paris, she wrote her parents a long and detailed letter about the trip. Border officials took her papers and were not going to let her proceed. Then, after they finally decided to let her go, there was no room for all of her luggage in the car. She had to share her compartment with a number of restless, yelling, complaining children. But, she allowed, since she must have looked so miserable, everyone was incredibly nice to her. Most important, the first leg of her journey to Budapest, then to America, was completed. But all that was secondary. What was most important was that she was getting farther and farther away from them, and that simple fact caused her enormous pain.

> I have to thank you for those twenty-nine beautiful years that only you, my dear dear Mami and Papi, were responsible for making so wonderful. And whatever the future will bring, I know that the worry-free and problem-less period of life has come to an end. I hope that God will make the life with Aladár happy. (I hope that he is going to be happy with me too.) But the closeness of our life together, and the blessing of having been born into your life, will never ever be substituted. Therefore I am just praying to be able to find a solution so that we will be able to meet very soon. And if you don't come to America, then I will leave Aladár there, I will save money, and wher-ever you are, I will come to visit you. There is one more thing that I want to ask you. Please take care of yourselves. Don't forget to take the medications—you have to take them. It is not enough to keep them in the drawer. The good and mighty should bless all of you, many, many warm and loving kisses, I miss you terribly. Your Hancsi

She spent nearly a week in Paris, trying to get to Budapest. Her trans-portation became an issue for the American ambassadors in Lisbon, Paris, and Budapest. Getting room on a flight from Paris to Vienna in December proved nearly impossible. She needed another piece of paper, this one an American official document that might hurry things along. From the American embassy in Paris came the "Application for Priority for Non-Military Air Travel on Foreign Routes . . . Or for Surface Trans-portation on US Controlled Missions." After she provided her name and passport number and birth certificate, the application required an expla-nation for why her trip was urgent: "Miss Kornfeld is proceeding to Bu-dapest on urgent mission for Hungarian minister to U.S."

That proved to be sufficiently urgent.

Fortunately there were many old friends of the family who lived in Paris and were eager to spend time with Hanna, so the week passed quickly. On December 14 she managed to get on a six-hour flight from Paris to Vienna. Once she arrived in Vienna, she was met at the airport by an American captain with whom, she shyly intimated, she indulged in her last flirtation. She ate at the officers club and stayed in an official American military hotel, enjoying some of the practical implications of her impending change of status. But she was shocked by what she saw and duly recorded it: "Vienna looks terrible, lots of ruins, the people are skinny, the stores all closed. There is no food. Terrible circumstances." In Estoril, without her daughter, my grandmother wrote Hanna another letter.

> *My dear, dear beloved heart, in my thoughts you are so close to me, and all the time I am with you, but alas I did not get any news, and I don't know anything since a telegram telling us that you have flown away from Vienna. . . . How was your wedding? When are you starting out? So many questions to which I do not know the answers. But you know that the invisible threads that join us and that across time and space connect you to my heart will never slacken and that the distance will make my longing, great love, even more palpable. I wish I could have been with you to be able to tell Aladár what a treasure he is getting in you, that the greatest sign of our love and trust is the fact that we let you go in this sad and uncertain world, in which only his person and love is a certain harbor. May God grant that he realizes this more and more and that you find in each other what is in you. Love, trust, and understanding are strengths that make everything in life bearable. . . . I don't want Puppa to know how much and how painfully I miss you.*

Finally, on December 18, Hanna boarded a flight to Budapest. Her fellow passengers included some Hungarian war criminals. Aladár and Lilly picked her up at the airport. My father wrote, "I had not seen her for twenty-one months, and I abandoned her between March 19 and April 14, and yet she said yes to my letter and agreed to come home after my appointment to Washington. . . . The tragic events of 1944 and 1945 subdued me so that even the pleasure of our reunion and the particular mercy shown to us from Above, manifested in this reunion, could not quite make either of us ignore the other facts."

Hanna and Aladár were, at last, together.

HANNA STAYED WITH JÁNOS Zwack and his family, and her days before the wedding were consumed with visits to friends, official lunches and dinners, and attempts to calm Aladár's fraying premarriage nerves. "I vividly remember how scared I was for a few days before the wedding," Aladár wrote in some rare sentences of emotional revelation. "When I first met Hanna more than five years before, I viewed myself as a permanent bachelor, since I viewed this as the only way to assure my independence, on which I firmly insisted. In spite of the solidity of our emotional connection, I was not sure I could live up to the obligations inherent in marriage, which I considered absolutely essential."

She also took inventory of the wreckage of her previous life. She went to Lendvay Street, up Andrássy Avenue, and saw the ruins of what they once had had. She heard shocking stories about the siege from old friends of the family who emerged from hiding. On December 22 the minister of nutrition in Hungary announced that wholesale famine seemed unavoidable and said that the mortality rate in Hungary exceeded the birth rate by a mind-numbing 50 percent. Aladár had been right. She had to see her country; she couldn't have imagined the circumstances in which people lived.

She received a letter from Ireg from Teta Liesel, her old baby nurse who had sheltered her brother Tom when he hid after March 19. She had married the head gardener at Ireg many years before and had heard about Hanna's impending nuptials. She congratulated her and begged her to visit Ireg just one more time, before she left "for the foreign country where you will be living for a while." Even though she knew that Hanna would likely not be able to come, if she did, "it would be the best Christmas joy." Liesel explained that "in other years, we spent Christmas with strange people because the house in Ireg was taken over by the Russians and it was a hospital. You cannot imagine what we found when we came back. It was totally robbed, and the furniture was all broken up. Again, all the best, my beloved Hancsi. I kiss you with much love. Your Teta."

A cold, dismal rain fell on Budapest on Sunday, December 23. The city looked as bleak as it ever had, the bridges still missing, concrete and glass and dirt in piles where once-solid buildings presided. And yet bright green shoots of hope began to appear. A new life was starting, not just for the fifty or so people who gathered for the wedding, but maybe, for Hungary, which at last had the opportunity to become the kind of democratic, civil society that the best of its citizens imagined it could be. People believed that something positive was going to emerge from the terrible mess they had all endured. In contrast to the passive misery of

Vienna, Budapest was brimming with activity. Despite the dismal weather, on every street corner basic commerce was humming; someone sold some food or cigarettes, or bits of candy, or books or lampshades or clothes.

The new mayor of Budapest, Ferenc Kővágó, officiated at the civil ceremony that took place the day before. The civil ceremony was even mentioned in a news broadcast on Hungarian radio, and in Portugal my grandmother's sister-in-law Erzsi rushed in to tell her that she had heard the news. The religious ceremony was held at a chapel in Maria Street.

Their friend Judit Máriássy was there. She had seen Aladár several weeks earlier and asked him to take her sister Katalin to America with him. He remembered Katalin's heroism when the Szálasi regime took over—she refused to take the oath of allegiance at the Foreign Ministry—so he agreed. It was the greatest gift he could have given his new wife, since Katalin became her closest friend for forty years, until her death in 1985.

Lilly took on the job of wedding planner, inviting the guests and greeting them when they arrived. For many of those assembled, this was the first time they laid eyes on each other since the siege. In other words, it was the first time that they could see who was still alive. Murmurs of happiness and shock and tears of joy filled the small, cold chapel. Judit's husband, Gen. Pál Almásy, who had been imprisoned by the Nazis, arrived and for the first time in months wore his uniform. Some of the guests who didn't know him were horrified—they thought he was a Russian soldier since the uniforms were so similar. Sarolta and Aladár Senior, a bit unsteady on their feet, entered with Lilly and Musi.

Then, arm in arm, my parents appeared and walked toward the altar. Everyone started to cry.

My mother, straight as a column, wore a black dress with an emerald-green belt and emerald earrings that she had borrowed from Vera Zwack. For a moment, my mother looked into the congregation and nearly cried that her family was not there. She composed herself quickly. Everyone there realized that this union was a miracle.

After the ceremony—the priest spoke about the gift of love and the enormous barriers that had stood in the way of the couple—Lilly had organized a small but very crowded reception. Everyone had something to say, a word of congratulations or a request for a small favor from the United States or some wisdom or advice for the uncertain future. Lilly introduced Hanna to Judit, whom she had never met. Judit said to her, "My sister is going to America. She is already on the boat. And I would like you to look after her."

Hanna, deeply acquainted with the worries sisters could have for one another, was moved by the request and agreed. She could not know then how easy that promise would be to keep, how much she would love Katalin, and how close they would become.

They spent an emotional Christmas with Aladár's family. As Hanna and Aladár were celebrated and exchanged very modest gifts, the foreign ministers of Great Britain, the Soviet Union, and the United States agreed to a twenty-one-nation peace conference that was going to take place in Paris in the summer of 1946. The family gathered around the radio and listened as Pope Pius XII, in his Christmas Eve message, appealed to the world for an end of totalitarianism and the beginnings of using "fundamental moral prerequisites of a true and lasting peace."

As they packed and prepared to leave for Washington, my father struggled with what to take. Was this a temporary assignment, or should he bring some more of his possessions to make it seem more permanent? The most painful choice involved his books. He was an avid bibliophile and over the years had collected an impressive library of more than six thousand volumes, some of which were old and valuable. He did not want to leave his parents' home denuded, so he left his books, etchings, carpets, and porcelain.

He packed four suitcases. Hanna and Aladár left Budapest on December 29. The weather was so bad, they were rerouted to Frankfurt—a shocking scene of utter devastation. They spent New Year's Eve huddled in the airport.

On the last page of Hanna's 1945 journal, there was one sentence: "I wish that everyone and everything could be as happy as I am and this was."

1946

The first representative in Washington was Aladár Szegedy–Maszák, who had worked in the old regime's foreign service. As a liberal and anti-Nazi, he had been arrested by the Gestapo, deported to Dachau, and freed by the Americans.... He was a highly respected diplomat who created good will for the country he represented though that good will had few practical consequences.

—PETER KENÉZ, *Hungary from the Nazis to the Soviets*

WASHINGTON POST, JANUARY 20, 1946

MME. SZEGEDY-MASZÁK
TYPICAL OUTDOOR WOMAN

Bride of the Diplomatic Corps
Finds Washington A
Fascinating New World

By Marie McNair

Newest, youngest, prettiest, "bridiest" member of the diplomatic circle is Mme. Szegedy-Maszák, wife of the first Hungarian Minister to Washington since the war began.

She's been married but three weeks and has been in Washington only two, and since she left Budapest to fly to the United States a whole new world has opened up to her. It's a world that still seems too wonderful to contemplate just for now, for the land of her birth offers strange and sorrowful contrasts.

The children are undernourished, there is very little food, the beautiful capital city of Hungary lies in half ruins. And there is very little happiness anywhere. In the spirit of the once rich, spoiled and beautiful women of Hungary, however, there is great hope, Mme. Szegedy-Maszák believes.

They struggled magnificently during the war and now have turned toward the task of rebuilding with an obsession-like zeal.

So quietly did the new minister and his bride slip into Washington that few people even know they are here. Well, they have a suite at the Carlton and are—yes, you guessed it—househunting. And that has taken up practically every moment of Madame's time since she arrived.

To date she has found nothing suitable, but with a philosophical shrug of her shoulders she explains, "It seems like such a minor problem—where to live—compared to the real troubles we all have."

Tall, straight as an arrow with crisp dark wavy hair almost to her shoulders, Mme. Szegedy-Maszák looks like the typical outdoor woman that she is. There's not an ounce of superfluous fat on her slender figure; her skin glows with a healthy tan and her hazel eyes, very direct, sparkle with wholesome living.

Before the war she spent many months of the year at her parents' country estate little more than one hundred miles from Budapest. There she rode every day, hunted and played lots of tennis. When the Germans overswept Hungary she fled to Portugal, returning later to her homeland to see what she could do to help.

In the meantime, Hanna Kornfeld, as she was then, had met the young diplomat whom she later was to marry. He was then with the Foreign Office and before that served with the Hungarian embassy in Berlin. Taken prisoner by the Nazis in Budapest, he spent months in a concentration camp in Dakar [*sic*], several more in Budapest, and was released shortly before the American liberation.

The bride of the Diplomatic Corps speaks English with a delightful English accent attributed, she says, to the number of English-born teachers in Hungary.

A good bridge player and one who likes to dance, Mme. Szegedy-Maszák will find herself being warmly welcomed in Washington.

CHAPTER 35

A Forced Landing

■
■   ■

I was astonished. A picture of my mother in the newspaper? *My*
mother?

That article and others were kept in an envelope in the secret leather
bag in my grandmother Marianne's closet on Patterson Street.

There was a nest of yellowed newspaper clippings: My parents waving at La Guardia when they had just landed in the United States. My
father accepting the keys to the city from Newark's mayor. A smiling
picture of both of them with the great conductor Eugene Ormandy. A
society story about a fabulous reception they hosted, *the* party of the
spring season. A political cartoon where my father, all jutting jaw and
jet-black hair, was smoking a prosperous cigar, reclining against bags and
bags of U.S. dollars, with the Capitol in the background and a singularly
sinister Uncle Sam shaking his hand, while in a corner were starving
Hungarian figures.

That one came later.

When letters containing these clippings arrived in Portugal, it "resembled a National Holiday," Puppa wrote to Hanna. "Starting with
Uncle Ali, they all stand in line to hear your news. Mami gives them out
with her usual kindness—'I may be nice enough to part with them.'
Somehow I am jealous that they think you are everyone's property; on
the other hand, I am proud to know that you are such a popular person."
Marianne's thrill in showing off her daughter and new son-in-law's tri-

umph in the United States almost compensated for how much she missed my mother.

More than twenty years after my grandmother enjoyed showing these clippings to an appreciative audience, I was very young, maybe ten years old. I remember that we were in her bedroom and she brought out the bag and put it on her bed, as her ancestors peered down at us from their images on the wall. The room was filled with afternoon warmth and light. Classical music played on the radio. My grandmother unfolded the pages carefully and warned me to be mindful of their fragility. I couldn't believe they were about my no-longer-young, not-exactly-pretty, and far-from "bridey" mother.

It was another peek behind the curtains at Patterson Street.

THEY LEFT PARIS ON Saturday, January 5, at three-thirty in the morning, and at first the starlit night painted their departure with magic and romance. But during the twelve-hour flight to Bermuda, all the doubts, the regrets, and the corrosive worry ambushed Hanna. To make matters worse, they were shown a short film entitled *What to Do in Case of a Forced Landing.* She wrote her parents, "I know exactly what to do, and it is certainly not what the film tells me."

At some point, high over the Atlantic, the solid month of strain and emotion and transitions and travel walloped her. She looked at her new husband dozing beside her and felt a stab of anxiety. She wrote to her mother, "I cursed the airplane and cursed America and could not understand the sense of what we were doing at all. I was so shaken up by everything." When they arrived in Bermuda the next day, a lieutenant in a magnificent Packard took them sightseeing before depositing them at a military base for a rest.

After a brief nap, they boarded another flight to New York. Five hours later they emerged for passport and customs inspection. Filling out the forms, my father hesitated at the question about their "race," which struck them both as peculiar given the recent war and especially when the newspapers were filled with reports from the Nuremberg trials that had just begun a few weeks earlier. There initial evidence showed that approximately four million Jews had been killed in concentration camps, and another two million had died in other ways. Aladár impatiently wrote, "Hungarian."

As they emerged from customs, on the way to the flight that would take them to Washington, they were greeted by a scrum of photographers and journalists, eager to report on the arrival of the new minister from Hungary and his bride. All they had really wanted to do was eat something, but instead they smiled and waved. She wrote her parents that she dreaded where the "idiotic photo with the Hitler-Salut" would appear. Her question was answered on Wednesday, January 9: on page four of *The Washington Post.*

There was a poignant irony to it all: after all the years they had spent longing for a "normal" courtship, a relationship untroubled by secrecy, conspiracy, and racist laws, they now had to cope with a much-too-public marriage, of interest to photographers and journalists. Even at home in Budapest, all the attention had made my mother self-conscious; here she was overwhelmed, a newlywed on a new continent, in the bull's-eye of several cameras pointed in her direction.

Finally on Monday, January 7, 1946, they arrived in Washington in the early evening. Stanley Woodward, the chief of protocol of the White House, greeted them, accompanied by the assistant head of the Southeast Europe division, Walworth Barbour. As they drove in an official State Department car through the city to the Carlton Hotel, the polished and patrician Woodward inquired about their trip, congratulated them on their marriage, and pointed out various points of interest. Hanna and Aladár sat in the back, glancing out the window, surprised by the parks and the trees and the long rows of modest two-story houses with generous lawns. This was the capital of the free world?

Despite some impressive government buildings, Washington appeared to be a small town in comparison to the great European cities they had known. Of course they knew that the war had not touched the United States, and yet the pristine houses and pleasant neighborhoods and streets were visually startling to both of them, seeming as they did to deny the reality they knew so well. An odd nostalgia for ruins infected them as they sat in that car and looked at their new home, a nostalgia that lingered for months. Eventually, incredibly, Washington even made Aladár nostalgic for Dachau.

When they arrived at the Carlton, one of Washington's finest hotels, Woodward and Barbour accompanied them to the front desk and made sure all the arrangements were in order. They said goodbye, shaking hands and promising continued contact. Finally the exhausted couple took the elevator to their room, following the porter who wheeled their bags, which looked far shabbier now than when they had been packed in Budapest. The porter unlocked the door to their room, closed the curtains, and accepted the tip from Aladár.

Hanna looked at Aladár, who was trying to hang a few things up, and then at the strange American hotel room, with its ridiculous bathroom. She felt so tired and depressed and overwhelmed, she just sat down and cried.

But imagine: less than a month after her farewell to Portugal, she had somehow assumed a completely alien identity, or several completely alien identities: a married woman, a diplomat's wife, an émigré in America— Hanna Szegedy-Maszák, on her passport. How was this possible? What on earth was she doing here? Clearly, she had made a terrible mistake. This was the forced landing she had dreaded, and contrary to her confident declaration that she would know *exactly* what to do, she didn't.

Not without the guidance and the presence of her family, her *real* family. And now that she had done everything that was expected of her, now that she had behaved in so many demanding circumstances in ways that would have made her parents proud, in ways that showed her breeding and her unusual gifts, she was ready to go home. Given the last two years of destruction and diaspora, "going home" meant going anywhere that her family lived but emphatically not Washington, D.C.

Of course she cried.

The Feeling I Could Go Home

Hanna's departure had been the first of many goodbyes for the family in Portugal. For eighteen months they had lived densely intertwined. Those who were held hostage in Vienna—Alfons Weiss, Hansi Mauthner, George Kornfeld, his wife, and their three-year-old son—were now free. Alfons went to Portugal and was reunited with his family, ambivalently by his wife and joyfully by his two sons and two daughters. Hansi Mauthner, who had become a morphine addict, traveled between Vienna and Budapest and was planning to settle back in Hungary. George and Elsie Kornfeld were in Innsbruck for a little while with their young son Stevie and were headed for Zurich. Edith Weiss had managed to get a Swiss visa and lived in Zurich. Mopi was still in Basel, and Baby, her husband, and two children and Stephen Mauthner were in Zurich.

Shortly before Christmas, Hanna's brother Tom and his cousin Martha had received their American visas and embarked for the United States. Magda Gábor's friendship with the head of the Pan Am office in Lisbon helped them get a ticket to New York when others were waiting for months. They arrived even before Hanna and Aladár. Tamás became Thomas. In order to "de-Jewify" his name, as he put it, and claim his rightful status as a baron, he inserted the quietly assertive *de* between his first and last name. He set a precedent for all who followed.

Nonetheless the core of the family, five of the six children of Manfred Weiss and their spouses and many of their children, were together. Annoying each other, supporting each other, providing social life and some intellectual framework, they sustained the essence of the world they had left in Budapest—the propinquity, the solidarity—but the two marble columns of power and influence were gone. In their place, to varying degrees for each family member, were simple gratitude, the nagging guilt of survival, and a terrible anxiety about the uncertain future.

News trickling in from Budapest triggered long-suppressed restlessness that spanned the generations. The younger cousins made plans, applied for visas, and imagined futures unmoored from the safety of their privileged position, though never completely severed from the dominating presence of their elders. Even as they all hoped to return to Hungary, America was clearly the best possible alternative, although the allure of Switzerland was also great.

They had heard that in Hungary, some people actually paid one hundred dollars for American visa application forms—blank forms that the State Department issued for free—to enterprising Hungarians, revealing as much about Hungarian entrepreneurial savvy as it did about the desperation to emigrate. These Hungarians mistakenly believed that these forms could help them jump the long line that preceded them to the United States. After all, Tom and Martha had managed. Those who remained in Portugal filled out papers, visited the American embassy in Lisbon, and wondered whether the United States or Switzerland would be more a comfortable place to start new lives.

Gradually the community in Portugal began to disperse. In the early spring, the Gábor family finally left to seek their fortune in the United States, where eventually they would become the punch line for any remark about Hungarians. Marianne wrote to Hanna that finally "Papa Gábor left. He was quite deaf because of the flu, but he was full of expectations that during his first visit to New York he would go straight to the diamond exchange and make a bundle. One of his daughters [Zsa Zsa] bought a big house in New York, and there they will have a wonderful apartment. Magda had her nose operated on. I never noticed that it was bad, but the whole family is now ready to make new conquests. I hope you have nothing to do with them, even though, for all their ordinariness, they are very helpful people."

Only Puppa remained distant from the feverish plans. She had managed in Portugal to replicate the outlines of her previous life in Budapest. She was once again engaged in an unacceptable romance, this time with

Luis Alsina. He was twenty years older than she, a Republican in the Spanish Civil War. His watercolors of the Portuguese light caroming off the walls and narrow streets of Lisbon resembled more transparent versions of Cézanne's oils of Mont Saint-Michel. He was terribly jealous, though. When Puppa walked with him and smiled spontaneously at a passerby, Luis would be angry and petulant for hours.

She was thirty-one years old and pulled in several different directions. Luis assumed that she was there for him alone. But Tamás Perczel, a not-very-handsome but incredibly nice friend of the family's from Hungary, had adored Puppa for years and, now that the war was over, wanted to marry her. Marianne approved of the match because she both liked and felt sorry for Perczel, whose own mother was indifferent to her son to the point of brutality. The family had always thought that at least one reason for her nastiness was that she was so vain, she could not abide her only son's bald, triangular head, big horizontal ears, unfortunate overbite, and, of course, thick glasses.

From the moment he met Puppa, he had fallen in love with her and desperately wanted to marry her. In January 1946 he proposed by letter, and she wrote him a tender but emphatic refusal that left her feeling guilty for weeks. She hated the idea that the friendship would end and was reassured, several weeks later, when she received a "very friendly, very civilized letter" from him, assuring her that their friendship would be for life, which it was. He visited Washington and proposed to her nearly every year of his life, and every year he received the same answer.

Then there was János Zwack. Coko had loved Puppa passionately since 1932, and while they had kept things neatly compartmentalized before the war, now he had decided it was time to divorce Vera and marry Puppa.

The tension between János and Vera was exacerbated by her bitterness that she and her family had been excluded from the deal and the great escape. As close as the families had been in Budapest, this snub had jeopardized Vera's and her family's lives. So it was easy to conflate the escalation of his affair with Puppa—many years before, they had agreed it would remain only an affair, but it was now morphing into something more threatening—with all these other matters. János had sent Puppa a letter shortly after Hanna and Aladár's wedding saying that he was going to divorce Vera and wanted to marry her. Marianne wrote Hanna:

As far as Puppa is concerned, she has not yet decided. I think she was pleased with J's letter, but I have the feeling that she is not as much in love as once she was. But she said, "I have the feeling that I could go home if I could be with him." If this feeling is really that strong and she would find a home, no one has the right to get involved. (It is a different matter that I am very sorry for Vera.) Puppa responded right away to say that they should not get a divorce, there will be time to make a decision when she gets home. No one can be more loyal than that. I just wish that this good soul should be happy, and not very un-happy, and find everything she wishes for in Coko.

Hanna did not waste any time before responding. "I only wish that Puppa could find the same happiness that I have discovered. Mami, I beg you to do everything for the Coko problem to go smoothly. János adores Puppa, and I am convinced this is the only good solution. Vera behaves fantastically generously, and we came to the conclusion that this is the only solution. Vera will certainly miss János terribly, but to stay together would be even worse, because he thinks exclusively about Puppa, speaks of nothing else. I am certain that he is the one person with whom Puppa will be happy."

Just to be clear: the family had no objection to Puppa—who had had a long affair with the husband of her mother's first cousin—now being the reason that this couple would divorce so that she could marry him. Trivial issues of middle-class morality did not trouble them when they defied understandable human emotions. They wanted Puppa to be happy. No moral judgment here. No high-minded homilies on the sanctity of marriage. But something held Puppa back. She wrote to Hanna in Janu-ary that "I wrote to János that I am coming home, but not to divorce. I also sent a telegram stating this."

At least part of her hesitation was due to her continuing affair with Luis. His vulnerability was well disguised by refined, macho bravado, but Puppa could still see the vague atmosphere of defeat that surrounded him. She was helplessly drawn to these sensitive, depressed men, ones whom she could in some way save, even redeem. It was her form of social work. In the winter of 1946 their affair—like the affair with Zwack in Budapest—was an open secret to the assembled family and probably one of the reasons that wrecking the home of a relative was considered a good option.

The war and the exhibit of pictures from the camps had changed Puppa's sense of herself in the world. The life of a detached intellectual had lost its charms. Guilt, which would ebb and assert itself throughout the coming years, was powerful in 1946. She just knew that in some way, without malice or even intention, she had withheld help that she might have given, and she knew that whatever happened, she would need to do things for other people. Maybe she would become a nurse.

The older generation also chafed at the constraints of refugee life, but most of their hopes and plans involved returning to Hungary. Móric was especially pained by his exile. "You know how I live here, dear Hanna. I live exactly the same way as when you were here. I nourish the old earth with philosophy. Péter and Fenyő both write that I can go home without hesitation, but I have to wait until the peace conference. I do not want to go home just now, and I have to see the situation more clearly, just as you do, before I make any decisions. Still, I know that I will not be at home in any place except Hungary."

"We did not get very much news from Budapest in a long time, but according to the newspapers things are not getting better," Marianne wrote to Hanna. She described, with some irritation at their florid anxieties, how worried her brothers Eugene and Alfons were because "Eugene is telling himself now that he and Ali are in great danger as war criminals."

Their concerns were exaggerated, stoked by Eugene's characteristic obsessive anxieties, but returning was still risky. There were rumors that anti-Semitism was on the rise again in Hungary, not that anyone assumed that it had disappeared. But life was so miserable there, with limited food and heat, and ruins everywhere, that everyone needed to blame someone.

Ferenc Chorin had already set his sights across the Atlantic on the United States. His return to Hungary would have been complicated, given his close association with the Horthy regime, and given that his masterminding the deal was still an open subject in the increasingly vicious Hungarian press. He considered going back, of course, but as passionate a patriot as he was, and as great a leader in the country as he had been, hardheaded realism, curiosity, and ambition trumped abstract values.

There was something compelling about all the possibilities in the postwar United States, and even as Chorin made short-term plans to

visit Switzerland and considered a permanent move there, he visited the
American embassy in Lisbon and organized the visa applications for his
family. His wife, Daisy, balked—but she balked at everything. The rest of
the family continued to wonder whether the United States or Switzerland would be a more comfortable place to start their new lives, and they
glanced back at Hungary as if they were on boats looking at a rapidly
receding coastline.

Efforts to reclaim some of their lost property, begun the previous year,
gained some momentum as lawyers were hired and assets were tallied. In
an effort to protect some of their assets, the six owners had signed over
their legal ownership of the Manfred Weiss empire to four of the Gentile
spouses of family members: the wife of Eugene Weiss, Annie Geitler; the
husbands of two of Elsa's daughters, Dr. Ferenc Borbély and Herbert
Margaretha; and Elsie Kavalski, George's wife, Móric and Marianne's
daughter-in-law.

The first step was to legally reestablish their ownership, which was
done by a document signed in Bern, Switzerland, in July 1946. The document stated that the six children of Manfred Weiss "had remitted one
part of their legal ownership unto us, who—according to the laws of that
time—were considered as Aryans, in order to exempt the concern from
the different anti-Jewish laws and regulations." The spouses of the family
members then went on "to declare that we considered this transfer of
ownership as purely formal and that the above-mentioned six heirs of
Manfred Weiss always remained and still are the only legal owners of the
concern." The paper was duly signed by each of them, in what constituted the first stumbling step to see if it would be possible to stake a
claim for the factories in Hungary.

It was hopeless. The factories were nationalized.

And so the months unfolded after my mother left. Her parents and
sister acknowledged the need to reconstruct their lives, but their efforts
often seemed like distracted recitations of familiar verses—do we return
home, can we reclaim some assets, where are the visas, how can we manage with this amount of money, what are the Chorins, the Weisses, the
Mauthners doing—for lunch, for dinner, for the rest of their lives? The
answers were just not clear.

CHAPTER 37

FOR ALADÁR ONLY—PRIVÁT!

▪ ▪

Everything in Hungary was in flux. The Soviet Union had not yet officially established its political sphere of influence and created the bloc of satellite countries that would define international relations for the next forty years, but Hungarians knew that by dint of their geography, some ill-considered leadership, and their historic bad luck, they would end up suspended between two miserable alternatives. The Soviets were initially restrained in taking complete control of the country. Stalin knew that in order to achieve his ultimate goal of regional domination, he needed to act relatively slowly. World War II had decimated the Soviet Union, and Stalin needed the support of the Western powers, or at least he needed not to alienate them by brash assertions of power in his Yalta prizes.

Never a particularly robust or indigenous party, the Hungarian Communists maintained strong connections with the Soviet Union. Following the end of the war, other parties sprang up and gained power. The Communists, the Social Democrats on the left, and the National Peasants Party and the Smallholders Party in the center-right formed a coalition that, at least at the beginning, operated cooperatively, culminating in elections in the fall of 1945 that were remarkably free and fair. Every Hungarian over the age of twenty was allowed to vote, unless they were ethnic Germans or had been convicted of a crime during the war, or charged with pro-Nazi activities.

The Smallholders Party triumphed during the elections on November 4, 1945, winning 57 percent of the popular vote. The Communists and the Social Democrats each won about 17 percent, and with all the other parties combined made up the difference. The outdated constitution preserved the monarchy in Hungary, so on February 1, 1946, the National Assembly approved Law I, which abolished all institutions of the monarchy and established the Republic of Hungary. Smallholders Party men Zoltán Tildy became the president of the republic and Ferenc Nagy became the prime minister. At the same time, hard-line Soviet Communists also assumed positions of power and influence, with Mátyás Rákosi becoming the deputy prime minister and Ernő Gerő the minister of commerce.

For this very brief period, the Republic of Hungary enjoyed a kind of euphoria that a free, autonomous, and democratic Hungary might actually exist. The optimism and pessimism of many Hungarians rose and plummeted like a sick child's fever chart. Those who remained—Aladár's parents, sisters, and cousins, not to mention many close friends—concentrated on reassembling whatever fragments remained from their old lives. In the words of the novelist Sándor Márai, "Like someone crawling on all fours in anguish during the moments of an earthquake and feeling his way with his palms, people searched for some kind of security in their daily lives."

Familiar social and professional points of reference linking the past—the past before the war—with the unfamiliar postwar present had been blown up, like the bridges linking Buda to Pest. The Hungarians in Budapest, many of whom were masters of improvisation, became more so as they repaired apartments, started businesses, created political parties, returned to work, educated their children, entertained their friends, and attempted desperately to keep pace with inflation by pawning the silver tea sets, the bejeweled tiaras, and the Old Masters that were once family legacies, or prizes from the abandoned properties of Jews, aristocrats, or others who would never return.

Lilly was determined that her brother not miss a moment of life in Budapest and wrote voluminous and detailed letters to him. She described their father's volatility ("Daddy's mood is terrible. If there is news about prices increasing, it is horrible to listen to him cursing, and saying awful things about the Jews"); the improved health of their mother ("Mami, thank God, is happy and well-balanced and full of energy"); and the demands of renovating an apartment, earning a living, and managing their money. "If we cannot sell the dining room set, we will cut it into pieces for heating purposes," she wrote. "They want to give us a couple of hundred thousand pengős for the entire set while the price of wood is already up to 300,000 pengős for a kilo." She begged him to write, both because she was desperate for news and because she was sick of answering the complaints of their parents.

Aladár's marriage and departure were a double trauma for Lilly, whose passionate devotion to her brother verged on the romantic. Her own marriage a failure, her other liaison with a married man extravagantly unsuccessful, her beautiful younger brother had always been the man who least disappointed her; on him she predicated her sense of security and her sense of the future. What happy times they had had together when he worked at the Foreign Ministry and they shared an apartment! She liked nothing more than to take care of him, nurture him, entertain with him, and luxuriate in the reflection of his status in her mirror. She had even managed to be enthusiastic about his courtship of Hanna.

At least in the beginning, Hanna seemed to love and admire Lilly as well. But when the letters to America started arriving, some with cautionary notes saying that the following several pages were "FOR ALADÁR ONLY—PRIVÁT," Hanna must have felt irritated. And then when some of those pages contained thinly veiled criticisms of her ("I hope that Hancsi is also able to be in some ways good for you, even as I know you are good for her" was a typical example), I can't imagine she was so secure and good-natured as not to be bothered.

Lilly was determined to do all that was needed to make the Budapest apartment their home as well. "I tried to arrange everything here in such a way that upon your return everyone would have his and her relative comfort," Lilly wrote. "My dear Hancsi, I hope you too will have a good time here, with us. The two rooms can be separated. . . . Of course, this is a different comfort from what you have over there, but based on the circumstances here, this place is fairly good." And then the finish, where Lilly could not resist activating the cattle prod of guilt: "Many, many hugs, much love and kisses for both of you from your endlessly loving, grateful and deserted old—Lilly." Aladár would have agreed to nearly anything. For her part, Hanna wrote to her parents, "I think with horror about living with them." Nonetheless the uncertainty of the future permitted, perhaps demanded, that she make a few unrealistic but comforting reassurances to Lilly.

The modest salary Lilly received from her job as a secretary and the additional support from Aladár and Hanna couldn't cover her expenses. In postwar Hungary those who were most successful were the expert black marketeers. Inflation rates were out of control. In April 1945 one dollar on the black market would fetch 250 pengős. At that time Hungary had to begin punitive reparation payments to the Allies—especially the Soviets—and the armistice agreement forced Hungary to furnish goods and services to 1.5 million troops in the Soviet occupying army. The combination of military defeat and ruinous payment requirements had created an economic catastrophe.

By August 1946 the exchange was one dollar for 4,600 quadrillion (thirty zeros) pengős. Indeed, the Hungarian inflation of 1946 has stood the test of time and continues to be regarded as the worst in economic history. Because the rate of inflation was between 10 and 12 percent every *hour*, nearly everyone was paid twice a day and would race to the stores—which were in fact mostly empty—in order to buy anything to eat before the price quadrupled. In fact, the only reliable currency was barter. In the streets of Budapest, scholars would barter rare books for loaves of bread; a bag of flour could purchase several Persian rugs; and a gold wedding band was worth a few days of groceries for a family. One couple had a thick gold chain and cut off pieces when the check arrived at a restaurant.

Hanna pulled together care packages from Washington and sent them to her in-laws to try to provide some small luxuries in the midst of the economic insanity. Lilly was grateful for her help. She hoped to visit the United States at some point but knew that her destiny was in Budapest. "Maybe I am not that young anymore"—she was fifty-three—"but I cannot imagine leaving the country," she wrote. "And to do it with the old parents is impossible. Even if I were alone, I could not leave those two graves here either, and start a new life, establish new roots, friends and life in a world that is foreign to me—alone."

When my father, who had his hands full representing his country in the United States, did not respond to her letters as quickly as she wanted, she wrote him, "You know, darling, I start to be worried that you will detach yourself from home, and you will forget about those good and pleasant times that you have spent here until March 19, 1944. You will also become estranged from us if you stop maintaining a written communication with people and friends here at home. This is not a rebuke. If anyone, it is me who understands and knows you, your nature."

For those in Hungary, the compelling and reassuring Technicolor drama was in the United States, with Hanna and Aladár in the starring roles. As 1946 unfolded, all eyes were turned west to America, a place that they could not fathom.

CHAPTER 38

The Happy Joint Endeavor

.   .   .

"Washington in wartime is a combination of Moscow (for over-crowding), Paris (for its trees), Wichita (for its way of thinking), Nome (in the gold rush days) and Hell (for its livability)," wrote Malcolm Cowley in *The New Republic* in 1946. The city that greeted Hanna and Aladár in the winter of 1946 was like an awkward adolescent after a particularly harrowing growth spurt, frantically trying to get organized around unexpected new dimensions. The New Deal and especially the war had created a boomtown. Between 1940 and 1945 the population of Washington doubled, with new demands for office workers, government bureaucrats, military personnel, journalists, and congressional staffers and a burgeoning service industry to satisfy them all. Now that the war was over, what had once been a transient population became permanent, but housing and other services—like schools, shopping, transportation, and roads—lagged far behind the demand.

The day after they arrived in Washington, Aladár traveled up Connecticut Avenue to the Hungarian legation on LeRoy Place to meet his staff. One of the new press attachés greeted him with a smile, saying, "*Habemus Papam,*" we have a pope. Aladár described his staff as "a heterogeneous group, thrown together by earthquakes and avalanches." Only three of them had ever worked in foreign affairs, and among the top members were a politician, a journalist, and inexplicably, an Africanist. Viktor Csornoky, the son-in-law of President Tildy, had already annoyed Aladár by giving a public interview to Hungarian radio, bidding farewell to the Hungarian people and acting like the man in charge. Hanna took an instant dislike to him and warned Aladár not to trust him. As Aladár entered his office, he met his secretary, Katalin Máriássy. He brought her greetings from her sister Judit in Budapest.

He was determined to maintain "a low profile, be modest, avoid notice, exaggerations, and flag waving, so that our honesty and trustworthiness could be established." During this first meeting, he advised other members of the legation that "before they tried to convince anybody of anything, they had to establish their own credibility." Or to put it more crassly, he quoted an old American saying that he had once heard: "Before you can sell anything, you have to sell yourself." They could really accomplish nothing, he said, without demonstrating both personal and national integrity. But as he looked around at the vivid personalities at the legation, he worried that each one of them probably understood what he just said in a totally different way.

Aladár went to the State Department, hoping to present his credentials to Secretary of State James Byrnes. Byrnes was unavailable, but Assistant Secretary of State Dean Acheson was there. Standing over six feet, Acheson did not quite tower over Aladár, but with his patrician bearing, brush mustache, and bespoke pin-striped suit, he reminded Aladár of the prototypical British diplomat. Perhaps the timing was wrong, but Acheson's reception was odd and distracted. After accepting his credentials with a few pro forma remarks, Acheson immediately began to describe a report he had just received from Gen. George Marshall about an armistice that had been signed between the Nationalist Chinese and the Communists. Shortly negotiations would begin, he said, to form a coalition government for all of China. Although surprised by both the news and the turn that the conversation took, Aladár mumbled a few bromides about the preservation of human rights in China being the strongest bulwark for peace. Acheson nodded and made it clear that the audience was over.

Meanwhile Hanna explored the city, got on the wrong tram that led her hours out of her way, wore the black suit from her wedding for her official photograph—"so that the official photo will be a wedding photo too"—bought a new hat at Garfinkel's department store that caused Aladár to burst out laughing when she modeled it, and started to look for a house, no easy endeavor given the shortage in Washington. Almost in spite of herself, she somehow managed to become a "presence" in the city, not a force to be reckoned with like the formidable hostess Perle Mesta, but rather a new and refreshing curiosity, a lovely bride with an exotic and admirable past, whose charm and war-scarred background attracted the attention of many people "who mattered." Her brother Tom had arrived in the city, much to her relief, and lived with them as he made his future plans.

The day *The Washington Post* article appeared about Hanna, Aladár presented his credentials to President Truman at the White House. Accustomed to European capitals and castles, he could not get over the modest informality of the White House, the absence of uniformed guards, the easy access. Squeezed between Truman's visit with the national officers of the Future of Farmers of America at eleven-thirty on Friday, January 18, 1947, and his meeting with the acting secretary of war Tommy Thompson at twelve-fifteen, the new minister from Hungary was scheduled to appear before the American president. Stanley Woodward, the chief of protocol, again greeted him and asked about his first ten days in Washington. Aladár said how pleasant the city was and how warm their welcome had been. Woodward then led him into the Oval Office.

Aladár glanced at the painting of George Washington over the fireplace, the fresh flowers on Truman's desk, and the family pictures. These were standard office features, of course, but the lack of pomp seemed to reveal something essential about the man himself. Truman welcomed him cordially, emphasizing the goodwill of the United States toward Hungary. The president hoped that the minister and his wife would be comfortable in America. Aladár thanked him and assured him that they had received a happy introduction and looked forward to their stay. He added that all of Hungary regarded the United States with enormous gratitude and hope. Ever the man of the heartland, Truman said that he would love to visit Hungary and study Hungarian agriculture and cattle breeding. He imagined that the country resembled the American Midwest. Aladár smiled and agreed that agriculture was one of Hungary's greatest treasures, but the devastation of the war had triggered a dire economic situation. He assured Truman that he would be welcomed both in the countryside and in Budapest should he ever find the time to visit. Aladár presented his formal speech and then was ushered out. The whole meeting lasted ten minutes.

The speech had been prepared carefully in Budapest and in Washington. It began with an expression of gratitude to the president for resuming diplomatic relations with a defeated country even before the peace treaty had been signed. He made a distinction between the previous regime with its "ruinous" policy, and the Hungarian people, whose suffering from that regime was immense. While the Hungarian people were responsible for laying the foundations of the reconstruction of their own country by their own efforts, it was also impossible to achieve without assistance from the United States: "Unfortunately, without assistance, the Hungarian people cannot create all the preliminary conditions of prosperity since prosperity and happiness within any country can be achieved only through international cooperation."

Three days later Truman's official reply accepted the letters "with which the Supreme National Council of Hungary accredits you as envoy extraordinary and minister plenipotentiary to the United States of America." After assuring the minister and his government of the goodwill of the United States, the statement also expressed gratitude "that the Hungarian government in entering upon official relations with the United States government has chosen a representative who through personal hardship and sacrifice has shown his devotion to humanity's common cause. The impulse to freedom is not circumscribed by the bounds of state or nationality."

One day a thick, formal invitation arrived for Mrs. Szegedy-Maszák from the White House. In beautiful calligraphy, Mrs. Truman requested "the pleasure of the company of Mrs. Szegedy-Maszák at luncheon on Tuesday, February 26, 1946, at one o'clock." Hanna dreaded the event, and on February 26, "fully dressed and terribly afraid," she arrived at the White House. Her heart sank, "and I got smaller by 5 cm," when she saw the seating chart that placed her as the honored guest on Bess Truman's right. There were thirty-six women, wives of congressmen and senators, and only one other foreigner, Mrs. Sajpay, the wife of the ambassador from India. Together they walked in pairs to the dining room, led by Hanna and Bess Truman. The food was, to Hanna's European palate, execrable. "A soup in which hazelnuts and almonds swam. Poultry with a horrible thing named sweet potatoes and some other garnishes of a similar kind. And then a green salad with grapefruit, oranges, and pears," she wrote to her mother. After dessert and coffee, the same parade marched out to the living room, where Hanna realized that as the guest of honor, she was responsible for leaving first. But when? "To my good fortune, the social secretary took pity on me and told me that it was time to leave."

In spite of her professed shyness and reputation for a lack of self-confidence, Hanna was made for diplomatic life: the many invitations, the life on the go, the occasionally interesting conversations. Most important was the conviction that she was helping Aladár in such a difficult and thankless enterprise. She sometimes accompanied him on his frequent visits to Hungarian communities throughout the United States. They went to Pittsburgh. "The trip was magnificent, the feast was touching, but to live in Pittsburgh must be horrible—smoke and an unimaginable quantity of chimneys," she wrote. When they visited the large Hungarian community in Newark—where they also received the golden key to the city—no limousine was available for transportation, so the local Hungarian-owned funeral home provided a hearse in which the VIPs toured the city.

Some of their travels were intended to raise money from the local communities for Hungarian relief efforts. One such trip was to Cleveland in May—where nearly eighty thousand people of Hungarian descent lived. They raised almost $15,000 for Hungarian relief. "Afterward in the lobby of the theater," Hanna wrote, "Aladár and I were put on the stage, and those who wanted, were invited to come and shake our hands. (How good it must have been for them!) A great many people were around us asking horrible questions, while I had to distribute autographs."

"I just want to say that I am terribly happy," Hanna wrote her parents. "If I were superstitious, I would be afraid that in the midst of so much pain, I have won the lottery. It is impossible to find the words to describe how good Aladár is to me and how he spoils me." No matter how inevitable their marriage was, no matter how many years they had spent getting to know each other under arduous circumstances, they had been curious and shy and regarded each other and their marriage with some trepidation. And yet they both missed their families and the European way of life. Homesickness would ambush them at odd moments—when they visited another émigré's home, perhaps, or didn't receive any mail for several days, or received several letters in one day. There was no real pattern to their longing, but America never felt quite right without the familiar and beloved voices that they now could only summon when reading letters. Because they were both in a completely new environment, untested and unknown, they depended on each other in ways that cemented their love affair. Aladár wrote, "America became a joint endeavor for us, coinciding with the beginning of our marriage, and because we were in a foreign country, we were probably more interdependent than we would have been at home."

The responsibility of his new job physically weighed on Aladár, and Hanna was terribly worried. She wrote her mother and father, "I went to the doctor's yesterday—relax, I am okay—and he examined Aladár too. He said that if he does not take care of himself and his nerves, he will not be able to bear this harried life. Aladár is exhausted, tired. He looks sick, and I do not know what to do. I feel responsible for him and watch powerlessly without being able to help." Some nights, in nightmares, he returned to the torments of Dachau.

As the new minister, he believed that his task was to ward off impending disasters as strenuously as possible, and the first one was economic. Hungary suffered a tremendous shortage of wheat, and worries about a winter of starvation loomed. He knew both from official reports and from letters from home that the new government would have no hope of survival unless it was able to bring food to the tables of the population. The rate of inflation was reminiscent of Germany in 1923, and he vividly remembered the images of children pushing wheelbarrows full of currency. Economic collapse was not merely a theoretical possibility but a very real option, and after the international wreckage from the war, the United States emerged as the only country capable of offering some support.

Aladár knew that any support Hungary received would be in direct proportion to America's perceived interests in the country. So he tried to convince the State Department, Congress, and anyone who would listen that aiding Hungary would serve not only Hungarian domestic concerns but the broader goal of universal peace. How could he attract both the trust and the attention of the United States? Being an attractive young diplomatic couple helped, but my father believed that because Hungary's relatively stable democratic government was actually the product of a multiparty election—as opposed to the single-party elections that had occurred in Romania and Bulgaria—the Americans would see it as the most sympathetic country in central Europe.

He was wrong.

As Peter Kenéz points out in *Hungary from the Nazis to the Soviets,* "By the spring of 1946 the United States gave up on Hungary, at least to the extent that it did not consider it worthwhile to extend material support." The reasons were complex, but from the vantage point of the United States, a marginal country, on the verge of starvation and bankruptcy, with a robust Communist Party that was getting more and more support from the Soviet Union was not a place where American interests seemed able to gain much foothold. As a result, the policy of the United States forced Hungary toward the Soviet Union in order to get any help whatsoever.

Meanwhile Hanna's brother Tom had been drafted and was stationed at Fort Sam Houston in Texas. "You curse the heat or the rain or the mud," he wrote, "and in the evening you are swearing when you can't go to sleep because there is so much noise, but even with all this I feel very well, I am a good friend of the guys, and I am delighted to be living without any problems or responsibilities." When he first arrived for the initial fitness evaluation, they all had to strip naked. It was so cold that they had been wearing hats; they discarded their clothes, but there was no place to put their hats. Tom observed that he finally could see what a "nudist orthodox synagogue was like." Eventually, out of a class of 180 in basic training, he was ranked third.

Gradually, beautiful Washington spring days began to outnumber the cheerless dark days of winter, reminding Hanna of the flowers and breezes of Estoril in Portugal. After a series of temporary and unsatisfactory rentals, Hanna found a home for them on 31st Street in northwest Washington. In April, society columnist Alice James reported in *The Washington Times Herald* that "invitations are being readied for a reception on April 9, to celebrate the opening of the minister's new residence. . . . The reception will be the first large fête given by the Hungarian Minister and his tall, slender, and chic wife who have been in town only since January."

The reception was in honor of two prominent Hungarian musicians: Eugene Ormandy, the conductor of the Philadelphia Orchestra, and Metropolitan Opera singer Alexander Sved. "If this particular reception was indicative of 'things to come' at the Legation of Hungary, then any invitation from the Minister and his wife undoubtedly will be a MUST in anyone's engagement book," wrote the society columnist Peter Carter.

At the same time, depressing letters arrived every day from Hungary, imploring them for help. "The poverty is horrible, and they have no money," Hanna wrote her parents. "Yesterday I got one from the wife of Szarvas, the caretaker of Derekegyháza. I forwarded her desolate letter to Edith. Another from Dudi Benke—her husband died and they are very badly off. You know, sometimes I am at the point of saying, 'Oh go away, you are breaking my heart.' But I know that this is the last thing I could ever do."

CHAPTER 39

A Visit from the Home Team

From their diplomatic perch, my parents were able to anticipate information that eventually appeared in the newspapers. The Communists in the government persuaded the Smallholders to create a Supreme Economic Council, an entity responsible for regulating the country's perilous economic life. While its ostensible purpose was to bring some rationality to an economy in shambles, in fact it was a way for the Soviets to reduce the private sector, nationalize industry, and tighten their grip on economic life. The Soviets required $200 million in war reparations from the Hungarian government. By making the exchange rate against the dollar artificially low, a decision made by the Soviet-dominated Communists within the Hungarian government, the goods were simply drained out of the country at bargain-basement prices.

In the end, two-thirds of the output of Hungarian industry was directed toward the Soviet Union, and the Manfred Weiss factories and Chorin Salgótarján ironworks and anthracite mining company were all nationalized. For the Manfred Weiss Works alone, 95 percent of its products were sent to the Soviet Union.

Hanna warned the family in Portugal that the demonstrations in Csepel "against the 'reactionaries' have evolved into anti-Semitic demonstrations. . . . We have heard that Takácsy has *not* been beaten *only* because he is *not* Jewish." No matter how alien America was to my parents, it had one similarity to Hungary that astonished them. The connection between Communism and anti-Semitism, a cherished Hungarian conceit, had its parallel expression in the United States.

In another letter, Hanna explained that the anti-Russian mood in the United States was growing in proportion to anti-Semitism, because so many of the local Communist Party members were also Jewish. "My most agonizing moments are when we are in social situations and people start saying that the Jews have been hated for two thousand years, etc. I feel so dishonest because I keep silent. I don't say that I am myself of Jewish origin." Once she had to go to a funeral of one of her "co-religionists. It was ghastly. His daughter—Mrs. Cafritz, whom I wrote about as being so rich and the cocktail party she gave in our honor—considered this a social occasion. . . . Except for the two daughters and me who wore black, everyone else was in colorful summer dresses." The small culture shocks accumulated.

The couple was invited to the White House on several occasions, and gradually the goodwill that Aladár had hoped he could foster began to reap some tangible benefits in terms of financial support for Hungary. Even while he was acting the ministerial role, being as conscientious and diligent as was his nature, in conversations with Hanna he wondered when he should resign. He knew that he could not be ambassador forever; he also knew that the political situation in Hungary was volatile. And then—how on earth would he make a living there? The same cul-de-sac of questions that bedeviled those in Portugal became part of the conversations between Hanna and Aladár in Washington. Should they remain here? Return home? Go somewhere in Europe? And do what? But as long as they were in Washington, they had work to do.

Aladár always considered diplomacy to be a very important job, but he lacked the arrogance of many diplomats. He would refer to himself as a "civil servant," and as minister he considered himself a Foreign Service officer. He once heard from an American journalist acquaintance that State Department officials were happier in Hungarian company than anywhere else, and Aladár always believed that it was because he had a great appreciation for how important it was to have good relationships with the midlevel officials and their immediate superiors. He felt that he was much too new and not important enough to exert much influence on the higher levels in the government.

When he arrived, he really believed that the United States had succeeded in solving the thorny problem of how a diverse group of people can live together in an organized fashion. Clearly this had been the central challenge in Europe—"European conceptual confusions," he called it—and one that Europe had clearly failed to address. He thought that the American leadership would show Europe how to extricate itself from the terrible political and economic crises during the process of rebuilding. The United States, strengthened by its European refugees, could clarify for the rest of the world basic political, social, and economic concepts involved in peaceful coexistence.

In a series of discussions with the prime minister's office, Aladár organized a visit of the Hungarian leadership to the United States. This group would include the prime minister and the leaders of the various political groups in Hungary, including the Communists. He attempted to focus the strategy and objectives of the American visit, then worked with some contacts in the State Department to see if those efforts would find support. The Hungarians decided that they needed the Americans on their side during the peace conference that would be held over the summer in Paris, where final decisions about borders and Soviet dominance were likely to be made. They also hoped that the United States might help Hungary with its financial crisis. During the war, the Nazis had raided the Hungarian National Bank and robbed it of over $30 million worth of gold bullion. At the end of the war, the Americans had recaptured the gold and kept it under the control of the American forces in Austria and Germany until some political stability could emerge in those countries. The gold could help create some long-overdue financial stability by making the Hungarian currency actually backed by something of real value, rather than the paper it was printed on.

In a major diplomatic coup, Aladár managed to secure an invitation to the United States for the leaders of the Hungarian government. The delegation received a formal invitation from the U.S. government and arrived in Washington on Monday, June 10. Prime Minister Ferenc Nagy was accompanied by Minister of Foreign Affairs János Gyöngyösi, Minister of Justice István Reisz, Pál Marik the interpreter, and Mátyás Rákosi, the deputy prime minister and a hard-line Communist.

Rákosi had been selected by Stalin to head the Hungarian Communist Party, after a long history of loyalty and service to the cause. Short, bald, and heavy, with a pugnacious face, he was a central casting version of the thuggish Communist. But he was also a gifted linguist and the only member of the visiting delegation who spoke English. He came from a poor Jewish family and had learned English in Britain before World War I. While he had been important during Béla Kun's brief and ill-fated government, he spent the interwar period being trained as a Comintern agent. Imprisoned in Hungary for nearly sixteen years, he went to the Soviet Union in 1940. He returned to Hungary at the end of October 1944 and maintained a relatively low profile. He rose to political power after the end of the war, during the free elections. He despised the United States with the same passion with which many Americans hated Communists.

"The legation is desolate. We were sure that the visit would not come through, but the Americans, contrary to their better judgment, invited them, and they, of course, grabbed the opportunity to come," Hanna wrote in dismay. "The whole visit might have been bearable without Rákosi, but with him it is a total curse."

They had very little time to plan the official visit—a matter of a week. But the Hungarian leaders arrived and attended a reception for 350 people, a small dinner with Dean Acheson at Blair House, a meeting and luncheon with members of the House Foreign Affairs Committee, and an out-of-town trip to visit the Tennessee Valley Authority. Ferenc Nagy even enjoyed a private meeting with Secretary of State Byrnes, who asked him what he wanted to accomplish by the trip. Nagy responded, through an interpreter, that the gold bullion would be a great help and that ensuring that Hungarian borders were secure would also be appreciated. While Byrnes acknowledged that he could do nothing about the borders, he did assure Nagy that the U.S. government would examine the question of the gold bullion and respond as quickly as possible.

The big question was whether President Truman would have time to meet with them, and after a series of exchanges, Aladár's good relations with Acheson and Chief of Protocol Woodward paid off. On Thursday, June 13, at eleven-fifteen, the Hungarian delegation would have fifteen minutes with the president of the United States. Emblazoned on the cover of a Budapest magazine called *Figyelő* was a picture of Aladár smiling behind President Truman, wearing a light-colored suit, and shaking the hand of Ferenc Nagy. The caption: "Everyone is smiling in the garden of the White House."

The Hungarians were impressed with the modesty and warmth of the president. Truman asked about the Danube as a political and economic factor in the life of Hungary and Central Europe. They were taken to the Rose Garden for another round of photographs, and as the photographers arranged the group in various configurations, Truman pointed out that even in America one could not escape dictatorship. That evening at a dinner hosted by Undersecretary Acheson at Blair House, the group met a number of distinguished Washingtonians including Justice Felix Frankfurter. Later in the visit, Acheson gave Nagy a memorandum that said that the U.S. government hoped to support the efforts of the people of Hungary to stabilize the economy and would unconditionally return both the gold bullion and the war booty that had been stolen from Hungary and captured by the Americans. Also, the Americans granted Hungary a line of credit for $10 million, then raised it by an additional $5 million. The delegation, with the exception of Rákosi, was thrilled.

The next morning the group flew to the Tennessee Valley Authority and saw a model rural development in which a single river provided electricity to an area larger than all of Hungary. As Aladár described the trip to Hanna, they nearly cried with laughter at Rákosi's leaden and reactionary responses. When the delegation ate at a workers' cafeteria—an unknown institution at that time in Hungary—the waitresses piled food onto the plates of the visiting dignitaries. The only one who finished all that he was given was Rákosi, who said, "This is the land of plenty. Why should we spare the Americans by leaving any food?"

As Prime Minister Nagy recalled, "Rákosi's criticism knew no limits, but we tried to overlook his efforts to spoil our impressions. In Tennessee he outdid himself as the enfant terrible." When he saw a farmer with patches on his pants, Rákosi crowed, "Look at those rags. All is not cream in America either." When they visited the actual power plants of the TVA, Rákosi raved about Soviet power plants. When they were shown prefabricated housing, Rákosi announced, "Once the bedbugs get into these houses, they will never get them out again." My father gently pointed out that in his experience, there were no bedbugs in the United States. "Don't you know," Rákosi retorted, "that bedbugs originated in this country and were exported from here to Europe and Russia?"

When the delegation finally left from New York, the coverage of the visit was generally rhapsodic. Hanna wrote to her aunt Edith that having been with "these people (although two of them are really all right), one realizes that our world is finished." Móric, writing from Portugal, offered his congratulations. He knew that the only reason the Americans had reacted with such warmth—indeed, the only reason the delegation was able to meet with the likes of Truman and Byrnes and walk away with such positive results—was because of Aladár and his leadership at the legation.

The return of the gold bullion might not stabilize the economy, "but it may help the Hungarian souls gain some trust in stabilization." "I hope you are very pleased with your success," Móric wrote. "During those few times in my life when I too enjoyed such success, I always felt as if there were more oxygen in the air and that I could breathe more easily, happily, and in a better frame of mind."

BY JUNE 1946, THE Weiss community in Portugal had dispersed. Erzsi and her children settled in New York. Her husband, Alfons, was in Switzerland and planned to join them later. The Chorins also went to Switzerland, though they were still waiting for their American visas to come through in Portugal. Eugene Weiss, his wife Annie, and their three children ended up in Switzerland as well.

Edith was one of the first to leave Portugal. She first went to Sweden to help her dying cousin, Henry de Wahl. After his death she went to Switzerland, where she joined the newly established Hungarian Committee of Assistance and became the person in charge of assistance to children. Soon after, though, she received her visa to go to the United States, and she arrived in New York.

Elsa and her daughters eventually were able to get visitors' visas to Switzerland, but they too had applied for precious American visas.

Hanna's brother George was also in Switzerland, working in a menial position. None of them were complaining, but to a greater or lesser extent they were all worried about money. The factories had been nationalized, so the family could not hope to get any compensation for them. When the Germans left Hungary—in fact, even before they left—they took out a great deal of the machinery, some of which was later found scattered in Germany and Austria. Chorin and his lawyers managed to extract some compensation for that from the war reparations.

The Swiss didn't give them permission to work or get an apartment so they lived in pensions. The family members were in various ways coping with the aftereffects of all they had gone through. When Memi

Mauthner needed a back operation in Zurich, she conscientiously told the doctor that she was of Jewish origin. He assured her that he didn't care.

Marianne wrote to Hanna that Puppa did not get a visa to the United States or to Switzerland, "and we can't leave her here alone because of the painter. She is much more with him than is proper, but she has so little joy in her life, and I can't give her anything better. To say goodbye would be very hurtful. If she just would find someone important finally." They were hopeful that Tom's military service would put them in a good position and that the American visas might still come through.

But the confidence that uncertainties might disappear in peacetime proved even more distant than anyone had anticipated.

CHAPTER 40

Paris

■ ■

On July 29, 1946, foreign ministers and their staffs from Hungary, Romania, Bulgaria, Italy, Finland, the United States, Great Britain, and the Soviet Union assembled in Paris and went to the grand Luxembourg Palace to negotiate the final peace treaty of World War II. My parents had hoped that my father would be spared the trip, but on July 24 he called my mother to tell her that he had to leave that night to go to New York, where he would catch a flight to Paris. Hanna was disconsolate.

They had been together intensely for eight months of colossal change, and his leaving pulled a rug out from beneath her. That night she wrote to him:

1946 JULY 26 FROM NYC

You know, my angel, I hate the passing of time, but now I would love to be through these days during which I have to live without you. Please, my dear, take care of yourself. I am chiding myself that I didn't give you more food to take. . . . My dear, dear, did you really need this? To have a wife who is so much in love with you? If I just knew that you were sleeping peacefully and the plane wasn't jumping too much in the air and that you got enough to eat and that you are well taken care of. My dear, if you are getting very depressed—and I am afraid that this will happen—do not forget how good God was to us. It all looked so hopeless, and in the end everything was resolved, and this

will be resolved too. . . . I cannot think of anything else but of you, and
I am longing for you. Good night, my dear. I am with you. Hancsi

Of course he would get depressed. Even with the success of the Hungarian delegation's U.S. visit, events in Hungary created a powerful undertow, dragging the country away from the secure shores of democratic autonomy. The Communists skillfully and aggressively went about destroying the country's civil society and creating such pressures on the fragile new coalition government that it could hardly keep up with their demands. In early July the Russian commander in Hungary ordered the purge of Hungarian political and youth organizations. They demanded that three Catholic youth organizations be disbanded as well as the Boy Scouts, since they were all considered to be breeding grounds for future members of the Smallholders Party, or at the very least future democrats, and therefore inimical to Soviet interests.

The Russian leadership also ordered that two of Hungary's most prominent conservative journalists be barred from practicing journalism in Hungary. Aladár's old friend Count Dessewffy, editor of the Smallholders' leading paper *Kis Újság,* was one of them. The other was György Parragi, who had been in Mauthausen with Móric and wrote editorials for the biggest government paper. The Russians went after members of the Smallholders Party who actually served in the government and demanded the ouster of an undersecretary in the Ministry of Justice. Anyone who was an anti-Marxist was vulnerable, and since the Communists were in charge of the Ministry of the Interior, there was a spree of arrests on political charges, many of them friends of the family. Gyuri Pallavicini, who had been in Dachau with Aladár and was from one of the oldest aristocratic families in Europe, was accused of being a monarchist—a crime of which he was probably guilty, whatever that means—and jailed.

The Smallholders' coalition government clung to power, systematically weakened at every opportunity by the Soviets, but still determined to govern as best it could.

Against this backdrop, the stakes for Hungary in Paris were monumentally high. As *The New York Times* headline from August 1 said, "Hungarian Regime Periled by Treaty: Loss of Territory and Soviet Opposition to Pro-Western Government Key Factors."

For Hungary, Trianon was always and forever a point of reference.

The loss of those territories and their promised reinstatement motivated Hungary's German alliance, and in November 1938, the Vienna Award had fulfilled those hopes. Now at Paris, borders were once more a central issue, and their very importance seemed destined to sabotage Hungary's entire future. A borderland between Hungary and Czechoslovakia, in which a few hundred thousand Hungarians lived, ended up dominating the talks for Hungary. As far as Transylvania was concerned, Hungarians hoped that it would appear on the agenda, but they could not force it at the risk of appearing irredentist, like an old resentful Trianon veteran determined to redraw borders that had already been secured.

The most contentious issues involved two parcels of land in Slovakia: a strip that included Rakovic, where Móric still had property, and the fifty-three-mile island of Csallóköz in the Danube, which was almost entirely inhabited by Hungarians. Before the talks officially began, the Czechoslovak delegation, boasting a new Communist leadership, was aggressive in approaching the Soviets and was rewarded at the beginning of the peace talks with an announcement by the Soviet Union that it had received these proposals "with sympathy and approval."

This was potentially disastrous for Hungary, as John MacCormac of *The New York Times* wrote from Paris on July 31. "To the Hungarian ears this means Moscow would support the desire of Prague to turn Czechoslovakia finally into a state of Czechs and Slovaks by deporting several hundred thousand Hungarians into Hungary." Moscow had no intention of giving Hungary any of Csallóköz. In fact, during the peace conference, the Czechs did everything they could to alienate the Hungarians and curry favor with the Soviets. For the Hungarian delegates, this posed a terrible problem. They argued that they could not possibly absorb that number of displaced people, no matter how beautifully they spoke Hungarian or how strongly they identified themselves as Hungarians.

Aside from these basic humanitarian issues, MacCormac reported, Hungary argued that the people deported from Czechoslovakia would constitute "a landless and jobless proletariat who, like the Greeks deported by Turkey during the First World War, will become ready victims of demagogy and extremism."

But perhaps that was exactly the point. With a new Communist prime minister in Czechoslovakia and an unreliable government in Hungary, Moscow was always happy to see Hungary systematically weakened. When Móric read this report, he was appalled and wrote to Aladár:

"It is shattering to think that people can be torn away from a land and their surroundings where they have lived for hundreds of years and then transplanted into a new territory, which, despite the same language, is not their homeland. Of course, thinking about the nation and not of human beings, we may come to a different conclusion."

No wonder Aladár's letters reflected his despair. He wrote to Hanna after a week that while he was not surprised at the mess, "it still made me depressed because the time and the difficulties and the disappointments made people even more bitter. The anarchy still goes on but with an accelerated tempo—a miracle is needed to stop this, and start the healing." But once more no miracle was forthcoming. The talks dragged on. By mid-August it was clear that he was going to be stuck there for months.

During that time he visited Hungary. Pleased as he was that his parents seemed cheerful and healthy, being in a country where so many bad things were happening and being separated from his new bride by such a huge distance depressed and disorganized him. He went to the funeral of a distant acquaintance, and that one event, for him, cast a pall over the entire visit. He wrote to Hanna on August 16, "I miss you here even more than I did in times past, and I am already extremely impatient for when we will see each other again. This separate way of life does not fit us, and this modern way of life just increases my nervousness."

His visit home began to crystallize a more profound and painful shift, one in which he realized that "there is no need for me to be here anymore." He was watching his country collapse in slow motion and could feel the inevitability of failure. He could not give up completely, but he was enough of a realist to appreciate that his job in Washington was clearly temporary. Only a year before had he returned to Hungary from Dachau. Even though physically the landscape had improved, politically and socially things had degenerated.

Back in Paris, the head of the Hungarian delegation, Foreign Minister Gyöngyösi, urged those gathered to create a peace treaty that would be more just and therefore more lasting than the one that had occurred after World War I, which had set the stage for World War II. He said that he was the representative of the new, democratic Hungary, heir to the democratic aspirations between 1848 and 1918. This was not the aggressive, revanchist Hungary that had allied itself with Germany but one that was committed to peace and autonomy. As for the push from Czechoslovakia to deport 200,000 Hungarians, Gyöngyösi rejected the proposal for political, moral, and economic reasons. "If the Czechoslovak government wants to get rid of the Hungarian minorities at all costs, then the Hungarian government would have to insist on the principle that people have a right to the soil on which they live."

But the Czech problem did not go away. "I hate to be here," Aladár wrote to Hanna, "but my responsibility is to do this until the end. I am in a raging temper. I hardly find any pleasure here. The only bright spot, maybe, is that in a totally worthless situation, we still somehow survive. They did not push us under the water yet. For how long this will be possible, I don't know, and I am not very optimistic. But to a certain small extent, we still hold the reins, and we receive some support from the Americans and the Anglo-Saxons. I have something to do with this, even if it is not too much, but it is still something."

His efforts were both noticed and appreciated. Behind the scenes, one of Prime Minister Nagy's deputies approached Aladár and asked if he would consider taking the job of foreign minister after the peace talks. "Well, my darling," Aladár wrote, "nothing of the sort can happen. I would resign from the embassy, and taking up the job of foreign minister is out of the question."

The inevitable confrontation between the Czechoslovaks and the Hungarians began on the week of September 17, nearly two months after the conference began. The Czechoslovaks publicly accused their Hungarian minority both of anti-Semitism and of fomenting efforts to undermine the nation of Czechoslovakia. They insisted that in the interest of the stability of the country, these 200,000 Hungarians had to be expelled. Aladár's "raging temper" found a suitable target, and he made a memorable speech in response, one that landed his sepia-toned picture on the cover of a Hungarian newsweekly.

"WE ARE FIGHTING!" the cover announces. "Aladár Szegedi-Maszak [sic], our envoy to Washington, delivers his great speech in Paris against Czechoslovak claims." The photograph captured Aladár's proudest moment at the peace talks, when "in a quiet tone and faultless English," according to the newspaper Magyar Nemzet, he confronted the Czechs with their distortions and lies. In a dramatic moment, he proved that there was no basis for the Czech accusation that the Hungarian population played an important role in the dissolution of Czechoslovakia, and he supported his argument with a quotation from President Eduard Beneš's own book, one of the few surviving copies of which Aladár not only possessed but had read. The foreign minister from Czechoslovakia looked astonished and quickly grabbed a piece of paper and wrote, "Do we have this book?" His Hungarian expert replied no. Aladár continued his discussion of the many centuries of Hungarian settlement in Slovakia and described the humanitarian, economic, and historical arguments against repatriation.

Later in the session, a Czechoslovak speaker declared that Aladár had lied and falsified quotations, because the book he had referenced did not exist. Aladár produced not only the volume but a photograph of the page in which Beneš described all the forces that conspired to destroy Czechoslovakia: the Sudenten German front, the Slovak front, the French and English front. Hungarians were not mentioned at all, a fact that was not lost on the Czechoslovak delegation. They immediately contacted Prague and requested copies of the book, but apparently there were none to be had. Since Beneš's political opponents had discovered that his writings furnished quite a bit of ammunition, he arranged for the Czech government to buy every copy of his work and store them for an indefinite period of time. No copies arrived in Paris.

Aladár spent his days in Paris working hard and visiting a few old friends. At the beginning of October, Lilly joined him, in a stopover on her way to Washington. The same week Móric arrived from Portugal. He finally received his French visa and was peripherally involved in the peace talks because of his property in Slovakia. It was his first trip away from Portugal, and he confessed that he was so utterly overwhelmed "in the big city, I was like a little peasant girl visiting Budapest for the first time." The shock was understandable: the last time he had been an independent man in charge of his own destiny had been in Budapest on March 18, 1944. Over two and a half seismic years had passed, many of them spent dislocated from every familiar, now-archaic touchstone of his existence. He was now on his own again, but the experience was a shock to his system. The presence of my father and Lilly, as well as many of his old friends, comfortably cushioned Móric's reentry into civilized independent life, and after settling in an inexpensive hotel, he began a quiet routine of visits and business.

This was a different form of waiting, but they were waiting nonetheless: Lilly for the ship that would take her to America, Aladár for the end of the peace conference, Móric and the rest of the family for something resembling their new life to begin.

Reunion

.

M y father's experience in Paris convinced him that any hope of making a positive new beginning in Hungary was futile. Finally, almost miraculously, a compromise emerged. Although three Hungarian villages would be a consolation prize given to Czechoslovakia, the 200,000 Hungarians would not be expelled. It was a victory of sorts; the much-discussed expulsion didn't happen because the Western powers aligned themselves with Hungary, and one of the many reasons they aligned themselves with Hungary was that Aladár managed to help persuade them that it was the right thing to do. Nevertheless, he wrote to Hanna, "it deeply depresses me that all our hopes end in failure. You cannot count on the Americans in important matters."

Only the first part of the final treaty dealt with territorial problems; the others focused on military, political, economic, and social stipulations. The Hungarian army could not be larger than 65,000 soldiers, for example, and Hungary could not produce nuclear weapons. In an especially humiliating requirement, Hungary had to pay more than $300 million in war reparations—$200 million to the Soviet Union and $100 million to Czechoslovakia and Yugoslavia—forcing her to financially support the very countries most determined to destroy her democratic autonomy. While the Allied armed forces were required to leave Hungary, the Soviet army was permitted to remain in order to keep contact with Soviet troops who were stationed in the Austrian Soviet zone.

Aladár listened with a kind of exhausted cynicism to the well-intentioned and hopelessly naïve words of American secretary of state Byrnes at the conclusion of the conference. "These treaties are not written as we would write them if we had a free hand. They are not written as other governments would write them if they had a free hand. But they are as good as we can hope to get by general agreement now or within any reasonable length of time.... Whatever political differences there may be among us," Byrnes told the assembled delegates, "we are firmly and irrevocably committed to the principle that it is our right and the right of every people to organize their economic and political destiny through the freest possible expression of their collective will. We oppose privilege at home and abroad. We defend freedom everywhere."

The Hungarian delegation left Paris after the closing session on October 15 and boarded the train to Budapest. Aladár left for America the next day.

This Paris assignment was a horrible trial for Hanna and Aladár. They had been separated so much, but it seemed especially cruel to have been married for eleven months, only to spend nearly three of them apart.

During this time they communicated with ease and tenderness. Aladár wrote to Hanna, "I miss you terribly because I can now see for myself how much I love you, and how intertwined we have become during the last eight months. It is such a big happiness to read a letter from you and imagine from them how you are doing, what you are doing, and how you love and miss me too."

As the weeks turned into months and the separation began to feel catastrophic, mere words seemed inadequate for expressing their feelings. When they passed their unofficial anniversary of September 18, Aladár had been working hard on his speech confronting the Czech delegation, and he felt dreadful for permitting yet another anniversary to pass without being together. "Oh my darling, I miss everything so much," he wrote. "Your hair, your eyes, your hands—the warmth and peacefulness when we are together. Imagine, my darling, I miss the common bedroom too. I just realized how much I miss you when I wake up during the night and do not see you next to me."

Hanna too felt unsettled and disorganized without him beside her. "Please, my dear, send me a telegram. I am terribly unsettled," she wrote. "Oh my God, if we could just be together again. I am always with you. Your very loving and longing, Hancsi." She kept busy during the time he was away. She entertained and was invited to both official and unofficial events. Katalin stayed with her, and they cemented their friendship. She visited New York, where her uncle Alfons had arrived. She even kept a watch on what was happening at the embassy and reported dutifully the activities there. Her brother Tom was on leave from the army and visited her for two weeks, and together they took short trips. The summer months were breathlessly hot and humid, and often she and Katalin would sneak into a movie simply because it was air-conditioned. But she was always a bit on edge, waiting for letters and missing him.

Her aunt Daisy had advised her that even though many perfectly happy couples had separate bedrooms, she should share a bedroom with her new husband. Both of them may have been shy about it, but the shyness disappeared when they were together. They made so many references to their secret life together: a green light that maybe was the signal for some special intimacy; *The New York Times* that perhaps ended up on the floor; a shy reference to a bit of trouble "after a monastic life" that could easily be fixed. Aladár suggested a little slap on the bottom that nearly made me blush. My mother wrote to him on their unofficial anniversary, September 18, and hoped that his speech was a great success. She continued, "If I think of how long ago you 'hit the horn,' I start feeling very sorry for myself. So at least we are on the same wavelength. I kiss you and wait for you. Hancsi." She told him that every evening she took out his picture and reread his letters. Aladár too referenced that special date: "I kiss you, my darling, even if not with as much trepidation as on September 18, 1940, on the Danube shore, but with great love."

So *that* was why September 18 had such significance. It was the anniversary of their first kiss. They had known each other for months, he had already visited her in Ireg several times, and they had gone on many long "educational" drives together. But finally, on that drive near the riverside village of Leányfalu, with trepidation and happiness, they had kissed.

Aladár returned home on October 17. Hanna wrote that when she heard that he was coming home, "I was so happy you could have made me catch birds." An added bonus was that Lilly was still on the boat, heading toward the United States, so they would have a few days of privacy. Hanna described their reunion in New York in a letter to her mother: "Aladár arrived at dawn on Friday. According to eyewitness accounts, we caused quite a stir because we greeted each other as if we had been separated for years. . . . I don't know how I deserve such happiness."

How could there not have been even the slightest glimmer of their great love affair in our house on Patterson Street? In the way that sound continues to travel to distant planets years away from its original source, I would have thought that the sheer power of what they once had felt would, many years later, at least leave a trace.

Is this the timeless and eternal secret that exists between parents and children? That our parents were once young and passionately in love? Have I ventured too deeply into their private world, the hot and sensual place where no child ever *really* wants to go, a place that parents must cordon off with a securely locked bedroom door? Or protected in letters written in a foreign language?

After all, we children don't want to know too much. We need to titrate revelations sufficient to shed light on our own egocentric selves. And yet when I read those letters, I felt the same kind of relief, even happiness, that I felt an hour after my father died, when my mother said to me, "You know, he *adored* me." Others would misunderstand the story when I told it, seeing it as an example of my mother's inability to comfort me, or as her failure to recognize me as a daughter who had just lost her father, or as her desperate staking of a claim—he adored *me*. My father had died that evening in his bed at Patterson Street, and my mother was now lighting her first cigarette and drinking her first sip of scotch without him. We were alone, and I could only smile and reply, "He sure did."

I knew that her statement was an astonishing and unexpected affirmation, not something competitive or hurtful. In the moments right after his death, during that sliver of time when she had not yet assumed the identity of "widow" after forty-three years of marriage, the couple who had yearned for each other and pored over letters and turned on the green lamp and "caused quite a stir," a couple who had never been present even in the shadows of my growing up, finally, with timid defiance, appeared in the pantry at Patterson Street right after my father's body had exited the front door for the last time. I briefly saw then what I discovered much later in these letters, something that had been concealed my entire life by the rigid and broad familial power structure at Patterson Street: emotions that had been obscured by the fog of my father's depressions.

For only a moment I could glimpse something that I had spent my life hoping to see: my parents' powerful love for each other. It took twenty years before the couple reappeared on the pages of letters that I needed to have translated. The translation extended far beyond the mere words. For the first time in my life, as a middle-aged woman, I felt the almost-mystical bedtime comfort of knowing that my parents were the centerpiece, the safe harbor, the true north of our family's story.

The Weiss Diaspora

・ ・

Hanna could not have been happier during the fall of 1946, and Puppa could not have been more unhappy.

As soon as Aladár returned, the couple went to the Poconos for an abbreviated and belated honeymoon before Lilly arrived and they resumed their hectic ambassadorial schedule. A visit to Trenton for Hungarian war orphans' relief, a trip to Philadelphia to honor composer Zoltán Kodály and his wife ("an extraordinarily unpleasant couple, old and petty," Hanna wrote to her mother), dinners with the Poles, a huge party at the Russian embassy, and an assortment of smaller social engagements, plus my father's forty-third birthday on November 19, "where he received magnificent treasures, a fountain pen, shirt, robe, and books." They went up to New York frequently as more and more family members started arriving there. During one of those trips, Magda Gábor summoned Hanna for the express purpose of showing off her new nose. Lilly was a welcome guest, and Hanna seems to have genuinely enjoyed her company. For Lilly, the two months in Washington marked the happiest time of her life, for the rest of her life.

Other good news came from America as well. Tom, who visited Washington whenever he had leave from the army, contributed to my grandmother's collection of newspaper clippings. He was only twenty-two, a private first class stationed in San Antonio, Texas. A story about him appeared in *The Pulse*, the Brooke Army Medical Center weekly paper. "Instructor Now at MDETS (Medical Division Educational Training

Services) Saw Nazis Overrun Europe," the headline announced. "It's a long road from an estate in Hungary to a classroom in MDETS of Brooke Army Medical Center. And in the six short years that brought Pfc Thomas de Kornfeld such a distance, there's been a bit of rough going." Tom's students "feel he is one of the best instructors the course has to offer." He is a "soft-eyed gentle voiced boy who does an outstanding job as instructor in anatomy and physiology. . . . You would find it difficult to envision the circumstances—glamorous, exciting and terrifying—which form his background."

The American visa was the brass ring they all hoped to grab, the finish line they all hoped to cross. Alfons Weiss and his family had arrived and settled in New York. But the Kornfelds mostly remained in Portugal, although Móric was still in Paris. Edith Weiss was in Switzerland with Ferenc Chorin, his wife Daisy, son Ferenc, and daughters Daisy and Erzsébet. Elsa Weiss Mauthner and her four daughters were in Switzerland, along with her son Stephen. Her other son, Hansi, had settled in Budapest and finally entered a sanatorium to quit his morphine addiction, while her other son, also Ferenc, remained in Portugal, determined to resurrect the great reputation of the Mauthner seed business. Puppa worked with him as a secretary, a job she enjoyed but one to which Luis and her parents objected.

George and his wife, Elsie, and the first de Kornfeld grandson were also in Switzerland, and my grandmother's brother Eugene Weiss had finally arrived there with his wife, Annie, and their three adult children, Alice, Annie, and George.

Puppa was sick of the lot of them. Since she and her mother remained in Portugal, they became the de facto messengers and secretaries for the entire family in Switzerland, who needed visas arranged, bags sent, dresses made, shoes ordered, and medicines mailed. For a few of them, the ever-present prewar identities of people of importance and entitlement reasserted themselves.

The entire family had applied for their American visas out of the embassy in Portugal, but they had also received visas to go to Switzerland for a brief period of time, since other relatives had already settled there, supported in part by a still-intact Manfred Weiss bank account. Even when thorny visa problems had been settled, going anywhere from Portugal—or coming back from Paris or Zurich—required finding available space on either flights or trains. With apparently so many Europeans getting resettled, reservations were difficult to come by. "It is a life of waiting, of senseless vegetation," Marianne wrote.

Móric stayed in Paris for several months and even acquired a *carte d'identité*, so he was spared some of the endless registrations with the police. He still imagined that something could be gained from the final peace documents, which had not yet been signed, and he still had some hope of regaining his family's old property in Rakovic, Slovakia. His wife missed him and simply wanted the whole issue to be resolved. Their marriage, which had begun with awful tensions and even the threat of a divorce, had matured into a deep and interdependent love. During their separation, Marianne wrote unhappily, "it is difficult without Papi, and every minute without him is a loss that cannot be regained."

Finally in December Marianne and Móric received their Swiss visas and joined the rest of the family for the Christmas holidays. Puppa remained in Portugal, still waiting for her Swiss visa. At last they were reunited with their son George and could admire and play with their grandchild, Stevie, whose infancy had been lost in the chaos of 1944. It did not take long for George's wife to resent her mother-in-law and brandish her petulance like an expensive new haircut.

In the morning Marianne was not allowed to visit because the apartment was being cleaned. At meals she was told not to talk to her grandson because that would make him eat poorly. For days on end, Elsie would come up with reasons why Marianne could not see her grandson. She wrote that she "tried to keep the three commandments for mothers-in-law: *schlucken, schweigen, schenken*"—to swallow, to be quiet, to give—but she felt sad that she and her beloved son were being estranged, first by the Nazis and now by Elsie. Yet she could understand George's calculation that it was far better for him to keep the peace at home at the expense of his mother than vice versa.

"It really would not hurt Elsie, whom I like, to be less stupid and more forthcoming in little things, as no one wants to know her secrets," Puppa wrote. Marianne was hurt and unhappy. After all this time apart, why couldn't things be easier?

Finally Puppa got the necessary travel papers. Luis was in Spain looking for some, for any, kind of work. With both her parents and her lover out of Portugal, Puppa was able to earn some money doing clerical work. Tom had sent her a typewriter, and she was getting much more agile on the keys. She even mastered rudimentary shorthand. When no one was there, she worked seven-hour days and earned what she described as " a fortune." For her parents, this kind of work was a very good thing but had to be consumed, like rich food, in moderation.

Luis was broke and unemployed, and his paintings did not have much of a market, although Puppa would bring one or two to Zurich to see if she could sell them at a gallery and even pocket the 10 percent commission. When he returned to Spain, he would work for restaurants or resorts and assist with the interior design. The disparity between a man not working and a woman earning money was too dissonant for his Spanish soul. "I know that people may ask, why don't I work? If I were living all alone, I would have to work too," Puppa wrote. "But they do not know what it is like to be with a very jealous person. It would be out of the question for me to work in an office if we were to get married, unless I found some work with the Ursuline sisters or some other religious orders."

Before they embarked on their separate journeys, Luis spent a week trying to pack for Spain. Puppa sat quietly mending his clothes and darning his socks as she watched chaos descend on his suitcase and frustration descend on Luis. Finally she offered to help him and tamed his confused efforts. It was a small thing—the hesitation, the capitulation—but the dynamic was repeated over and over again in things small and large. She could not shed her ambivalence about their affair. Even though its impermanence was never articulated, they both knew that when her parents got their visa to America, she would accompany them.

Her mood was not improved by having to be in Switzerland, a place she had always detested. But after all the horrible devastation in Europe, the unseemly, smug, prosperous "neutrality" of Switzerland irritated her even more. Leaving the verdant warmth of Portugal for Zurich in December seemed like a terrible idea, and everywhere she turned someone looked ill. Her father had recovered from a stubborn bronchitis, but her mother looked pale and thin. That did not include the collection of elderly aunts, uncles, and younger cousins with their many trips to many doctors addressing many medical complaints. And then the conversations! For too many family members, life had stopped on March 19, and they "worry about the dresses they left with the gardener, or the jewels at the Bank of Commerce or talk about 'having been somebody.' I cannot bring much enthusiasm to these subjects, and that is a great sin!"

At the end of 1946 word came from Lisbon that the Chorins had finally received their U.S. immigration visas. It was a wrenching departure for Marianne, for whom the fragmentation of the family forced an unnatural way of life. She knew Europe, but America was so exotic and strange, even though it was the future they were all likely to embrace.

In January 1947 the Chorin family flew from Lisbon to New York, an especially long trip as the planes stopped in Ireland and Newfoundland. They arrived in New York in the midst of a huge snowstorm. New York was teeming with people, and the bedraggled group managed to get a room in a horrible hotel on upper Broadway. Alfons Weiss, now the seasoned American, took his exhausted family for lunch at the nearest Horn & Hardart, the legendary automat, where you threw twenty-five cents into a slot, and out came a sandwich. "Uncle Ali said this is the way people eat in America," his niece Daisy recalled decades later. "Needless to say, my mother was ready to turn around."

They had finally reached their ultimate destination. Ferenc Chorin was sixty-eight years old, an age when most people were retired. But he was determined to start a new life. "Make the best of it," he would say. If anyone in the family knew how to do it, he did.

Their community in Europe was getting smaller and smaller.

Then some wonderful news came in from Washington, just in time for Christmas. Hanna was pregnant. Her parents were ecstatic—indeed, it was the kind of news that raised the spirits of the entire family. The letters of joy and congratulation flew across the Atlantic. Móric wrote to Hanna and Aladár immediately after Hanna called with the news. "I think of you so much with so many warm wishes and hopes and expectations. . . . What a wonderful thing it would be to be your child. Our impatience to come has grown."

1947

By the rivers of Babylon,
There we sat down, yea, we wept,
When we remembered Zion.
We hanged our harps upon the willows in the midst thereof.
For there they that carried us away captive required of us a song
And they that wasted us required of us mirth, saying
Sing us one of the songs of Zion.
How shall we sing the Lord's song in a strange land?

—PSALM 137

CHAPTER 43

Salami Tactics

In 1947 my father stood briefly in the spotlight of history. He played a medium-size role in an epic tragedy of an easily dismissed country.

His name appears in chapters, or paragraphs, or footnotes, in books and in scholarly articles about the collapse of democracy in Hungary, about the creation of the Iron Curtain, and about the immediate postwar history of that benighted country. He is the main character in front-page stories and in official State Department records. *The Congressional Record* cites him several times. And this is just in English. In Hungary, people knew his name for decades, because even in Hungary ours is an unusual name. But there they officially knew him as a spy, or a traitor, or a coward, or an American tool. However, some, quietly, considered him a hero.

He had faced a catastrophe in his country and had tried everything he could, for the last but most prominent time in his life, to change the course of history. "I view the events from the distance imposed by failure," my father once told my Hungarian cousin Mihály. He had thought that he could actually persuade the Americans to help in creating the circumstances and the political will to sustain a free and democratic future for his country. And even as he would write my mother that things were hopeless and he was discouraged, he continued to try.

In early 1947 Hanna and Aladár appeared to be the epitome of a content and secure diplomatic couple. They entertained visitors and other diplomats; they were invited to concerts and then to state dinners at the White House. They traveled to Hungarian communities and welcomed visiting Hungarian dignitaries. Hanna translated among the guests in German, French, English, and Hungarian. They raised money for Hungarian war orphans, and she volunteered for Save the Children and the Red Cross.

Another glowing report appeared in the society pages of *The Washington Post*:

> The warmth of the welcome extended to their guests by the Minister of Hungary and Mrs. Szegedy-Maszák at their reception of the Hungarian Minister to Paris Dr. Pal Auer yesterday afternoon from 6 to 8 pm was reflected in the brilliant red gladiolas standing in large vases around the comfortable living room, library and dining room. . . . The front of the bodice of Mrs. Szegedy-Maszák's long black afternoon gown was of cloud blue and she wore a long string of pearls and clips.

She was nearly three months pregnant then; I wonder if she was showing yet.

But beneath this surface calm, Aladár worked, first systematically and then with increasing frustration and desperation, to enlist the help and attention of the American State Department so that it would express some official concern about the Communist intimidation in Hungary's political life. In late 1946 and early 1947, the Communists had already removed various promising leaders and closed down innocuous organizations like the National Association of Young Farmers' Clubs and the Catholic Youth Association and nearly two hundred similar groups. Gen. V. P. Sviridov from the Soviet High Command accused them of being "terrorists" and "underground fascist organizations" in which "youth were taught to rise up against the Red Army and to hate the Soviet Union as well as Hungarian Democracy."

Another politician was arrested on phony charges; another journalist was fired; another loyal Muscovite Communist was put in a position of power over key government offices like the Interior Ministry and the Ministry of Commerce. The technical term, "salami tactics," described the way in which, sliver by sliver, Hungarian Communists systematically eviscerated the native political and civil society, leaving it so frightened and crippled that totalitarian control became inevitable. Maybe those who had some faith that Hungary might become a free and democratic republic believed that after the crimes of Nazism had been uncovered and prosecuted, the world would not stand idly by and watch a similar single-party rule of terror and intimidation and imperial ambitions. Every postwar peace treaty gave assurances that countries would be able to enjoy some self-determination. But treaties are made to be broken, and whatever lessons World War II might have taught were often conveniently forgotten.

After the impressive Smallholders victory in November's free elections, the Hungarian Communist Party, supported by the Soviet Union, had forced a "coalition" government in which representatives from parties that received small fractions of the popular vote were given power. The Communists had already grabbed control of the Interior Ministry and did not relinquish it after the election. By 1947 they had already created a network of vicious secret police and utterly corrupt "people's courts." A new organization of secret police was formed called the State Defense Department—in Hungarian, the Államvédelmi Osztály, known forever as the dreaded ÁVO. They settled in at 60 Andrássy Avenue, an address that had established its pedigree for terror when it was Arrow Cross Party headquarters.

The head of ÁVO, working hand in glove with the Soviet secret police, the NKVD, was a vindictive and sadistic Hungarian Communist named Gábor Péter. With the exception of Lászlo Rajk and a few others, most of Hungary's top Communist leaders were of Jewish origin, which did little to set the stage for some national soul searching regarding the extermination of Hungary's Jewry. Some had been imprisoned in concentration camps; others had been in the Soviet Union. Péter lost no time in rounding up political unreliables, also known as democrats and members of the Smallholders Party, in smaller towns and villages throughout Hungary. He encouraged a web of informants who furthered their careers by destroying the livelihoods of others. So called "right-wing" elements in public service were fired all over the country, adding up to over eighty thousand people.

For years this office assembled a dossier on my father, officially entitled "Reports of Military Police and Others Concerning the Person of Aladár Szegedi[sic]-Maszák." One of the first entries, posted in October 1945, provided a unique interpretation of my parents' relationship: "Concerning Washington, the rumor persists that Aladár Szegedi [sic]-Maszák will be the envoy there. In order to obtain the trust of the capitalists, he has asked for the hand of Baroness Kornfeld who is momentarily in Lisbon. This happened when SzM was still in Paris following deportation."

Report number 641, dated December 1, 1945: "The Hungarian legation could have left for Washington if it weren't for the unclear reasons for the postponement of the wedding of the envoy: A SzM originally scheduled it to be held in Lisbon but changed to Budapest. One of these days the bride will arrive, in a special airplane, and possessing a Russian entry permit. . . . Our opinion of this problem is that Baroness Hanna Kornfeld will do everything according to directives from her parents, to prepare the return of the families Weiss, Chorin and Kornfeld."

Constantly referring to Hanna as "Baroness" was not a gesture of respect. It was a way of further emphasizing that she was a prominent member of a despised class that should be, if not eliminated, then thoroughly mistrusted. In May 1946 a different source, who apparently had read neither the earlier reports nor the newspapers, reported:

> Members of the Workers Party involved with foreign policy object to the assignment of Szegedy-Maszák because of his relation to the family Chorin. It is well known that Sz.M's wife is Anna [sic] Chorin, of whom nobody in the best of faith can claim is of democratic inclination. It is common knowledge that she is a faithful adherent to the rule of world capitalism. Within the Smallholders Party as well as within the Workers Party there is deep concern about the problems of having the husband of an industry baroness representing democratic Hungary in democratic America.

And so on.

Curiously, in reading through the dossier, the informants seemed at least initially to find it difficult to criticize my father directly. His major liability was my mother. Even as a young man he "distinguished himself with his judicious nature. He was very intelligent and hungry for learning . . . [and] possessed a wide range and varied body of knowledge. Besides political science, he was also well versed in literature and the arts." A later entry stated that my father had been in Dachau, and "the deportation psychologically transformed Szegedy-Maszák permanently, and at present he is a totally pessimistic person." At least in some cases, someone who actually knew my father personally was accurately informing on him.

Dachau was not the only reason why he was pessimistic. He had simply to look at the dynamics in the government to see the dangerous trajectory. The small indigenous Communist Party in Hungary had once turned to Moscow for support to further its aims, but by the fall of 1946 and then almost completely by 1947, the roles were reversed, and the Soviet Union manipulated the Hungarian Communists in order to advance its grand design. Prime Minister Nagy and President Tildy kept trying to govern in a democratic fashion, through appeasing the noisiest and most aggressive of their coalition members. But the dynamic was tantamount to Eagle Scouts trying to demonstrate their high-mindedness by including the Mafia in their troop.

The longer the Smallholders were in power, the better the quality of life for most Hungarians. The cities had been cleaned up and repaired, a new temporary bridge linked Buda and Pest, and the economy had stabilized. The Communists needed to create a crisis of confidence in the ruling party, and in January 1947 they succeeded by accusing the Smallholders of conducting a right-wing conspiracy to overthrow the democratic republic of Hungary. László Rajk, the Communist minister of the interior who had the face of a matinee idol and the heart of an assassin, told Tildy that the Interior Ministry was going to get to the heart of this "conspiracy." Then the Communists planted stories in newspapers intimating the cancer in the body politic and singled out young leaders in the party as the malignancies. Once more the Smallholders were put on the defensive.

From Washington, Aladár could see that a trap was being set. In early January he visited with the man who met him at National Airport eighteen months before, Walworth Barbour, associate chief of the division of Southern European affairs at the State Department. (He later became the U.S. ambassador to Israel.) My father asked him if the United States could publicly express its interests "in maintaining the democratic elements in Hungary," because doing so would help Prime Minister Ferenc Nagy cope with the most recent crisis created by the Communists. He reminded Barbour that the U.S. ambassador to Hungary had told Ferenc Nagy not to abandon his electoral mandate by making concessions to the Communists.

With surprising alacrity, Secretary of State George Marshall sent a cable to the American embassy in Budapest that acknowledged the internal strains on the Hungarian government and the importance of "buttressing U.S. political support of democratic elements in Hungary" not just with material and economic aid but also—and here was the tricky part—politically. On the one hand he was not averse to making some public statement of U.S. support, but he worried that "there may be factors which would suggest that such statement would only complicate PriMin's position."

Marshall's good intentions and diplomatic niceties were quaint irrelevancies in a game where the Communists played by their own ruthless rules. On January 20 they announced that they had found the ringleader of the conspiracy, none other than the Smallholders Party secretary Béla Kovács. Aladár had met him several times in Budapest and thought him "friendly and good-humored . . . a tough-minded, versatile politician who filled a variety of posts in his party, all of them well. He courageously and decisively stood for a true democracy and for a rule of law. He argued with the Communists, for which he ultimately fell victim to the Russian and Communist vengeance." He was also one of the most charismatic and popular leaders of the Smallholders Party and the editor of Dessewffy's old paper, *Kis Újság*. The Communist leader Rákosi despised him for many reasons but especially because Kovács had long urged the leaders of the Smallholders Party like Ferenc Nagy to stand firm and not be so accommodating with the Communists.

Aladár too wanted to urge Nagy to stop being so amenable and to assert his authority, but he could not communicate directly to the prime minister. Everything he wrote was subject to the scrutiny of the Communists in the Foreign Ministry. He thought the Americans might help him, perhaps by letting him use their channels of direct communication, but they refused. They could not completely trust Nagy, Barbour said, and if this were discovered, "the Soviets would have grounds to charge us with intervention on behalf of the Smallholders similar to their intervention in support of the Communists to which we object."

Kovács was given no trial, even in the completely corrupt "people's courts." At the end of February, he was taken to ÁVO headquarters, where he was interrogated and tortured by Gábor Péter. These brutal sessions broke him completely, and emotionally and physically debilitated, he was escorted for a brief visit home, which had been completely ransacked by Soviet officers, before he was arrested again. His wife was assured that he would be home in a few days. She waited for him for *nine years* while he rotted in a Soviet gulag. My father referred to him not just as "one of the innumerable victims but a martyr, whose principles, behavior, and courage brought down on him the vengeance of Rákosi and of the Soviet power."

In March and April the United States and Great Britain sent several diplomatic notes that protested Russian activities, but they were met with total silence. Meanwhile in Hungary, the pressures on Nagy were getting more intense. He was forced to fire five parliamentary deputies and three more cabinet ministers, who were tried in the "people's courts." Many were sentenced to death. Against this backdrop, Aladár was ordered to apply for Hungary's membership to the United Nations, which made it the first former Axis country seeking to join. *The New York Times* reported that "Mr. Szegedy-Maszák pointed out that the treaty of peace between Hungary and the twelve nations with whom she had been at war had been signed in Paris more than ten weeks ago. He added that the Republic of Hungary wished to join all other peace-loving nations in the international organization as soon as possible."

In May, Hanna and Aladár were invited to Hyde Park to visit Eleanor Roosevelt with Mrs. Tildy, the wife of the Hungarian president, who was then visiting the United States. Mrs. Roosevelt wrote in her journal, "We live up here in the country under the illusion that we are cut off from the world and that few people will come our way. But last week we had the pleasure of several foreign visitors. We had a visit from two delightful representatives from Uruguay, Mr. and Mrs. Fontania; then a visit from Mrs. Zoltán Tildy, wife of the President of Hungary, who was accompanied by the Hungarian Minister to this country, Aladár Szegedy-Maszák, and his wife. We also had a writer from Great Britain, Mr. Luscombe, and a member of the United Nations subcommission on minorities and discrimination, Mr. McNamara of Australia. I felt that we were importing a little bit of the United Nations into the countryside of New York State."

Mrs. Tildy began her visit in mid-April, and by the time she boarded the Pan American flight to Brussels on May 28, the democracy in her country was on the verge of collapse. The photograph in *The New York Times* shows Mrs. Tildy standing on the aircraft steps at La Guardia, as Aladár in a pin-striped suit kisses her hand. In ten days he would lose his job and his country. The image of that hand being kissed marks the end not just of an official visit but of an entire world.

CHAPTER 44

Demonstratively Dejected

■

■   ■

While my father may have glanced at his picture in *The New York Times* on May 29, the most important story appeared on the pages of the Washington *Evening Star*, which reported, "A high Hungarian source said today that the Russians in an official note had accused Premier Ferenc Nagy and two other officials of complicity in a recent plot to overthrow Hungarian democracy." The two other officials were the foreign minister, my father's boss János Gyöngyösi, and the speaker of the House, a Catholic priest named Béla Varga. The source of this revelation was the "confession" of Béla Kovács.

While Mrs. Tildy was flying home, the Hungarian News Service announced the details of Kovács's so-called confession that conveniently implicated the entire leadership of the Smallholders Party in the destruction of Hungarian democracy. The report claimed that the Smallholders had approved connections between the party and an alleged émigré Hungarian army in the British zone of Austria. Furthermore, it claimed that a Smallholders-organized secret antigovernment, anti-Soviet underground had been created in August 1945 and in March of the following year to provide an illegal army in western Hungary with guns and armaments so that it could seize power. Kovács also "confessed" that the Smallholders planted conspirators in every part of the government and organized a Hungarian "countergovernment" in exile. Kovács's signature appeared on this document.

Communists and left-wing, pro-Soviet members of the Smallholders

Party demanded Ferenc Nagy's resignation. Nagy was in Switzerland at the time, so they kidnapped his four-year-old son in Hungary and held him as a hostage. Over several tense days in early June, Nagy refused to resign, but he finally capitulated when his son was brought to him. Béla Varga escaped to Vienna, but Gyöngyösi remained in Hungary.

As Ferenc Nagy lost power, other members of his cabinet fled, and a new "provisional" leadership was installed, it became clear that the United States was going to do nothing. It was reluctant to act alone, and Great Britain—which was overextended in lending aid to the civil war in Greece—refused to engage in a similar battle in Hungary. As Bertram D. Hulen reported in *The New York Times* on June 1,

> Official circles today gave it as their opinion that it would be difficult to take effective counter-measures against the extension of the iron curtain to Hungary through Russia's apparent plan to dominate the Hungarian government and control the army. It was felt that the coup seemed to rule out any chance of applying the Truman Doctrine as in the case of Greece and Turkey, since the Budapest Government was not one to which the United States would extend aid on a practical basis . . . .Washington may be urged by Aladár de Szegedy-Maszák, the Hungarian Minister, to do something. His position is looked upon as largely helpless in the circumstances. He has been in touch since the crisis developed but only to seek information. He has not formally requested any action, it was said.

Another artifact of the Cold War: rather than back a popular, democratically elected government in Hungary that was in danger of being swallowed up by the Soviets, the United States turned its back on Hungary to back unpopular generals in Greece against a truly popular Communist movement.

On June 2 Aladár delivered a six-page letter to Secretary of State George Marshall in which he described the cataclysmic turn of events in Hungary and asked for American intervention. He explained that the entire future of Hungary as an economically, socially, and politically independent state was at stake. Economically, he explained, the Soviet Union was determined "to achieve the economic enslavement of Hungary and her complete integration into the Russian economic system," which would mean the "establishment of a Russian industrial colony in Hungary on the traditional pattern of exploitation."

He described the destruction of the political infrastructure by the Communists and wrote, "Hungary is therefore . . . on the verge of being engulfed by Russian and Communist expansion. In spite of the silent but stubborn struggle to establish and maintain free democratic institutions, Hungary is facing subjugation by a large occupation army, by a permanent drain on an impoverished economy, and by a small minority, which is not only in control of the police, but has armed its own followers as well."

As for the "confession" of Béla Kovács, he wrote, "I am not in a position to say that Béla Kovács did not sign this deposition. As a former prisoner of the German Gestapo and inmate of the Dachau Concentration Camp, I do know, however, that people under pressure can be induced to sign almost anything, especially if they are denied the basic human right to an eventual fair and open trial."

He closed the letter saying:

Appointed by the duly elected Hungarian Government to represent Hungary in the United States and enjoying the freedom from fear in this free country on behalf of the avowed majority of the Hungarian people, I have the honor to lodge a solemn protest against the totalitarian aggression of which my country has fallen victim. Mindful of the generous economic and political assistance the Government and the People of the United States have extended to Hungary, I have complete reliance that the Government of the United States will assume its responsibilities under the agreements and the declaration of principles referred to above and will take the appropriate action towards the restoration of the independence and democracy in Hungary.

I have the honor, Mr. Secretary, to be,

> *Your obedient servant.*
> *Aladár Szegedy-Maszák*
> *Minister of Hungary*

The Hungarian government demanded that Aladár return to Budapest. He refused, saying that he did not recognize the government as being legitimate. One week after the crisis began, on Thursday, June 5, *The New York Times* reported:

BUDAPEST'S ENVOY TO U.S.
DEFIES REDS

WASHINGTON, June 4—Aladár de Szegedy-Maszák, the Hungarian Minister to the United States, and seven members of his staff refused today to recognize the legality of the new Communist controlled Government in Budapest and remained at their posts. . . . They refused to resign or even to notify the Budapest government of their attitude since this might be construed as implied recognition of its legality. The rest of the legation staff sat quietly by, offering no interference and transacting no business.

In a statement at his press conference, my father provided readers and listeners with a brief history of Hungary since the elections of 1945.

It was our hope that our country, after so much struggle and oppression, would finally participate in the blessings of a true democracy. We recognized the fact that we had to establish friendly relations with our neighbor, the Soviet Union, and we hoped that Soviet Russia would assist us in our democratic efforts. . . . Deeply upset by the tragic developments in our country, which will impose new hardships on our suffering people, we have decided not to recognize the legality of the new Hungarian government formed under force. It is our firm conviction that the so promising and hopeful evolution which was begun by the election of 1945 and interrupted by foreign interference will be resumed as soon as the Hungarian people will be given the opportunity to express their will freely and will achieve its aim: a free and democratic Hungary will become a reality in a world of peace, progress and democracy.

The day this was reported, President Truman called the Hungarian coup "outrageous." The United States sent a strong note to Russia accusing the Soviets of illegally interfering in Hungarian affairs, but the gesture fell short of Aladár's hopes and objectives. He wanted the United States to refuse to recognize the new Hungarian government. Such a refusal could mean that the United Nations would then investigate what had happened, and the Smallholders would have a formidable ally and might be able to reestablish some sort of autonomous, democratic rule.

Ambassador Arthur Schoenfeld was leaving his post in Budapest. The Americans had the option of *not* replacing him as another way of demonstrating their seriousness. Unfortunately, the State Department had already announced that Selden Chapin was going to be the next American ambassador to Hungary. If they could be persuaded not to send him, the Soviet Union might see that the United States took its interference in Hungarian domestic affairs seriously.

On the afternoon of June 5, Aladár was invited to the State Department for a meeting with H. Freeman Matthews, the director of the Office of European Affairs; John D. Hickerson, the deputy director; and his old friend Walworth Barbour. Hickerson told Aladár that he had been invited so that the three of them could express their admiration to him for the courageous step that he had taken in the light of recent developments in Hungary. I picture my father sitting there, tense, exhausted, worried, and profoundly alone as he faced three men who were professionally talented at severing their empathy from geopolitical pragmatism. He had one card left to play.

He asked what his status in the United States was now, since he had already informed the State Department that he didn't consider the new government of Hungary to be legitimate and was not prepared to execute its orders. He reminded them that he had not resigned, and he hoped to continue relations with the U.S. government. He didn't wait for their answer before laying down his card. What were the American intentions regarding the appointment of Selden Chapin as ambassador to Hungary?

Mr. Chapin will be proceeding to Budapest, Mr. Hickerson replied.

The game was lost.

Hickerson described Aladár as being "demonstratively dejected," a strong expression for a State Department memo. His country, his family's security, and his future hung on that sentence: *Mr. Chapin will be proceeding to Budapest.* Under these circumstances, Aladár then said, "The U.S. should consider my mission as terminated and that I have resigned."

Aladár tried to explain that continuing U.S. relations with Hungary "would be contrary to the course contemplated by this Government to protest developments which led to the Government's installation." Couldn't they see the contradiction?

The trio that were gathered there thought Aladár was the one who failed to understand something important. "The minister seemed unable to comprehend our intention that Mr. Chapin assume his post," Barbour wrote. Then Matthews said that the United States was determined to follow the course that seemed best for Hungary and asked if "the Minister would feel that we would be serving that end in withdrawing our representation as would be necessary if we continued to maintain official relations with him?" Did Aladár really believe that his ministerial position was more important than an American presence in Budapest?

Aladár paused and "after profound reflection said, 'no' we should by all means maintain ourselves in Hungary. But that he had hoped that some middle course could be found whereby it would be possible to 'keep the door open.'"

During that profound reflection, Aladár watched all his fragile hopes turn to ash, as when he incinerated the files on March 19. All his most persuasive arguments, all his responsibilities as the Hungarian minister to the United States, finally reached the terminus with his quiet *no.* He was completely defeated. Here is where the reading of this dispassionate diplomatic note becomes for me almost unendurable, even knowing how civilized and well-intentioned, how consummately professional the gathering was.

Matthews pointed out that "we could not have it both ways and that we had to take one course or the other." His disagreeable job now completed, it was time for the gracious host to replace the executioner. "Mr. Matthews assured the minister, at length, that we would be happy to have him continue to reside in this country with such members of his staff as would wish to do so as private citizens and that we would welcome friendly contact with him in that private capacity." If ever the minister wanted to let them know anything of interest, well, by all means they would be delighted to hear it.

This gave Aladár enough time to collect himself so that he could, at least, finish the meeting with some dignity intact. There were still formalities to enact. "The Minister, although obviously depressed, assured Mr. Matthews of his appreciation of this Government's Courtesies to him while on official mission, of his constant desire not to embarrass the U.S. government in any way and declared on leaving that in all the circumstances he considered his official mission as concluded." He said that he had planned to have a press conference on June 6 and wondered if they had any objections if he released the letter that he had written to

Secretary of State George Marshall. They assured him that there was no objection.

He walked into the State Department as the Hungarian minister and left it as an exile. He took a cab to the legation offices on 3129 Le Roy Place and packed his things. Eighteen months after he and my mother arrived, so full of hope, so exhilarated by America, it was all over. He was nearly forty-four years old, was about to become a father for the first time, and for the second time in three years, was unemployed. This time he was without even a country he could call his own.

Paces Back and Forth

The newspapers called him a "self-deposed Hungarian Minister." The morning after his meeting at the State Department, he held a press conference at home on 31st Street. The stories about the press conference were divided into several predictable sections: "Ex Premier Plans U.S. Trip" described Ferenc Nagy's plans to come to the United States; "Charges Soviet Aggression" and "Vacate Legation Offices" explained that only three people—who supported the new government because they were either opportunists or Communists or both—had refused to resign and they held the fort.

The subhead for the last section seemed more like stage directions than a newspaper article: "Paces Back and Forth." My father had met with the *Evening Star* reporter for an interview before the official press conference, which the paper described: "Obviously aroused by events, he paced back and forth through the house while answering questions. Now he was on the back porch, then on the ground floor office, next in the hall, then in the living room, and then back in the hall, out the front door and back and forth in front of the house—finally back inside again."

The man, "aroused by events" who had walked miles through Budapest after March 19 as he awaited his arrest, was driven by the same engine to walk some more. A photographer from *Life* magazine showed up, and the nine members of the legation who had followed Aladár's lead were photographed. Aladár stood in front of the group, looking like a leading man about to ask for a drink or an assignation, leaning a bit on his right leg, hand in his left pocket, his head tilted down, so he looked up with cool dignity and stared straight into the camera. When they removed the diplomatic plates from their car, *Life* magazine captured that moment as well.

In the MovieTone archives, I discovered the thirty-six-second clip of my father's resignation speech. He stands in front of some bushes, wearing a double-breasted suit and looking at once stricken and in complete control. He nods briefly at the cameraman and starts to speak with a shockingly heavy Hungarian accent: "I refuse to recognize the new Government which was imposed upon Hungary by Russian and Communist pressure. I refuse to comply with its orders, and I refuse to return to Hungary. I raise my voice of protest on behalf of the Hungarian people and am confident that free people everywhere will listen to it."

I hadn't seen my father talk in the twenty-three years since his death. His face was the same, younger of course, the jaw cleaner, the hair darker, the brow unfurrowed. I imagine some people watching the clip in theaters might not have understood what he was saying because of his thick accent. I replayed it dozens of times, wishing that the cameras had kept rolling and I could see him walk away.

After the press conference, Aladár wrote a letter to H. Freeman Matthews. It was not an official letter to the State Department but a personal one, addressed to Matthews at his home on Woodland Drive. He thanked him for having seen him the day before and apologized that, "as a consequence of a manifest mistake, I discussed with you certain questions, instead of limiting myself to a purely personal basis." He must have been tormented by having talked about the ambassadorial appointment. How unprofessional. The arguments of Matthews were so airtight, he could not have countered them.

He then continued his apology: "I am also very sorry for having been bitter about certain things, but I hope that you will realize what it means for me to have to stand idly by, for a second time within three years, when the independence of my country is being lost. This time, however, my responsibilities are greater than in March, 1944."

How could H. Freeman Matthews, for all his illustrious experience in diplomacy, as a comfortable American, possibly understand what standing "idly by, for a second time within three years, when the independence of my country is being lost," meant for my father? As my grandfather wrote from Switzerland, "Occasionally it seems that we have buried not only the past but the future as well."

On June 18 Malvina Lindsay of *The Washington Post* wrote a short society column called "Displaced Diplomats, Exile Strikes." "How does it feel to lose one's country overnight?" she asked with surprising empathy. "Americans can only guess." She wrote about the ten men and women who "recently walked out of the Hungarian Legation in Washington to become exiles, because their conviction would not permit them to serve their new government. Nearly all had resisted and suffered under Nazi rule. One had been in a concentration camp. One, while in a Gestapo prison, had lost parents and all near relatives. Others had been robbed of their possessions and lived meager, dangerous lives under Nazi occupation. All had come to America tired and saddened by their ordeals but eager to help build a new Hungary."

Then Lindsay focused on the women, "reputed addicts of comfort and security," who were behind the scenes. She did not name any names, but it was easy to recognize my mother, "expecting her first baby in five weeks. She was reared in comfort, became a needy exile during the war. Asked how she will get along, she smiles and says: 'This is easy. My husband isn't in a German prison camp as he was three years ago, but in a beautiful, free country. We are together and that is the most important thing.'"

Hanna was not just putting up the brave front, presenting a cheerful face to the world while inwardly grieving. She meant it, with the kind of moral and transcendent clarity that comes from facing death and from comforting a man she loved after his nightmares of camp life. And she was moved by the surprising expressions of support and sympathy that came in the wake of his decision. Their landlord told them not to worry about the house they were renting—they could live there for the entire summer without even thinking of making a move. Others invited them and complimented them and were genuine in their desire to help in any way they could.

The future was unclear, of course, but Hanna was healthy and hugely pregnant; Aladár may have been a nervous wreck, but he was safe, and they were together. Her brother Tom was out of the army and living with them, being incredibly helpful and also providing her with comforting Kornfeld ballast.

Letters streamed in from Europe. Puppa wrote, "Even though I am in Portugal, my thoughts were more in America than here. . . . I am happy that people are so nice because I remember from 1944 how much more susceptible one is to every human kindness and how welcome every small human kindness is."

CHAPTER 46

Making the Best of It

In New York, the Chorin family slowly adapted to the bizarre new country in which they found themselves. Ferenc Chorin, sixty-eight years old, set about rebuilding the family fortune with the same energy he applied to nearly everything else. He was "making the best of it," as he told everyone in his heavily accented English. For a man of his compulsive energy and resilience, the previous three years of sitting in Portugal and floating around in Europe had been a kind of imprisonment. Not that he hadn't been intellectually occupied—figuring out what was going to happen to the family's assets, determining strategies for securing compensation from the Germans for war reparations, managing the remaining money to ensure that it would provide for them now and in the future—were vitally important activities. But what he had needed was a secure base of operations, and now finally, in New York, he had one.

Chorin, his wife Daisy, and their children, Erzsébet, Daisy, and young Ferenc, lived in a hotel while they looked for an apartment. They had two and a half rooms and a small kitchen, designed for the preparation of the simplest of meals, but for the first time in their lives, the family cooked for themselves. Daisy nearly set the kitchen on fire at least once by forgetting something cooking on the stove. Ferenc approached the preparation of breakfast with the spirit of an explorer venturing into uncharted territories; he became acquainted with the details, reporting with some concern that American eggs were completely different from Hungarian ones. When they were dropped into boiling water, something yellow leaked out immediately, unlike the noble Hungarian egg, which reposed, dignified and intact, in its egg cup.

Eventually the family moved into a huge apartment at 1000 Park Avenue, which had plenty of room for them plus Daisy's sister Edith and a parade of visitors from Europe. My father always referred to the New York branch of the Hungarian diaspora as "Atlantis" because it was a perfectly preserved, now extinct, ancient civilization. Friends and acquaintances slowly arrived in New York, and the Chorin home became, as it had been in Budapest, the center of activity. Chorin was the wise elder statesman, working behind the scenes to unite this argumentative, shipwrecked group.

None of it would have been possible without his extraordinary business acumen. Within three years he capitalized a pharmaceutical company, a shipping firm, and with the help of Hungarian chemists, a chemical enterprise in Brazil, with investor groups that he organized. He invested with one of the kings of New York real estate, William Zeckendorf. And when the Austrian immigrant Charles George Bludhorn needed some venture capital, Chorin was one of the men he turned to. The company he formed became Gulf + Western. But even as Chorin established himself in America, part of him always planned, or longed, to return to Budapest.

For Hanna, the presence of the family in New York was tremendously reassuring. Slowly the broad outlines of their prewar lives were beginning to take shape. On the Upper East Side of New York, recent Hungarian immigrants joined those from previous generations. There were Hungarian bakeries, grocery stores, and restaurants. Many old friends whose fate had been uncertain appeared in search of a job or at least a good meal. Hanna and Aladár visited the city frequently.

As in New York and Washington, so it was in Europe: obsessive preoccupation with the events in Hungary, legions of worries about the future, and now a shared sense of dislocation. After Aladár resigned, Hungarian ministers throughout Europe, many of them old friends of the family, followed: in Paris, in London, and in Rome. One by one they refused to recognize the new Hungarian government. Later in June, Ferenc Nagy emigrated to the United States with his wife and children, just one year after his triumphant state visit to America, this time as a refugee.

The Kornfelds remained in Europe still trying to secure American visas. Letters to my parents arrived from Paris, Zurich, Sils-Maria, Territet, and then, back again, once more from Lisbon. Like Dutch miniatures, with whole worlds captured in small frames, the reports of dinners eaten, walks taken, friends visited, trips taken, are vivid and varied. Yet the same names, the same themes, the same worries reappear like a roll call: the health of various family members, second- or third-hand reports from Hungary that things were either not quite so bad or very bad, appreciation for letters from Hanna and gentle chastisement about the lack of letters from Tom. In every letter there was some mention of concern about Puppa and the painter, about George and his family, hints about some financial compensation for property and material, and most important, urgent updates on the status of the prized visa applications.

The quest for the precious American visa was all-consuming and marked by magical thinking, endless gauntlets, and quirky schemes. At one point rumor had it that farmers would get preferential treatment. Móric was reproached by one of his lawyers for not "choosing the straight 'farmer preference' path [but] the serpentine 'displaced person' path with a 'typical capitalist perversity.' " A New York law firm urged him to "prove to the United States consul in Lisbon that he is an experienced farmer and that he has again the intention of engaging in farming in the United States."

In one such filing, Baroness Morris Kornfeld, née Marianne Weiss de Csepel, was described as having taken "complete charge of the work on the poultry farm to take in about 15,000 fowls, the fruit farm of an area of 40 Hungarian cadastral acres and as a bee keeper." Móric was engaged in "cattle breeding, the improvement of seeds, and on specialized lines of the agricultural industry like the growing of hops, castor, soya-beans, etc." Puppa was portrayed as having "charged herself with the personal conduct of the gardening work and the vineyard of an area of six Hungarian cadastral acres on the estate of her parents at Felsőireg."

The lawyer in New York also suggested that they wait to buy their farm until after arriving in the United States: "Mr. Strisak of the Jewish Agricultural Society would be pleased to assist in the selection of a farm, but they feel that they first should discuss with [Móric] his personal qualifications in order to determine the type of agricultural occupation for which he is best suited."

Little did the lawyer know that Móric already owned several thousand acres of ranchland in Alberta, Canada, purchased in the 1920s when two Canada-bound Hungarian bachelor barons had asked them to be investors. Móric had been prepared to turn them down, but the ever-fatalistic Marianne had said that one never knew what the world would bring, so they invested. Over the years, the two thousand acres of the Bow River Ranch enjoyed mixed success, so gradually their share grew.

In fact, the type of agricultural occupation for which Móric was best suited was as a baron who owned a six-thousand-acre model estate in a Hungary before land reform, supporting a large staff of full-time agricultural workers who could live in homes provided by that estate and regular brigades of seasonal workers who helped with the harvest.

Tallying the losses of the valuables that had once been in Ireg or in the apartment on Lendvay Street preoccupied the family, especially Marianne. She must have closed her eyes and returned to the many rooms of her old homes, taking mental inventory of silver and porcelain, paintings and carpets, baroque and Biedermeier furniture. Long lists of items, carefully typed and annotated, were sent to various authorities in charge of compensation. Móric's extraordinary library of rare books and his collections of silver and porcelain, paintings and statues, and works of medieval art and rugs were all gone.

Before March 1944 the family had gathered a portion of their valuables and stored them in two bank vaults. They had also stored crates of paintings, silver, porcelain, and old books with the gardener at the old Manfred Weiss estate on Budakeszi Street, where Alfons and his family had lived.

The Germans had taken most of the booty on what was known as the "treasure train," in order to protect the valuables from the Russians who were not, in a western European sense, connoisseurs. When the Russian army arrived, it did appropriate large portions of Móric's library. Today his ex libris can be seen in the Russian library of Nizhny Novgorod, and some of his precious woodcarvings are at the Grabar Institute in Moscow. Some financial assets were in the American zones in Austria and Germany, and lawyers attempted to get some compensation for those lost items.

During this time Móric and Marianne lived a strange and itinerant life, moving from one city to another, meeting up with family members, then going their separate ways, only to meet up again in another city. "We now live in total uncertainty as far as our travel plans are concerned," Marianne wrote in a typical letter. They did not go to the United States as farmers or as visitors. They would spend two more years in Switzerland before the American visas finally arrived.

Timsi

■
■ ■

They called their baby Timsi, which is pronounced in the Hungarian fashion *Tim-shee*. In my mother's jewelry box was a gold locket with his name, all in capital letters. They didn't know if they would have a son or a daughter, so the name had an androgynous quality and with a meaning known only to them.

Timsi was due in July. The trauma of Aladár's recent resignation was still fresh but was mitigated by the joyful distraction of his first child's impending birth. The child represented a future that was not bleak and abstract but hopeful and real. To begin their new life as Americans with an American baby augured well. Hanna could practically hear the quiet chatter of knitting needles across the ocean, as blankets, hats, booties, and little sweaters were lovingly created by both sets of grandmothers and aunts. Advice for the prospective new parents was imparted across great distances.

The most strident and emphatic one came from Sarolta, who had been waiting her whole life for the opportunity to bestow this wisdom. After all, she was not the head of the Hungarian Catholic Women's League for nothing. The first grandchild would be a Szegedy-Maszák, and that alone made him special.

As soon as she learned about the pregnancy, Sarolta enumerated Hanna's obligations during the next months in order to physically, intellectually, and spiritually groom the next Szegedy-Maszák in utero. "To develop the healthy body of the future descendant it is a must to follow the doctor's instructions, because the consumption of certain foods significantly contributes to the healthy condition of the new life," she wrote. "Today's medical science is more advanced than earlier. This means that the future generation should be physically better than the previous one was." As far as she was concerned, Hanna's spiritual and emotional life was a tincture that directly poured into the cells of her fetus, and it was up to my mother to make sure that these ingredients were of the highest quality.

> In regard to the emotional issues, the future mother has to start to establish her relationship with God. One has to think about the little newcomer with uplifting and colorful thoughts. The future mother has to develop all the nice and noble things that were received from God because this way the child will be a part of all these things. Intellectually too, one has to strive for the highest in this condition by reading relevant materials, enjoying art and music, conducting a religious life. Through all of this the superior mission of the soul can be developed in the child. My dear Hanna, I will send you one of Aladár's photos taken in his childhood. He really was a beautiful child. According to old wives' tales, if you look at the photo every day, your child will look like the person in the photo. And now Aladár, my dear son, be especially and to an even greater extent gentle to your wife in order to make sure that Little Timsi will also be such a gentle person.

I love to imagine my mother's reaction to this letter and wonder if she and my father were able to read it together and laugh just a little at the long to-do list. Or if he thought she needed to read and absorb the instructions with the seriousness with which they were offered. There had to be someone, perhaps Katalin or even Tom, with whom she could share it and see humor in its utter humorlessness. Not that it wasn't good advice, but it reads more like instructions for an especially demanding merit badge than tender advice from a future grandmother.

On the other side of the family, Marianne was terribly unhappy not to be there to help her daughter with the birth of her first child, so she deputized her youngest sister Edith to travel from New York and help. As nervous as a cat and having never had a baby herself, Edith managed to antagonize nearly everyone at Columbia Hospital for Women throughout the night until finally, at 7:44 in the morning on July 29, 1947, despite the presence of his great-aunt Edith, Aladár Thomas Szegedy-Maszák was born. He was the fourth Aladár Szegedy-Maszák in one hundred years.

Dr. Miller Willard Boyd said he wished all his patients were as calm and stoic and quiet as Hanna, though he vowed that as much as he liked her, he would never deliver another one of her children if her aunt were in the Washington metropolitan area.

Like fireworks, telegrams shot out from Washington to Sils-Maria, where Marianne and Móric were, to Puppa in Lisbon, and to the Szegedy-Maszáks in Budapest. And then telegrams rebounded in other directions. The Kornfelds sent congratulations to the Szegedy-Maszák grandparents, and the whole scattered army of cousins and aunts and uncles saluted the newest member of the family. "*Magnum Gaudium,*" Ferenc Chorin wrote. "I want to wish that you and the little pretender to the throne will live in a better and more harmonious world and that he will continue the family tradition. Even though he was born as an American citizen, may he help in the resuscitation of Hungary, and before that, be a cause of your great happiness."

The present, the past, and the future were all contained in Móric's letter:

> The little arrival came into a world that is changing. He couldn't have come at a better place than to you, from whom he can inherit so many positive and exceptional qualities. And with God's help, you will raise him to be able to assume his place in a better and more just world. It is true that it is a little bit too early to talk about this, but when I imagine the little boy, I feel a warmth around my heart, and I have to smile to think about him already as a man. Yet it comes with such a fantastic speed. Hancsikám, as I remember when you were this "old," like your son is now, we hardly took a few breaths until you became this age. And look, here is your son, who in my thoughts I already accompany to the future when he is a grown man.

Marianne's joy and curiosity and sheer maternal gusto could barely be contained: "When did it start? Were you very uncomfortable, dear Hancsikám? Did everything go smoothly? How does little Aladár look? How does he behave? Will you be able to feed him? Are you very uncomfortable with the warm weather? How long will they keep you in the clinic?"

She had borne four children and worried that since the little boy was born at 7:44 in the morning, my poor mother had had a "bad night," and she wished that she had been there with her. And then, ever gracious, she thanked my father, with "an extra special loving kiss . . . for making Hanna so happy. I cannot quite imagine you as a serious father, and I hope that I will soon get pictures from my dear beloved two Aladárs." And again, the complex uncertainty of the world intruded on this simple moment of happiness: "I also hope that he will live in a quieter and better world, in the creation of which you will, I hope, still play an active and important role. God be with you, my dear beloved children, with inexpressible love, I kiss you. Your extremely happy, Marianne."

Letters and telegrams of congratulation continued into August. Each aunt, uncle, cousin, friend, acquaintance, and sibling weighed in, their words practically soaring with happiness. Messages of congratulation arrived from perfect strangers who mentioned that they had been in Cleveland or Newark when my parents were there, had followed my father's courageous break with the Communists, and just wanted to celebrate this news with them.

Timsi's fingerprints and footprints decorated his birth certificate, and they capture the squirming vitality of an infant even now. Little Aladár *was* a beautiful baby: he had dark hair, large dark eyes, long tapered fingers, and one of those personalities who visibly delighted in the love and attention he received. In one photograph, my father holds him tight, and the two Aladárs beam at each other. Every baby is a joyful miracle, and I cannot claim that the birth of my oldest brother was even *more* joyful and *more* miraculous than all the others at the Columbia Hospital for Women that day. But for my parents and their parents, the long, painfully uncertain, hard-fought prelude to the birth of this little Aladár meant that when he finally did burst into the world, he reassured, renewed, and redeemed them all. The future in America, all of a sudden, became a kind of a friend, and it was because he was in it.

Hanna was surrounded by helpers. Edith had returned to New York and then went to Europe with the Chorin family, whose European withdrawal symptoms had become so severe, they had to leave New York. The mountains of Switzerland, Gstaad, and Territet were their preferred destinations and would remain so for the rest of their lives. Katalin Máriássy lived with them, as did Tom, as he deliberated about returning to school. Hanna luxuriated in new motherhood and received dozens of small gifts from Europe, each new grandmother and aunt eager to indulge little Timsi.

There he is yawning. Or looking at his hands. Or with his fist at his mouth. Or peeking with large dark eyes over my mother's shoulder, and yes, there is the faint outline of a widow's peak, just like my father's. In one photograph he lies in his stroller with a deeply satisfied smile on his face, beneath a knitted blanket, wearing a crocheted hat and sweater. His cheeks are full and healthy, and he looks as perfect a baby as one is ever likely to see. By the time he was three months old, he could raise his head. Obviously a genius.

After so many years of pondering the decision, and after promising while he was in Dachau, Aladár had converted to Catholicism that summer, and Timsi was baptized at Blessed Sacrament Church in Washington. Aladár looked for a job, enjoyed a few speaking engagements, and waited for some offer that seemed right. He had saved enough during his brief reign to support his new family for a year, but certainly money from the Kornfeld family helped. Of course, he worried.

He wrote to Lilly, "In terms of being employed, we have problems. . . . I am thinking of getting a university job, but I did not do anything yet . . . , and with a little child, I do not want to go to Utah or Wisconsin, where offers were made." In a later letter he said that my mother and his son "feel excellent and are in great spirits," but he worried about money and thought about taking out a loan to start—shockingly, to me—a farming business.

He was certain that eventually they would return to Hungary, though uncertain about what that would actually mean. The only thing that was clear was that throughout the summer and early fall, little Timsi thrived, and my parents were happy with a sense of completion they never again enjoyed.

The Remorseful Revolutionary

Puppa remained in Portugal, although she occasionally visited her parents in Switzerland. Her relationship with Luis kept her in Lisbon, and there were no more mentions of János Zwack or speculations about a divorce from Vera. Now the question was whether she should stay with the man everyone referred to as "the painter." That they were having an affair was obvious to everyone, but whether the affair would lead to marriage was still open.

"The painter," Móric wrote Hanna, "is still a very sympathetic cultured man, but he is a very touchy, jealous hypochondriac who loves to be pampered and wouldn't be a very easy husband. How much of this is love and how much is Puppa's desire to be independent, no one can determine."

The desire to be independent—what a familiar theme. When I was a teenager in the late 1960s and early 1970s, I aspired to be like Puppa. So brilliant, so marriage hating and autonomous. Hers was a rebellion that resulted, not in censure by the family, but in a kind of eminence. She was a feminist who loathed feminists. She gave me Virginia Woolf and Radclyffe Hall to read, even as she was openly contemptuous of Gloria Steinem and Betty Friedan and their braless acolytes and bullhorns on the evening news.

During this time of women's liberation, when marriage seemed unnecessary since living together was so easy, Puppa would share her own unconventional romantic history with me. Her affair with János Zwack taught me, at age fourteen, that there was nothing wrong with having an affair with a married man as long as you had no interest in marrying him. I did not see this approach as being servile and a terrible form of self-sacrifice. I saw it as being forward thinking and free. Just like my aunt.

In her third-floor bedroom, on the wall over her bureau, was a watercolor of a Lisbon street, spare and flat and angular and luminous. Near the bottom of the street, a woman in blue, with a copper pot on her head, tilts in an arabesque. During my adolescence, in a haze of cigarette smoke, I heard about Puppa's affair with Luis. I learned that she had had an abortion and that he was jealous and interesting and tiring. She spoke about the affair in much the same rueful and abstract way as she spoke about her abandoned dissertation on medieval Hungarian cities. From these conversations, I learned that she was always in control and always a little detached so that no man ever really owned her. That, I thought, was a good thing.

But then I read her 1947 letters to my mother and her parents and realized that when she showed me the unconventional path, she had used a thirty-year-old map from which all the details, the emotional texture, and the raw pain had been erased. In the letters the messy details remain preserved, as if in formaldehyde, and I see my venerated thirty-three-year-old aunt sounding like a confused, tormented adolescent in love with the wrong guy.

In Portugal, distant from the family life she found so suffocating, she wrote her parents a long letter. She assured them that now that she was on her own, Luis was "much more concerned about appearances," so they didn't have to worry. Presumably, he would not touch her in public or have a tantrum in a café or leave her hotel room first thing in the morning before breakfast.

Now that the first battle for her freedom was won, she confessed to her parents "how hard it was to let me go for different reasons, and for this I cannot be thankful enough. All the wind is taken out of my sails, and never again will I be a good revolutionary. . . . You will not have any more of these problems with me, and I am very sorry that lately I have been so unpleasant. Something in my head was wrong. . . . I promise to resolve everything intelligently, and you will not have to be ashamed because of your 'black sheep' daughter."

Her parents probably knew that this did not signal the end of the affair, but they still responded with love. Their letters to Hanna were outspoken in their concern about Luis. He had fought in the Spanish Civil War on the side of the Republicans, so he could not easily return home. Did this reveal something more worrisome about his past? They contacted friends in Spain who did some checking. And when they visited Portugal, they tried to talk with Luis about his intentions.

Marianne wrote Hanna, "My discussion with the painter did not clarify anything—just as I thought. He said it would be better for him if he did not love her so much, because his life then would be easier. There was nothing in his life he has to hide, and if he learned that we made inquiries, this would hurt him so much that he would run away or take Puppa with him. In the end he stammered that he is nervous, but in better health than Puppa. I have to confess that all this was said in a nice way. I do not think Puppa would be happy with that man for a long time. How good God was to us concerning Aladár—we never had even one minute of anguish."

Puppa would refer to him with uxorious ease. "Luis sends his love," she would write, or "Luis was very impressed" by something Aladár had done. But several sentences later she would explain that she was planning to become a lab technician and move to America if she could get the visa. Another possibility would be to move to Switzerland to be trained there. She studied typing and shorthand formally and kept her sister apprised of the progress that she was making in both. As long as the visa proved elusive, however, and as long as her parents remained in Europe, and as long as Luis clung to her and loved her, she remained with him.

For years.

In one long stream-of-consciousness letter to Hanna—"you will think that this letter will fit a Freud psychoanalysis," she wrote—she contemplated my mother's pregnancy and looked into the future with uncanny prescience. "If you have a daughter," she wrote, "you can bring her up and say, 'See, I did it this way because it is the way it should be done. You can do what you want, but if you look at your old aunt, then you will think about it twice.'"

When I first read this passage, I felt a snag of embarrassment. My adolescent self stood between my mother and my aunt. But my mother did not have the temerity to say, "I did it this way" (not that I would have listened anyway), and I turned to my "old aunt" eagerly, brimming with curiosity, admiration, and an eagerness to replicate her life in my own. I never *thought twice* until I had made too many of the same mistakes. I never *thought twice* until I realized that what was right for her was wrong for me. I never really *thought twice* until everyone who mattered, including her, was dead.

I had been bewitched by a complicated alchemy of the force of her presence, the quiet resignation of my parents, and the crazy timing of popular culture. Reading her letters, I saw that she too had suffered and been bewitched by very different but no less irrational or potent or unlucky forces. The map of the life of "freedom" and independence that she had once shown me led nowhere but to a life as a lab technician, living with her parents and her sister's family. She had been the most dutiful of sisters and daughters growing up, of course, but many of the most important parts of growing up—achieving self-sufficiency, autonomy, adult relationships outside the family—had simply not been a part of her life. She had forgotten that. Or I had.

When I read her letters, though, the romance of her romance was barely visible. As the year wore on, she became more restless and more eager to settle down. She asked Hanna to ask Tom to look around at what laboratory possibilities there were, "what schools are teaching it, and if there is hope to get accepted in one of them. Don't talk about this as I hate it if they talk about me . . . but I have had it with hotel life and would like to stay in a place where there is a possibility of staying for a lengthy time."

She vowed that if things began to improve, if the police were nicer to her when she checked in to renew her residence permit, if she could begin to have some hope for the future, if Luis found more lucrative work, she would go to Fatima. Some or all of these things might have happened, because she did go to Fatima. "Do not think that I am crazy and all of a sudden that I became a religious maniac," she wrote Hanna, whose recently converted husband had already vowed to go to Lourdes. "But somehow this is the only thing I can still rely on: that God will help. I very much rely on this and believe it."

The Large Wound Fate Inflicted

. . .

On the first day of November, All Saints' Day, Timsi began to cry with an intensity not from complaint but from pain. He was unable to eat properly, but when Hanna took him to the pediatrician, her concerns were dismissed. A new mother. (A Hungarian at that.) Hysterical. Over-reacting. Go home and relax. Just a little colic.

But it was not a little colic. The little boy was sleepless. His legs curled up. No one could see that one part of his bowel had folded inward, creating a blockage, and everything in that small space was backed up. Brand-new intestines were inflamed, constricted, and swollen. All his parents could see was that this radiant, healthy little boy was miserable and wasting away.

The condition is known as intussusception, and I learned that it strikes boys more frequently than girls, that it weirdly occurs mostly in the spring and fall, and that the babies are usually between five and ten months of age. Little Aladár, demonstrating precocity even then, was just a bit older than three months. Treatment within the first twenty-four hours generally results in complete recovery. Delays in treatment can lead to further complications, including irreversible tissue damage, perforation of the bowel, infection, and death.

But the pediatrician failed to perform an exam that would have alerted him to the problem. He just told Hanna not to worry. Little Aladár screamed and writhed in pain for much of the night and part of the next day. When they brought the baby back to the doctor the next day, he changed his mind. There was blood in the little boy's diaper—a classic symptom they call red currant stool. He told my parents to take him to the emergency room at Children's Hospital.

Timsi was immediately admitted. Perhaps they could save him. Hanna and Aladár watched as their baby was wheeled into the operating room. They smoked and waited. Timsi survived the operation, but the doctor offered no reassurance, only sympathy. Hanna's breasts were still full of milk. She and Aladár and Tom stood in little Aladár's room, watching as each breath seemed to take him farther away from them. He had stopped crying. They would have given anything to hear his cry again.

Early in the morning of November 4, 1947, he died, a perfectly unnecessary death.

Nothing compared to it. Not the Nazis, not Dachau, not Rákosi. Their devastation was absolute, infinite, shocking. They had not slept for two days. Stricken with a grief that seemed beyond enduring, they returned to a home that was still redolent of his presence—his clothes, his smell, his diapers and blankets and small soft toys. They would never hold him again or see him smile or marvel at what he could do.

Later that morning Tom took care of the onerous details. He sent telegrams to his parents and other relatives. Unable to rest, he went to Blessed Sacrament Church, where only a few months before Aladár Thomas Szegedy-Maszák had been baptized. He walked to the residence of the priests and knocked on the door. There was no answer. He knocked again, and there was still no answer. The door was open, so he stepped in. "No sooner had I stepped in than one of the distinguished clergy came down," Tom recalled. "And he said, 'This is a private home. You have no business standing here.' And I said, 'I am sorry, Father, but I came to tell you that the child of one of your parishioners has died. And we have to make arrangements for a funeral.'"

The mood shifted.

One of the saddest funerals took place at Blessed Sacrament several days later, and I picture it sharply, as if I had been there. I know the crimson darkness of that church, the large and properly gruesome crucifix on the transept wall. The many stained-glass windows depicting the life of Jesus, with the supporting richly colored cast of saints, Mary and Joseph, lambs of God and angels. The wood-carved Stations of the Cross on the walls, with Jesus falling the first time, Jesus being crowned with thorns,

Jesus nailed to the cross. But the Via Dolorosa did not have imprisonment in a concentration camp. Or losing your country twice in three
years. Or burying your first child, your perfect son. The stone statue of
Mary holding the baby Jesus, who in turn holds a chalice with a Eucha-
rist, must have seemed almost like a reproach. At least Mary had had her
son for thirty-three years. And the dark red carpet, the beautiful filigreed
altar, my parents and Tom and Katalin in the front row. The tiny casket.
The tears.

The only Catholic cemetery was half an hour away, past Washington's
poorest neighborhoods. They arrived at the children's section, with the
little crosses economically inscribed with one year for both birth and
death. They watched as his casket was lowered into the grave. How could
they leave him there all alone, in the cold earth for eternity, under the
darkening November sky?

After receiving the telegram on November 4, Móric immediately sat
down to write.

My dear Children,

*Just a few words with the deepest of sorrow. I want to do this with
affection and delicacy so that I do not increase the pain of the large
wound that fate has inflicted on you. That it has inflicted on us,
because the little boy who just left us was one of the happy hopes of our
future. At a time of such dreadful loss, it is good to remember two
things: Life goes on with its duties and demands, with its beauty and
purity, with its pleasures and sorrows. The second thing you must
think about is the love that surrounds you, and that while everybody
has to fight this battle in his own soul, he or she is not alone. You are
not alone. You must appreciate more deeply than ever before what
parental love is, and you must know that our love is with you. Think
of this, my dear children, when the house seems so empty and the
world is so dark. With inexpressible love and yearning, Papa.*

From Budapest, Sarolta wrote her own anguished letter of love and
sorrow. She tried to reassure them that she frequently felt "the little angel
around me. I spontaneously open my arms wide to embrace him. I know
he is up there protecting us all, and his biggest problem is how to make
your pain and sadness easier." She urged them, "My darlings, accept that

this is not reversible and make preparations for the little newcomer who will be sent by God and for whom I pray daily. The little darling who just departed will stay in our soul, and we will keep his memory with love. He will be the liaison between us and God, so that our requests will all be answered with his love."

Puppa wrote immediately. She "could not find the words to tell you and Aladár how much my heart hurts. It is always bad to be so far away, but at times like this, every letter, every word is insufficient to tell you that I am with you and that it hurts me that I cannot be with you when you are hurt. . . . I always have felt that you are the one I would like to safeguard against all grief. It is terrible that the ones I love so much should suffer such great pain."

Aladár kept a file of the hundreds of letters and condolence notes that they received in Hungarian, German, English, and French. The shock, the love, the inadequacy of the words need no translation but spoke to something quite beautiful that my parents inspired. Most striking were how many of the notes were from new American friends, speaking with warmth and caring that would have taken a European decades to utter.

Little Aladár hovered like a phantom infant presence throughout our lives. His baby pictures dominated our parents' bedroom. The perfect new baby on a sea of white, his head resting on his right ear, his gently curled fist by his cheek. He stared out with his large dark eyes, forever present. Every Palm Sunday my mother would change the dried-out palm that draped this picture in their bedroom, the only tender motherly gesture for her firstborn that remained to her.

Hanging near my mother's side of the bed was a series of small photographs of him with my parents, in his crib, in his stroller, propped up on a chair. Only one other baby picture was in their room—that of my brother Andy, who was born eleven months after Little Aladár died.

My brothers and I each made Little Aladár's acquaintance at different times in our lives. We would ask our mother about the picture, and she, in a gentle but strangely dispassionate way, would explain that this was Little Aladár, our oldest brother, who got very sick and died when he was a baby. For children, this seemingly reassuring fact actually diminished his importance. He was *just* a baby. Not like us. We would all indulge in wondering what our lives would have been like if he had lived.

Once, after my brothers had tormented me with unusual relentlessness, my father had comforted me by saying that Little Aladár would have protected me, had he lived. I had my fantasy oldest brother, my protector and confidant.

I didn't realize that the deeper meaning was how much his presence would have protected us all, especially my parents. This loss above all others reverberated through our lives, but we were not even aware of it.

When I was eleven or twelve, I sat in a dressing room at Woodward & Lothrop department store with my mother as she tried on dresses. I was preoccupied by breasts at the time, having just managed to persuade my old-fashioned mother that I needed a bra because my friend Gail, whose mother knew these things, advised that if you jumped up and down and your breasts moved, you needed a bra. Desperately I jumped.

I never saw my mother naked, so my mother in a slip, whether in her bedroom or in a dressing room, was as close as I ever came. That afternoon, with the brazen curiosity of a young adolescent, I evaluated her collapsed breasts. She noticed. "When Little Aladár died," she said slowly, almost reluctantly, "my breasts were still full of milk, and very uncomfortable. The doctors told me that I should put heavy, hot towels on them to make them feel better. I did, for weeks and weeks, but, well, they were never the same . . ." she trailed off, almost apologetic. My mother had never confided in me like this before; in her vulnerability, she had disrobed more than I had ever imagined possible. The scene goes dark here. I vaguely remember escaping from the small room, charging into the glare of the store to find my mother another dress in another size.

But she was made of sterner stuff than my father. She was more resilient or perhaps just less damaged. A week after they buried Timsi, Puppa replied to a letter from my mother. "You wrote that I should tell you about myself but there is not very much of interest to say. . . . This last week I 'lived' more in Washington than here." She valiantly tried, describing her knitting and her visa challenges and some translations that she was doing. "I can't begin to tell you how much I thought about you all last week and how much my heart aches." I can see my mother asking others for news, begging for some distraction, keenly aware that she had to follow her father's advice and remember that "life goes on, with its duties and demands, with its beauty and purity, with its pleasures and sorrows." Three months later she was pregnant again.

My father never recovered. His namesake's death destroyed something in him forever. For several months after he would sit in the living room, staring into space for hours. My mother tried to help him as best as she could, but this suffering was so different from when he had returned from Dachau. Then he had reached out and she comforted him; now he disappeared, and she too was bereft. Gradually he crawled out from beneath the boulder of his pain and loss, but part of him carried that boulder for the rest of his life, even through the birth of three more children.

On Little Aladár's first birthday, my parents went to the cemetery. The small white marble cross was still not ready. Aladár wrote to Lilly, "You can imagine the mood of both of us. We did not speak about it, but were thinking about one thing: how much happiness the little newcomer brought us, how happy we were as long as he was with us. By now he would be running or at least he would be toddling around. We did not want to increase each other's pain, but when we looked at each other, we felt and knew that we were thinking about the same thing. . . . But, with God's help, there will be another grandchild."

Every year, in his journal, my father would reflect on how old Little Aladár would be. It has been fifteen, twenty, thirty, thirty-three years since Little Aladár was born, he would write. On his thirtieth birthday, he wrote,

> Source of enormous joy and hope, ninety-nine days later, horrible, never quite bygone, pain. At that time I didn't realize it, but it became clear only in retrospect that his premature death also meant the end of any hope to return home. That a fourth Szegedy-Maszák with this name was not to be, interrupted a tradition that I had hoped would continue. Even so, I thank God, because his birth and the ninety-nine days of his life helped me through the shock of becoming a stateless, homeless person. He gave me the joy of birth and the vision, the touch of one's own child. When he first smiled at you because he may have recognized you, I discovered what it meant to be present at the creation of a human being's first personal relationship.

Ninety-nine days. One afternoon, or maybe during a sleepless night, desperate with grief, he had tried to quantify a loss that was unquantifiable and just sat and counted each day they had spent together. Day after day after day.

In July 1951 my parents were living in Washington with their two sons, Andy (who was born in 1948) and Peter (who was born in 1950). Aladár commuted between Washington and New York at the time. He wrote to a friend in Washington that he was planning to be there at the end of the month because "it was, as you may recall, the birthday of our son Aladár who died." Little Aladár was born on July 29; my brother Peter had turned one on July 26. But he made not even a mention of the first birthday of his youngest son.

As the years went on, my father grew even more deeply depressed. "Tomorrow Little Aladár would be thirty-two years old," he wrote. "I wonder how he would have developed. What he would be like compared to his three very different siblings. I wonder if his premature death spared him from more than what he lost. These are melancholy, painful, worrisome parental thoughts. They have no answers." A year later he and my mother visited his grave. "It still hurts," he wrote. "Again, I am thinking more frequently about suicide, this possibility returns involuntarily. My Maszák great-grandfather, my uncles Miklós, Árpád, and Putyu, in three generations quite a few chose this way. They might have considered it a way out. Obviously it was a dead end."

Aladár celebrated his forty-fourth birthday three weeks after the death of Timsi, although there could not have been much celebration. I am shocked by his youth and shocked to realize that in all the most meaningful ways, his life ended at forty-four.

On New Year's Eve the Kornfelds were in Zurich with the Chorins and the Mauthners. Puppa greeted 1948 with Luis in Lisbon. George was in Vienna with Elsie's family. Hanna and Aladár and Tom were in Washington. "It is easy to say goodbye to the past year, not only because of the great grief, but the year was so broken up and scattered as no year had ever been before," Móric wrote in his New Year's letter to my parents. "It was a bad year. We wish for ourselves and for all of us that the New Year will get us together and that what happens will not be too different from what we hope for."

Marianne wrote a hasty postscript to her husband's letter. "My dears, in this mysterious new year, you are the first ones to whom I send my warm and loving kisses. I have just returned from the Chorins, where everybody, including us, spoke about everything except what was oppressing our soul. My thoughts, filled with loving yearning, are with you and Puppa, and I hope that you have felt them. May God preserve you from any more pain. My kisses and love, Mami."

God declined her request.

Epilogue

A story has no beginning or end; arbitrarily one chooses
that moment of experience from which to look back or from
which to look ahead.

—GRAHAM GREENE, *The End of the Affair*

Epilogue

.   .   .

After Little Aladár died, my parents had to cope with the details of employment and immigration and build some kind of future from the few fragments of optimism and resilience left to them. But their loss informed everything they did. On December 9 Aladár wrote a letter to the visa division of the State Department in which he asked about the status of their visas. He had been told by a State Department official in June that under Section 19/c of the Immigration Act of 1917, the birth of a child would enable them "to have our immigration status changed without having to leave the United States. In this connection, I wish to inform you that on July 29th a son—Aladár Junior—was born to my wife. To our great sorrow our child died on November 4th. In view of this fact our eligibility to have our immigration status changed under the above quoted legal provision does not exist at the present time."

Telling Mr. Alexander about Little Aladár's death may or may not have been necessary in the strict bureaucratic functioning of the world, but my father simply had to share the catastrophe with anyone he could. Maybe he needed to hear another expression of shock and sympathy; maybe he had to unburden himself so someone else would bear witness. He may have still been so grief stricken and disorganized that nothing could happen without it being the central point of reference.

My brother Andy was born in October 1948. My mother's self-confidence had taken a mortal hit when her first baby died. She never stopped blaming herself for flawed maternal instincts that hadn't pushed through all barriers, like recalcitrant American doctors, to save her son. When Andy was born, she persuaded her cousin Daisy to come down from New York and help her care for him. Her mother was still in Europe, and she needed the presence of someone from the family. She also knew that she would have to be the one to revive Aladár. She was the only person who could give him a reason to keep going.

Aladár had cobbled together some jobs. The Library of Congress, for example, had asked him to help compile their Hungarian catalog. He was also active in émigré affairs, and in February 1948 he appeared once more in *Life* magazine in a "Life's Visit" section. He stands without a suit jacket on, in profile, reading some papers. Nearby Tom and Alexander Szász, a former counselor from the embassy, stand beside a cumbersome old copy machine. "Hungarian mimeograph operators turn out anti-Communist peasant union literature," the caption reads. It would be his last appearance as a subject in print until his obituary decades later.

He would have loved to become a professor somewhere, but as he lacked a Ph.D., no decent American university was interested in hiring him. Eventually he found work with Radio Free Europe; then he discovered that the CIA funded it, so he quit. Finally the Voice of America hired him and put him in charge of their Hungarian service. The Voice at that time was based in New York, so he would work in New York Monday through Friday, staying in a small room at the Chorins' Park Avenue apartment, then would come back down to Washington for the weekends, an arrangement that never made sense to me.

Until I realized that by that time, in early 1949, my grandparents had arrived in the United States. Since Tom was a veteran, they had received preferential treatment and finally managed to secure American visas. They moved in with my parents in a house they had bought in Chevy Chase, Maryland, and Móric Kornfeld became Maurice de Kornfeld.

The arrival of Móric and Marianne brought a seismic shift for Hanna. After nearly four years of separation, she concentrated on making her parents welcome in America. By this time, all of Marianne's brothers and sisters had immigrated to the United States.

New fatherhood and a new profession may have dulled the pain of Aladár's terrible losses, but 1949 brought more tragedy to his life. The most vicious Stalinist period in Hungary's history had begun, and his family in Budapest was especially vulnerable. They would have been anyway because of his public repudiation of the Communist Hungarian government, but Lilly refused to keep a low profile. She spent time at the American embassy, visited American contacts, and acted as if she wore a cloak of invulnerability, or ex post facto diplomatic immunity, even as she became more and more distraught in her letters to her brother.

In January 1949 she wrote:

> *I think so much about what I should do, but there are not too many options, because we are in a mousetrap. There is no way out. To leave illegally is almost impossible. I could somehow manage the monetary matters, but to liquidate everything unnoticed is not possible. At the same time how long will they let us stay in the apartment, how long will they allow Api his retirement that represents the basis of our exis- tence, at least on paper, is something that no one can predict. It can change from one day to the next.*

The first months of 1949 brought one blow after another. On Febru- ary 7, Lilly was arrested and indicted for espionage. In March a cousin, István Moldoványi, who was a mechanical engineer at Csepel, was ar- rested by the secret police, and a few days later his wife was informed that he had died suddenly at Gábor Péter's dreaded 60 Andrássy Avenue. Aladár Senior, who was eighty-two, and his brother, who was seventy- three, were told that they would no longer receive their pensions. In June Musi's husband, Károly, a fifty-two-year-old chemical engineer, was fired and had little hope of getting another job.

Aladár wrote a former colleague at the State Department in July 1949: "Lilly was sentenced to life imprisonment and not five years as reported to you. My father was deprived of his pension. My brother-in-law lost his job. My uncle was deprived of his pension. My cousin was murdered at Andrássy ut. 60. To what extent am I responsible for this score, I do not know." He went on to ask if the United States could do anything for them, even though he knew that the question was "very silly." The more pressing question was his own "serious dilemma: Can I go on working for the Voice or for the Hungarian exile movement in the belief that the U.S. would ultimately help Hungary while I am unable to secure any help for my family?"

Lilly was in prison for seven years. During that time my brother Peter and I were born. In 1956 she was freed. Initially she could not bring her- self to leave the building that had held her against her will. When she

finally left, she ran into a cousin, Mihály, and his mother, who were astonished to see her. Mihály's mother asked where she was going, and
Lilly responded with her customary insouciance, "To the hairdresser."
She kept some of the 1920s Soviet production novels that she had been
forced to read in prison, and pieced together her life with the financial
help of the de Kornfeld family. Aladár's parents, the class enemies that
they were, had been kicked out of their apartment and deported to the
countryside, where they lived with a resentful peasant family. His father
died in that exile.

But Sarolta returned to Budapest, and Lilly found a place for both of
them to live. She took care of her mother, whose health was always
deemed fragile, until she died at ninety-eight. After Sarolta's death, Lilly
collapsed emotionally. My father's guilt never ceased. In 1970 he wrote in
his journal, "I begged Lilly to be cautious, not to play a role in society, but
she continued to go to the Americans, she was proud to be the only
Hungarian who visited them. . . . She was arrested and until today she
keeps saying that all this happened because of me. The poor soul, individual responsibility was never her strongest suit . . . but when I go to
confession, Lilly is my greatest reason for remorse."

The difference between the lives of the Kornfelds and the Szegedy-
Maszáks, the enormous abyss between ease and privilege and suffering
and deprivation, was tragically underscored in the postwar years.

In June 1950 Puppa left the painter forever and arrived at La Guardia,
where her parents were waiting. They went to the Chorins' apartment on
Park Avenue. Puppa had described a bustling home filled with friends,
all Hungarian refugees; everybody talked in a rush about musicals and
films. "I was the little goose who came from the country," Puppa said.
"And all of a sudden, everyone was running right and left. I thought they
were all crazy. The telephone rang, the friends were coming, there were I
don't know how many people at the dinner table." She paused. "The
funny thing is, six months later, I was running, too."

Puppa went down to Washington and lived in the house in Chevy
Chase for several months until they all moved to a large, sunny house in
Scarsdale, New York. Aladár commuted to the city. Puppa was trained as
a lab technician and worked at New York Hospital.

Tom finished his undergraduate education at George Washington
University, spent a miserable year at Georgetown University Medical
School, then transferred to Harvard. He married a lovely American nurse

from Berlin, Wisconsin, had four children, and became a famous anes-
thesiologist. He is considered one of the fathers of respiratory therapy.
He is also one of the foremost translators from English to Hungarian
and vice versa.

His brother George divorced Elsie in 1948, married another Austrian
woman, and moved to the United States in 1951 becoming George de
Kornfeld. Elsie decided that since her name had been affixed to the Csepel factory as one of its owners, she deserved to be paid for her ownership
and sued the family for millions. The suit dragged on for years, until in
1956, she was paid $47,044 (about $380,000 in today's dollars). George
had a distinguished career as a hotelier and was general manager of the
Plaza in New York and the Carleton Towers in London, as well as the
Mayflower in Washington, D.C.

In 1954 the Voice of America headquarters were moved to Washington, D.C., and the family moved once again. Hanna and Marianne
looked for houses and then bought the house on Patterson Street, where
I was brought after I was born, also at Columbia Hospital for Women.
By this time my father had stopped driving simply because he didn't like
to drive in America. He worked downtown and began to garden with the
focus and single-mindedness with which he approached anything he
cared about. Zinnias, tulips, snapdragons, soaring roses and peonies, de-
mure pansies and delicate freesia, some lavender lined the front walk, and
only now do I wonder if it was a small, romantic homage to the lavender
they had shared in Ireg. A voluptuous weeping cherry tree was in the
front yard. The garden was vivid and beautiful, and the house always had
fresh flowers in it. In the basement, seedlings in his preemie unit struggled under grow lights, and in the backyard there was a greenhouse. The
fishpond was turned into a compost heap.

Aladár spent hours outside tending his garden. It was the one domain
at Patterson Street that was unambiguously his own. I once asked him if
he had gardened in Hungary, and he said he hadn't. He only began in
America, because he had seen so much death and destruction—he
"wanted to watch things grow." When each of us had our first Holy
Communion, he planted two fruit trees in our honor. My brother Andy
had peach trees, Peter had apple trees, and I had two sour cherry trees.
All ten cousins would gather for Easter egg hunts that seemed to take
hours. On summer nights we would sit on the side porch and fireflies
sparkled in the grass and in the sky, and even in darkness the garden was

beautiful. Conversations in different languages surrounded me when guests were there. It was, for me, the safest place on earth.

When Hanna and Aladár arrived in America, the rest of the family had still been in Europe. My parents were married just to each other for three lambent but challenging years, until everything changed and my father was married to my mother's family. Every day Hanna teetered between her life as a daughter and her life as Aladár's wife. Not that tensions among the in-laws made these identities incompatible. Quite the reverse—harmony reigned. But the comity and civility imprisoned them. The process was so slow, the reasons to be grateful so numerous, and the loss of their primacy so basic, they could not have acknowledged it to each other, much less to their children.

My poor mother. She was always so conscientious, so intent on being the good and loving daughter. She was a wife and mother, married to a Hungarian husband, and raising American children. Like the prodigal son's well-behaved and unrewarded brother, Hanna's status slipped with the arrival of her sister. Aladár wrote in his journal about "the family's collective narcissism. Somehow everything relates to the family, for everything that happens there is a particular procedure or some sort of axiom. In this respect I feel myself to be more emancipated, despite my attachment to everything my father, mother, and their families represented."

My father wrote this when he was seventy-six years old. The arrival of the Kornfelds, happy as it was, exacted an enormous price. My father was already deeply depressed. Battered by history and circumstances, financially drained by the demands of his family in Hungary, already in debt to the Kornfelds, he could not welcome them and also be the master of his house. He surrendered. And Hanna could not fight that battle alone.

In December 1962 Móric celebrated his eightieth birthday, which George arranged at the Mayflower Hotel in Washington. All the grandchildren sat around a big table, surrounded by what seemed to be hundreds of other tables with famous émigré Hungarians celebrating him. Móric and Marianne's golden wedding anniversary was on June 17, 1963, and we all gathered in the Chorins' apartment for a fancy dinner. Each of us presented my grandparents with a single strand of golden wheat and recited a poem. (*For everything that happens there is a particular procedure or some sort of axiom.*) I always loved the poems, the events, and the festivities. I didn't realize how much my father resented them.

That was the last joyful event in the life of the family. Ferenc Chorin died on November 4, 1964, Edith in August 1967, and Móric died, with strange best-friend symmetry, on November 4, 1967. He had been sick with the flu for a few days, but his breathing became labored. Around ten at night they called the ambulance. I stood at the curve of the stairway at Patterson Street and watched as he was carried down on a stretcher. The ambulance lights flashed across my grandmother's face, and after everyone left, my father and I prayed the Our Father together. The next morning I awoke early and heard my mother downstairs. She was cleaning, a default activity that I grew to share during times of pain and sadness. "Is Grandfather okay?" I asked. I had never seen my mother cry before, and the fact that she was struggling not to cry was nearly as momentous for me as the fact that she shook her head no. "Is he dead?" She nodded. She now would mourn both her father and son on November 4.

His funeral was the first and last "great" funeral I remember. Hungarians from all over the country packed the church. Many people spoke, and they too had had illustrious histories long ago: a prime minister, a foreign minister, a bishop. I couldn't understand a word they said. So Catholic and formal was the funeral, there was no trace that the man whom they all mourned had been born, indeed had lived half his life, as a Jew. I was twelve years old then and knew the family history, but only now do I wonder if anyone who sat in the crowded church, or lined up in the funeral cortège that snaked across many blocks as we made our way to Rock Creek Cemetery, or listened at the freezing graveside as an old Hungarian priest sang the national anthem of Hungary, quietly recited the mourner's kaddish.

Fewer people attended my grandmother's funeral six years later. During the last year of Marianne's life, Lilly had visited us for several months, and this was a sore point for my mother; she still suffered the terrible combination of guilt and irritation that Lilly managed to inspire. Lilly would sit and watch high-decibel soap operas, and her presence at the dining table made everyone nervous. Finally, reluctantly, Lilly returned to Hungary.

A series of small strokes led to my grandmother's precipitous decline. She lost her way in our house; she asked to be taken out of the car when she was sitting in the living room; she needed to have her meat cut. I was a junior in high school and preoccupied with my own ridiculous world, but I watched my mother and Aunt Puppa tend to her with the respect and deference that she had commanded throughout her life. And finally, with two of her sisters from New York and several of their daughters flanking her bed, she died in the hospital one soft April dawn. The funeral was large and dignified, and I remember very little about it. Much to the astonishment of Washington's émigré community, Puppa assumed the head of the table after her mother's death.

At some point in the 1960s, my parents fulfilled the dream that Aladár had discussed with Francois Fauré, his friend in Dachau. It was not the little country house in the Badacsony region of Hungary that he had envisioned, and it was not designed by his French architect friend from the Dachau hospital. It was a little country house in Bluemont, Virginia, about two hours away from Washington. At last Aladár had his own modest domain. They furnished it and bought sheets and towels, dishes and silverware. Hanna's friends threw a housewarming to set them up with teakettles and festive cups, pots and pans, and the rest of the accoutrements that make up a couple's first home. The modest ranch-style house sat on enough land for a large garden and even a small orchard. When you looked out the living room window, on a clear day you could see the vast Blue Ridge Mountains.

Aladár was retired by this time and planned to work on his memoirs there. But he did not drive, and my mother had become painfully inflexible, too tied to her family life at Patterson Street. My parents would drive to Bluemont once a week, usually on Wednesday and sometimes with friends. They worked tirelessly in the garden, weeding and trimming and clipping and planting; they paused to eat the sandwiches they brought from home, then worked into the afternoon. They would collect buckets of flowers—white and pink feathered peonies, statuesque irises—put them in the backseat along with the trash from their lunch, and drive back home.

They owned that property for over ten years and never once spent the night.

Hanna no longer felt safe alone with Aladár, especially in what she considered the wilderness. The next house was less than half a mile away, but she couldn't face it. Aladár had accommodated himself to so many losses; he accepted this one, too. He never woke up in his own home with his wife. Yet behind their Patterson Street bedroom door, I often heard happy chatter, the clatter of laughter, and the murmur of a serious conversation.

My father died a few months before his eighty-fourth birthday. He had maintained the energy and appearance of a much younger man as he grew older. He would go on constitutionals every morning and stop at Blessed Sacrament to pray. He retired from the Voice of America in 1968 and began to write his autobiography, a voluminous project. His serious clinical depression was euphemistically referred to as "pessimism." Day after day his journal entries throughout the 1970s and into the 1980s record his struggle. The antidepressant of choice at the time was Valium, and he would write, with astonishment, that he was becoming even more depressed "despite the two Valium that I took." He complained of his memory faltering and his focus disappearing. To read it and to understand just a little bit about the effects of a benzodiazepine was to watch a man deteriorating because of the cure as much as the illness.

In 1987 he developed a blood dysplasia and began living, he said, on "borrowed platelets," which he received from monthly, then biweekly blood transfusions. In March 1988 at our house on Patterson Street, my mother, aunt, two brothers, and I stood around his bed and watched as he slowly surrendered and died. When we realized that his ragged breaths had stopped forever, together we said the Our Father. Later that evening my mother said, "You know, he adored me," and I was so reassured. His manuscript was unfinished. He had spent twenty years on it and never lived to see it published. Finally my mother and Puppa and our cousin Mihály arranged for it to be edited and published, and the two volumes finally appeared in Budapest bookstores.

Hanna and Puppa lived happily together at Patterson Street for the next thirteen years. When I became a mother, I discovered a new connection with my own mother. She revealed herself to me, and we chatted about nursing, about crying, about the first steps of a child, and about the ease or difficulties of our respective births. She was playful with my daughter, Joia, with a patience and delight I didn't remember from my own childhood. It was standard grandmotherly indulgence. For hours they would play library, where my mother was the eager patron and Joia the efficient librarian. But Puppa felt a special bond with my daughter. She cared for her and protected her and took her to the third floor, where they made paper dolls together.

In 2001 my mother began to lose weight. She and Puppa came over for lunch. As we sat in our sunroom, I realized that my mother was jaundiced. She was diagnosed with pancreatic cancer and managed one more heroic Christmas with all of us. On January 12, 2002, she died. Puppa described her sister in a long, private essay written just for me: "There are people in this world who are unknown. There are no great inventions or earth-shattering deeds in their lives. But in the circle in which they live, they are important and memorable because they make that small world of theirs a better place. Hanna was one of them."

Puppa could no longer live alone at Patterson Street. She was an indomitable, energetic, still-driving eighty-eight-year-old, but the house was too large for her to keep on her own. Though determined and disciplined and always so present for us all, she nevertheless moved to an assisted living facility in Arlington, Virginia. With her usual grace and self-discipline, she adapted to her much-reduced circumstances with ease. She was also lucky. She never became sick or addled, was always brilliantly aware and acute, and slowed down a bit, but at ninety she still went places on her own, read complicated books, and lavished attention on each one of us. When I began to work on this book, she translated innumerable letters, articles, and poems. I have pages and pages of yellow legal pads covered with her handwriting as she meticulously returned to her own past, and the past of her family, for me.

No one lived at Patterson Street anymore. The house was badly in need of repair. The gardens were overgrown and neglected, so my brothers, my aunt, and I finally decided to sell it. The Blessed Sacrament Church and parochial school bought it.

Puppa was diagnosed with pancreatic cancer in May 2008. She died on a beautiful June day. She did not leave a trace of Luis in her life except for the painting of the street with the woman walking. But János Zwack's picture was on her bedside table; his letters, shuffled a bit as if recently read, were in the drawer.

Blessed Sacrament tore down the house on Patterson Street to make a playground.

I felt as if I had been complicit in the murder of a friend.

The house that had sheltered us all, its large formal rooms echoing with so many languages. The gardens my father tended in a domain that was his alone. The smell of cigarettes and dust and sherry, the heavy curtains separating rooms, the attic filled with mysterious papers and my grandmother's lace trousseau. The big balconies where we would play Ping-Pong, or smoke cigarettes, or sit in the spring. The hot, still, beautiful summer nights on the side porch. None of the old trees remain.

After two world wars and a revolution, Lendvay Street is the French embassy, Ireg is now a school for mentally disturbed children, and the Weiss palazzo on Andrássy Avenue is the official guesthouse of the Hungarian government. Csepel continues to be a factory. After the collapse of Communism in 1990, it was broken up into smaller factories. Schwinn made bikes there, and Estée Lauder made lipsticks. These landmark buildings are not what they were, but they exist with the stubborn, old-fashioned determination not to be undone by historical cataclysms. I like to think that in a few long-forgotten corners, there exists a trace of someone who once lived there, a scrap of paper, a bit of cloth, a thimble, an old book with an ex libris.

So maybe it is fitting that while my ancestors all lived big and visible lives in Hungary, big and visible buildings should remain. But when theirs became an American story, with its immigrant anonymity and its Hungarian anachronisms, the place where most of it took place—the house where they all lived longer than in any other place in their lives—disappeared as if it had never existed. What once was a protected fortress against the world is now a parochial school soccer field. "Most things boil down to people, or at least most houses to those who live in them," observed the British writer Henry Green. So what was once Patterson Street boils down to my grandparents and my aunt, my brothers, and me, and a love story of grandeur and tragedy between my mother and my father.

ACKNOWLEDGMENTS

When I was in the midst of writing this book, a friend asked me how I was progressing. "Great," I replied. "I have already written 200 pages."

"And those are just the Acknowledgments," she said, knowing me a little too well.

Were I able to give each person who helped me the space that he or she is due, then two hundred pages might be sufficient. These acknowledgments, therefore, are inadequate to express my gratitude to so many people who gave generously of their time and talents to help me write this book.

My parents' gifts to me continued long after their deaths. My father's writings were revelations. Aladár and Hanna's story and the way that they lived their lives inspired me in ways that I wish I could have expressed more articulately when they lived. I only hope that this book does them justice.

Often writers say that their editors have become treasured friends. In my case, the process was reversed. Julie Grau was my dear friend, who broke her and her co-publisher Cindy Spiegel's rules by taking on this project. When she did, I knew that it would be in the best of hands, not only because of her brilliance as an editor, but because of her heart and her insight. She transformed a sprawling manuscript into a book that is true to what I had hoped and better than I had dreamed. Spiegel & Grau has been a wonderful place to work. My special thanks to Laura Van Der Veer for her patience, enthusiasm, and lightning response rates. Additional and heartfelt thanks to the immensely talented designers Greg Mollica and Barbara Bachman, the steady and unflappable production editor Kelly Chian, and the meticulous copy editor Janet Biehl, all of whom showed the book tremendous care.

Flip Brophy from Sterling Lord Literistic traveled the opposite path, beginning as a consummate professional and ending as a close friend. She was patient, focused, tough, and incredibly warm and kind. From the very beginning, she believed in this book as if she too had been to Patterson Street and also wanted their story told. Her team at Sterling Lord, Julia Karden and yet another brilliant Hungarian Szilvia Molnar, could not have been more helpful.

A liability of a book that took several years to write is that several people who helped me immeasurably are not alive to see it. My aunt Puppa, shared her stories, sat for hours translating, opened her life to me with an unselfishness that characterized her entire approach to life. Possessing a prodigious memory for historical context and family events, she wrote like an angel herself.

Judith Mariassy translated my father's diaries, papers, and letters. Knowing him as well as she did, she was able to make his voice as true in English as it was in Hungarian. She shared insights from times in Berlin, dark days in Hungary, and beautiful times at Patterson Street. Gabriella Mauthner, was selfless in sharing her memories and helping me sort out the many family stories. In Budapest, Peter Zwack sweetly and patiently shared his thoughts and memories of the time and of his parents. Josephine Woll read and critiqued early chapters, and Nancy Berkopf Tucker, a distinguished China scholar and brilliant writer, accompanied me on my writer's journey, pointed out problems, and offered solutions, with ease, tact, and focus despite her cruel illness.

My brothers, Andrew and Peter Szegedy-Maszák offered me endless practical and moral support. Andy read parts of the manuscript, provided always helpful observations, generously offering his own memories, insights, and encouragement with humor and precision. Peter patiently filmed a long series of video interviews with our aunt Puppa, meticulously asking her questions and revealing layers of the story that would have been out of reach for me. He has been a tireless cheerleader, with profound insight and understanding that he generously shared.

I must also thank the wonderful writer and editor (and sister-in-law) Elizabeth Bobrick for her help at crucial moments while I was writing. I must also thank the fantastic (sister-in-law) Debra Thomas who often provided a safe harbor. A shout-out to my nieces, Katalin and Andrea Szegedy-Maszák, for their enthusiasm and support.

After my father died in 1988, my uncle Thomas J. de Kornfeld took on the formidable task of translating his unwieldy, one-thousand-page manuscript from Hungarian to English, realizing with wisdom that we might, one day, be curious about our father's work. As the only person who could match my grandfather's erudition, he also translated his writings. Whenever I needed something untangled, translated, revealed, he and his wife Helen responded with grace and alacrity.

In Hungary, members of my father's family were unfailingly generous with their assistance. My cousin Mihály Szegedy-Maszák was my father's closest confidante and most respected younger relative. He helped to turn my father's life work into a published book, and helped steer me away from painful mistakes and toward a deeper understanding not only of a singular man but also of a complicated country. His daughter Zsuzsanna, herself a respected academic, was enormously helpful in reading the manuscript and correcting some mistakes, as well as offering her own scholarship on the painter, Miklós Barabás. Sándor Sperlágh spent hours helping me untangle some of the more inaccessible Moldoványi stories and offering familial insights and encouragement.

Daisy von Strasser has managed to combine roles of surrogate mother, close friend, learned adviser, wailing wall, and book writer herself. Her wonderful book about her father, Ferenc Chorin, was an invaluable source of detail and historical context. With humor and generosity, she shared her vivid memories of her childhood growing up in this extraordinary family.

Other family members also were my cheerleaders, sources of insight, solace, and rich narratives: Annie Weiss, Martha Nierenberg, John de Csepel, Mary Radcliffe, Thomas de Kornfeld Jr., James de Kornfeld, Christine Hannouche, Francis Rath, Anne Smith, Alexander Borbely, and Maria Widemer.

Several researchers in Budapest, London, Berlin, and Washington applied their prodigious scholarship to giving this book some historical heft: fellow Hungarian Marvin B. Fried, from the LSE, combed Kew Gardens Archives and discovered some gold, Rick Moss did the same with the State Department Archives in College Park, MD. Agnes Szechenyi found remarkable documents in the Security Archives in Budapest, and Gabriel Fawcett provided invaluable documents on Becher from Berlin.

The Missionhurst community gave me the physical space and spiritual support that infused every page of this manuscript. My special gratitude to Father Michael Hann and Father Joe Giordano for the special care that they took of their writer in residence, as well as to Fathers Randy Gonzales, Anselm Malonda, Bill Wyndaele, Charles Phukuta, Joseph Dewaele, John B. Peters, and Leo Zonneveld. Additional thanks to Clara De La Cruz and Sonca Nguyen whose kindness was a daily joy.

Judy Katona's early translations opened the new world for me and launched this project. Throughout my work, Ferenc Katona provided incredible assistance, supporting me as if it were his own book, adding details of family history and deep understanding of Hungarian history.

Deborah Duffy was an astute guide from the moment I set down to write this story to its final chapter.

My great friend and wonderful editor Wray Herbert helped me to conceptualize the book with a line drawing on a napkin that organized my chaotic thinking.

Bob Keeler went through the manuscript as a brilliant editor and loving friend who provided an invaluable jumpstart of self-confidence when I most needed it.

Despite the demands of her job in Kabul, Alissa J. Rubin offered perceptive insights, poems, and intuitive understanding of this project.

Wendy Zevin has proven herself to be as gifted with subtitles as with friendship. Walking many miles, she followed the progress of my work with care and enthusiasm often helping me break through a logjam.

Though scattered now across the country, Kathleen Currie, Amy Cunningham, Sheila Kaplan, and Teresa Riordan were my dream team of immensely talented fellow writers, wonderful supporters, and treasured friends.

In many ways this book started nearly twenty years ago, when I was an Alicia Patterson Fellow. Thank you to Peggy Engel for her patience and support.

For their support, food, curiosity, kindness, and friendship, for reading the manuscript and believing in this project, my deepest thanks to: Annamaria Almasy, Ilona Almasy, Charles and Betty Alexander, Tyler Anbinder, William M Arkin, Robert Sam Anson, Adam Berry, Molly Bingham, Mark Bisgeier, Anita Blackman, Laura Brothers, Bill Buzenberg, Estelle B Campbell, Warren I Cohen, Beth Corning, Joy Chen, Laurie Chester, Steve Connors, Janice Farrell Day, Istvan Deák, David de Csepel, Jack and Gini Diskin, Adele D'Ari, Susan Polk Dugan, Margie, John and Katie Fehrenbach, Nina Fisher, Charles Gati, Deepika

Green, Katalin Gimes, David Goldstein, Sharon Grigley, Robert Hardi, Ruth Heiten, Hilary Henkin, Bill Hogan, Alexis Jetter, Gabor Kadar, Maria Kovacs, Valli and Stelios Kirimlis, David LaRoche, Drew Lawrence, Charles Lewis, Susan Loewenberg, Antonio Louça, Gail Larocca, Alex Levin, Margaret Lorber, Caroline Mayer, Gloria Mancco, Elizabeth, John, Charlie, and Emma Marshall, Kati Marton, Vic and Catherine McGrady, Debbie Mesce, Ann Moline, Joan Mower, Annie Moyer, Julia Ferrill Niemann, John Newman, Marc Niesen, Istvan Palffy, Dawn Penfold, Charles Piller, Allen Pusey, Anne Scott Putney, Sarabeth Rees, Sara Rimer, Len Rubenstein, Enid Rubin, Maureen Scance, Jackie Schaeffer, Judith Schweitzer, Astrid Sheil, Jay Starr, Jamie Stevens, Nick Stevens, Julia Sweig, Amir Tahami, Reed Thompson, Jay Tolson, Matyas Vince, Ellen Walsh, Ellen Wayne, Claudia Wiegand, Laurie Westley, Katalin Zanello, Laura Zigman, Anne Zwack.

Finally, there are four people who have held often uncomfortable ringside seats in watching this book become a reality. My stepchildren, Nick and Lea Xenakis, have expanded their Greek identity to become honorary Hungarians, and done so with grace and love. My beloved daughter Joanna LaRoche spent her earliest years on Patterson Street, and experienced some of the sweetness of the life that I describe. With the great intelligence of her heart, generosity of spirit, and her intuitive diplomatic brilliance, I can see in her so many of the qualities embodied by her ancestors. My loving and tireless husband Stephen N. Xenakis, believed in this project with the kind of passion that he brings to all his most cherished convictions. His love and fierce support made my distant dream of writing this story a reality. I could not have done it without him.

Arlington Virginia, 2013

NOTES

This book is a memoir that has relied on long interviews with my family members and on their unpublished and published writings, letters, and journals. In order to provide the necessary historical context, I have also relied on scholarly books and articles, archival research in the National Archives and Records Administration (NARA) in Washington, D.C.; declassified documents from British Intelligence at the National Archives (NA) at Kew Gardens in London; and at the archives and the library at the U.S. Holocaust Memorial Museum, also in Washington. I visited Budapest several times and went to Dachau Concentration Camp Memorial Site. I have also gone back to newspapers and periodicals of the time, both in English and in Hungarian. In the course of working on this book, I interviewed approximately eighty family members, family friends, regional experts, and historians.

CHAPTER 1: YOU SEE, I USED TO LIVE HERE

During my first trip to Hungary, I recorded my experiences in a journal. The quotation from Csicsery-Rónay, *My First Book of Hungary*, appears on its first page. Particularly helpful for this and all the chapters dealing with the lives of the Kornfelds was the introduction by Agnes Szechenyi to *Reflections on Twentieth Century Hungary*, a book of my grandfather's writings that were collected and translated by Thomas de Kornfeld and edited by Szechenyi and de Kornfeld. Varga, "Manfred Weiss: Profile of a Munitions King," offers great detail about Weiss's business and professional history in the social and political context of Hungary. My interviews in Budapest with my father's cousin's son, Mihály Szegedy-Maszák, his daughter Susan Szegedy-Maszák (who is an art historian and has written about Miklós Barabás), and Sandor Sperlagh, a cousin from the Moldovány side of the family, were invaluable in filling out my father's family story. Mihály Szegedy-Maszák's essay, "Diplomatic Illusions," written as an afterword to *Autumnal Retrospections*, offered family history and the political, literary, and social context, as well as deep insights into my father's legacy and psychology. I have also used my father's diary from 1929, an unpublished essay that Maria de Kornfeld wrote about her past, and interviews and e-mail correspondence with the eminent historian István Deák.

CHAPTER 2: THE ARIZONA

My father's memoir, *Az ember öszel visszanez—: Egy volt magyar diplomata emlekiratai-bol* (*A Man Looks Back From the Autumn of His Years: Memoirs of a Hungarian Diplomat*) was published in Budapest eight years after his death. Thomas de Kornfeld translated the memoir into English and chose the title, *Autumnal Retrospections*. Those two volumes provide the historical and biographical underpinning for a great deal of this book. The description of the Arizona by the English visitor is from Fermor, *Between the Woods and the Water,* p. 26.

CHAPTER 3: THE DRAFT BOARD

Cartledge, *Will to Survive,* provided me with the best historical overview of Trianon, the interwar period, and Hungary's involvement in World War II. For my father's reflections on that period, I used the journal that he kept from his early adulthood. Additional background on the political situation and industrial concerns about the Weiss Manfred Works comes from declassified documents at the NA (C 8042/61/21).

CHAPTER 4: IREG

The Ireg guestbook is now at the Hungarian National Museum. A microfilm copy of the July 28, 1940, edition of the newspaper *Magyar Nemzet* is at the Library of Congress. On the special relationship between Hungary and Great Britain, I found Bán, *Hungarian-British Diplomacy 1938–1941,* and Frank, "Anglophiles," extremely helpful.

CHAPTER 5: SEPTEMBER 18

My information about Margit Huszár comes from interviews with Judith Mariássy, who worked for the Hungarian embassy in Berlin shortly after Aladár served there, and from my interview with Mihály Szegedy-Maszák. The descriptions of the Danube Bend and other areas near Budapest draw on the 1937 guidebook Megyery, *Budapest Scrap Book*. Ann Bridge's description of the scene comes from her memoir *Facts and Fictions.*

CHAPTER 6: NEVER IN HUNGARY

I was fortunate enough to recover several small pocket calendars from both Hanna and Aladár for the years 1941–45. I have used them throughout to track their comings and goings. The historical information came from Cartledge, *Will to Survive;* Aladár's memoir; and the British historian C. A. Macartney's two-volume *October Fifteenth; A History of Modern Hungary.*

CHAPTER 7: JEWISH QUESTIONS

A number of sources, interviews, and published material, helped me tease out the complicated relationship between Hungary and its Jewish population. Among the most valuable books were Braham's monumental *Politics of Genocide;* Deák, *Essays on Hitler's Europe;* Kovács, *Liberal Professions and Illiberal Politics;* and Patai, *Jews of Hungary.* My grandfather Móric Kornfeld's observations on the Jewish Laws appeared in "From Trianon to Trianon," an essay in his *Reflections on Twentieth Century Hungary.* A dispatch from the Department of State, Division of European Affairs, dated December 13, 1938 (NARA Dispatch no. 1285), entitled "The Situation of the Jews in Hungary" states that the anti-Semitic movement "appears to be directed against the 'big' Jews—the industrialists, financiers, bankers and others in positions of great economic importance. . . . Although he was replaced by another Jew, Mr. Chorin, the General Manager of the bank, was forced to give way to a Christian friend of the Prime Minister." The memo points out that "many Hungarians have expressed their horror at the brutality and inhumanity of events which recently took place in Germany." I owe an enormous debt of gratitude to Ferenc Katona, former archivist for the U.S. Holocaust Memorial Museum, who in extensive interviews contributed much historical and social context and gave me many insights into the life and times of Hungarian Jewry.

CHAPTER 9: THE SATANIC NATURE OF HIS CHARACTER

The Wannsee Conference is chillingly described in Braham, *Politics of Genocide,* pp. 229–37. I also relied on Cartledge's treatment of the political background and of the influence of the war on internal Hungarian politics in *Will to Survive,* pp. 402–15).

CHAPTER 10: INERTIA AND A DECISIVE MINDSET

Móric Kornfeld wrote the personal essay "The History of Ten Weeks in 1944," as he said, to comply "with the urging of my family and relate the history of those ten weeks when I was a prisoner of the German Secret Police (Gestapo)." This essay is included in his *Reflections on Twentieth Century Hungary,* pp. 145–85. Here he also expresses his thoughts on why the family did not emigrate.

CHAPTER 11: A CHRISTIAN ENTERPRISE

The background information on the Weiss Manfred business comes from a number of different sources, including writings of Ferenc Chorin that appear in Strasser and Bán, *From Andrássy Ut to Park Avenue.* The bombing of Budapest is described in "Budapest Raid Studied," *The New York Times.* September 6, 1942.
Cartledge, *Will to Survive,* Braham, *Politics of Genocide,* and Macartney, *October Fifteenth,* provided me with historical background, and Aladár's memoir, once more, offered the rest.

CHAPTER 12: WHAT ABOUT HUNGARY?

Aladár's memoir, journals, and *Hungarian Studies* article (published under the pseudonym Pál Szegedi) are the main sources for this chapter. Mihály Szegedy-Maszák's "Diplomatic Illusions" was extremely helpful in providing the broader context. I found additional historical resources in Macartney, *October Fifteenth*, and Braham, *Politics of Genocide*. The Himmler memo can be found online as "Hitler authorizes Himmler to sell off Jews for foreign currency, December 10, 1942," http://www.fpp.co.uk/Himmler/docs1942/Vermerk101242.html. The original document is in the Bundesarchiv, Schumacher collection, file 240/I.

CHAPTER 13: SPIDERWEBS

I expanded on the story of this period of the war and my father's work by consulting declassified primary sources from the British NA in London and from the American NARA in Washington. At the NA, I consulted the Foreign Office, Political Departments, General Correspondence from 1906–1966, or FO371. The secret memorandum "M. Szegedy-Maszák's visit to Stockholm: Future of Hungary" was filed on March 20, 1943; see NA registry no. C3046/1421/21. A note from F. K. Roberts in the Home Office to Sir Owen O'Malley, the British ambassador to Hungary, said, "You should avoid any suggestion that His Majesty's Legation have had any sort of contact with Szegedy-Maszák or that His Majesty's government take any special interest in his visit. As you know. The whole question of our attitude towards Hungary is at Present under consideration." A confidential memo from the office of Strategic Services (NARA no. NND877092) provided a vivid description of Hungary at the beginning of 1943. The information about Böhm comes my father's memoir and also from a conversation with Maria de Kornfeld.

CHAPTER 14: THE USUAL BOUNDLESS OPTIMISM

Ferenc Chorin's observation about the regent can be found in his "Notes by Francis Chorin About the Events Affecting Him and His Family after March 19, 1944," in Strasser and Bán, *From Andrássy Ut to Park Avenue*, p. 95, Daisy's book about her father. Horthy's visit to Klessheim is described vividly in Macartney, *October Fifteenth*, and in Admiral Nicholas Horthy, *Memoirs*. Macartney writes in depth about the Szegedy-Maszák memorandum in *October Fifteenth* on pp. 162ff. The memorandum received a great deal of attention in the British Foreign Office, as seen in a secret report on August 23, 1943, stating that "Copies of this memorandum are being sent to the Central Department of the Foreign Office, the Ministry of Economic Warfare, the Ministry of Information, the Foreign Office Research Department, and to Major Neame." The dismissive reaction to the memo was contained in an August 23, 1943, memo (NA, registry no. C 9609/385/21).

CHAPTER 15: A PROMOTION INTO THE ABYSS

Aladár's memo containing his reflections about his promotion was dated September 1, 1943 (NA, London, registry no. C10149) and was sent to "the Central Department of the F.O., the M.o.I., the M.E.W., the F.O. Research Department and to Major Neame." The memo ended with this observation: "We must make clear to the British that they must let us have a little time to wait for the opportunity of taking upon ourselves the great risk [of abolishing all troop transports]. Without this small 'reprieve from the gallows,' our whole plan will be ruined." The description of the fall of Mussolini comes from Aladár's memoir, *Autumnal Retrospections*. Details of Operation Margarethe come from Macartney, *October Fifteenth*, Braham, *Politics of Genocide*, Cartledge *Will to Survive*, and Fenyo, *Hitler, Horthy, and Hungary*. The description of the scene at Derekegyháza comes from Strasser and Bán, *From Andrássy Ut to Park Avenue*.

CHAPTER 16: MARCH 19

The main sources for this chapter are Kornfeld, "The History of Ten Weeks in 1944," in *Reflections on Twentieth Century Hungary;* Strasser's introduction to her and Bán's *From Andrássy Ut to Park Avenue;* Ferenc Chorin's "Notes by Francis Chorin About the Events Affecting Him and His Family After March 19, 1944," (ibid., pp. 93–110); and Szegedy-Maszák, *Autumnal Retrospections,* which stops at the end of 1943; an unpublished addendum covers the years until 1947. Operation Margarethe has been described by many historians, especially the trio of Braham, *Politics of Genocide,* Cartledge *Will to Survive,* and Macartney, *October Fifteenth,*. A memo from the Office of Strategic Services dated March 20, 1944 (NARA no. NND750140) provides a window into the sense of the occupation from the outside world.

CHAPTER 17: AT THE FOREIGN MINISTRY

In addition to the sources I used for Chapter 16, for this chapter I also used Zweig, *Gold Train,* and Cesarani, *Becoming Eichmann*. The extraordinary unpublished diary by Countess Éva Dessewffy offers great detail and insight into this period.

CHAPTER 18: SAYING GOODBYE ALL OVER AGAIN

Kornfeld's and Chorin's recorded experiences (see notes to Chapter 16) are the main sources for this chapter. The description of what happened in Parliament comes from *Autumnal Retrospections*.

CHAPTER 19: ENOUGH PRIDE AND ENOUGH HUMILITY

Once more, my source was Kornfeld's and Chorin's essays on their imprisonment (see notes to Chapter 16).

CHAPTER 20: HONORABLE CONFINEMENT

Aladár described his arrest and imprisonment in his diaries and in the unpublished addendum to *Autumnal Retrospections*. I also consulted Countess Dessewffy's unpublished memoir.

CHAPTER 21: ENTER BECHER

Becher appears in a number of books on the deals that the Nazis made with wealthy Jews. For a book entirely about him, see Serebro with Sellschop, *Beyond Redemption?*. Fenyvesi, "Portrait of a Plunderer," which focuses on Becher, was written for the U.S. Holocaust Commission. I used a number of other books as background for this chapter, especially Bauer, *Jews for Sale?*; Bower, *Nazi Gold;* and Kádár and Vági, *Self-Financing Genocide*. Becher was interviewed at length about the Manfred Weiss affair before the Eichmann trial by the Bremen District Court, "In the Murder Case Against Adolf Eichmann, an Examination of the witness Kurt Becher" (pp. 9, 10, 11). The Manfred Weiss case is discussed in Braham, *Politics of Genocide*, pp. 2:517–18, 520–21). For a transcript of the Eichmann Trial, see Nizkor Project, *Trial of Adolf Eichmann*.

CHAPTER 22: A FAMILY REUNION

NARA documents provide several accounts of this transaction, especially "Description of the Transaction of the Family Manfred Weiss: Made in May–June 1944," NARA no. NND765008, as well as in documents no. NND877092, NND 750140, and NND750140. The NA's Public Record Office also has a number of documents about the transaction: nos. FO /39 264, C 9669/15/21, and C9245/15/21. Gabriella Mauthner was interviewed in "I Have to Tell Everybody Where I Belong." Finally, Antonio Louça, the Portuguese historian and documentary filmmaker, interviewed family members for his documentary on the deal, *La Lista de Chorin*, that appeared on Portuguese television in 2010. He very kindly shared his interview transcripts and a copy of the documentary with English subtitles. *The Times* of London covered the arrival of the family in "Hungarian Jews Fly to Lisbon: Financial Deal with the Germans," June 29, 1944. The Churchill document can be found in the Prime Minister's Personal Minutes, Serial no. M.928.4.L10410. Scribbled on the bottom of the statement is the note: "Like to comment. We have entirely no intention of hunting them down."

CHAPTER 24: A NEW ERA OF CAPTIVITY

The historical background comes from Cartledge, *Will to Survive*, Braham, *Politics of Genocide*, and Macartney, *October Fifteenth*. Aladár's unpublished addendum to *Autumnal Retrospections* describes his time in prison. The unpublished journal of Éva Dessewffy describes the scene with the bridges. "Records Relating to the Research and Analysis Jewish Desk," at NARA, in RG 226, Entry 191, Box 1, outlines the picture of the destruction of Hungarian Jewry as it was happening in 1944.

CHAPTER 25: DACHAU

When I visited Dachau in 2010, I saw the camp in its pristine and museumlike state. The Comité International de Dachau, the House of Bavarian History, and the Dachau Concentration Camp Memorial Site published three volumes that I consulted extensively: *The Dachau Concentration Camp, 1933–1945,* and two volumes edited by Benz and Distel, *Dachau and the Nazi Terror,* vol. 1, *Testimonies and Memoirs,* and vol. 2, *Studies and Reports.* I also used my father's *Autumnal Reflections.* Two articles in the *British Medical Journal* describe the medical experiments in Dachau: Rosencher, "Medicine in Dachau," and Weindling, "Human Guinea Pigs and the Ethics of Experimentation." But the most valuable source was Paul Berben, *Dachau 1933–1945: The Official History,* Munich: LIPP, 1986. Additional sources include Selzer, *Deliverance Day;* Cesarani, *Becoming Eichmann;* and Padfeld, *Himmler.*

CHAPTER 26: THE SIEGE

The observation "not only fanatics but criminals" appears in John Lukacs's introduction to Ungváry, *Siege of Budapest,* p. xvii. "Relief and Rescue Work for Jewish Refugees" comes from NARA, Security Classified Intelligence Reports, XL series, 1941–1946, Entry 19, RG 226. Macartney's description of the siege can be found in *October Fifteenth,* vol. 2; the reference to Christmas appears on p. 463. Further information comes from Aladár's *Autumnal Retrospections,* Braham, *Politics of Genocide,* and Cartledge, *Will to Survive.*

CHAPTER 27: DISPLACED PERSONS

Ferenc Chorin refers to the arrival of the Gábors in "Notes by Francis Chorin About the Events Affecting Him and His Family After March 19, 1944," in Strasser and Bán, *From Andrassy Ut to Park Avenue,* p. 110. The story about Magda Gábor summoning Chorin is told in his daughter's introduction to the book on p. 25. Edith Weiss's letter is in the privately held family collection of correspondence.

CHAPTER 28: THE DAY OF DELIVERANCE

This chapter relies on the Dachau sources mentioned in the notes to Chapter 25, especially Selzer's *Deliverance Day.* Most of the chapter, however, is gleaned from Aladár's unpublished addendum to *Autumnal Retrospections* and from his private diaries of the 1970s and 1980s.

CHAPTER 29: BROKEN AND WITHOUT A JOB

The references to the effects of the war in Hungary come from Cartledge, *Will to Survive,* p. 433. Everything else appears in Aladár's unpublished addendum.

CHAPTER 30: THE ICE OF MISTRUST

The State Department document is dated May 10, 1945, and appears in NARA's State Department files as no. 864.00/5–1045. The correspondence among Ambassador O'Malley, the Foreign Office, Chorin, and Kornfeld can be found in the Public Record Office, registry no. R 8330/26/21. Chorin's August letter to Marosy can be found in Strasser and Bán, *From Andrássy Ut to Park Avenue*, p. 134. Fenyö's letter is also available in this volume. For the context of Edith Weiss's work, see Ben-Tov, *Facing the Holocaust in Budapest*.

CHAPTER 34: THE LOVE THAT MAKES LIFE BEAUTIFUL AND HAPPY

The State Department files concerning Aladár's appointment can be found in NARA's General Records of the Department of State, RG 59, Box 2601. Aladár's description of his activities following his appointment can be found in the unpublished addendum to his memoir.

CHAPTER 35: A FORCED LANDING

Marie McNair's article in *The Washington Post* was published on January 20, 1946, and was among my grandmother's prize possessions. My father described their arrival in Washington in his memoir addendum. Brinkley, *Washington Goes to War*, paints a vivid portrait of the city at the end of 1945 and the beginning of 1946.

CHAPTER 37 FOR ALADÁR ONLY—PRIVÁT!

Cartledge, *Will to Survive*, offers a good overview of the Hungarian world at the time. I also used both Kenéz, *Hungary from the Nazis to the Soviets*, and Kertesz, "Peacemaking on the Dark Side of the Moon." The Sándor Márai observation "Like someone crawling . . ." comes from his *Memoir of Hungary: 1944–1948*, p. 138. Hungary's appalling inflation rate is described in Kertesz, "Peacemaking," on p. 488 and more deeply in Bomberger and Makinen, "The Hungarian Hyperinflation and Stabilization of 1945–1946."

CHAPTER 38: THE HAPPY JOINT ENDEAVOR

My description of Washington draws from Brinkley, *Washington Goes to War*, where the Malcolm Cowley quote on "Washington in wartime" can be found. Aladár and Hanna's activities are recorded in the unpublished addendum to *Autumnal Retrospections* and in their letters. President Truman's schedule can be found in the Truman Library online, http://www.trumanlibrary.org/calendar/main.php?currYear=1946&currMonth=1&currDay=18. The official letters are in Aladár's files. Hanna described her lunch at the White House in her letters to her mother. The "United States gave up on Hungary" passage from Kenéz, *Hungary from the Nazis to the Soviets*, can be found on p. 122.

CHAPTER 39: A VISIT FROM THE HOME TEAM

Once more Kenéz, *Hungary from the Nazis to the Soviets*, was important for me in setting the scene in Hungary. Aladár described the visit from the Hungarians in detail in his unpublished addendum. State Department documents at NARA contain information as well. Nagy, *Struggle Behind the Iron Curtain*, offers another perspective on the event and additional detail. The periodical *Figyelö* put my father and Truman on the cover of its June 29, 1946, issue. "The President's Calling List . . . ," *The Washington Post*, June 14, 1946, reported that the visit occurred at 11:15.

CHAPTER 40: PARIS

The Paris Peace talks have been written about in many places, but I consulted Cartledge, *Will to Survive;* Kenéz, *Hungary from the Nazis to the Soviets;* Kertesz, "Plight of Satellite Diplomacy"; Nagy, *Struggle Behind the Iron Curtain;* Gati, *Hungary and the Soviet Bloc;* and Gati, *Bloc That Failed.* In addition, documents in the State Department files at NARA describe the events in Paris. John McCormac's articles about the conference for *The New York Times* are cited in the text. The *Figyelö* issue in which my father discusses the problems in Czechoslovakia is dated September 28, 1946.

CHAPTER 43: SALAMI TACTICS

Once more Cartledge, *Will to Survive;* Kenéz, *Hungary from the Nazis to the Soviets;* Kertesz, "Plight of Satellite Diplomacy"; Gati, *Hungary and the Soviet Bloc;* Gati, *Bloc That Failed;* and Nagy, *Struggle Behind the Iron Curtain*, were helpful for this chapter. Declassified State Department documents at NARA also reveal the unfolding political crisis. The dossier on my father is among recently declassified documents from the Historical Archives of the National Security Services (Szolgálatok Történeti Levéltára, ABTL 3.2.4 K-1393). John McCormac, "How the Communists Took Over Hungary," *The New York Times*, June 8, 1947, provides a gripping narrative of the events. Eleanor Roosevelt's comments on Hanna and Aladár's visit to Hyde Park were published in a "My Day" column that can be found at http://www.gwu.edu/~erpapers/myday/displaydoc.cfm?_y=1947&_f=d000650.

CHAPTER 44: DEMONSTRATIVELY DEJECTED

The citations from *The New York Times* appear in the text. Aladár's letter to Secretary Marshall, dated June 2, 1947, is in his private papers and also in *Foreign Relations of the United States, 1947, Eastern Europe, the Soviet Union*, vol. 4. (Washington, D.C.: Government Printing Office, 1947), pp. 304–307. The State Department's memorandum of conversation, dated June 6, 1947, is at NARA, no. NND760050/864.00/6–647.

CHAPTER 45: PACES BACK AND FORTH

Aladár's letter to H. Freeman Matthews, June 6, 1947, is in his files and can also be found in NARA's State Department files, no. NND760050/864.00/6–647. The Movie-Tone clip can be found in the archive at www.movietone.com, under the heading "Hungarian Foreign Minister."

CHAPTER 46: MAKING THE BEST OF IT

The Chorin story is told in Strasser and Bán, *From Andrássy Ut to Park Avenue.*

EPILOGUE

The experiences of the Szegedy-Maszák family are described in Palasik, "Deportations from Budapest and Their Western Echo," but are also revealed in my father's writings and in my interviews with Mihály Szegedy-Maszák. The observation "Most things boil down to people . . ." can be found in Green, *Pack My Bag*, p. 1. When the Patterson Street house was torn down, Maria de Kornfeld and I shared a sense of loss. In "Epitaph for a House," handwritten on a yellow legal pad, she explained, "The hope was that after I left, a family with young children would move in and the story would start anew. But it did not happen. The house was thought to have aged too much. It was sold and the decision of the new owners was to demolish it. At this time, it is an empty shell, waiting to be killed. It is a sorry sight for people who walk by, but for me it is more than that. If you look closely and listen, you can see behind the boarded-up windows, with your minds' eyes and ears, laughter and sighs, the patter of little feet, the hesitant steps of old people, a procession of people who have died a long time ago and just live on in my mind, as I look at the house. But then, as is the law of nature, from death comes rebirth. The house will be gone, but on the lawn that will replace it, there will be laughter, also some tears, children will play, run around, and never know that once a house stood there, a home for many years."

Adams, Cindy. *Jolie Gabor*. New York: Mason/Charter, 1975.

American Institute of Public Opinion, *The Gallup Political Almanac for 1946*. Princeton, N.J.: Clarke Press, 1946.

Bán, András. "Friends of England: Cultural and Political Sympathies on the Eve of War." *Hungarian Quarterly* 40, no. 153 (Spring 1999).

————. *Hungarian-British Diplomacy 1938–1941: An Attempt to Maintain Relations*. London: Frank Cass, 2004.

Baross, Gábor. *Hungary and Hitler*. Astor Park, Fla.: Danubian Press, 1970.

Bauer, Yehuda. *Jews for Sale? Nazi Jewish Negotiations, 1933–1945*. New Haven and London: Yale University Press, 1994.

Becher, Kurt. Testimony. "In the Murder Case Against Adolf Eichmann, an Examination of the Witness Kurt Becher." June 20, 1961, Bremen District Court.

Ben-Tov, Arieh. *Facing the Holocaust in Budapest: The International Committee of the Red Cross and the Jews In Hungary, 1943–1945*. Dordrecht, Netherlands: Martinus Nijoff, 1947.

Benz, Wolfgang, and Barbara Distel, eds. *Dachau and the Nazi Terror: 1933–1945*, vol. 1, *Testimonies and Memoirs*. Dachau: Verlag Dachauer Hefte, 2004.

————. *Dachau and the Nazi Terror: 1933–1945*, vol. 2, *Studies and Reports*. Dachau: Verlag Dachauer Hefte, 2004.

Berben, Paul. *Dachau 1933–1945: The Official History*. Munich: LIPP, 1986.

Bomberger, William A., and Gail E. Makinen. "The Hungarian Hyperinflation and Stabilization of 1945–1946." *Journal of Political Economy* 91, no. 5 (October 1983).

Bower, Tom. *Nazi Gold: The Full Story of the Fifty-Year Swiss-Nazi Conspiracy to Steal Billions from Europe's Jews and Holocaust Survivors*. New York: HarperCollins, 1997.

Braham, Randolph L. *The Politics of Genocide: The Holocaust in Hungary*. Vols 1–2. New York: Columbia University Press, 1981.

Bridge, Ann. *The Portuguese Escape*. London: Chatto and Windus, 1958.

————. *The Tightening String*. New York: McGraw-Hill, 1962.

————. *Facts and Fictions: Some Literary Recollections*. New York: McGraw-Hill, 1968.

Brinkley, David. *Washington Goes to War*. New York: Alfred A. Knopf, 1988.

"Budapest Raid Studied." *The New York Times*, September 6, 1942, p. 18.

Cartledge, Bryan. *The Will to Survive: A History of Hungary*. London: Timewell Press, 2006.

Cesarani, David. *Becoming Eichmann: Rethinking the Life, Crimes, and Trial of a "Desk Murderer."* New York: Da Capo Press, 2004.

Chorin, Ferenc. "Attacks Against Hungarian Industry and Support of the Anti Nazi Press Memorandum to the Government." Hungarian National Archives-Z-248, Bundle 9, Item 220.

"Country Reports, 1940–1947: Portugal and Hungary." British Foreign Office Archives, Kew Gardens, London.

Csicsery-Rónay, István. *My First Book of Hungary*. New York: Franklin Watts, 1967.

Davidson, Basil. *Scenes from the Anti-Nazi War*. New York and London: Monthly Review Press, 1980.

Davidson, Eugene. *The Trial of the Germans: Nuremberg, 1945–1946*. New York: Macmillan, 1966.

Dart, Dorothy R. ."Chronicle of International Events for the Period November 16, 1945–February 15, 1946." *American Journal of International Law* 40, no. 2 (April 1946): 431–471. .

Deák, István. *Essays on Hitler's Europe*. Lincoln: University of Nebraska Press, 2001.

Dessewffy, Bársony Éva, "Az a Sok Tal Lencse" ("Those Many Dishes of Lentils"), The 1944–45 Journal's of Countess Gyula Dessewffy, unpublished manuscript. United States Holocaust Museum Collections Division, Archives. Box 17, 10.436.03 15 *(Aladár Szegedy-Maszák papers)*

Fenyo, Mario D. *Hitler, Horthy, and Hungary: German-Hungarian Relations, 1941–1944*. New Haven and London: Yale University Press. 1972.

Fenyvesi, Charles. "Portrait of a Plunderer: SS Col. Kurt Becher." Unpublished manuscript, July 10, 2000.

———. *When Angels Fooled the World: Rescue of Jews in Wartime Hungary*. Madison: University of Wisconsin Press, 2003.

Fermor, Patrick Leigh. *Between the Woods and the Water; On Foot to Constantinople from the Hook of Holland: The Middle Danube to the Iron Gates*. New York: Viking Penguin, 1986.

Frank, Tibor. "Editing as Politics: József Balogh and *The Hungarian Quarterly*." *Hungarian Quarterly* 34, no. 129 (Spring 1993).

———. "To Comply with English Taste: The Making of *The Hungarian Quarterly*, 1934–1944." *Hungarian Quarterly* 44, no. 171 (Autumn 2003).

———. "Anglophiles: The Anglo Saxon Orientation of Hungarian Foreign Policy, 1930s Through 1944." *Hungarian Quarterly* 47, no. 181 (Spring 2006).

Gati, Charles. *Hungary and the Soviet Bloc*. Chapel Hill, N.C.: Duke University Press, 1986.

———. *The Bloc That Failed: Soviet–East European Relations in Transition*. Bloomington: Indiana University Press, 1990.

Gerö, András. *The Jewish Criterion in Hungary*. Boulder, Colo.: Social Science Monographs, 2007.

Ghali, Paul. "Millionaire Chorin Buys Nazi Freedom." *Syracuse Herald-American,* July 1, 1944, 9.

Gilbert, Martin. *Churchill: A Life.* New York: Henry Holt. 1991.

———. *Holocaust Journey: Traveling in the Search of the Past.* New York: Columbia University Press, 1997.

Green, Henry. *Pack My Bag: A Self-Portrait.* New York: New Directions, 1992.

Hanebrink, Paul A. *In Defense of Christian Hungary: Religion, Nationalism and Anti-Semitism, 1890–1944.* Ithaca and London: Cornell University Press, 2006.

Held, Joseph, ed. *The Columbia History of Eastern Europe in the Twentieth Century.* New York: Columbia University Press, 1992.

Hoff, George. "The Manfred Weiss–SS Deal of 1944." *Hungarian Studies* 7, nos. 1–2 (1991–92).

Horthy, Admiral Nicholas. *Memoirs.* Edited and translated by Andrew L. Simon. Safety Harbor, Fla.: Simon, 2000.

Ignotus, Paul. *Hungary.* New York: Praeger, 1972.

Kádár, Gábor, and Zoltán Vági. *Self-Financing Genocide: The Gold Train, the Becher Case, and the Wealth of Hungarian Jews.* Budapest: Central European University Press, 2001.

Kállay, Nicholas. *Hungarian Premier: A Personal Account of a Nation's Struggle in the Second World War.* New York: Columbia University Press, 1954.

Kenéz, Peter. *Hungary from the Nazis to the Soviets: The Establishment of the Communist Regime in Hungary, 1944–1948.* New York: Cambridge University Press, 2006.

Kertesz, Stephen D. "The Plight of Satellite Diplomacy." *Review of Politics* 11, no. 1 (January 1949): 26–62.

———. "Peacemaking on the Dark Side of the Moon: Hungary, 1943–1947." *Review of Politics* 40, no. 4 (October 1978): 469–98.

Kornfeld, Maria. Unpublished letters and essays. In the author's possession.

Kornfeld, Móric. *Reflections on Twentieth Century Hungary: A Hungarian Magnate's View.* Edited by Agnes Szechenyi. Translated by Thomas and Helen de Kornfeld. Boulder, Colo.: Social Sciences Monographs, 2006.

Kovács, Maria M. *Liberal Professions and Illiberal Politics: Hungary from the Habsburgs to the Holocaust.* Washington D.C.: Woodrow Wilson Center Press and New York: Oxford University Press, 1994.

Krausz, Tamás. *The Soviet and Hungarian Holocausts: A Comparative Essay.* Translated by Thomas J. and Helen D. de Kornfeld. Boulder, Colo.: Social Science Monographs, 2006.

Lampedusa, Giuseppe di. *The Leopard.* New York: Pantheon, 1960.

Laqueur, Walter. *The Terrible Secret: Suppression of the Truth About Hitler's "Final Solution."* New York: Henry Holt, 1998.

Lendvai, Paul. *The Hungarians: A Thousand Years of Victory in Defeat.* Translated by Ann Major. Princeton, N.J.: Princeton University Press, 2003.

Lewin, Rhoda G., ed. *Witnesses to the Holocaust: An Oral History.* Boston: Twayne, 1990.

Liddell Hart, B. H. *The History of the Second World War.* New York: G.P. Putnam, 1970.

Louça, Antonio. *A Lista de Chorin.* RTP documentary, 2008.

Lukacs, John. *Budapest 1900.* New York: Grove Press, 1988.

———. *The Hitler of History.* New York: Vintage Books, 1998.

———. *At the End of An Age.* New Haven: Yale University Press, 2002.

Macartney, C. A. *October Fifteenth: A History of Modern Hungary, 1929–1945.* 2 vols. Edinburgh: Edinburgh University Press, 1957.

Márai, Sándor. *Memoir of Hungary, 1944–1948.* Budapest: Corvina, in Association with Central European University Press, 1996.

Matloff, Maurice. *The War Department: Strategic Planning for Coalition Warfare, 1943–1944.* Washington D.C.: Office of the Chief of Military History, Department of the Army, 1959.

Mauthner, Gabriella. "I Have to Tell Everybody Where I Belong." Interview by Lajos Erdélyi. http://www.hhrf.org/hhrf/index.php?oldal=478.

McCullough, David. *Truman.* New York: Simon & Schuster, 1992.

Megyery, Ella de. *Budapest Scrap Book.* Budapest: Dante Press, 1937.

Mellanby, Kenneth. "Medical Experiments on Human Beings in Concentration Camps in Nazi Germany." *British Medical Journal* 1, no. 4490 (January 25, 1947): 148–50.

Montgomery, John Flournoy. *Hungary: The Unwilling Satellite.* Millington, N.J.: Vista Court Books. 1993.

Muggeridge, Malcolm, ed. *Ciano's Diary.* London: William Heinemann, 1947.

Nagy, Ferenc. *The Struggle Behind the Iron Curtain.* New York: Macmillan, 1948.

Nemeth, Andor, ed. *Hungary with Illustrations, Maps and City Plans.* Budapest: Lloyd Guide Books, 1932.

Nizkor Project. *The Trial of Adolf Eichmann.* Session 61, parts 1–9. http://www.nizkor .org/hweb/people/e/eichmann-adolf/transcripts/Sessions/Session-061-01.html.

O'Malley, Sir Owen. *The Phantom Caravan.* London: John Murray, 1954.

Padfeld, Peter. *Himmler.* New York: MJF Books, 1990.

Palasik, Mária. "Deportations from Budapest and Their Western Echo," *Big Brother's Miserable Little Grocery Store: Studies on the History of the Hungarian Secret Service After World War II.* Budapest: L'Harmattan Kiadó, 2012.

Pastor, Peter. *Hungary Between Wilson and Lenin: The Hungarian Revolution of 1918–1919 and the Big Three.* Boulder, Colo.: East European Quarterly, 1976.

Patai, Raphael. *The Jews of Hungary: History, Culture, Psychology.* Detroit: Wayne State University Press, 1996.

Pelényi, John. "The Secret Plan for a Hungarian Government in the West at the Outbreak of World War II." *Journal of Modern History* 36, no. 2 (June 1964).

Rath, Elizabeth Chorin. Unpublished diary, 1943–1946.

Rosencher, Henri. "Medicine in Dachau," *British Medical Journal* 2, no. 4485 (December 21, 1946).

Sachar, Howard M. *Dreamland: Europeans and Jews in the Aftermath of the Great War.* New York: Alfred A. Knopf, 2002.

Selzer, Michael. *Deliverance Day: The Last Hours at Dachau.* Philadelphia and New York: J.P. Lippincott, 1978.

Serebro, Harold, with Jacques Sellschop. *Beyond Redemption? The Nazi Colonel Who Saved Jews and Plundered Their Wealth.* Johannesburg: Westmoreland and Trent, 2007.

Sereny, Gitta. *Into that Darkness: An Examination of Conscience.* New York: Vintage Books, 1983.

———. *Albert Speer: His Battle With the Truth.* New York: Vintage Books, 1996.

Simons, Marlise. "Nazi Gold and Portugal's Murky Role." *The New York Times,* January 10, 1997.

Stokes, Gale, ed. *From Stalinism to Pluralism: A Documentary History of Eastern Europe Since 1945.* New York: Oxford University Press, 1991.

Strasser, Daisy Chorin von, and Adrás Bán. *Az Andrássy úttól a Park Avenue-ig: Fejezetek Chorin Ferenc életéből (1879–1964).* Budapest: Osiris Kiadó, 1999.

———. *From Andrassy Ut to Park Avenue: Chapters in the Life of Francis Chorin (1879–1964).* Unpublished translation.

Szalai, Anna, ed. *In the Land of Hagar: The Jews of Hungary: History, Society and Culture.* Tel Aviv: Beth Hatefutsoth, 2002.

Szegedy–Maszák, Aladár. *Az ember ősszel visszanez—: Egy volt magyar diplomata emlekirataibol.* Edited by Laszlo Csorba. Budapest: Europa Konyvkiado, 1996.

———. *Autumnal Retrospections.* 2 vols. Unpublished translation by Thomas J. de Kornfeld.

———. Unpublished letters and diaries. In author's possession and at the Szechenyi Library in Budapest and at the U.S. Holocaust Memorial Museum.

Szegedy-Maszák, Mihály. "Diplomatic Illusions." Afterword to Szegedy-Maszák, *Autumnal Retrospections.* Unpublished translation by Thomas de Kornfeld.

Szent-Miklosy, Istvan. *With the Hungarian Independence Movement: An Eyewitness Account.* New York: Praeger, 1988.

Sinai, Miklós. "Hungary on the Threshold of War." *Hungarian Quarterly* 36, no. 137 (Spring 1995): 101–109.

Szita, Szabolcs, and Sean Lambert. *Trading in Lives? Operations of the Jewish Rescue Committee in Budapest, 1944–1945.* Budapest: Central European University Press, 2005.

Tamási, Miklós, and Krisztián Ungváry. *Budapest 1945.* Translated by Thomas J. and Helen D. de Kornfeld. Budapest: Corvina, 2006.

"The Third Session of the Council of Foreign Ministers, New York, November 4–December 12, 1946," *Foreign Relations of the United States, 1946. Council of Foreign Ministers.* Vol. 3 (Washington, D.C.: Government Printing Office, 1946), pp. 965–1563ff

Ungváry, Krisztián, *The Siege of Budapest: 100 Days in World War II.* New Haven: Yale University Press, 2006.

Varga, László. "Manfred Weiss: The Profile of a Munitions King." In Michael K. Silber, ed., *Jews in the Hungarian Economy 1760–1945.* Jerusalem: Magnes Press Hebrew University, 1992.

Walters, E. Garrison. *The Other Europe: Eastern Europe to 1945.* Syracuse, N.Y.: Syracuse University Press, 1988.

Weindling, Paul. "Human Guinea Pigs and the Ethics of Experimentation: The *BMJ*'s Correspondent at the Nuremberg Medical Trial." *British Medical Journal* 313, no. 7070 (December 7, 1996).

Weiss, Alfons. Unpublished memoir, 1986.

Werfel, Franz. *The Song of Bernadette.* New York: Viking Penguin, 1968.

Zwack, Anne Marshall. *If You Wear Galoshes, You're an Émigré: Peter Zwack, a Memoir.* Budapest: Ab Ovo, 2001.

Zweig, Ronald W. *The Gold Train: The Destruction of the Jews and the Looting of Hungary.* New York: William Morrow, 2002.

In addition, broad runs of newspapers and journals were consulted; it is impossible to list every article that proved useful.

LIST OF ILLUSTRATIONS

Front of jacket photo (from left): George Kornfeld, Manfred Weiss, Marianne Kornfeld, Maria Kornfeld, Edith Weiss, Hanna Kornfeld (in front), Daisy Weiss, Eugene Weiss, Moric Kornfeld (standing in front)

Title page: Daisy Weiss's wedding to Ferenc Chorin on September 21, 1921, in the back of the home on Adrássy Avenue. From left: Alfonse and Erzsebeth (Erzsi) Weiss, unknown child, Maria Kornfeld, Marianne Kornfeld, George Kornfeld, Moric Kornfeld (standing), Ferenc Chorin, Daisy Weiss, Alfred Mauthner standing behind them between his daughter Baby and his son Francis (Ösci), Gabor Weiss standing between Daisy and Manfred Weiss (seated), Hanna Kornfeld, Manfred Weiss, Eugene Weiss (standing), Elsa Mauthner, Mopi Mauthner, Zseni Eissler (sister of Manfred Weiss) holding Istvan Mauthner, Annus Mauthner

1940: (top left) Manfred Weiss; (top right) Alice de Wahl; (bottom) Sarolta, Aladár and Lilly Szegedy-Maszák

1941: (top left) Kornfeld children circa 1936: Puppa (Maria), Thomas, George, Hanna; (top right) winter at Derekegyhaza; (bottom) Hanna, astride a horse in Ireg

1942: (left) The Weiss house on Andrássy Avenue; (right) Maria Kornfeld

1943: Sunning in the summer at Ireg: Nina Adamczyk (a Polish refugee Marianne had taken in), Esther Domony (wife of Moric's cousin Peter Domony), Hanna, and Janos Zwack

1944: (top) The factory at Csepel; (bottom left) Daisy and Ferenc Chorin en route to Portugal; (bottom right) Aladár in prison uniform

1945: (left) Aladár and Hanna surrounded by American soldiers on their way to the United States; (right) a letter from Aladár to Hanna

1946: (clockwise from left) The young diplomatic couple, Hanna and Aladár, together and separately

1947: Aladár (left) and Hanna (right) holding little Aladár (Timsi)

Epilogue: (upper left) Timsi's grave; (upper right) the house on Patterson Street; (bottom) the Szegedy-Maszak Family: Hanna, Marianne, Peter, Andrew, and Aladár

MARIANNE SZEGEDY-MASZÁK is a journalist whose work has appeared in *The New York Times Magazine, Esquire, The New Republic, Newsweek, The Los Angeles Times,* the *Bulletin of the Atomic Scientists,* and *Psychology Today,* among others. She has worked as a reporter at the *New York Post,* an editor at *Congressional Quarterly,* a professor of journalism at American University, and as a senior writer at *U.S. News and World Report.* She has won awards for her journalism from the National Alliance for the Mentally Ill, the National Mental Health Association, and the American Psychoanalytic Association. The recipient of a Pulitzer Traveling fellowship and the Alicia Patterson Foundation fellowship, Szegedy-Maszák has been an officer on the boards of the Center for Public Integrity and the Fund for Independence in Journalism. This is her first book.

ABOUT THE TYPE

This book was set in Caslon, a typeface first designed in 1722 by William Caslon. Its widespread use by most English printers in the early eighteenth century soon supplanted the Dutch typefaces that had formerly prevailed. The roman is considered a "workhorse" typeface due to its pleasant, open appearance, while the italic is exceedingly decorative.